Thirukkural
(TRANSLITERATION)
தமிழ் - Thamizh - English

காலக்கண்ணாடியில் புதுப்புதுத் தோற்றங்கள்
Kalakk Kannadiyill Puthupputhuth Thotrangkal
**A glasnost spectrum of an encrypted life
guide thro' the prism of time**

Transliteration :
aided by **Murasu Convertor**
English Version :
J. Narayanasamy

சுரா பதிப்பகம்

An imprint of Sura Books (Pvt) Ltd.

(ISO 9001 : 2000 சான்றிதழ் பெற்ற நிறுவனம்)
சென்னை

விலை ரூ.*140.00*

THIRUKKURAL (TRANSLITERATION)

© வெளியீட்டாளர்கள்

இந்தப் பதிப்பு : மார்ச், 2008

அளவு : 1/8 கிரவுன்

பக்கங்கள் : 408

விலை: ரூ.140.00

ISBN: 81-7478-525-6

சுரா பதிப்பகம்
[An imprint of Sura Books (Pvt) Ltd.]

தலைமை அலுவலகம்:
1620, 'ஜே' பிளாக்,
16-வது பிரதான சாலை,
அண்ணா நகர்,
சென்னை-600 040.
☎ 91-44-26162173, 26161099

கிளை அலுவலகம்:
XXXII/2328, நியூ கலாவதி சாலை,
பி.எஸ்.என்.எல். எதிரில்,
சென்னொத் கிளாஸ் அருகில்,
பலாரிவட்டம், எர்ணாகுளம் - 682025.
☎ 0484-3205797

டி. கிருஷ்ணா பிரஸ், சென்னை-600 102 இல் அச்சடிக்கப்பட்டு,
சுரா பதிப்பகத்திற்காக [An imprint of Sura Books (Pvt) Ltd.]
1620, 'ஜே' பிளாக், 16-வது பிரதான சாலை, அண்ணா நகர், சென்னை - 600 040 இல்
திரு. வீ.வீ.கே. சுப்புராஜ் அவர்களால் வெளியிடப்பட்டது.
தொலைபேசி எண்கள்: 91-44-26162173, 26161099. தொலைநகல்: (91) 44-26162173.
e-mail: enquiry@surabooks.com   website: www.surabooks.com

03 08 2400

AnbaLippu

iLamaikkum,varungkaalach samuthaayaththiRkum

Dedicated to : Youth and Posterity

ACKNOWLEDGEMENTS

Grateful thanks to all those patrons and friends who had extended help in formulating and bringing out this book on ThirukkuRaL and to Mr. V.V.K. Subburaj of M/s. Sura Books (Pvt) LTD. and his staff, who took much pains to publish this book and encouraging me all along.

A KEY TO TRANSLITERATION OF THAMIZH WORDS TO ENGLISH VERSION

உயிர்	**vowel**	த்	th
அ	a	ந்	n-
ஆ	A/aa	ப்	p
இ	i (ie)	ம்	m
ஈ	I (ee)	ய்	y
உ	u (vu)	ர்	r
ஊ	U/uu (vuu)	ற்	R
எ	e (ae/ye)	ல்	l
ஏ	E (aee/yae)	வ்	v
ஐ (அய்)	ai (ay)	ழ்	z (zh)
ஒ	o (vo)	ள்	L
ஓ	O/oo (vou)	**உயிர்-மெய்**	**vow/cons.**
ஔ (அவ்)	ou (av)	க	ka
ஃ	aq	ங்	nga
இனஒற்று	**conjunct**	ச	sa/cha
க்	ck	ஞ	nja/gna
ச்	ch	ட	ta/da
ட்	tt	ண	Na
த்	tth	ன	na
ப்	pp	த	tha
ர்	tr	ந	n-a
ற்	tR	ப	pa
மெய்	**consonant**	ம	ma
க்	k	ய	ya
ங்	ng	ர	ra
ச்	s/ch	ற	Ra
ஞ்	nj/gn	ல	la
ட்	t/d	வ	va
ண்	N	ழ	za (zha)
ன்	n	ள	La

v

PREFACE

ThirukkuraL is neither a Testament, nor a Scripture, or a Heavenly Dispensation; it is a Treatise on Social Life. It is the embodiment of enlightened wisdom; the hallmark of an ancient civilization, with a rich heritage, tradition and culture reflected in a distinctive language and diction.

It is a literary masterpiece of verses with poetic excellence, brevity and crispness, rhythm and syntax, easy to grasp and remember.

It is a lighthouse guiding the ships of Virtue, Wealth and Love; a treasure-trove of knowledge based on reasonable, analytical, practical, scientific and worldly outlook; moulded in the norms of virtue, aesthetics, kindness, hospitality, sociability, munificence, service, etc. cemented in family life.

It is not constrained by the tenets of any religious faith or dogma but adopts and highlights the virtues in many of them, in tune with innate senses.

The expositions are framed in three parts containing 133 Chapters of ten verses each.

This attempt to present 'ThirukkuraL in English' (following the original verses with interpretations in Tamizh) is not a translation but a simple rendering in a language of common usage, more in prose than in verse, of ideas from the depths of wisdom of a peerless Seer, whose vision transcends time and place. This is meant to convey ThiruvaLLuvar's message to those who are more at ease with English.

The approach is to have a fresh look, not shackled by pre-conceived notions of times yore; to highlight the relevance to present day life and times ahead, of norms which can be kept in mind and adopted day to day, to enrich our lives.

5, T.G. Sambandam Road,   **J. Narayanasamy**
Coimbatore - 18. India.   *Author*

E. VENKATESALU, M.Ed.   Coimbatore-44
     Secretary
S.N.R. Sons' Charitable Trust

FOREWORD

As every lover of Tamizh knows THIRUKKURAL 'the book of All Times' has been rendered into almost all the leading languages of the world. The translators of this great work have taken to the task as a labour of love.

The earlier works on *ThirukkuraL in English* by great authors like G.U. Pope, Rev. Drew and John Lasarus, Rajaji, V.V.S. Iyer, Yogi Suddhaanandha Bharathi, Kasturi Srinivasan and others were done atleast some decades back; they are either in English metric verses or in prose, appealing to the intelligentsia.

The author of this book has taken pains to use simple English so that, he can reach the common people possessing a working knowledge of this international language. At the same time, he has been able to render it in two line couplets with rhythm, syntax and diction wherever it naturally fits in and adorns.

It is not an easy job to bring out the spirit of the learned couplets of the original into a foreign language, but an honest attempt has been made in this volume to explain the multifaceted approach of the genius of *ThiruvaLLuvar*.

No area of human thought has been left untouched by this great inspiring monumental literary work by the Tamizh Saint. He has delved deep into all aspects of life of the people of his times, like values and morals, family and social life, service and munificence, dignity and manners, agriculture, economics and trade, health and medicine, politics and statecraft, management and human relations, communication skills, administration and intelligence, romance and chaste wedlock. Like Shakespeare, he has been a *Jack of all trades,* and has left his mark shining on all that he has touched.

ThiruvaLLuvar has rendered his great treatise in such a way that it has sustaining interest even after 2000 years. If only we follow his advice at least from now on, we can regain our past stature among the Comity of Nations and shine as a model for others to follow.

E. Venkatesalu.

Dr. P. PARAMESWARAN
(formerly Professor of English,
PSG College of Arts and Science)

136, R.G. Street
Coimbatore - 641 001

A NOTE OF APPRECIATION

When there are already so many translations and commentaries, both classical, scholarly and literary as well as modern and simple, on the greatest Tamil classic 'ThirukkuraL', one needs courage, confidence and scholarship to add yet one more to these.

That Mr. J. Narayanasamy has all these qualities of character is proved by the valuable and thought-provoking book of his. An industrial entrepreneur by profession, he has been cherishing interest for Tamizh in his heart ever since his boyhood. His predilection for the study of ThirukkuraL especially, is borne out by this book which is the fruit of his labour of love for many years. It carries the stamp of devoted scholarship. The proof of this is seen in his concise account of his approach to the work in Tamizh and English and the illustrations ranging from Chankam (Sangam) works to Paratitacan (Bharathidasan) that he gives to elucidate the text.

The author's purpose has been to follow a thoroughly rationalistic approach, eschewing superstitions, religious and 'preconceived notions of times yore'. His aim has been to highlight the relevance of Kural to 'present day life and times ahead'. He has succeeded admirably in his endeavours. The book is very appropriately dedicated to youth and posterity.

His notes on Godly feeling as the noblest conception of humanity are well argued. He affirms that TiruvaLLuvar has not spoken about creation, forgiving sins, luck, attaining mukti, raising palms, begging the favour of gods, receiving boon, surrender, the cycle of births and deaths that the soul is said to experience depending on the good and bad deeds etc. which are superstitious and religious and which are in no way related to or fit for our social life. However, TiruvaLLuvar has explained many constructive principles which religions have accepted. 'Penance', according to the author, is performing ones duties well in social life and true renunciation is the discordance, in any situation, of avarice and improper desires.

His interpretation of 'paka(la)van' as *Sun* (1), 'VaalaRivan' as *the learned, the pure* (2), 'malarmicai ekinan manadi cerntar' as *those who follow the light of nobility* (3), 'venduthal vendamai ilan adi' as *the one above likes and dislikes* (4), 'iRaivan' as *the great benefactor* (5), 'poRivayil aintu avithan' as *controlled senses of body, eyes, ears, nose and mouth* (6), 'thanakkuvamai illaathan' *as the peerless* (7), 'aRavali anthanan' as *those who have swum the sea of virtues* (8), 'enkuNathan' as *the adorable guides* (9), and again 'iRaivan' as *the great protector* - all these carefully avoid the name of God - *KadavuL - (as TiruvaLLuvar has not mentioned it in any couplet)*. His interpretations are detonative and not connotative, while all the above phrases were taken to mean God by many other commentators.

His explanation of KuraL 37 in Tamil is very ingenious indeed. He takes good care to steer clear of moral connotations. So also is the explanation of 'immai-maRumai, orumai-ezhumai' (ezhupiRappu-p.18). 'Teyvam' in kural 43 is taken as divinity and explained in Tamil as 'those who guided by doing rare acts in their lives'. His interpretation of kuraL 55 is at once apt and happy.

Though VaLLuvar has spoken about abjuring flesh meat, the author has argued convincingly that in the present context of population explosion, scarcity of available food and shortage of nourishing nutrients, abjuring flesh meat completely is very difficult (p. 60). Similarly his explanation of abstaining from killing is enlightening (pp. 61-63). His exposition of soul-force (vuyirppatRal) and the happenings activating life in the body are instructive and illuminative.

We may go on writing about his many other interpretations which are worthy contributions to the understanding of Kurazh in the context of our present day world. My hearty congratulations to the author for his valuable contribution to Tamil literature and I hope - not in vain - many such great works from him would see the light of day in future.

P. Parameswaran

INTRODUCTION TO THE TEXT

Part I – VIRTUES

Chapters 1-4 Prayer, enlighten the righteous path, taking guidance and following the footsteps of seers, savants and persons of vision, for realizing the infinite manifestations of primordial matter in Nature; and speak of the greatness of ascetics, the importance of rain and emphasizes virtue as the basis of all thought and action.

Chapters 5-24 on **Domestic Virtues,** explain the primeness of family and social life, the role of spouses, wealth of children, kindness of love, of words, hospitality, equity, humility, discipline, and forbearance; and warns against the evils of adultery, envy, coveting, slander, vanity, etc.

Human being are rational and social animals. Humanity has the unique qualities of honour and dignity, modesty and shame, laughter and speech, besides an orderly social life. Rational human beings live in full awareness of their duty to family and society, to contribute fully to common good and live in fame (Ch. 22-24).

Chapters 25-38 on **Ascetic Virtues,** touch on a status, ripe with experience in family and social life, to aim at perfection by adopting compassion and grace, penance (even in family life), conscience of instability, truth and veracity, renunciation and existence in harmony with Nature, abjuring vileness and imposture, anger, greed, fraud, flesh-meat, harm and killing.

Part II – WEALTH AND WELFARE

In chapters 39-63, Politics and Governance, Chapters 39-46 deal with the qualities of a ruler, the importance of education and good listening, understanding wisdom, cherishing good company, seeking aid of the worthy, eschewing crime and meanness.

Chapters 47-73 are of special significance. In the distant past, 2,000 years back, in the culture and tradition of a society which Thirukkural reflects, there had been keen and wonderful insight into what are considered as **modern concepts of management sciences,** such as Human Relations Development and Effective Communication Skills.

Chapters 47-50 speak of the ways and means to assess strength, choosing time and place, and acting after due deliberations.

Chapters 51 and 52 elaborate the methods to test and then trust people, evaluating their aptitudes; entrusting jobs suited to them, and the art of delegation and follow up.

Chapters 53-63 specify the norms of good governance, cherishing kith and kin, humanism with considerate foresight, intelligence, motivation and will-power, pervasive efforts, overcoming obstacles and the need to guard against complacence and sloth, tyranny and terrorism.

In chapters 64-73, Cabinet and Governance, Chapters 64, 66-70 speak of the qualities and attributes of ministers, ambassadors, envoys and administrators surrounding the ruler, and of purity, firmness and mode of actions. Chapters 65, 71-73 explain **communication skills** in eloquence, the method of understanding and reading minds of people, the manner of dealing with assemblies of audience and councils of the wise.

Chapters 74 and 76 elaborate on the greatness of a **sovereign country,** its wealth of produce, hills and forests, water and mineral resources; the means of making wealth and its value.

Chapters 75, 77 and 78 deal with the glory of **defence** in fortresses, reputation of army and heroism of warriors.

Chapters 79-95: Friendship and Alliance, Chapters 79-91 elaborate the different aspects and niceties that distinguish traditional and ripe relationships, comradeship, fellowship and friendship and the ways to avoid harmful and false acquaintances, to guard against folly, shallowness, and defiance; appraising enmity and internal discordance and the need for nobility in hostility and not offending the great.

Chapters 91-95 speak of the virtue of **food as medicine,** diagnosis and treatment of diseases; and caution against female infatuation, of women without virtue, and the harm of liquor and gambling.

Chapters 96-108: Merits and Miscellany, deal with nobility of social life, devotion to social causes, qualities of dignity and pride, sublimity, mannerism and sensitivity to shame.

Chapter 104 highlights the primacy of **farming** as a devoted service to society.

Chapters 101, 105-108 cover the harmful nature of **futile wealth,** the pains of **poverty** seeking alms, dreadfulness of **beggary** and the meanness of **cowardice,** which harm human dignity.

Part III – LOVE LIFE

Chapters 109-115 complement **romance in love,** with the lovers admiring and extolling beauty and charm of each other, revelling in the language of signs, enjoying the joy of intimacy and ecstasy of love. In the proses, there is wailing on the loss of decorum and longing for the clamour of relatives and society to speed up the process of wedlock.

Chapters 116-130 elaborate the situation after the **charm of bridal union in wedlock.** When the male goes off on duties and avocations, trade and business to amass wealth for a better life, he leaves the spouse forlorn. The passion of love and pangs of separation manifest in different forms of pain to the mind and body, such as pining in sorrow, wailing in paleness, pallor of loneliness, cursing the eyes, the eve; relating visions of dreams, withering of limbs, conversing and chiding the soul, failing in modesty, signalling symptoms of passion, throbbing and longing for reunion.

Chapters 131-133 converse on the **finesse of bouderie,** that is, when the lovers meet after long separation, expression of resentment and pleasure in the form of feigned sulking and pouting, that enhances the pleasure of love.

On an overall view of the text, some salient features emerge, which are worth taking note of:

1. The concept of Almighty is not explicit anywhere in the text; but it is left to one's own feeling and realization of the forms of primordial matter, that is Nature (couplet 370)

2. Life on earth is a process of evolution. The terminology used is 'making' (385 and 1062) and the concept of 'creation' or any equivalent term, is conspicuous by its absence.

3. Life on earth is meant for worthy living in full flow, in discipline and fame. Family and social life of virtue is better than renunciation for saintly order (46, 48)

4. There is no concern for any 'before or after' life. Speaking of cause and effect, the text says one's actions of the forenoon are repaid the same afternoon (319); one's own actions are responsible for one's greatness or meanness (505) and while it is the duty of parents to foster children, the latter's wealth is the effect of their own actions. (63)

5. The text stands firm witness to the high esteem in which women were and deserve to be held in family and society on the vital roles played by them (51-60, 907, 924, 974, 1101, 1137, 1272, 1280), not minding the inhibitions, restraints and mental, physical constraints and taboos imposed historically by a male dominated society denying equal opportunities.

6. Enlightened societies in the modern world lay stress on three main aspects of life, viz. humanism, equality of womanhood and advancement of the downtrodden. *Thirukkural* lays stress on humaneness in various chapters (esp. in 4, 8-14, 16, 22-25, 30, 32, 53, 58, 79, 81, 99, 100, 103)

7. A solemn and binding duty is cast on societies and governments the world over to foster and uplift the weak and downtrodden who form substantial sections of population suffering under extreme poverty and disability. *Thirukkural,* while being critical of seeking of alms and begging caused by poverty and meanness (Ch. 105-108) directs pointed attention to the following facts:

   (a) Duty to uplift society is more important than charity contributions to individual causes and hospitality (225)

(b) Social wealth is a Trust, like a commune well or fountain for water, like fruits of neighbourhood trees, like medicinal plants, and service-centres, duty bound to aid the deserving in need of help (211-220)

(c) It is the duty of government to protect the accrual of wealth by encouraging and aiding entrepreneurs, technicians and artisans to preserve and develop their skills (560)

(d) Governments and managements should always keep dear to their minds the interests of workers, whose steady hands keep the world on stride (520)

(e) Governments and societies should eradicate discrimination on the basis of birth or work (972)

(f) The dedication and involvement to develop farming and industry should be a penance in social life. The causes for a few benefiting from the labour of many, while many live on the labour of a few, should be eliminated (266, 270)

(g) While all citizens are equal to the rulers, the government should perceive by merit and help the weak, according to their needs (528)

8. Above all, vigilance and alertness of the people are essential for the governments to behave and avoid/correct wrong actions (899)

9. On the lighter side, there are hilarious comparisons between the passion of love and liquor and folly to establish the supremacy of love, besides the similarities of yields of love and sugarcane in sweetness; (couplets 838, 921-930, 1080, 1145, 1201, 1281)

10. There are as many as 17 couplets dealing with adorning eyes, lips and other parts, with their beauty enchanced by jewels, which are exclusive complements to ladies (couplets 575, 911, 919, 1081, 1089, 1101-102, 110, 113, 114, 124, 134, 135, 262, 273, 275 and 1329)

NOTES ON THE TEXT OF THIRUKKURAL

1. With a view to enable the reader to follow the original text and understand its meaning, compound words have been split up, and a vocabulary guide is given for words in rare use, in appendix I

2. The English version is given in two line couplets, in simple modern language, avoiding antique and tough metric verses. A dictionary of words considered hard for young students and people with limited understanding of the language is also given in appendix II

3. It has been a basic approach to find new ideas and explanations acceptable and useful to the present day society. It is the richness of KuRaL that it is so deep as to yield new ground to the extent we dig and probe.

4. Besides the group headings under each chapter (preamble , domestic virtues and grace in Part I Virtues; politics, defence, governance, friendship, and mannerism in Part II Wealth; romance in love and chaste wedlock in Part III Love Life) emphasis has been laid to highlight the ideas on management sciences, strategies, human relations and communication skills. For each group and at the beginning of each chapter summaries and gist of the text are added.

5. As a novel attempt special essays are added on concept of Almighty; the origin, growth and energy of life, functioning mechanism of life in the body, with a scientific approach.

6. Thoughts expressed at different places of the text on similar themes have been grouped as follows:

   a. The esteem of women (p. 8, 126)
   b. Non-violence and saving lives (p. 17)
   c. World and people (p 19)
   d. Birth and life (p 22)
   e. Cause and effect (p 12)
   f. Crime and punishment (p 110)
   g. Present, future; singular, multiple (p. 13)

    h. Seeking alms and death (p 137)

    i. Intoxication of liquor and passion (p 288)

7. The concept of saving lives, or abstaining from killing, has been changing in its import and practicability with progressive findings in modern science. There are unlimited micro organisms unseen in the universe and life of the species is impossible without destroying other living organisms. In the present context it can at best be taken only as an extension of non-violence and abstaining from deliberate and crude methods of harming living beings.

8. Earlier it was considered for the origin of life a seed or semen is essential. But latest findings have proved that life can be originated and grown by cloning of tissue cells.

9. So many of KuRaL's concepts and codes have stood the test of time. But a few based on the customs and beliefs of olden days have been modified by current knowledge, such as:

    a. The shadow of earth on the moon in lunar eclipse was considered as the figure of a snake (1146)

    b. Women of chastity can command the clouds to rain (55). This is at best a lofty praise of the usefulness of such women to family.

    c. The ship on sea cannot sail on land (496). This has been pushed back by the modern invention of amphibious vehicles that run on land and sea on a thin bed of air.

10. The significance and relevance of chapter 93 on ABSTAINING FROM DRINKS are all the more important now in the face of widespread addiction to alcohol and drugs damaging lives.

11. The tenets of chapter 94 about GAMBLING deserves special emphasis to counteract the lure of elusive 'luck' and prevalence of betting, slot machines and lotteries which de-motivate and sap the enthusiasm and devotion to fair means and sustained hard labour.

12. In the present context of war mongering, terrorism and sole dependence on multiplying arms and weapons of mass destruction, the teachings of chapters 86 - 88 on strategies

for getting rid of the spirit of defiance, nobility in hostility, appraising and overcoming enmity deserve deep consideration of all right thinking people who seek and respect peace.

13. Modern day life has increasing imbalance between mental and physical work, growing stresses and strains. People are attracted by easy availability and affordability to gorge on endless varieties of food rich in fats, protein and carbohydrates resulting in fattiness, hyper tension, heart diseases and diabetics.

The rustic wisdom and common sense in the sayings of Chapter 95 on natural medicine and methods of treatment recommend food itself as medicine, in measured units and quality, to maintain and preserve a sound mind in a healthy body by balancing intake of proper food sufficient for the energy needs of the environment, growth, work and exercise.

14. The strength of a worthy nation depends not only on its geographical location, resources in land, water, minerals, flora and fauna, but primarily on the skills and character of its people in efficiently utilising them to increase wealth, defence, proper governance, and indomitable courage to face natural and man-made disasters and rebuild without dependence on outside help. (Ch. 74)

15. On the subject of crime and punishment, there is no scope for seeking or granting pardon for sins. Deliberate actions of harm and evil are crimes (*kutRam*) which deserve to be punished (549, 550, 561). Pain boomerangs on those who cause it to others (319, 329) .

Index to Contents

Chapter Headings

PART II: WEALTH
39–63 POLITICS & GOVERNANCE

64–73 CABINET GOVERNANCE

பகுதி *1* – அறத்துப்பால்
pakuthi 1 - aRaththuppAl
Part I - VIRTUES

May happiness and prosperity thrive in this world

PART 1: VIRTUES

WINDOW TO THE TEXT

Group 1: Chapters 1-4: Prayer and Preface

Like a mirror reflecting the light of images, knowledge of the mind and inner wisdom of the soul are reflected in our deeds and expressions. Seers and seniors of sublime qualities and grace bestow traditional benediction on the worthy. The magnificence of Primordial Matter (the concept of Almighty) transcends our vision and is beyond praise. No tradition is known in *Thamizh* of the ordinary blessing the high and mighty. The vocabulary adopted in *KuRaL*, like reverence (*vaNakkam*), adherence (*vazipAdu*), glorifying (*poutRal*), worship (*thozukai*) appear more apt in the fitness of things to adore the virtuous, the peerless savants and pure benefactors.

Saint Vivekananda, a seer of Indian thoughts, has classified the various paths as;

Unison of mind and soul with Nature, the highest

Meditation in renunciation and penance the middle,

Recitation of verses and names the lower and

Idol worship the lowest of all avenues.

The later two do not find any place in *KuRaL Oothal* (134, 834) means only acquiring knowledge by study and memorisation.

According to *Thamizh* tradition, the Sun (*pakalavan*) has been the known source of light and all energy sustaining life (*gnAyiRu*), and the first among the solar system (*Aathavan*). The words *Pakavan* and *Aathi muthalvan* denote the core atom of matter that constituted the Universe (*Andam*)

It is noteworthy, Saint ILangkovadikaL, commenced the preface of epic *SilappathikAram* in praise of the Sun, the Moon and Rain.

Classification of primordial matter as Space (*idam, veLi*), Universe (*vuuzhi, aNdam,*) the suspended stellar and solar systems (*gnAlangkaL*), the sky (*viN, visumbu, vAnam*), the moving planets (*kOLkaL*), the revolving & rotating earth (*ulaku,*

vaiYam), and the elements (bUthangkaL) contained in space viz:
air (vaLi, kaatRu), fire (thee), water (neer) and land (nilam, maN);
their qualities, configurations, movements and consequential
effects were known in depth to the bare eyed scientists of ancient
Thamizh Naadu in the centuries well before Christ.

Their civilization was well matured and cultured in
identifying the world of lands and seas as continents, nations,
cities, and the country side as habitats (vuur), colonies (kompai)
and hamlets (saeri); and a finer distinction between house (manai)
and home (veedu, illam). Societies comprised of kith and kin,
clan and professional castes, friends and comrades.

The dream of splitting the atom was ingrained in their
imagination, to encompass seven seas within the core of atom
(ThiruvaLLuva maalai); the idea to split the core of the atom
into thousandths (Thirumanthiram) portrays the beauty and
sophistication of a sharp intellect. That civilization had setbacks
due to natural disasters and historical reasons of occupation
and forced interaction of alien concepts based on religious
thoughts, which shattered the coherence, realism and confidence
of the people by the burden of ideas on instability. But its innate
culture has survived from total obliteration (as had happened to
ancient Greek, Roman and Egyptian civilizations) thanks to the
sustaining influence of its rich language and literature, a mainstay
of its past traditions.

Movements for renaissance and rationalistic thoughts have
started to grow in the 20th century, to revive and refurbish
ancient values as guides for the future, in tune with modern
scientific trends.

In the words of Saint Vedhadri, for those who have matured
thinking, the path of enlightened wisdom is the best; for others
true religion should be a guide to disciplined life.
Dr.S.Radhakrishnan has stated that simple humanism free from
blind dogmas and stale customs is pure religion.

There are no religious values (samayam) higher than kindness
and truth. The animal trend of musk and rutting, addicted to
dogmas as drugs (matham) is dangerous to society. Wars and

terrorism are madness and vandalism in the names of religions; history and current events testify. This is neither religion nor rational humanism.

WHAT IS DIVINITY

Divinity, Life and Knowledge are still abstract concepts. The word God (*KadavuL*) is not found in *KuRaL*. In usage it is taken to mean something that transcends our mental faculties. Life is a function which throbs inside and motivates functioning of our mind and body. Arising in the depths of our subconscious mind (*aanmaa* - soul or spirit) and throbbing in our physical mind, Divinity is a matter of our feelings. It has been said that God is the noblest conception of humanity. To understand this clearly and realise its impact, the codes, edicts and tenets of *ThirukkuRaL* are invaluable guides to refine and direct our lives.

Again it was Saint Vivekananda who said that for those who cannot understand and realise divinity in their minds, it is rather good they give up blind belief on it.

KuRaL has not advocated any belief or faith outside rational ethics. In fact the words belief or faith (*nambikkai)* are nowhere therein. What we need to cultivate is confidence that motivates forward looking, positive and upward trends in life. Beliefs that cause setbacks, stagnation, *lais-sez-faire* attitudes or negative actions are harmful to growth of humanity. A mind-set of happy go lucky life to eat and sleep will not lead us anywhere.

In our endeavours to understand divinity the following quotes may throw some light.

"Leave this chanting and singing and rolling of beads
Whom does thou worship in the lonely dark corner
of a temple with doors all shut;
Open thy eyes and see that thy God is not before thee
He is there where the tiller is tilling the hard ground
And the path maker is breaking stones.
He is there with them in Sun and shower,
With his garments covered in dust

Put off thy holy mantle and
Even like him come down into the dusty soil
Come out of thy meditations and
Put aside thy flowers and incense
What harm is there if thy clothes are tattered and stained
Come and meet him and stand by him
In his toil in the sweat of thy brow."

Geethanjali by Rabindranath Tagore

"Where are you searching for God
Not seeing him here in human form
All the populace who work from dawn to dusk
To make their livelihood are the forms of God"

Periyasaamith Thooran
Editor, *Thamizh Kalaik kazanjsiam* (Encyclopedia)

"The God of life resides inside and outside you
He is the form of your body
Follow and adhere to His appearance of the
Clear manifestations in the fullness of Nature" Saint
Vivekananda

You deem installed statues as Gods, shower flowers,
Come around it and chant – where from are these hymns?
When the Almighty is within you, will the statues speak?
Do the frying pan and ladle know the taste of vegetables?

Mystic Sivavaakkia Sithar

In Part II – Wealth, Chapter 39 and in *KuRaL* couplets 388, 432, 436, 541, 547, 564, 690, 733, 778, the word Divine refers to the Protector, Leader, King, and Emperor.

It is more appropriate to deem chapters 1 - 4 as part of Virtues, referring to the mighty seers, people of sublimity, who have attained realization of truth and the ultimate state of happiness, and to be guided by them in our lives, conscious of the rich and vivid manifestations of Nature.

In ancient *Thamizh Changkam* literature like *TholkAⁿiyam, PuRanAnURu, Kaliththokai, NatRRiNai, PathitRRup Paththu,*

Pattinap Paalai, Paththup Paattu, Paripaadal, in about 25 places divine refers the King. At 5 places in *Paripaadal* and 2 places in *AhanAnURu* only, divine refers to God. In *Thamizh* the word *Theivam (thaeippathu)* could mean Fire caused by rubbing. In olden days people out of awe, fear and respect for natural phenomenon of fire, lightning, thunder, storms etc. started worshipping them as divine manifestations of nature. Evolved out of this were the concepts of *Kanthan* (tree), *Murugan* (beauty), *Maalavan* (the black), *MaayOn* (the illusory, glorious).

In tune with ancient *Thamizh* cultural traditions, in *ThirukkuRaL*, divine refers to the great with rare qualities who guide and lead the human race. The 'divine of heaven' has been a lofty imagination in usage. In *KuRaL,* couplets 5 and 10 also divine can be taken to mean the King as protector and the Sublime as guides.

The word *Pakavan* in *KuRal* is unique, purely of *Thamizh* origins. In *Silappathikaaram* and *MaNimaekalai* it denotes a proper noun and in *Innaa NaaRpathu* it is used in general. No other literary work in *Thamizh* refers to primordial matter (*AathiPakavan)* as God. When annotated as *Aathi + pakavu* it means the original core atom (i.e. element of primordial matter in space) and *An* is a terminal suffix of honour.

The word *muthal* appearing in couplets 449, 941, 948, 1304 denotes principal, first, origin and basic. It chiefly refers to first of matter (*muulap poruL*). According to Indian thoughts *and saangkiya* philosophy of knowing self, original matter in nature, as the first cause (etymological noun) that initiated the process of evolution. The theory of evolution expounds that Space, Matter and the Universe originated and developed from the first cause, the core atom.

The word *iyatRRal in couplet* 385 conveys the process of evolving, making, cultivating, producing, manufacturing or changing one or more into different products. It has been established in science that matter can neither be created nor destroyed, but only changes forms. In the same connotation of the word *iyatRRal,* in couplet 1062 the words *ulaku iyatRRiyaan* reasonably means those who have devised the social systems of law and governance. It is far fetched to bring in any idea of creation (*padaippu*). In fact such a word is not found in KuRaL, and it is alien to its ethical codes and ancient Thamizh civilization and cultural traditions.

Group 2: Chapters 5 - 24: Domestic Virtues

Chapter 5: Family Life

Family as a sacred institution in social life, is the earnest of virtues, basic to protect and promote other virtues. *KuraL* deems it as the foremost of virtues. Initiation of the primitives from scattered livelihood to the path of progress commenced in cooking food, farming, handicraft, trade etc. Family life commenced when relations between man and woman were sanctified in marriage and they started living in houses, as a forerunner to the formation of societies.

This basic culture commenced as one of the ancient civilizations in Thamizh's land (in the continent of Lemuria, south of Asia, also known as Dravidian culture) and had grown and refined into a civilization rich in language, literature, fine arts, virtues, rational ethics, manners and codes of behaviour, developing into organised governments of monarchy with established systems of education, law and justice. This group of *kuRaL* chapters commencing from Family life (5) to Fame (24) deal with different aspects of family and social life.

In earlier times, up to 1900 AD, in consideration of traditional occupations, economy, thrift, cooperation and security, people of two to three generations lived in joint families. Fast changes occurred in the 20th century shrinking families to husband, wife and children up to adolescence. With increasing prominence of the concepts of equality of men and women; educational, employment and social opportunities, economic independence and self-reliance the concept of beautiful home, sweet home is painfully receding, yielding place to arrangements of living together for sex, sharing daily chores, comradeship and such other considerations. As a result, the number of children with dual mothers/fathers, in the care of nannies, in child care centres, in school and college dormitories and old age parents in senior's or rescue homes are disconcertingly increasing. A mind-set of greater understanding and tolerance are the need of the day to save and protect the ideal concept of families.

The word Divine (*theyvam*) occurring in kuRaL couplets 43, 50, 55, 619, 702, and 1023 refers to the Great of rare qualities who have stood as guides to humanity. This view is reinforced by the following:

"Say the name of Truth is Divine, else
Know the names recited of 'divines' are false"

Poet Subramania Barathi

"Mother and Father are the foremost divines"

Saint poet Avvaiyaar

"The chaste woman of dignity glorified
by the great as Divinity"

Silappathikaaram on KaNNaki

Those who have found fame in history by their acts of heroism, valour and the mighty force of their skills to save humanity from enmity, cruelty and hunger, are known as divine protectors. Those who have achieved rarer deeds in society, by kindness of love, sublime qualities and manners, integrity and chastity and contributed to sustain virtues are known as divines of their clans. It has become a tradition to revere and worship them as great saviours and guides by raising memorials for them. It is noteworthy that *kuRaL* 43 places divine next to forbears in priority for a households' duty to cherish and sanctify..

Chapter 6: Partner in Life

In the context of the age of *ThirukkuRaL*, 30 BC, in praising the glory of women in clear and emphatic terms, VaLLuvar's rare courage and contributions are outstanding. It has been the ethical code of *'VaLLuvam'*, the cult of ancient *Thamizhs* to respect women and place them at the altar of glory. The following couplets stand testimony to this:

What is greater than chaste women (54)

Women of modesty are far higher in glory (907)

The glory of women is serene and unsurpassed (1137)

The unique qualities of womanhood are:

Strength of chastity (54, 974)

Beauty of modesty (924, 1124)

The charm and grace of womanliness (1272, 1280)

'Kings respect the sophistication of women'

- PuRan-aanURu 68

Another poem in PuRan-anURu -115, says:

'Mission of duty is the lifeline for men,

For women of household men are lifeline'

implying that men primarily shouldered external responsibilities of defence, politics of state, trade and commerce while women took to managing the household and stood by to help in farming, handicraft etc. to support families.

In the changed circumstances of today, women have besides their responsibilites in the household, to take up opportunities in society and public life as well. They are gaining equality, a due share of and respect in life. For this it is essential for them to come out of the narrow circle of their paternal homes, husband and children and enlarge their visions of society and the world. Skills and independence are not things that others give them to take; they have to achieve and sustain them by the dint of their own efforts and self-help.

Ladies esp. in the Orient and East are tradition bound and are even now in a dual mind-set seeking independence of actions at the same time feeling sentimentally comfortable to play a secondary role to husbands. Perhaps they are not keen on poet Barathi's dream of 'complete equality of men and women in life'

Chapter 7: Wealth of Children

The basic duty of parents is to make their children learned and noble; KuRaL specifies it as their responsibility in the nature of things, which they perform without any expectation of gratitude or reward. This shines well in comparison to the unique munificence of rain; a gratitude pure, sans recompense (211).

The sense of duty of *Thamizs* is highlighted in *PuRan-anuuRu* 312 in the words of a mother blessing her son on his way to war:

'My primary duty is to beget and bring up

A noble warrior is moulded by the father.

The king grants and ensures good behaviour

To attack the elephant and win is duty of the lad'

In society as in defence, life will enrich and prosper if people perform their duties sincerely. *KurRaL* 63 emphasizes that descendents should not rely on wealth of forbears, but earn their fortunes by the dint of their own skills and endeavours. It is a significant forethought of evolution in couplet 68 that 'growing knowledge and skills of youth down generations makes life all the more pleasant in the world.'

Chapter 8: Kindness of Love

Kindness born out of love helps to bind families, make societies cohesive and strengthen nations. It is essential to refine humanity from negative aspects of violence, desires, jealousy etc. by spreading and sustaining the message of love on all species of life.

Chapter 9: Hospitality

The greatness of inviting and honouring needy and deserving guests with a smile on the face and a liberally extended hand.

'Utilise wealth of land and water

Produce food that saves body and life

Who give food save precious lives'

– PuRan-aanURu 18

Like the vigilant and studious ants

that hurry with food grains to uplands

Foreseeing rains that shower on time,

We, our kith and kin in large groups go

From the bards house, hands full of food,

who heal the pain of hunger and retrieve'

– PuRan-aanURu 173

The quality of householders going in search of and feeding the Seers and Saints who have renounced the world, shrunk their bowels, seeking to enlarge the light of their inner self, is praised in *kuRaL* couplets 86 and 283.

Chapter 10: Sweetness of Expression

Saying things of substance in courteous tones, pleases and attracts the listeners. Those who desire to succeed in family duties and save honour of the society, have to overcome the evils of anger, envy, harsh words etc.; speak soft, gain friendship and respect from others for a life of merit. An expression is sweet and good that springs from the purity of mind, blossoms with a smiling face, and goes with a message of kindness and love, carefully avoiding faulty lines.

Even in information technology, effective communication skills with a persuasive and delicate approach, refined manners of speech convince and yield good results. Rough and tough attitudes run the risk of being ignored or rebutted in negatives.

Chapter 15: Not to covet others' spouse

In matters of personal discipline and mental firmness women are deemed on a higher plane of modesty and chastity. (974, 1011). *KuRaL* 1311 says the bosom chest of men are thrown wide open for many women to gaze and embrace, meaning that men are more vulnerable and susceptible to extra marital relations. This chapter, as also the subsequent ones (91, 92) are warnings and edicts to men against such a mind-set, infatuations and hankering after women of dominance and doubtful character.

With increasing awareness, social and economic independence of women, the offensive habit of coveting others' spouses is a diminishing phenomenon. Even if the description of women in couplet 141 as the husbands property could mean a wealth of the family, there can be no disputing that it is a reflection of the olden days practice of women occupying a secondary place in family and society.

Chapter 16: Forbearance

To bear with wrong doings and harmful acts of others, and to refrain from retaliation, is goodness of character, expected of the affected. Actions by mistake are follies (*thavaRu*) which can be corrected by conscious effort, to make them realise their mistakes, be ashamed and willing to correct them is the best way to prevent their recurrence (655, 987). Of course this is meant for people sensitive to shame, and cannot apply to the mean minded who will listen only to the language of the rod. (1077-78).

While on this, it is necessary to make a distinction between forbearance and pardon. The concept of pardoning crimes and sins is alien to *Thamizh* culture and the codes of *KuRaL* There is no remedy for crime. The sinners have to bear the brunt of it. Who sows harm cannot expect to harvest grain. According to the well laid edicts of *KuRaL,* there is no reference to pardon.

Evil deeds follow as our shadow and ruin us (208)
˙The punishment to violent harm.. (314)
Sickness of pain rebounds on the giver (320)
Protect from internal crime with a strong arm (549)
Banish terror by hard (capital) punishment (550)

In criminal jurisprudence, there is no room for others bearing punishment for a criminal. In this view the idea of one pardoning others of their crimes is out of place. Even in present day democracies the right to excuse punishment for undeliberate harm are vested as an exceptional power on the President/ Governors of States, to be exercised cautiously on merits.

Present (immai), Future (maRumai), Singular/Integral (orumai), ascend/ rise (ezumai), succession/everlasting (ezupiRappu):

These words of long traditional usage, found in couplets 62, 98, 107, 126, 398, 538, 835, 904, 1042, and 1315, have been subjected to confused and wrong interpretations, linking them to a concept of rebirth (*maRupiRavi*) which does not find mention in *kuRaL*. They can be taken in the ordinary sense constructively to mean family life-renunciation, a bright time ahead, swelling growth, a rein of succession of seven generations.

Similarly the expressions 'an exciting new world, the world of the high, heavenly, sky high' etc. occuring in couplets 50, 58, 86, 213, 222, 234, 247, 290, 346 and 353 are customary phrases of lofty imaginary concepts to denote praise (as substantiated by the phrase 'sky high appearance' in *kuRaL* 271) , which have no authentic support or elaboration in *kuRaL*. It will be wise to take a rational view of these things in tune with present day realities.

Chapter 17: Desist from Envy

The reference to 'the wreaks of envy floating in riches and the good suffering poverty' in *kuRaL* 169, is against nature and contrary to moral values. Such occurrences have not only to be identified for what they are but subjected to reform by stern measures.

Chapter 22: Awareness of duty to society

The importance and benefits of healthy interaction and cooperation for the advancement of society is well recognised. People have learned the qualities of diligence of the ants, faithfulness of the dogs, community and sharing without concealing of the crows, steadfastness of reptiles (lizard - *udumbu*) and the sense of dignity and honour of the deer (*kavari maan* - yak). For the purpose of safety, cooperation and confabulation, community living has been evolved as a unique feature among humanity. Besides the objects of sustaining family traditions, succession and hospitality, cherishing and protecting social welfare is a noble task. Common good is ahead of self interests, and it has to be performed as a duty without expecting returns.

Chapter 23: Contribution

The compassion to share and patronize lives (322) giving out in measures to the needy (477) are praiseworthy virtues. Contribution in conjunction with service to society can benefit a wider area of needs, merits fame (231, 232), has the eminence of divinity (382, 387), is the nobility of social duty (953, 1057), utility of wealth (1006), the ultimate purpose of industrious farming (1035) and many other virtues.

Chapter 24: Glory

The glory of the ones who seek public good and serve without any aim on rewards, survives and stands even after they pass out. The factors contributing to glory and praiseworthiness are divine wealth (5), virtues (39), family life (59), forbearance (156), veracity (296), worthy community (457), non-complacent alertness (532-3), sustaining fame (966), shunning avarice (1003), so on and so forth.

Group 3: Chapters 25 - 38: Ascetic Virtues

Kindness of love with a clear perception of life and realities matures into compassion and grace of the mind and soul. Following the expositions on family and social life based on virtues, this group elaborates, with grace as the foundation, a life sans the vices of fraud, pretension, vileness and imposture, deceit, greed, anger, violent harm etc. and pursuing qualities of veracity, non-violence, self-realization, penance and renunciation of desires, lead to sublimity and unification with nature.

Chapter 25: Compassion

Grace as the greatest of wealth, the righteous path capable of clearing darkness, fear and distress and leading to self introspection and renunciation of desires is expressed vividly.

Chapter 26: Abjuring flesh meat

This concept has to be viewed in the context of the circumstances prevailed and values adopted 2000 years back, based on compassion, as enunciated in couplets 251, 251,254. In couplets 253, 257 and 258 this code is related to ones inner conscience, and in 255, 256, 259, 260 as in pursuit of non-violence.

If people feel sentimentally that meat eating is against ones ethical norms, or consider for environmental reasons of physical state and age, nature of work, food habits and health condition, that vegetarian food is the best suited, they will do well in sticking to their views. But the ideas about 'killing to eat' have a different connotation in present day life, which will be discussed later in chapter 33.

In the present day phenomenon of exploding population, abject poverty, scarcity and non-availability of food and proper nutrition in vast regions of the world, as also the extreme climatic conditions of the polar and desert regions where people cannot afford any means of vegetarian food to give them the required calories of energy, it is not only inevitable but essential to depend on food from animal flesh. Even in countries depending and thriving on agriculture, for economic and practical reasons people cannot forgo the vast wealth of fish, crabs, turtles etc from seas, rivers and ponds. Poultry, pig, sheep and other animal/ bird farming is part of present day culture to augment resources. In the eyes of scientific reasoning food from either grains, vegetable or animals does not make any major difference, as all are living organisms.

The question of religion should not interfere in this as Christians, Muslims, Buddists and even a vast majority of Indian religions accept and share with non-vegetarian food. In realism it is best left to the conscience and convictions of the individual concerned.

Chapter 27: Penance

To face and bear with miseries and distress with firmness and determination, as we do in fasting; to refrain from doing things that cause harm and pain to others and to perform our duties in an upright and mature manner is real penance. Mental strength, kindness and humility are essential to sustain fasting. Penance can be performed even in family and social life by those who cultivate and ripen their mental attitudes. It has the power to achieve and attain what we aim and seek with pervading effort. It purifies and invigorates ones mind and body. It is wrong to misuse the powers of penance.

Chapter 28: Vileness & Imposture

Cheating in the garb of penance and sainthood, a life of pretence, wrong deeds of a stained mind in the form of renouncers are evils to be wary of and identified for de-weeding and destruction. Certain religious beliefs esp. of the East, that dipping and bathing the body in pure waters of rivers and seas considered holy, is a way of curing stains and sins of the mind, are repudiated by *kuRaL* couplets 278 and 298 which assert that purity of mind is to be found in veracity of the tongue and virtue of actions. There is a famous verse in Telugu (a Dravidian/ Indian language) that says

'There is no merit or virtue, carrying your sins stored in mind and going to Varanashi to dip in Ganges water,'

Chapters 29-32:

Deal with the mental torture, harm and evil in coveting and looting; the excellence of veracity of truth that does not harm; the prowess of controlling and banishing vehemence and anger; realizing and desisting from painful harm.

Chapter 33: Non-violence

It could not be easily comprehended and asserted as to how this was interpreted and treated in the olden days of VaLLuvar. However it will be safe to take that the thought of saving lives prevailed as an extension of the code of not inflicting painful harm, and abjuring the violent ways of killing by goring bodies, for the heck of it as in hunting, destructive wars, feuds etc. *KuRaL* 109 mentions avoiding 'cruelty of wounding to death'. That is a virtue higher than veracity, the right path to a positive and constructive environment. It is the manifestation of kindness and compassion, and a duty to society to share with, patronize and preserve all living organisms (322).

At the same time, banishing terror by the hardest punishment (550), culling out thorny shrubs from their roots young (879) and destroying foes who defy (880) are not crimes but inevitable duties. Destroying weeds and pests that harm crops and environment is essential for healthy living. In the light of current scientific knowledge, plants and micro organisms are living beings as humans and animals. Even 2000 years back *kuRaL* has hinted at the life cycle and sensitive nature of plants and flowers"

A tender flower withers in our breath (90)

The lilly droops down in shame (1114)

In the air we breathe and the water we drink
exist millions of micro organisms; in the grains
we eat stay living cells; in the palms that sap
water from ground and yield tender nuts from head,
taking energy from sun light, life's mechanism throbs.

We are all familiar with plants that are touch sensitive, that sleep, breathe, take water and nutrients from ground by capillary action and grow; they are very much alive as humans and animals. Even stones and earth have living organisms in them. Life is a struggle for existence and survival of the fittest in evolution, and no life can survive without causing harm or destroying other lives.

But the vegetarians cannot avoid and have no qualms in eating vegetables and plants or consuming milk from animals, which in nature is meant for their calves. Most of those who advocate vegetarianism for non-violence have no hesitation in using silk from worms killed, wool and skin from animals for clothing and foot-ware. Domesticating and employing animals for work is taken in stride as growth of civilization; Can we make it fully free from harm or cruelty? Animals are grown, as we grow grain, pulses and vegetables for food. If all the animals in disuse are to be maintained for life there won't be enough fodder for them in the world; if all the eggs laid are hatched to chicks will there be enough space to accommodate? Therefore on a practical outlook the best that could be aimed is to avoid cruelty to all species. Mercy killing has come to be recognised in human race.

Chapters 34 & 36:

To know and abide by the truth as to what are stable virtues in the world - like kindness, love, contribution and glory, and the unstable ones that expand, roll off and shrink - like wealth, time that waits for no one and the throb of life that commences and ends its activity automatically. To achieve clarity of what is true and ultimate wisdom, what cause happiness and pain, what is the real nature of matter, how to get rid of the blind notions about rebirth; to appreciate the true objectives of family life, penance and renunciation, and the means of overcoming lust, wrath and folly; to seek eternal truth and attain unison with Nature. These are analysed in depth.

Chapters 35 & 37:

The ethics of *kuRaL* does not accept the concepts of Buddism and Janinism about abandoning social life and opting renunciation as the better; but endorses the fact that insatiable desires and greed are the basic causes of pain and sorrow in life.

Like the tidal waves that ebb and rise to the shores

by the force of hot air currents, desires are endless.

Real sacrifice is to burn the burden of boundless lust

Life can be reformed and refined only by curbing greed, with a firm attitude of mind, resolute that 'we do not need what we can do without'. Control and deployment of our senses, free from vacillations, towards the ultimate truth of nature is renunciation pure.

Chapter 38: Natural Phenomena

KuRaL variously describes this as stable nature (370), true knowledge (373), nature of the world (373, 637), proper procedures by the laws of nature (547). In short it deals with the behaviour of the forces of nature, caused by the environment.

In sociology and political science it refers to the rules of discipline, governance and justice. Life on earth is an unceasing endeavour to shape and mould our environment to congenial surroundings, knowing that the forces of nature are omnipotent and cannot be overcome; the response of a rational human being to the seemingly irrational universe. However, ceaseless striving with confidence will muster strength that moulds ones environment to success (620). Nature is not poor. It has all the elaborate wealth. To live in happiness in tune with nature is never against the codes of grace and penance. The fruits of nature are for decent enjoyment. Not to be overwhelmed and drowned in them is the true knowledge of self-realisation.

THE FUNCTIONING AND MOTIVATION OF LIFE

Birth (*piRavi*) refers to the consequential object of life on earth in *kuRaL* couplets 133, 339, 345, 351, 357, 358, 361, 362, 972, 1002, 1026 and 1315. The nature and mechanism of life is like electricity. It flows, throbs and activates movement thro' a medium, namely the body. Without the body there is no life, no function. When the body ceases functioning, it is the symptom of end of life. Life by itself is no substance of mass but the function of matter, and hence not apparent but abstract.

Like alcohol produced by biochemical reactions, fermentation and transformation of certain ingredients like starch, enzymes and sugars, complex combinations of the elements of matter-air, water, fire and earth- evolve substances like the body; and the energy of matter originates life to function.

The ancient *Thamizh* grammar of 6th century BC, *Tholkaappiyam* defines that the body (matter) is the medium for the origin of life (*'meyyin vazhi athu uyir thOnRum nilaiyae'* 1-18). Life cannot be seen separately from a functioning body; it cannot exist without a body. The death of a body is the extinction of throbbing life, resulting in deterioration, disintegration and deformation of matter in the body.

It is again *Thirumanthiram* the 3rd century AD book of *Thamizh* philosophy that says, life is one with the body; with the destruction of the body life extinguishes, life that has the power to sense, think and act, born with the body goes with it (*vudambaar aziyin vuyiraar azhivar 3-13, Oruvanumae udaloudu vuyir thaanae 2-9, unnuyir poum udal okkap piRanthathu 1-4*). *Avvaik kuRaL* says there is no sensual feelings of life without the body (*udambinaalanRi uNarvuthaan illai*). One of the *Thamizh* epics *MaNimaekalai* says knowledge that senses the character of perpetual movement- joining together and separating of atoms of elements in matter- is known as life, and it ends with the

4

destruction of the body mass (*avvakai aRivathu vuyir enappadumae; avvuNarvu av-vav buuthaththu azhivukaLil vevvaeRu piriyum* 27-119, 267).

The sensing function of life is known as the inner mind or soul (*aazh manam-aanmaa)*, it has no dimension or mass; it pervades the body. The functioning state of life is survival and flourishing; its sensual state is awareness, thinking, knowledge and actions. Its manifestations are throbbing of heart, movement of limbs, skills, wisdom, execution of deeds etc.

Commencing from couplet 31 *kuRaL* deals with various aspects of life, its nature, throbbing and functioning state in about 61 places, comparing and distinguishing, plaiting and figuratively referring to it with the body. The import of all these is that it is a shapeless functioning/motivating instinct and force of energy. It is not a physical matter, or elements or atoms; it is not cell of the bodý, but its character. That it has no existence outside the body and it is only functional, is reinforced by the references to it as a verbal function (vuyirppa– 880), the state of life (255, 290), living life (392), end to life (476), all life depends on flesh (1013). In *Malayaazham* (a branch language of *Thamizh*), the ceasing of life is described as the juice, the energy has gone (*saththu pOyee*). Living is a survival instinct sensing the environment. The scientific name of life is *'homo sapiens sapiens'* (I know and I know that I know).

Modern science has invented machines like MRI (magnetic resonance imageing) wherein the internal organs of the body and their movement can be seen multi-dimensional in live telecast . It has been established that our mind is not in the heart (which had been customarily referred to as the repository of feelings), but in our brain's nerves, a centre called 'limbic'. If we assume that our brain is a computer, the nervous system functions as a software. The energy that makes it functional is the life system; like electric power, its force is felt at the end loads, like the burning of a light, rotation of a machine, the sound on an amplifier etc.

The evolution of life on earth is considered accidental by chance. As electric energy produced by chemical changes, so the evolution of the mechanism of life's throbbing.

According to Charles Darvin's theory of evolution, long time after the formation of the earth spun off from the Sun, and precipitation of water on it, in a warm pond on its periphery, micro carbon atoms in the process of a continuous chain reaction of complex chemical changes, combined, separated and multiplied themselves repeatedly up to a stage of functioning to form molecular cells that grow and double up themselves, which is called the origin of life.

In the concepts of *KuRaL* also the terminology used is evolving, producing (385, 1062), multiplying, organising and distributing. On the question whether life energy is stationed in the sperm cells and ovaries, or as part of the brain structure, latest findings have asserted that it is in the metabolism of all living cells. The processes of protoplasm converting food into nutrients and proteins into enzymes is the functioning of life. In all living cells, the core nucleus DNA (deoxyribose nucleic acid) has about 46 variety of chromosomes. In each chromosome there are over 40,000 atoms charged with life in the form of chemical acids. The genes in chromosomes are of two types RNA and DNA. They survive with a characteristic energy of involuntary self motion, constantly changing and multiplying themselves. The fountain nucleus for DNA are four types of acidic atoms A G C T. Scientific explorations for probing the basic characteristics and type spectrums of genes are progressing fast, to solve more mysteries in the realm and rhythm of biology.

In farming for cultivation of plants like sugar cane, plantains we use saplings, not seeds; for cross breeding of plants we join young branches. In a more sophisticated way it has now become possible since 1997 to clone tissues of animal or human cells for reproduction of parts or whole bodies, initiate life and growth cycles. This is a significant development radically changing and replacing the idea of creation. Scientists have already succeeded in producing sheep, cattle and cats. Human reproduction is also on the cards, but old religious taboos, as usual against any scientific invention, stand as great hurdle.

The progress of genetic research is greatly helping developments in farming, medicine and biology. With the help of charts and type tests on the characteristics of DNA atoms knowledge is gained on the causes of heredity, genetic diseases and birth abnormalities for curing and preventing them.

Knowledge is not hereditary; no one is born a genius. Circumstances and environment shape and mould life's qualities. From childhood to adult age, in tune with environmental conditions, the rate of growth of millions of tissue cells is fast. By this process the brain rejuvenates and maintains growth. The developments in research on brain are revolutionary. It can lead to finding out as to how the human mind is evolved and shaped.

FUNCTIONING OF LIFE IN OUR BODY

For a better and closer appreciation of the inputs in *ThirukkuRaL* on Penance, Renunciation and Realization of Truth the deep analysis and researches made by ascetic sage *yogi* Vedathiri about *yoga* (meditation, concentration and unification) for command and control of the powers in the mystic circle fistula of the anus, to generate the elixir (energy) for prolonging life (*kaayakalpa kuNdalini yoegam*) throws more light.

To acquire in the growth of human thoughts the faculties of grace, facility of mind and soul, material wealth and health, by overcoming illness; to protect youthfulness and to prolong life by distancing death, the aforesaid yoga practice advocated in the poetry of mystic saints of yore shows the right path. This has been tested and experienced in finesse by means of critical scientific and psychological tests.

The form of species is the integrated movement in unison of the body (1), throb of life (2), semen-egg (3), life magnetism (4) and mind (5) . Our body cells have balanced pressure of magnetism on all sides. Its particles charged with life have the characteristics of continuous self rotation, expansion and multiplication. Depending on the count of particles and the pressure of magnetism the cells maintain their form and setup and functionalize the mind and body maintaining temperature and pressure of the blood, making adjustments to the effects of external temperature, humidity and pressure. Magnetic energy of the cell particles depends on the quantity and quality of seminal-ovary egg fluids. These are required in sufficient quantities for the equilibrium and uniform functioning of the body and mind. One part of this internal magnetism functioning thro' the tissues, governs the body metabolism and the other part thro' the brain tissues, activates and controls the microwave movement thro' the nerves system. Any disorder or weakness in the disciplined functioning of the aforesaid five components, cause pain, illness and death. Coordinated and balanced inputs of nutrition, rest, work, sex, thought etc. are essential for normal and steady functioning of life. A self balancing mechanism to correct disorders in health is available in the body. It is also immune to disturbances to some extent. When the disorders are intense and increasing, we have to organise and re-orient our physical and mental exercises and food habits.

Impact of the external environment, and magnetic influence of the Sun, planets and stars around the world also marginally affect the life and body functions. Magnetism from the core of the earth attracts body magnetism. Life's mechanism exerts a balancing and unifying force of body magnetism. When the latter is stronger the body registers growth in the first 35 years of youth and after that it starts to fatigue and feeble. The sixth sense has the faculty to feel and try to overcome to some extent the forces and methods of nature. As our body ages in course of time, making use of our thinking power, it is possible to retard the rate of slow down of our life force and delay death. By increasing density and strength of seminal fluids it is possible to control energy of life functions, by our senses (268, 269).

When we attain a state of fulfilment in life, it is possible to subdue mental faculties (349). When functioning of both the mind and body stop, life subsides and extinguishes in the body.

This is the stage of integration with nature which sages called samaathi (stable unison). That stage can be attained by the induced process of recycling sexual vital fluids, diminishing deterioration and wastage, ripening and purifying its energy in the form of waves at the fistula and push them up the vertebrae and merge with the brain's waves. This method of integrating body and mental exercise is the rare achievement of mystic sages, called the art of *kundalini yoga.*

Only by special interest and deep involvement or maturity and ripeness in family life, and a detachment attained by clear thinking, the full dimension and import of many couplets of *kuRaL* in chapters 25, 27, 34 and 37 can be appreciated.

THE CONCEPT OF TRANQUILLITY IN KURAL

The word home (implying its tranquillity) has been mentioned only once in KuRaL. This Thamizh word has a multifaceted dimension of liberty, freedom, calmness, contentment, detachment, seclusion, redemption etc. Home is a place which protects us from external environmental impacts of sun, wind, rain, wild animals and foes and affords physical rest, mental peace and calmness. As an embodiment of family life, home is distinct from a house. It also means liberty from troubles, and completeness in tranquility. The kuRaL couplet 791 containing this word renders in English as:

'Courting friendship without searching evaluation is a

bad risk, redemption is scarce once friendship is held'

In this the word connotes that there is no redemption, separation from worthy friendship. Beyond this and the codes of virtue, wealth and happiness ThiruvaLLuvar has not gone into any unseen, abstract concept like salvation, which is ingrained in many religions; benefits of health acquired by virtuous means, a family/social life and happiness attained thereby, have no apprehension about what happens after death.

KuRaL 501 says that one's attitude and capability of handling fears about life, determine their ability and courage in facing affairs of life. This has totally ignored the Northern and Western religious codes of salvation (refuge) after death. Ancient Thamizh codes and ethics of life called 'VaLLuvam' of many centuries before Christ, asserts full and total dimensions of life in virtues, wealth and happiness, and nothing beyond integration and unison with nature. There is nothing lacking in this concept in fullness of life. This prevailed up to 6th century AD.

Nachchinaarkkiniyaar, a scholar interpreter of *Tholkaappiyam* has asserted that Tholkaappiyar, ThiruvaLLuvar and Akaththiyar in Thamizh tradition have not spoken about 'salvation', a concept alien to Thamizh culture, which the process of thoughts and words cannot conceive.

'Happiness, wealth and virtue' merged in kindness of love'
                    Tholkaappiyam, poruL, kaLavu 1.
'You patronise, virtue and wealth'

                    - *PuRan-aanURu* 28 & 31.
'Neither wealth, nor virtue or happiness can
reside in submissive servitude to women'

                    kuRaL 909.
'If you think of good alone there will be no fear or shame of
and no refuge to seek after death'   Thirumanthiram
                    7- 34.
'Virtue as the lamp, wealth as the wick and happiness as oil
VaLLuvar has ignited the flame of short couplets that
drive away the darkness of ignorance and light knowledge'
                    ThiruvaLLuva Maalai.
'People of worldly wisdom said   three codes, in introspection
realize they are virtues, wealth and happiness'
                    Thirumangkai AaLvaar SiRiya Thirumadal 5-8

The verses cited reflect the views of KuRaL 754 and 755 that material wealth enables to achieve virtues and happiness in life if acquired in grace and kindness.

A peaceful and fulfilling family life is the objective and purpose of home; this was beautifully laid out in *Tholkaappiyam, PoruL, kaRpu 6 -thavam.*

'In the prime of life after achievement of happiness
Living with the safety and affection of children,
And the virtuous company of kith and kin to cherish
and perform duties to society, is the purpose of life'

The same idea has been stressed in kuRaL 265, 370 that the discipline of fasting is the best of peace in family life, and attaining glory in social life is the harmony in nature.

Even in Sanskrit language of the north, in the era of Kalidaasa and Vathsaayana up to 4th century AD, only the trilogy concept of virtue, wealth and happiness was prevalent.

In the middle ages after Sangam era in Thamizh, with the spreading influence of the northern based philosophies of religion, the interpretation of home as refuge, salvation crept in. Pursuit of wealth and happiness were considered impediments in achieving the goal of salvation.

In *vaisaedigam* philosophy of the North the attainment of 'home' for the 'soul' is considered as the stage where, in the absence of rebirth and loss of body, the 'spirit' stays at the feet of the Lord, without entering another body. Gradually the idea of salvation started gaining ground pushing back the primacy of materialism and happiness, which were interpreted as sins, receded. After Kavudilya and Vaathsaayanar in the North and ThiruvaLLuvar in the South, there have been no authentic treatise on Materialism or Happiness for many centuries. After the Thamizh sangam age, the tradition of treating life as *akam* (love and family) and *puRam* (social existence) have been suppressed by invading religions; commencing from 6-7 century AD the four fold concept of virtues, wealth, happiness and salvation has dominated.

In the conservative brahminical religion of India, discriminating human according to race, colour and origins of beings birth and dividing society into four strata according to the codes of Manu, only the self accredited brahmins are qualified to the fortification of salvation. Renunciation and the right to teach scriptures were denied to those described by them as 'lower' castes. They also contend that the sanctity of their scriptures will be spoiled if handled by others and in languages other than Sanskrit.

As the scriptures and the way to salvation are shut off to those others, it is beyond their reach and they need not bother about them. Of late in the 20th century, Thamizh scholars like V. Kaliyaanasundaram (thiru vi.kaa), M.Varadarajan (mu.vaa) and A.S Gnanasambandan (Aa Sa Gna) had worked for rejuvenation of the old sangam literary concept of *Akam* (virtue, happiness, penance, renunciation and realization of self) and *PuRam* (materialism and social life). We can be thriving self-fulfilled without any worry about the abstract 'salvation'.

1. இறை வணக்கம்
iRai vaNakkam
PRAYER

(EULOGIZING THE SACRED HARMONY BETWEEN DIVINITY -
ALMIGHTY NATURE- AND HUMAN KNOWLEDGE)

அகர முதல எழுத்துஎல்லாம் ஆதி
பகவன் முதற்றே உலகு.   1

akara muthala ezhuththuellAm aathi
pakavan muthatRae ulaku

A is the first letter of languages; the
Sun is the origin of planet Earth

கற்றதனால் ஆய பயனென்கொல் வாலறிவன்
நற்றாள் தொழாஅர் எனின்.   2

katRathanAl aaya payanenkol vAlaRivan
n-atRAL thozAar enin

Of what avail education is, if one does not
admire and follow the learned, the pure

மலர்மிசை ஏகினான் மாணடி சேர்ந்தார்
நிலமிசை நீடுவாழ் வார்.   3

malarmisai eakinAn mANadi saern-thAr
n-ilamisai n-eeduvAz vAr

Those who follow the light of nobility, live
in fame that survives the world

வேண்டுதல் வேண்டாமை இலான்அடி சேர்ந்தார்க்கு
யாண்டும் இடும்பை இல.   4

vaeNduthal vaeNdAmai ilAnadi saern-thArkku
yANdum idumpai ila

Who are guided by the one, above likes and dislikes,
face no impediments in life

இருள்சேர் இருவினையும் சேரா இறைவன்
பொருள்சேர் புகழ்புரிந்தார் மாட்டு.   5

iruLsaer iruvinaiyum saerA iRaivan
poruLsaer pukazhpurin-thAr mAttu

Ignorance and faults afflict not those, who gain
benevolence in the grace of the great

பொறிவாயில் ஐந்துஅவித்தான் பொய்தீர் ஒழுக்க
நெறிநின்றார் நீடுவாழ் வார்.   6

*poRivAyil ain-thuaviththAn poytheer ozukka
n-eRin-inRAr n-eedu vAzvar*

Controlled senses of body, eyes, ears, nose and mouth
and disciplined life, ensure fame and survival

தனக்குஉவமை இல்லாதான் தாள்சேர்ந்தார்க்கு அல்லால்
மனக்கவலை மாற்றல் அரிது.   7

*thanakkuuvamai illAthAn thALsaern-thArkku allAl
manakkavalai mAtRRal arithu*

Distress does not afflict those, who adopt
the path of the peerless great

அறஆழி அந்தணன் தாள்சேர்ந்தார்க்கு அல்லால்
பிறஆழி நீந்தல் அரிது.   8

*aRaazi an-thaNan thALsaern-thArkku allAl
piRaazi n-een-thal arithu*

Swim the seas of wealth and happiness, guided by
those who have swum the sea of virtues

கோளில் பொறியில் குணம்இலவே எண்குணத்தான்
தாளை வணங்காத் தலை.   9

*kOLil poRiyil kuNam-ilavae eNkuNaththAn
thALai vaNangkAth thalai*

What worth are our still senses, lest they bow in
reverence to, and are guided by the adorable

பிறவிப் பெருங்கடல் நீந்துவர் நீந்தார்
இறைவன்அடி சேரா தார்.   10

*piRavip perungkadal n-een-thuvar n-een-thAr
iRaivanadi saerA thAr*

Swim the vast sea of life and survive,
seeking guidance of the great

2. வான் சிறப்பு
vAn siRappu
IN PRAISE OF RAIN

(RAIN FROM THE CLOUDS IN THE SKY ARE ESSENTIAL FOR ALL
LIFE ON EARTH, AS FOOD FOR GROWTH, TO REPLENISH THE
SOURCES OF WATER ON EARTH, AND TO MAINTAIN VIRTUES; IT
IS A GIFT OF NATURE WITHOUT RECOMPENSE)

வான்நின்று உலகம் வழங்கி வருதலால்
தான்அமிழ்தம் என்றுஉணரற் பாற்று.　　　　11

vAnn-inRu ulakam vazangki varuthalAl
thAnamiztham enRuuNaraR pAtRu

Pure water is the Elixir of life; the
world survives and thrives on rain

துப்பார்க்குத் துப்பாய துப்பாக்கித் துப்பார்க்குத்
துப்பாய தூஉம் மழை.　　　　12

thuppArkkuth thuppAya thuppAkkith thuppArkkuth
thuppAya thUum mazai

Water is food essential, and it helps
growth of all inputs for life on earth

விண்இன்று பொய்ப்பின் விரிநீர் வியனுலகத்து
உள்நின்று உடற்றும் பசி.　　　　13

viNinRu poyppin virin-eer viyanulakaththu
uLn-inRu udatRRum pasi

If clouds fail to rain, hunger will strangle
the world, girted though by vast seas

ஏரின் உழாஅர் உழவர் புயலென்னும்
வாரி வளங்குன்றிக் கால்.　　　　14

aerin uzAar uzavar puyalennum
vAri vaLangkunRik kAl

Agriculture suffers mainly, if rains
are inadequate for cultivation

கெடுப்பதூஉங் கெட்டார்க்குச் சார்வாய்மற்று ஆங்கே
எடுப்பதூஉம் எல்லாம் மழை.　　　　15

keduppathUum kettArkkuch chArvAymatRRu aangkae
eduppathUum ellAm mazai

Failed or excess rains destroy; seasonal
rains help lift up the afflicted

விசும்பின் துளிவீழின் அல்லால்மற்று ஆங்கே
பசும்புல் தலைகாண்பு அரிது.   **16**

visumpin thuLiveezin allAlmatRRu aangkae
pasumpul thalaikANpu arithu

Sights of greenery and prosperity are
rare in the world when rains fail

நெடுங்கடலும் தன்நீர்மை குன்றும் தடிந்துழிலி
தான்நல்கா தாகி விடின்.   **17**

n-edumkadalum thann-eermai kunRum thadiththuezili
thAnn-alkAthu aaki vidin

The seas, sources of clouds, lose their depth
and richness in the absence of rains

சிறப்பொடு பூசனை செல்லாது வானம்
வறக்குமேல் வானோர்க்கும். ஈண்டு.   **18**

siRappodu pUsanai sellAthu vAnam
vaRakkumael vAnOrkkum eeNdu

Celebrations and propitiations for the high
become rare if rains dry up

தானம் தவம்இரண்டும் தங்கா வியன்உலகம்
வானம் வழங்கா தெனின்.   **19**

thAnam thavamiraNdum thangkA viyanulakam
vAnam vazangkAthu enin

Penance and munificence do not thrive in
the world without the gift of rains

நீர்இன்று அமையாது உலகுஎனின் யார்யார்க்கும்
வான்இன்று அமையாது ஒழுக்கு.   **20**

n-eerinRu amaiyAthu ulakuenin yAryArkkum
vAninRu amaiyAthu ozukku

Droughts destroy social virtues and stress
the indispensability of water for life

3. நீத்தார் பெருமை
n-IththAr perumai
GREATNESS OF ASCETICS (RENUNCIATION)
(PEOPLE WHO DISDAIN THE PLEASURES AND PAINS OF FAMILY
AND SOCIAL LIFE, OR AT A MATURE STATE, RENOUNCE ALL
DESIRES AND OPT FOR A DETACHED SAINTLY MODE OF LIFE)

ஒழுக்கத்து நீத்தார் பெருமை விழுப்பத்து
வேண்டும் பனுவல் துணிவு.   **21**

ozukkaththu n-eeththAr perumai vizuppaththu
vaeNdum panuval thuNivu

Saintly disciples are the objects of
glory, the testaments eulogise

துறந்தார் பெருமை துணைக்கூறின் வையத்து
இறந்தாரை எண்ணிக்கொண் டற்று.   **22**

thuRan-thAr perumai thuNaikkURin vaiyaththu
iRan-thArai eNNikkoN datRRu

Glory of the ascetics counts higher than
all those who lived and left this world

இருமை வகைதெரிந்து ஈண்டுஅறம் பூண்டார்
பெருமை பிறங்கிற்று உலகு.   **23**

irumai vakaitherin-thu eeNduaRam pUNdAr
perumai piRangkitRRu ulaku

Discerning and righteous perception of matter
and spirit brightens and glorifies the world

உரனென்னும் தோட்டியான் ஓர்ஐந்தும் காப்பான்
வரனென்னும் வைப்பிற்கோர் வித்து.   **24**

uranennum thOttiyAn oorain-thum kAppAn
varanennum vaippiRkuoor viththu

Mental strength controls the senses of those
who are the seeds of greatness

ஐந்துஅவித்தான் ஆற்றல் அகல்விசும்பு உளார்கோமான்
இந்திரனே சாலுங் கரி.   **25**

ain-thuaviththAn aatRRal akalvisumpu uLArkOmAn
in-thiranae sAlum kari

Powers of self-control are the themes of
tales on destruction of the wicked

செயற்குஅரிய செய்வார் பெரியர் சிறியர்
செயற்குஅரிய செய்கலா தார்.   26

*seyaRkuaRiya seyvAr periyAr, siRiyar
seyaRkuariya seykalA thAr*

Rarer deeds are signs of greatness,
lesser mortals achieve no success

சுவைஒளி ஊறுஓசை நாற்றமென்று ஐந்தின்
வகைதெரிவான் கட்டே உலகு.   27

*suvaioLi uuRuoosai n-ARRamenRu ain-thin
vakaitherivAn kattae ulaku*

Name and fame are for those who diligently employ
their senses of taste, sight, touch, sound and smell

நிறைமொழி மாந்தர் பெருமை நிலத்து
மறைமொழி காட்டி விடும்.   28

*n-iRaimozi mAn-thar perumai n-ilaththu
maRaimozi kAtti vidum*

Wisdom and glory of the great are reflected
in the scriptures of their land

குணம்என்னும் குன்றேறி நின்றார் வெகுளி
கணமேயும் காத்தல் அரிது.   29

*kuNamennum kunRaeRi n-inRAr vekuLi
kaNamaeum kAththal arithu*

Anger of those who have reached the heights of character,
though rare and momentary, is unbearable

அந்தணர் என்போர் அறவோர்மற்று எவ்வுயிர்க்கும்
செந்தண்மை பூண்டொழுக லான்.   30

*an-thaNar enpOr aRavOrmatRRu evvuyirkkum
sen-thaNmai pUNdozuka lAn*

Who tread the path of righteousness with grace, love
and affection are fit to minister the souls

4. அறன் வலியுறுத்தல்
aRan valiyuRuththal
EMPHASIS ON VIRTUE (RIGHTEOUSNESS)

சிறப்புஈனும் செல்வமும் ஈனும் அறத்தின்ஊஉங்கு
ஆக்கம் எவனோ உயிர்க்கு.　　　　　31

siRappueenum selvam eenum aRaththin-uungku
aakkam evanO uyirkku

Righteousness is a great achiever; it
affords wealth and stature in life

அறத்தின்ஊஉங்கு ஆக்கமும் இல்லை அதனை
மறத்தலின் ஊஉங்குஇல்லை கேடு.　　　　32

aRathinuungku aakkamum illai athanai
maRaththalin uungkuillai kaedu

Adherence to righteousness shapes up virtues
and its negligence spoils life

ஒல்லும் வகையான் அறவினை ஓவாதே
செல்லும்வாய் எல்லாம் செயல்.　　　　33

ollum vakaiyAn aRavinai oovAthae
sellumvAy ellAm seyal

Be righteous and active all round in life
and persist ceaselessly and relentlessly

மனத்துக்கண் மாசுஇலன் ஆதல் அனைத்துஅறன்
ஆகுல நீர பிற.　　　　34

manaththukkaN mAsuilan aathal anaiththuaRan
aakula n-eera piRa

Purity of mind is righteousness personified;
other formats are hollow sounds

அழுக்காறு அவாவெகுளி இன்னாச்சொல் நான்கும்
இழுக்கா இயன்றது அறம்.　　　　35

azukkARu avAvekuLi innAchsol n-Ankum
izukkA iyanRathu aRam

Righteousness is a virtue unblemished by
envy, anger, greed and insult

அன்றுஅறிவாம் என்னாது அறம்செய்க மற்றது
பொன்றுங்கால் பொன்றாத் துணை.   36

anRuaRivAm ennAthu aRamseyka maRRathu
ponRungkAl ponRAth thuNai

Act virtuously from the start and persist;
that earns fame beyond your life

அறத்துஆறு இதுவென வேண்டா சிவிகை
பொறுத்தானோடு ஊர்ந்தான் இடை.   37

aRaththhuaaRu ithuena vaeNdA sivikai
poRuththAnOdu uurn-thAn idai

Success in righteousness is like riding a palanquin;
failure is like languishing under its burden

வீழ்நாள் படாஅமை நன்றுஆற்றின் அஃதொருவன்
வாழ்நாள் வழியடைக்குங் கல்.   38

veezn-AL padAamai n-anRuaatRRin aqthoruvan
vAzn-AL vaziyadaikkum kal

Miss not a day doing good things right; those
are the stones paving the path of your life

அறத்தான் வருவதே இன்பம்மற்று எல்லாம்
புறத்த புகழும் இல.   39

aRaththAn varuvathae inpammatRRu ellAm
puRaththa pukazum ila

Happiness comes from righteous virtues; acting
otherwise is unworthy and infamous

செயற்பால தோரும் அறனே ஒருவற்கு
உயற்பால தோரும் பழி.   40

seyaRpAla thOrum aRanae oruvaRku
uyaRpAla thOrum pazi

It behoves to act righteously; virtue
protects one from blemishes

5. இல்வாழ்க்கை
il vAzkkai
FAMILY LIFE (AN INSTITUTION)
(IS AN INSTITUTION TO PROTECT ITS MEMBERS, ANCESTRY,
EXTEND HOSPITALITY TO RELATIVES AND FRIENDS AND SERVE
THE NEEDY IN SOCIETY)

இல்வாழ்வான் என்பான் இயல்புடைய மூவர்க்கும்
நல்லாற்றின் நின்ற துணை.   41

ilvAzvAn enpAn iyalpudaiya mUvarkkum
n-allARRin n-inRa thuNai

Family life is the best protection to aid
one's parents, spouse and children

துறந்தார்க்கும் துவ்வா தவர்க்கும் இறந்தார்க்கும்
இல்வாழ்வான் என்பான் துணை.   42

thuRan-thArkkum thuvvA thavarkkum iRan-thArkkum
ilvAzvAn enpAn thuNai

A householder is patron to the renouncers,
the have-nots and the protected

தென்புலத்தார் தெய்வம் விருந்துஒக்கல் தான்என்றாங்கு
ஐம்புலத்தாறு ஓம்பல் தலை.   43

thenpulaththAr theyvam virun-thuokkal thAnenRuaangku
aimpulaththuaaRu oompal thalai

Family is an institution preserving heritage, divinity,
hospitality and relationships, besides one's dignity

பழியஞ்சிப் பாத்தூண் உடைத்தாயின் வாழ்க்கை
வழிஎஞ்சல் எஞ்ஞான்றும் இல்.   44

pazianjsip pAththUN udaiththAyin vAzkkai
vazienjsal enjnjAnRum il

The journey of life is secure in the family with a mission
of hospitality, and wary of blemishes

அன்பும் அறனும் உடைத்தாயின் இல்வாழ்க்கை
பண்பும் பயனும் அது.   45

anpum aRanum udaiththAyin ilvAzkkai
paNpum payanum athu

A family bound in love and virtues
is the purpose and essence of life

அறத்தாற்றின் இல்வாழ்க்கை ஆற்றின் புறத்தாற்றில்
போஒய்ப் பெறுவது எவன்.   46

*aRaththuaatRin ilvAzkkai aatRin puRaththaatRin
pOyp peRuvathu evan*

Dignified family life accomplishes better
than saintly or priestly orders

இயல்பினான் இல்வாழ்க்கை வாழ்பவன் என்பான்
முயல்வாருள் எல்லாம் தலை.   47

*iyalpinAn ilvAzkkai vAzpavan enpAn
muyalvAruL ellAm thalai*

Devotion to family life keeps one ahead
of those toiling in other streams

ஆற்றின் ஒழுக்கி அறன்இழுக்கா இல்வாழ்க்கை
நோற்பாரின் நோன்மை உடைத்து.   48

*aaRRin ozukki aRanizukkA ilvAzkkai
n-ORpArin n-Onmai udaiththu*

The path of righteousness in family life
is more saintly than the saint's

அறன்எனப் பட்டதே இல்வாழ்க்கை அஃதும்
பிறன்பழிப்பது இல்லாயின் நன்று.   49

*aRanenap pattathae ilvAzkkai aqthum
piRanpazippathu illAyin n-anRu*

Family life is the embodiment of righteousness;
if it guards against blame, it is finer

வையத்துள் வாழ்வாங்கு வாழ்பவன் வான்உறையும்
தெய்வத்துள் வைக்கப் படும்.   50

*vaiyaththu vAzvAngku vAzpavan vAnuRaiyum
theyvaththuL vaikkap padum*

Success in the ideals of family life raises
one sky-high in fame, as a guide

6. வாழ்க்கைத் துணைநலம்
vAzkkaith thuNai n-alam
PARTNER IN LIFE
(DEVOTED TO THE SPOUSE AND SUPPORT IN SUSTAINING AND
ENHANCING THE PRESTIGE OF THE FAMILY)

மனைத்தக்க மாண்புடையள் ஆகித்தற் கொண்டான்

வளத்தக்காள் வாழ்க்கைத் துணை.   **51**

*manaiththakka mANpudaiyaL aakiththaR koNdAn
vaLaththakkAL vAzkkaith thuNai*

A virtuous wife is a partner in life; she keeps
the family happy within its means

மனைமாட்சி இல்லாள்கண் இல்லாயின் வாழ்க்கை

எனைமாட்சித் தாயினும் இல்.   **52**

*manaimAtchi illAlkaN illaayin vAzkkai
enaimAtsith thaayinum il*

What is in life without a wife, who can
uphold the dignity of a family

இல்லதுஎன் இல்லவள் மாண்பானால் உள்ளதுஎன்

இல்லவள் மாணாக் கடை.   **53**

*illathuen illavaL mANpuaanAl uLLathuen
illavaL mANAk kadai*

A noble wife is everything in a family;
without her there is nothing

பெண்ணிற் பெருந்தக்க யாவுள கற்புஎன்னும்

திண்மையுண் டாகப் பெறின்.   **54**

*peNNin perun-thakka yAvuLa kaRpuennum
thiNmaiuN dAkap peRin*

Chastity is the greatest virtue of a wife; which
keeps her on a higher pedestal in life

தெய்வம் தொழாஅள் கொழுநன் தொழுதுஎழுவாள்

பெய்யெனப் பெய்யும் மழை.   **55**

*theyvam thozAaL kozun-an thozuthuezuvAL
peyyenap peyyum mazai*

**A wife who revers her husband as the first and
foremost guide, is like seasonal rains in summer**

தற்காத்துத் தற்கொண்டான் பேணித் தகைசான்ற
சொற்காத்துச் சோர்விலாள் பெண்.   56

*thaRkAththuth thaRkoNdAn pENith thakaisAnRa
soRkAththuch sOrvilAL peN*

**Guarding self, tending spouse, relentlessly protecting
family honour are hallmarks of a housewife**

சிறைகாக்கும் காப்புஎவன் செய்யும் மகளிர்
நிறைகாக்கும் காப்பே தலை.   57

*siRaikAkkum kAppuevan seyyum makaLir
n-iRaikAkkum kAppE thalai*

**Fullness of character guards ladies from
subjugation and protects their freedom**

பெற்றான் பெறின்பெறுவர் பெண்டிர் பெருஞ்சிறப்புப்
புத்தேளிர் வாழும் உலகு.   58

*petRRAn peRinpeRuvar peNdir perunjsiRappup
puththELir vAzum ulaku*

**Right companionship in life earns name and fame
for a wife, in a happy new world of a family**

புகழ்புரிந்த இல்இலோர்க்கு இல்லை இகழ்வார்முன்
ஏறுபோல் பீடு நடை.   59

*pukazpurin-tha ililOrkku illai ikazvArmun
aeRupOl peedu n-adai*

**'The mind is without fear and the head is held high' when
you are joined by a praiseworthy partner in life**

மங்கலம் என்ப மனைமாட்சி மற்றுஅதன்
நன்கலம் நன்மக்கட் பேறு.   60

*mangkalam enpa manaimAtsi maRRuathan
n-ankalam n-anmakkat pERu*

**Family life is a bed of roses and incense when adorned
with a loving wife and gifted children**

7. மக்கட்பேறு
makkat pERu
WEALTH OF CHILDREN

(OF ALL THAT PEOPLE ACQUIRE THE WEALTH OF TALENTED
CHILDREN IS THE BEST AND LONG STANDING; IT IS WISE TO
TRAIN THEM TO SHAPE THEIR FUTURE WITH THEIR OWN SKILLS)

பெறுமவற்றுள் யாம்அறிவது இல்லை அறிவறிந்த
மக்கட்பேறு அல்ல பிற.　　　　　　　61

peRumavaRRuL yAmaRivathu illai aRivaRin-tha
makkatpaeRu alla piRa

Intelligent and knowledgeable offspring
are invaluable assets of a family

எழுபிறப்பும் தீயவை தீண்டா பழிபிறங்காப்
பண்புடை மக்கட் பெறின்.　　　　　　　62

ezupiRappum theeyavai theeNdA pazipiRangkAp
paNpudai makkat perin

Evils dare not touch for generations families of
high tradition, and free from blemishes

தம்பொருள் என்பதம் மக்கள் அவர்பொருள்
தம்தம் வினையான் வரும்.　　　　　　　63

thamporuL enpatham makkaL avarporuL
thamtham vinaiyAn varum

Children are the best assets of a family; they earn
their wealth by their own toil and sweat

அமிழ்தினும் ஆற்ற இனிதேதம் மக்கள்
சிறுகை அளாவிய கூழ்.　　　　　　　64

amizthinum aatRRa inithaetham makkaL
siRukai aLAviya kUz

Be it porridge from the bowl of the poor, it tastes
sweeter than nectar, with the tender touch of kids

மக்கள்மெய் தீண்டல் உடற்குஇன்பம் மற்றுஅவர்
சொல்கேட்டல் இன்பம் செவிக்கு.　　　　　　　65

makkaLmaey theeNdal udaRkuinpam matRRuavar
solkaettal inpam sevikku

A soft embrace soothes your body and nerves; the
babe's lovely words ring music in your ears

குழல்இனிது யாழ்இனிது என்பதம் மக்கள்
மழலைச்சொல் கேளா தவர்.   66

*kuzalinithu yAzinithu enpatham makkaL
mazalaichsol kaeLA thavar*

Babel of our tender ones is sweeter than the melodies
of the flute and the yazh (a la guitar)

தந்தை மகற்குஆற்றும் நன்றி அவையத்து
முந்தி யிருப்பச் செயல்.   67

*than-thai makaRkua-atRRum n-anRi avaiyaththu
mun-thi iruppach seyal*

The duty of parents to children is to groom
them as leaders of elite assemblies

தம்மின்தம் மக்கள் அறிவுடைமை மாநிலத்து
மன்னுயிர்க் கெல்லாம் இனிது.   68

*thammin-tham makkaL aRivudaimai mAn-ilaththu
mannuyirk kellAm inithu*

Growing knowledge and skills of youth down generations
makes worldly life all the more pleasant

ஈன்ற பொழுதிற் பெரிதுஉவக்கும் தன்மகனைச்
சான்றோன் எனக்கேட்ட தாய்.   69

*eenRa pozuthiR perithuuvakkum thanmakanaich
sAnROn enakkaetta thAi*

Elation of a mother hearing others praise her children
is greater than the pleasure of begetting them

மகன்தந்தைக்கு ஆற்றும் உதவி இவன்தந்தை
என்னோற்றான் கொல்எனும் சொல்.   70

*makanthan-thaikku aatRRum uthavi ivanthan-thai
enn-OtRRAn kolenum sol*

The help children can render their parents is to gain
recognition for their penance to beget them

8. அன்புடைமை
anpudaimai
KINDNESS OF LOVE

(LOVE AND AFFECTION ARE THE QUALITIES OF MIND. KuRaL
PLACES LOVE NEXT TO VIRTUES)

அன்பிற்கும் உண்டோ அடைக்கும்தாள் ஆர்வலர்
புன்கண்நீர் பூசல் தரும்.   **71**

anpiRkum uNdO adaikkumthAz aarvalar
punkaNNeer pUsal tharum

Kindness born of true love, hardly
controls tears for the distressed

அன்புஇலார் எல்லாம் தமக்குஉரியர் அன்புடையார்
என்பும் உரியர் பிறர்க்கு.   **72**

anpuilAr ellAm thamakkuuriyar anpudaiyAr
enpum uriyar piRaRku

To the loveless other possessions are of no use
the loving ones give out everything

அன்போடு இயைந்த வழக்குஎன்ப ஆருயிர்க்கு
என்போடு இயைந்த தொடர்பு.   **73**

anpOdu iyain-tha vazakkuenpa aaRuyirkku
enpOdu iyain-tha thodarpu

The body encore of bones is activated by life;
kindness is motivated by love of the deserving

அன்புஈனும் ஆர்வம் உடைமை அதுஈனும்
நண்பென்னும் நாடாச் சிறப்பு.   **74**

anpueenum aarvam udaimai athueenum
n-aNpuennum n-AdAch siRappu

Love generates aspirations for kind acts; that
in turn springs up natural friendship

அன்புற்று அமர்ந்த வழக்குஎன்ப வையகத்து
இன்புற்றார் எய்துஞ் சிறப்பு.   **75**

anpuRRu amarn-tha vazakkuenpa vaiyakaththu
inpuRRAr eythunj siRappu

From a tradition of love in life flows the
pleasure and grace of humanism

அறத்திற்கே அன்புசார்பு என்ப அறியார்
மறத்திற்கும் அஃதே துணை.　　　　76

aRaththiRkae anpusArpu enpa aRiyAr
maRaththiRkum aqthae thuNai

To say love is virtue's aide is not to know
valour is sustained by patriotic love

என்பில் அதனை வெயில்போலக் காயுமே
அன்பில் அதனை அறம்.　　　　77

enpil athanai veyilpOlak kAyumae
anpil athanai aRam

As the Sun blazes the worms, virtue
burns the loveless souls

அன்புஅகத்து இல்லா உயிர்வாழ்க்கை வன்பாற்கண்
வற்றல் மரந்தளிர்த் தற்று.　　　　78

anpuakaththu illA uyirvAzkkai vanpARkaN
vatRRal maramthaLirth thaRRu

A life bereft of the bond of kindness in
love is like a sapless desert bloom

புறத்துஉறுப்பு எல்லாம் எவன்செய்யும் யாக்கை
அகத்துஉறுப்பு அன்பி லவர்க்கு.　　　　79

puRaththuuRuppu ellAm evanseyyum yAkkai
akaththuuRuppu anpi lavaRku

Love is the life instinct activating the body;
without it, body and limbs are in vain

அன்பின் வழியது உயிர்நிலை அஃதுஇல்லார்க்கு
என்புதோல் போர்த்த உடம்பு.　　　　80

anpin vaziyathu uyirn-ilai aqthuillArkku
enputhOl pOrtha udampu

The throb of life is in love; in its absence
the body is a bundle of bones and skin

9. விருந்தோம்பல்
virun-thOmpal
HOSPITALITY
(HOSPITALITY IS A SOCIAL RESPONSIBILITY TO TAKE CARE OF
GUESTS WITH KINDNESS SYMPATHY AND GRACE)

இருந்தோம்பி இல்வாழ்வ தெல்லாம் விருந்தோம்பி
வேளாண்மை செய்தற் பொருட்டு.   81

irun-thoompi ilvAzva thellAm virun-thoompi
vaeLANmai seythal poruttu

Enterprise and earning for homely life are
to discharge the duty of hospitality

விருந்து புறத்ததாத் தானுண்டல் சாவா
மருந்தெனினும் வேண்டற்பார் றன்று.   82

virun-thu puRaththAth thAnuNdal sAvA
marun-thueninum vaeNdaRpAR RanRu

Even if it be nectar, to keep out guests
and to eat is an unworthy act

வருவிருந்து வைகலும் ஓம்புவான் வாழ்க்கை
பருவந்து பாழ்படுதல் இன்று.   83

varuvirun-thu vaikalum oompuvAn vAzkkai
paruvan-ththu pAzpaduthal inRu

To treat guests who seek us everyday, with affection,
is to insure our lives against spoils in primeness

அகன்அமர்ந்து செய்யாள் உறையும் முகன்அமர்ந்து
நல்விருந்து ஓம்புவான் இல்.   84

akanamarn-thu seyyAL uRaiyum mukanamarn-thu
n-alvirun-thu oompuvAn il

Wealth thrives in their home in happiness, who
rejoice in entertaining the guests who deserve

வித்தும் இடல்வேண்டும் கொல்லோ விருந்தோம்பி
மிச்சில் மிசைவான் புலம்.   85

viththum idalvaeNdum kollO virun-thOmpi
michchil misaivAn pulam

Yields flourish their fields who relish treating guests, eat
the last, and do not mind cooking grain of seeds

செல்விருந்து ஓம்பி வருவிருந்து பார்த்திருப்பான்
நல்விருந்து வானத் தவர்க்கு.   86

selvirun-thu oompi varuvirun-thu pArththiruppan
n-alvirun-thu vAnath thavarkku

Who come out to feed the sages and renouncers, await
their usual guests, are revered guests of noble souls

இனைத்துணைத்து என்பதுஒன்று இல்லை விருந்தின்
துணைத்துணை வேள்விப் பயன்.   87

inaiththuNaiththu enpathuonRu illai virun-thin
thuNaiththuNai vaeLvip payan

Hospitality is penance at home; its reward is
matched by the quality and grace of guests

பரிந்துஓம்பிப் பற்றுஅற்றேம் என்பர் விருந்தோம்பி
வேள்வி தலைப்படா தார்.   88

parin-thuoompip paRRuaRRaem enpar virun-thoompi
vaeLvi thalaippadA thAr

Of what avail is toil and earnings; if the duty of
hospitality fails, hold is lost on everything

உடைமையுள் இன்மை விருந்துஓம்பல் ஓம்பா
மடமை மடவார்கண் உண்டு.   89

udaimaiyuL inmai virun-thuooimpal oompA
madamai madavArkaN uNdu

Possession is deprivation for those who fail,
in folly, to tend and treat guests

மோப்பக் குழையும் அனிச்சம் முகந்திரிந்து
நோக்கக் குழையும் விருந்து.   90

mOppak kuzaiyum anichcham mukamthirin-thu
n-Okkak kuzaiyum virun-thu

A tender flower withers in our breath; the guest
is shattered by an indifferent wry look

10. இனியவை கூறல்
iniyavai kURal
KINDNESS IN WORDS
(SWEETNESS OF EXPRESSION)
(SWEETNESS OF MANNER OF TALK- KINDNESS OF EXPRESSION SPRINGS FROM A MIND FULL OF VIRTUOUS LOVE)

இன்சொலால் ஈரம் அளைஇப் படிறுஇலவாம்
செம்பொருள் கண்டார்வாய்ச் சொல். 91

*insolAl eeram aLaiip padiRuilavAm
semporuL kaNdArvAych chol*

**Sweet words laced with love, free from
deceit, are the gift of the enlightened**

அகன்அமர்ந்து ஈதலின் நன்றே முகன்அமர்ந்து
இன்சொல னாகப் பெறின். 92

*akanamarn-thu eethalin n-anRae mukanamarn-thu
insola naakap peRin*

**Saying sweet things with a smile, is as
good as munificence of a kind soul**

முகத்தான் அமர்ந்துஇனிது நோக்கி அகத்தானாம்
இன்சொல் இனதே அறம். 93

*mukaththAn amarn-thuinithu n-Okki akaththAnAm
insol inathae aRam*

**Earnest words from the mind, conveyed
with a smile, have virtue in them**

துன்புறூஉம் துவ்வாமை இல்லாகும் யார்மாட்டும்
இன்புறூஉம் இன்சொ லவர்க்கு. 94

*thunpuRUum thuvvAmai illAkum yArmAttum
inpuRUum inso lavarkku*

**The woe of unfriendliness does not afflict
those who instil mirth by sweet words**

பணிவுடையன் இன்சொலன் ஆதல் ஒருவற்கு
அணியல்ல மற்றுப் பிற. 95

paNivudaiyan insolan aathal oruvaRku
aNiyalla matRRa piRa

Those adorned with modesty, speaking sweet
truth, do not need other decorations

அல்லவை தேய அறம்பெருகும் நல்லவை
நாடி இனிய சொலின்.

96

allavai thaeya aRamperukum n-allavai
n-Adi iniya solin

Pursuing virtue in the goodness of
fruitful words, vanishes harm

நயன்ஈன்று நன்றி பயக்கும் பயன்ஈன்று
பண்பின் தலைப்பிரியாச் சொல்.

97

n-ayaneenRu n-anRi payakkum payaneenRu
paNpin thalaippiriyAch chol

Graceful words of kindness, endowed in
courtesy, yield fruitful good deeds

சிறுமையுள் நீங்கிய இன்சொல் மறுமையயும்
இம்மையும் இன்பம் தரும்.

98

siRumaiyuL n-eengkiya insol maRumaiyum
immaiyum inpam tharum

Sweet words free from deceit afford everlasting
pleasure in life and fame beyond it

இன்சொல் இனிதுஈன்றல் காண்பான் எவன்கொலோ
வன்சொல் வழங்கு வது.

99

insol inithueenRal kANpan evenkolO
vansol vazangku vathu

Who perceive seeds of goodness in sweet
words have no mind for harsh things

இனிய உளவாக இன்னாத கூறல்
கனியிருப்பக் காய்கவர்ந்து அற்று.

100

iniya uLavAka innAtha kURal
kaniiruppak kAykavarn-thu atRRu

None having ripe fruits will relish raw ones; who will
speak harsh when sweetness can achieve good

11. செய்ந்நன்றி அறிதல்
seyn-n-anRi aRithal
GRATITUDE

(DUTY BORN OUT OF LOVE BEGET GRATITUDE TO THE KINDNESS
OF OTHERS; IT IS BEST OF MANNERISM TO VOLUNTEER HELP
WITHOUT EXPECTATION OF GAINS)

செய்யாமல் செய்த உதவிக்கு வையகமும்
வானகமும் ஆற்றல் அரிது.　　　　101

seyyAmal seytha uthavikku vaiyakamum
vAnakamum aatRRal arithu

Voluntary help from unforeseen quarters is,
in quantum, worth heaven and earth

காலத்தி னால்செய்த நன்றி சிறிதுஎனினும்
ஞாலத்தின் மாணப் பெரிது.　　　　102

kAlaththi nAlseytha n-anRi siRithueninum
gnAlaththin mANap perithu

Help without motives, in an hour of need, though
a little, is greater than the world in kind

பயன்தூக்கார் செய்த உதவி நயன்தூக்கின்
நன்மை கடலினும் பெரிது.　　　　103

payanthUkkAr seytha uthavi n-ayanthUkkin
n-anmai kadalinum perithu

Help, not weighed down by gains, outweighs
the sea in quality and good effects

தினைத்துணை நன்றி செயினும் பனைத்துணையாக்
கொள்வர் பயன்தெரி வார்.　　　　104

thinaiththunai n-anRi seyinum panaiththunaiyAk
koLvar payan-theri vAr

Willing help, though a millet in size, benefits
discerning users like a palmyra

உதவி வரைத்துஅன்று உதவி உதவி
செயப்பட்டார் சால்பின் வரைத்து.　　　　105

uthavi varaithuanRu uthavi, uthavi
seyappattAr sAlpin varaiththu

Measure not the effect of help, by the giver,
it measures up to the stature of beneficiary

மறவற்க மாசுஅற்றார் கேண்மை துறவற்க
துன்பத்துள் துப்பாயார் நட்பு.   106

maRavaRka mAsuaRRAr kaeNmai thuRavaRka
thunpaththuL thuppAyAr n-atpu

A friend in need is a friend in deed; do not
forget him or forsake comrades

எழுமை எழுபிறப்பும் உள்ளுவர் தங்கண்
விழுமம் துடைத்தவர் நட்பு.   107

ezumai ezupiRappum uLLuvar thamkaN
vizumam thudaiththavar n-atpu

The memory of those who help heal grief and
pain, shall be cherished forever in gratitude

நன்றி மறப்பது நன்றுஅன்று நன்றுஅல்லது
அன்றே மறப்பது நன்று.   108

nanRi maRappathu nanRuanRu nanRuallathu
anRae maRappathu nanRu

Do not be ungrateful, but do forget at once
the folly of a genuine friend

கொன்றுஅன்ன இன்னா செயினும் அவர்செய்த
ஒன்றுநன்று உள்ளக் கெடும்.   109

konRuanna innA seyinum avarseytha
onRun-anRu uLLak kedum

Let not your mind be wounded cruelly by a friend;
think of the good deeds he has been worth

எந்நன்றி கொன்றார்க்கும் உய்வுண்டாம் உய்வில்லை
செய்ந்நன்றி கொன்ற மகற்கு.   110

enn-anRi konRARkum uyvuNdAm uyvuillai
seyn-n-anRi konRa makaRku

Other virtues may be ignored in meritless
life, no one can survive ingratitude

12. நடுவு நிலைமை
n-aduvu n-ilaimai
EQUITY AND UPRIGHTNESS

(EQUITY IS STRAIGHT FORWARDNESS IN JUSTICE. THERE CAN BE
NO EQUITY BETWEEN TRUTH AND FALSEHOOD, GOOD AND BAD,
EXISTENTS AND ABSTRACTS)

தகுதி எனஒன்று நன்றே பகுதியால்
பாற்பட்டு ஒழுகப் பெறின்.　　　　　111

thakuthi enaonRu n-anRae pakuthiyAl
pARpattu ozukap peRin

Equity is uprightness in thought and conduct
always guided by a rational mind

செப்பம் உடையவன் ஆக்கம் சிதைவுஇன்றி
எச்சத்திற்கு ஏமாப்பு உடைத்து.　　　　112

seppam udaiyavan aakkam sithaivuinRi
echchaththiRku aemAppu udaiththu

Wealth earned by equitous behaviour
will protect oneself and posterity

நன்றே தரினும் நடுவுஇகந்துஆம் ஆக்கத்தை
அன்றே ஒழிய விடல்.　　　　　113

NandRae tharinum naduvuikanthuaam aakkaththai
AndRae oziya vidal

Even when apparently potential of good
gains, devious methods are detestable

தக்கார் தகவுஇலர் என்பது அவரவர்
எச்சத்தால் காணப் படும்.　　　　114

thakkAr thakavuilar enpathu avaravar
echchaththAl kANap padum

One's position in society is judged by what has
been achieved in life, fame or blame·

கேடும் பெருக்கமும் இல்அல்ல நெஞ்சத்துக்
கோடாமை சான்றோர்க்கு அணி.　　　　115

kaedum perukkamum ilalla n-enjsaththuk
kOdAmai sAnROrkku aNi

Ups and downs are but common in life, equity
in thought and actions is virtue of the wise

கெடுவல்யான் என்பது அறிகதன் நெஞ்சம்
நடுஒரீஇ அல்ல செயின். 116

keduvalyAn enpathu aRikathan n-enjsam
n-aduoreei alla seyin

Deliberate acts of vice are verily known
as sure guides to destruction

கெடுவாக வையாது உலகம் நடுவாக
நன்றிக்கண் தங்கியான் தாழ்வு. 117

keduvAka vaiyAthu ulakam n-aduvAka
n-anRikkaN thangkiyAn thAzvu

Mishaps in life to an upright person are
not viewed by the world as decline

சமன்செய்து சீர்தூக்கும் கோல்போல் அமைந்துஒருபால்
கோடாமை சான்றோர்க் கணி. 118

samanseythu seerthUkkum kOlpOl amain-thuorupAl
kOdAmai sAnRORk kaNi

The scales of justice are held on even balance
by people of virtue and integrity

சொல்கோட்டம் இல்லது செப்பம் ஒருதலையா
உள்கோட்டம் இன்மை பெறின். 119

solkOttam illathu seppam oruthalaiyA
uLkOttam inmai peRin

Justice is seen to be done when the
judge is upright in words and deeds

வாணிகம் செய்வார்க்கு வாணிகம் பேணிப்
பிறவும் தமபோல் செயின். 120

vANikam seyvArkku vANikam paeNip
piRavum thamapOl seyin

A trader is true to himself who weighs his
interests, even with his customers'

13. அடக்கம் உடைமை
adakkam udaimai
HUMILITY AND SELF-CONTROL

(CONTROLLING ONE'S MIND AND TONGUE, FORBEARANCE WITHOUT
OSTENTATIOUS BEHAVIOUR, RESPECT TO ELDERS, SUBMISSION IN AN
ASSEMBLY AND ABHORING ANGER, SHAME AND EVIL)

அடக்கம் அமரருள் உய்க்கும் அடங்காமை
ஆரிருள் உய்த்து விடும்.　　　　　　　121

adakkam amararuL uykkum adangkAmai
aariruL uyththu vidum

Humility earns lasting fame, grace and wisdom;
waywardness casts gloom and darkness

காக்க பொருளா அடக்கத்தை ஆக்கம்
அதனின்உஙகு இல்லை உயிர்க்கு.　　　　122

kAkka poruLA adakkaththai aakkam
athaninuungku illai uyirkku

Guard the valuable asset of self-control,
none else is more productive for life

செறிவுஅறிந்து சீர்மை பயக்கும் அறிவுஅறிந்து
ஆற்றின் அடங்கப் பெறின்.　　　　　　123

seRivuaRin-thu seermai payakkum aRivuaRin-thu
aatRRin adangkap peRin

Wisdom and self controlled ways of life
earn everlasting name and fame

நிலையில் திரியாது அடங்கியான் தோற்றம்
மலையினும் மாணப் பெரிது.　　　　　124

n-ilaiyil thiriyAthu adangkiyAn thOtRRam
malaiyinum mANap perithu

Firmness in principles and a serene outlook
appear greater than a mountain

எல்லார்க்கும் நன்றாம் பணிதல் அவருள்ளும்
செல்வர்க்கே செல்வம் தகைத்து.　　　　125

ellArkkum n-anRAm paNithal avaruLLum
selvarkkE selvam thakaiththu

Humility is virtue alround for everyone
it adds richness to other wealth

ஒருமையுள் ஆமைபோல் ஐந்துஅடக்கல் ஆற்றின்
எழுமையும் ஏமாப்பு உடைத்து.　　　　126

*orumaiyuL aamaipOl ain-thuadakkal aatRRin
ezumaiyum eemAppu udaiththu*

Self-control of senses, like a tortoise, focussed
on results, affords everlasting protection

யாகாவார் ஆயினும் நாகாக்க காவாக்கால்
சோகாப்பர் சொல்லிழுக்குப் பட்டு.　　　　127

*yAkAvAr aayinum n-AkAkka kAvAkkAl
sOkAppar solizukkup pattu*

Control on tongue is more important than on others;
else our own words lead us to disaster

ஒன்றானும் தீச்சொல் பொருள்பயன் உண்டாயின்
நன்றாகாது ஆகி விடும்.　　　　128

*onRAnum theechchol poruLpayan uNdAyin
n-anRAkAthu aaki vidum*

An indecent word of evil intent, though may be
productive of some gain, spoils everything else

தீயினால் சுட்டபுண் உள்ளாறும் ஆறாதே
நாவினால் சுட்ட வடு.　　　　129

*theeyinAl suttapuN uLaaRum aRAthae
n-AvinAl sutta vadu*

A fire burnt wound heals with scars; but sores
caused by a tongue lash never heal

கதம்காத்துக் கற்றடங்கல் ஆற்றுவான் செவ்வி
அறம்பார்க்கும் ஆற்றின் நுழைந்து.　　　　130

*kathamkAththuk katRadangkal aatRuvAn sevvi
aRampArkkum aatRin n-uzain-thu*

The wise in control of tempers are safe,
protected by a stream of virtue

14. ஒழுக்கமுடைமை
ozukkam udaimai
DISCIPLINE AND CONDUCT

(DISCIPLINE IS MANIFESTATION OF VIRTUE FROM A PURE MIND.
MANNERISM EXHIBITS ONES DISCIPLINED LIFE. ACTS ARE MORE
MERITORIOUS THAN WORDS)

ஒழுக்கம் விழுப்பம் தரலான் ஒழுக்கம்
உயிரினும் ஓம்பப் படும்.　　　　　　　131

*ozukkam vizuppam tharalAn ozukkam
uyirinum oompap padum*

Discipline sustains dignity; it is like life
to the body, to cultivate and protect

பரிந்துஒம்பிக் காக்க ஒழுக்கம் தெரிந்துஒம்பித்
தேரினும் அஃதே துணை.　　　　　　　132

*parin-thuoompik kAkka ozukkam therin-thuoompith
thErinum aqthae thuNai*

Patronize good conduct in you; by any
reckoning, it is your best companion

ஒழுக்கம் உடைமை குடிமை இழுக்கம்
இழிந்த பிறப்பாய் விடும்.　　　　　　　133

*ozukkam udaimai kudimai izukkam
izin-tha piRappAi vidum*

Decorum and discipline are social virtues
indiscipline makes life miserable

மறப்பினும் ஒத்துக் கொளல்ஆகும் பார்ப்பான்
பிறப்புஒழுக்கம் குன்றக் கெடும்.　　　　　　　134

*maRappinum ooththuk koLalaakum pArppAn
piRappuozukkam kunRak kedum*

Scriptures can be recapitulated by reading on;
discipline ignored is reverence lost out

அழுக்காறு உடையான்கண் ஆக்கம்போன்று இல்லை
ஒழுக்கம் இலான்கண் உயர்வு.　　　　　　　135

*azukkARu udaiyAnkaN aakkampOnRu illai
ozukkam ilAnkaN uyarvu*

Envy of an impure mind is never constructive;
without discipline aspirations fail to rise

ஒழுக்கத்தின் ஒல்கார் உரவோர் இழுக்கத்தின்
ஏதம் படுபாக்கு அறிந்து.   136

*ozukkaththin olkAr uravOr izukkaththin
aetham padupAkku aRin-thu*

Who understand the travails of misconduct; they
do not falter from the strength of discipline

ஒழுக்கத்தின் எய்துவர் மேன்மை இழுக்கத்தின்
எய்துவர் எய்தாப் பழி.   137

*ozukkaththin eythuvar maenmai izukkaththin
eythuvar eythAp pazi*

Good conduct is the path for achieving nobility;
indiscipline leads to disgrace and slur

நன்றிக்கு வித்தாகும் நல்லொழுக்கம் தீயொழுக்கம்
என்றும் இடும்பை தரும்.   138

*n-anRikku viththAkum n-allozukkam theeyozukkam
enRum idumpai tharum*

Decorum is the seed of virtue; bad conduct
is the source of pain and suffering

ஒழுக்கம் உடையவர்க்கு ஒல்லாவே தீய
வழுக்கியும் வாயால் சொலல்.   139

*ozukkam udaiyavarkku olkAvE theeya
vazukkiyum vAyAl solal*

People of righteous mind and conduct never
utter foul words even by a slip of tongue

உலகத்தோடு ஒட்ட ஒழுகல் பலகற்றும்
கல்லார் அறிவுஇலா தார்.   140

*ulakaththOdu otta ozukal palakatRRum
kallAr aRivuilA thAr*

Learning is to acquire knowledge for a disciplined
social life, in a world of everlasting wisdom

15. பிறனில் விழையாமை
piran il vizaiyaamai
REFRAINING FROM ADULTERY
(COVET NOT OTHERS' WIFE)

பிறன்பொருளாள் பெட்டொழுகும் பேதைமை ஞாலத்து
அறம்பொருள் கண்டார்கண் இல்.   141

piRanporuLAL pettozukum paethaimai jnAlaththu
aRamporuL kaNdArkaN il

Who have realised the benefits of virtue do not
commit the folly of sighing for other's wife

அறன்கடை நின்றாருள் எல்லாம் பிறன்கடை
நின்றாரின் பேதையார் இல்.   142

aRankadai n-inRAruL ellAm piRankadai
n-inRArin paethaiyar il

Of the clumsy ones, outside the periphery of virtue,
who languish at the doors of others are the worst

விளிந்தாரின் வேறுஅல்லர் மன்ற தெளிந்தார்இல்
தீமை புரிந்துஒழுகு வார்.   143

viLiththArin vaeRuallar manRa theLin-thAril
theemai purin-thuozuku vAr

Who misbehaves with the wife of a trusted friend
is no different from the dead - both are senseless

எனைத்துணையர் ஆயினும் என்னாம் தினைத்துணையும்
தேரான் பிறனில் புகல்.   144

enaiththuNaiyar aayinum ennAm thinaiththuNaiyum
thaerAn piRanil pukal

There is no elation in life for those who long for
other's wife, without even a forethought

எளிதென இல்இறப்பான் எய்தும்எஞ் ஞான்றும்
விளியாது நிற்கும் பழி.   145

eLithuena illiRappAn eythumenj jnAnRum
viLiyAthu n-iRkum pazi

One who takes to adultery as a trifle easy
is burdened with enduring guilt and grief

பகைபாவம் அச்சம் பழிஎன நான்கும்
இகவாவாம் இல்இறப்பான் கண்.   **146**

*pakaipAvam achcham paziena n-Ankum
ikavAvAm iliRappAn kaN*

Enmity, pretence, fear and guilt are the
handy armours dear to adulterers

அறன்இயலான் இல்வாழ்வான் என்பான் பிறன்இயலாள்
பெண்மை நயவாத வன்.   **147**

*aRaniyalAn ilvAzvAn enpAn piRaniyalAL
peNmai n-ayavAtha van*

Those who adopt a virtuous way of family
life, refrain from coveting vainful lust

பிறன்மனை நோக்காத பேராண்மை சான்றோர்க்கு
அறன்ஒன்றோ ஆன்ற ஒழுக்கு.   **148**

*piRanmanai n-OkkAtha paerANmai sAnROrkku
aRanonRO aanRa ozukku*

The supreme valour of not eying other's wife
is the vital virtue of a disciplined life

நலக்குஉரியார் யாரெனின் நாமநீர் வைப்பின்
பிறற்குஉரியாள் தோள்தோயா தார்.   **149**

*n-alakkuuriyAr yArenin n-Aman-Ir vaippin
piRarkkuuriyAL thOLthOyA thAr*

Good life on this earth of stormy seas, is
for those who clasp not other's spouse

அறன்வரையான் அல்ல செயினும் பிறன்வரையாள்
பெண்மை நயவாமை நன்று.   **150**

*aRanvaraiyAn alla seyinum piRanvaraiyAL
peNmai n-ayavAmai n-anRu*

Who are prone to ignore other virtues waywardly
should at least desist from the lust of adultery

16. பொறையுடைமை
poRaiyudaimai
FORBEARANCE

(BEARING WITH THE IGNORANCE OF OTHERS WHO CAUSE HARM
PAIN AND INSULT; RESTRAINING ANGER AND REPRISAL)

அகழ்வாரைத் தாங்கும் நிலம்போலத் தம்மை
இகழ்வார்ப் பொறுத்தல் தலை.　　　　　151

*akazvAraith thAngkum n-ilampOlath thammai
ikazvArp poRuththal thalai*

As mother earth bears with those who dig it
for gain, it is best to forbear abuses

பொறுத்தல் இறப்பினை என்றும் அதனை
மறத்தல் அதனினும் நன்று.　　　　　152

*poRuththal iRappinai enRum athanai
maRaththal athaninum n-anRu*

To bear with transgression is good; it will
be still better to fully forget insults

இன்மையுள் இன்மை விருந்துஒரால் வன்மையுள்
வன்மை மடவார்ப் பொறை.　　　　　153

*inmaiyuL inmai virun-thuorAl vanmaiyuL
vanmai madavArp poRai*

Shying away guests is dearth in poverty;
bearing with fools is power in strength

நிறையுடைமை நீங்காமை வேண்டின் பொறையுடைமை
போற்றி ஒழுகப் படும்.　　　　　154

*n-iRaiudaimai n-eengkAmai vaeNdin poRaiudaimai
pOtRRi ozukap padum*

Integrity is protected forever when tolerance
is cultivated and practised consciously

ஒறுத்தாரை ஒன்றாக வையாரே வைப்பர்
பொறுத்தாரைப் பொன்போல் பொதிந்து.　　　　　155

*oRuththArai onRAka vaiyArae vaippAr
poRuththAraip ponpOl pothin-thu*

Forbearance is a precious possession like gold;
proneness to punish is low in social esteem

ஒறுத்தார்க்கு ஒருநாளை இன்பம் பொறுத்தார்க்குப்
பொன்றும் துணையும் புகழ்.   156

oRuththArkku orun-ALai inpam poRuththArkkup
ponRum thuNaiyum pukaz

Retaliation might give one momentary pleasure;
but forbearance sustains lasting glory

திறன்அல்ல தற்பிறர் செய்யினும் நோநொந்து
அறன்அல்ல செய்யாமை நன்று.   157

thiRanalla thaRpiRar seyyinum n-Ononthu
aRanalla seyyAmai n-anRu

Harmful deeds might cause pain; even in the
face of grief, refrain from acting unjust

மிகுதியான் மிக்கவை செய்தாரைத் தாம்தம்
தகுதியான் வென்று விடல்.   158

mikuthiyAn mikkavai seythAraith thAmtham
thakuthiyAn venRu vidal

Win over by your nobility, those who may
cause anguish by senseless pride

துறந்தாரின் தூய்மை உடையர் இறந்தார்வாய்
இன்னாச்சொல் நோற்கிற் பவர்.   159

thuRan-thArin thUymai udaiyAr iRan-thArvAy
innAchsol n-ORkiR pavar

Tolerance to abuses outside of wits
is like purity of renouncement

உண்ணாது நோற்பார் பெரியர் பிறர்சொல்லும்
இன்னாச்சொல் நோற்பாரின் பின்.   160

uNNAthu n-ORpAr periyar piRarsollum
innAchsol n-ORpArin pin

One who forbears offensive tongues, is greater
than those who forsake food in penance

17. அழுக்காறாமை
azukkARAmai
DESIST FROM ENVY

ஒழுக்காறாக் கொள்க ஒருவன்தன் நெஞ்சத்து
அழுக்காறு இலாத இயல்பு.   161

ozukkARAk koLka oruvanthan n-enjsaththu
azukkARu ilAtha iyalpu

The stream of discipline flows free from
a mind cleansed from the dirt of envy

விழுப்பேற்றின் அஃதுஒப்பது இல்லையார் மாட்டும்
அழுக்காற்றின் அன்மை பெறின்.   162

vizuppaetRin aqthuoppathu illaiyAr mAttum
azukkAtRin anmai peRin

When you redress the mind from the fault
of envy, you see the path of glory

அறன்ஆக்கம் வேண்டாதான் என்பான் பிறன்ஆக்கம்
பேணாது அழுக்கறுப் பான்.   163

aRanaakkam vaeNdAthAn enpAn piRanaakkam
paeNAthu azukkaRup pAn

One who eyes the growth of others with
envy, forfeits the wealth of virtue

அழுக்காற்றின் அல்லவை செய்யார் இழுக்காற்றின்
ஏதம் படுபாக்கு அறிந்து.   164

azukkAtRin allavai seyyAr izukkAtRin
aetham padupAkku aRin-thu

Who knows the woes and pains of evil deeds
dares not to do or think wrong, out of envy

அழுக்காறு உடையார்க்கு அதுசாலும் ஒன்னார்
வழுக்கியும் கேடுஈன் பது.   165

azukkARu udaiyArkku athusAlum onnAr
vazukkiyum kaedueen pathu

The dirt of envy in one's own mind is sure
to wreak, even when a foe fails to hit

கொடுப்பது அழுக்கறுப்பான் சுற்றம் உடுப்பதூஉம்
உண்பதூஉம் இன்றிக் கெடும்.   166

*koduppathu azukkaRuppAn sutRRam uduppathUum
uNpathUum inRik kedum*

Envy on others' munificence deprives food
and clothing to one, and to kith and kin

அவ்வித்து அழுக்காறு உடையானைச் செய்யவள்
தவ்வையைக் காட்டி விடும்.   167

*avviththu azukkaaRu udaiyAnaich seyyavaL
thavvayaik kAtti vidum*

The cauldron of envy deprives the light of wealth
and casts the gloom of woeful want

அழுக்காறு எனஒரு பாவி திருச்செற்றுத்
தீயுழி உய்த்து விடும்.   168

*azukkARu enaoru pAvi thiruchchetRuth
theeyuzi uyththu vidum*

Despicable envy spoils good wealth and
drowns one in the swirlpool of evil

அவ்விய நெஞ்சத்தான் ஆக்கமும் செவ்வியான்
கேடும் நினைக்கப் படும்.   169

*avviya n-enjsaththAn aakkamum sevviyAn
kaedum n-inaikkap padum*

The wreaks of envy floating in riches, and the good
suffering poverty provoke serious thought for remedy

அழுக்குற்று அகன்றாரும் இல்லை அஃதுஇல்லார்
பெருக்கத்தில் தீர்ந்தாரும் இல்.   170

*azukkutRu akanRArum illai aqthuillAr
perukkaththil theern-thArum il*

The envious rarely prosper in peace
and the virtuous rarely lose

18. வெஃகாமை
veqkAmai
COVET NOT OTHERS' WEALTH

நடுவுஇன்றி நன்பொருள் வெஃகின் குடிபொன்றிக்
குற்றமும் ஆங்கே தரும்.   171

*n-aduvuinRi n-anporuL veqkin kudiponRik
kutRRamum aangkae tharum*

Lose equity and covet honest wealth of others;
guilt sticks on and destroys social values, sure

படுபயன் வெஃகிப் பழிப்படுவ செய்யார்
நடுவுஅன்மை நாணு பவர்.   172

*padupayan veqkip pazippaduva seyyAr
n-aduvuanmai n-ANu pavar*

Shy the shame of disgraceful acts;
covet not unjust benefits deviously

சிற்றின்பம் வெஃகி அறன்அல்ல செய்யாரே
மற்றின்பம் வேண்டு பவர்.   173

*sitRRinpam veqki aRanalla seyyAr
matRRinpam vaeNdu pavar*

Seeking the pleasures of glory, do not
ignore virtues and covet fleeting joys

இலம்என்று வெஃகுதல் செய்யார் புலம்வென்ற
புன்மையில் காட்சி யவர்.   174

*ilamenRu veqkuthal seyyAr pulamvenRa
punmaiil kAtsi avar*

Control your senses and see the truth,
without coveting in the guise of want

அஃகி அகன்ற அறிவுஎன்னாம் யார்மாட்டும்
வெஃகி வெறிய செயின்.   175

*aqki akanRa aRivuennAm yArmAttum
veqki veRiya seyin*

Of what avail one's subtle wisdom is, to one
who covets others' wealth in a rage

அருள்வெஃகி ஆற்றின்கண் நின்றான் பொருள்வெஃகிப்
பொல்லாத சூழக் கெடும்.   176

aruLveqki aatRRinkaN n-inRAn poruLveqkip
pollAtha sUzak kedum

Take to the righteous path of compassion;
fall not from grace coveting others' wealth

வேண்டற்க வெஃகியாம் ஆக்கம் விளைவயின்
மாண்டற் கரிதாம் பயன்.   177

vaeNdaRka veqkiyAm aakkam viLaivayin
mANdaRk karithAm payan

Shun the gains of covetous wealth;
its fruits are bitter to taste

அஃகாமை செல்வத்திற்கு யாதுஎனின் வெஃகாமை
வேண்டும் பிறன்கைப் பொருள்.   178

aqkAmai selvaththiRku yAthuenin veqkAmai
vaeNdum piRankaip poruL

Covet not other's possessions; that virtue
protects one's wealth from shrinking

அறன்அறிந்து வெஃகா அறிவுடையார்ச் சேரும்
திறன்அறிந்து ஆங்கே திரு.   179

aRanaRin-thu veqkA aRivudaiyArch chaerum
thiRanaRin-thu aangkae thiru

The wise who do not covet, gain beautiful
wealth, on a righteous path

இறல்ஈனும் எண்ணாது வெஃகின் விறல்ஈனும்
வேண்டாமை என்னும் செருக்கு.   180

iRaleenum eNNAthu veqkin viRaleenum
vaeNdAmai ennum serukku

The pride of freedom from greed yields
success; mindless coveting brings ruin

19. புறம் கூறாமை
puRam kURamai
DESIST FROM SLANDER
(REFRAIN FROM BLAMING OTHERS BEHIND THEIR BACK,
BLACKMAILING, EXAGGERATING FAULTS, SPINNING TALES ETC)

அறம்கூறான் அல்ல செயினும் ஒருவன்
புறம்கூறான் என்றல் இனிது.　　　　　181

aRamkURAn alla seyinum oruvan
puRamkURAn enRal inithu

Though not professing virtues and acting vile,
abstaining from slander is something to relish

அறன்அழீஇ அல்லவை செய்தலின் தீதே
புறன்அழீஇப் பொய்த்து நகை.　　　　　182

aRanazeei allavai seythalin theethae
puRanazeeip poyththu n-akai

A false grin at the face and back-baiting are
worse than ignoring virtues to act at will

புறங்கூறிப் பொய்த்துஉயிர் வாழ்தலின் சாதல்
அறம்கூறும் ஆக்கம் தரும்.　　　　　183

puRamkURip poyththuuyir vAzthalin sAthal
aRamkURum aakkam tharum

Death in pursuit of virtue's gain is better
than a dubious life of slander

கண்நின்று கண்ணறச் சொல்லினும் சொல்லற்க
முன்நின்று பின்நோக்காச் சொல்.　　　　　184

kaNn-inRu kaNaRach sollinum sollaRka
munn-inRu pinn-OkkAch chol

Even while having to use harsh words, face to face,
do not slander, unmindful of consequences

அறம்சொல்லும் நெஞ்சத்தான் அன்மை புறம்சொல்லும்
புன்மையால் காணப் படும்.　　　　　185

aRamsollum n-enjsaththAn anmai puRamsollum
punmaiyAl kANap padum

A mind devoid of virtues is exposed of
meanness, by a back-baiting tongue

பிறன்பழி கூறுவான் தன்பழி யுள்ளும்
திறன்தெரிந்து கூறப் படும்.   186

piRanpazi kURuvAn thanpazi uLLum
thiRantherin-thu kURap padum

Who slander others' faltering shoud be
fixed to realise their own follies

பகச்சொல்லிக் கேளிர்ப் பிரிப்பர் நகச்சொல்லி
நட்பாடல் தேற்றா தவர்.   187

pakachchollik kaeLirp piripppar n-akachcholli
n-adpAdal thaetRRA thavar

One who cannot cultivate friends with a
smile, back-baits to separate comrades

துன்னியார் குற்றமும் தூற்றும் மரபினார்
என்னைகொல் ஏதிலார் மாட்டு.   188

thunniyAr kutRRamum thUtRRum marapinAr
ennaikol aethilAr mAttu

Who make much of the faults of close friends,
what will not they do to aliens

அறன்நோக்கி ஆற்றுங்கொல் வையம் புறன்நோக்கிப்
புன்சொல் உரைப்பான் பொறை.   189

aRann-Okki aatRRumkol vaiyam puRan-Okkip
punsol uraippAn poRai

The world bears, alas as a burden of virtue,
back-baiters with mean minds

ஏதிலார் குற்றம்போல் தம்குற்றம் காண்கிற்பின்
தீதுஉண்டோ மன்னும் உயிர்க்கு.   190

aethilAr kutRRampOl thamkutRRA:m kANkiRpin
theethuuNdO mannum uyirkku

Realization of our own faults, as seen of
others, sustains life without harm

20. பயனில சொல்லாமை
payanila sollAmai
AVOID SPEAKING IN VAIN

(OUR TONGUE IS SECURED IN A PLACE NON-POLLUTED, SAFE
AND WET; LET IT NOT WANDER IN VAIN TALK)

பல்லார் முனியப் பயன்இல சொல்லுவான்
எல்லாரும் எள்ளப் படும்.　　　　191

pallAr muniyap payanila solluvAn
ellArum eLLap padum

Indulgence in silly banter, to the contempt
of many, attracts alround scorn

பயனில பல்லார்முன் சொல்லல் நயனில
நட்டார்கண் செய்தலின் தீது.　　　　192

payanila pallarmun sollal n-ayanila
n-attArkaN seythalin theethu

Vain talk in an assembly, despised by many,
is worse than unkind deeds to friends

நயனிலன் என்பது சொல்லும் பயனில
பாரித்து உரைக்கும் உரை.　　　　193

n-ayanilan enpathu sollum payanila
pAriththu uraikkum urai

Revelling in useless blabber, easily shows
up one as 'good for nothing'

நயன்சாரா நன்மையின் நீக்கும் பயன்சாரப்
பண்புஇல்சொல் பல்லா ரகத்து.　　　　194

n-ayansArA n-anmaiyin n-eengkum payansArap
paNpuilsol pallA rakaththu

Vain words of inconsequence in an assembly
rob one of any gains or goodness

சீர்மை சிறப்பொடு நீங்கும் பயன்இல
நீர்மை யுடையார் சொலின்.　　　　195

seermai siRappodu n-eengkum payanila
n-eermai udaiyAr solin

Grace and glory desert the worthy, when they
utter silly words of inconsequence

பயன்இல்சொல் பாராட்டு வானை மகன்எனல்
மக்கட் பதடி யெனல்.   196

payanilsol pArAttu vAnai makanenal
makkaL pathadi enal

One who prides in idle nonsense, is chaff
from grain rather than human in sense

நயன்இல சொல்லினுஞ் சொல்லுக சான்றோர்
பயன்இல சொல்லாமை நன்று.   197

n-ayanila sollinum solluka sAnROr
payanila sollAmai n-anRu

Words may be unpleasantly harsh, as
need be, but avoid useless quack

அரும்பயன் ஆயும் அறிவினார் சொல்லார்
பெரும்பயன் இல்லாத சொல்.   198

arumpayan aayum aRivinar sollAr
perumpayan illAtha sol

The wise in pursuit of worthy gains,
refrain from speaking without stuff

பொருள்தீர்ந்த பொச்சாந்தும் சொல்லார் மருள்தீர்ந்த
மாசறு காட்சி யவர்.   199

poruLtheern-tha pochchAn-thum sollAr maruLtheern-tha
mAsuaRu kAtchi yavar

People with clear vision, above the clouds
of doubt, speak not without substance

சொல்லுக சொல்லில் பயனுடைய சொல்லற்க
சொல்லில் பயனிலாச் சொல்.   200

solluka sollil payanudaiya sollaRka
sollil payanilAch sol

When you have to speak, choose fruitful words,
else better not resort to sweet nothings

21. தீவினையச்சம்
thIvinai achcham
FEAR OF EVIL DEEDS

(DREADING EVIL DEEDS. WHILE CARRYING OUT OUR DUTIES AND
FUNCTIONS, THEY SHOULD NOT CAUSE ANY HARM, FAULTS OR CRIME)

தீவினையார் அஞ்சார் விழுமியார் அஞ்சுவர்
தீவினை என்னுஞ் செருக்கு.   201

theevinaiyAr anjsAr vizumiyAr anjsuvar
theevinai ennum serukku

Evil doers fear not harming, but may take
pride; the worthy will keep the ill aside

தீயவை தீய பயத்தலால் தீயவை
தீயினும் அஞ்சப் படும்.   202

theeyavai theeya payaththalAl theeyavai
theeyinum anjsap padum

A fire kindles other fires to spread and burn;
evil begets dire evils to dread harm

அறிவினுள் எல்லாம் தலையென்ப தீய
செறுவார்க்கும் செய்யா விடல்.   203

aRivinuL ellAm thalaienpa theeya
seruvArkkum seyyA vidal

Keep off from harm even to fighting foes;
that soars up knowledge to wisdom

மறந்தும் பிறன்கேடு சூழற்க சூழின்
அறம்சூழும் சூழ்ந்தவன் கேடு.   204

maRan-thum piRankaedu sUzaRka sUzin
aRamsUzum sUzn-thavan kaedu

Forget of scheming evil to others; remember
virtue keeps a close vigil on evil doers

இலன்என்று தீயவை செய்யற்க செய்யின்
இலன்ஆகும் மற்றும் பெயர்த்து.   205

ilanenRu theeyavai seyyaRka seyyin
ilanaakum matRRum peyarththu

'Nothing to lose' is no excuse to evil deeds;
they will cause you to lose yourself

தீப்பால தான்பிறர்கண் செய்யற்க நோய்ப்பால
தன்னை அடல்வேண்டா தான். 206

theeppAla thAnpiRaRkaN seyaRka n-OyppAla
thannai adalvaeNdA thAn

Seeking protection from pain and suffering,
think not of wounding others' sensitivity

எனைப்பகை உற்றாரும் உய்வர் வினைப்பகை
வீயாது பின்சென்று அடும். 207

enaippakai utRArum uyvar vinaippakai
veeyAthu pinsenRu adum

One may survive the assault of foes, but the
rebound of one's own evil is deadly

தீயவை செய்தார் கெடுதல் நிழல்தன்னை
வீயாது அடிஉறைந்து அற்று. 208

theeyavai seythAr keduthal n-izalthannai
veeyAthu adiuRain-thu atRRu

Evil deeds are sure to ruin the doer, as our
shadow follows wherever we go

தன்னைத்தான் காதலன் ஆயின் எனைத்தொன்றும்
துன்னற்க தீவினைப் பால். 209

thannaiththAn kAthalan aayin enaiththuonRum
thunnaRka theevinaip pAl

Those who love their life, dare not pursue
evil, however trivial it may be

அருங்கேடன் என்பது அறிக மருங்குஒடித்
தீவினை செய்யான் எனின். 210

arungkaedan enpathu aRika marungkuoodi
theevinai seyyAn enin

One who avoids the wrong path of evil
is aware of and secure from its ill effects

22. ஒப்புரவு அறிதல்
oppuravu aRithal
DUTY TO SOCIETY (SOCIALISM)
(SOCIAL RESPONSIBILITY TO SERVE THE DESERVING NEEDY IS
ONE OF THE BASIC TENETS OF KuRaL LIKE ,VIRTUES, LOVE,
HONOUR AND JUSTICE)

கைம்மாறு வேண்டாக் கடப்பாடு மாரிமாட்டு
என்ஆற்றுங் கொல்லோ உலகு.   211

kaimmARu vaeNdAk kadappAdu mArimAttu
enaatRRung kollO ulaku

Rain is unique in munificence; social duty
is gratitude pure, sans recompense

தாளாற்றித் தந்த பொருள்எல்லாம் தக்கார்க்கு
வேளாண்மை செய்தல் பொருட்டு.   212

thALaatRRith than-tha poruLellAm thakkArkku
vaeLANmai seythal poruttu

Earning by toil is to deploy material wealth
and efforts in service of the deserving

புத்தேள் உலகத்தும் ஈண்டும் பெறலரிதே
ஒப்புரவின் நல்ல பிற.   213

puththaeL ulakaththum eeNdum peRalarithae
oppuravin n-alla piRa

There is no better gain to seek in life, now
or in times ahead, than service to society

ஒத்தது அறிவான் உயிர்வாழ்வான் மற்றையான்
செத்தாருள் வைக்கப் படும்.   214

oththathu aRivAn uyirvAzvAn matRaiyAn
seththAruL vaikkap padum

You live a fuller life in compatible social service;
otherwise you are a corpse with a feeble throb

ஊருணி நீர்நிறைந்து அற்றே உலகுஅவாம்
பேரறி வாளன் திரு.   215

uuruNi n-eern-iRain-thu atRRae ulakuavAm
paeraRi vALan thiru

Wealth with a person of worldly wisdom is
a well of life amidst a village commune

பயன்மரம் உள்ளூர்ப் பழுத்துஅற்றால் செல்வம்
நயனுடை யான்கண் படின்.   216

payanmaram uLLUrp pazuththuatRRAl selvam
n-ayanudai yAnkaN padin

A neighborhood tree bearing edible fruits is a treat
to all, like wealth in the hands of the kindly

மருந்தாகித் தப்பா மரத்துஅற்றால் செல்வம்
பெருந்தகை யான்கண் படின்.   217

marun-thuaakith thappA maraththuatRRAl selvam
perun-thakai yAnkaN padin

Wealth in the trust of the worthy, is a wholesome
medicinal tree of lasting benefits

இடனில் பருவத்தும் ஒப்புரவிற்கு ஒல்கார்
கடனறி காட்சி யவர்.   218

idanil paruvaththum oppuraviRku olkAr
kadanaRi kAtsi avar

At the call of duty to serve society, do not
halt even in a season of shortages

நயனுடையான் நல்கூர்ந்தான் ஆதல் செயும்நீர
செய்யாது அமைகலா வாறு.   219

n-ayanudaiyAn n-alkUrn-thAn aathal seyumn-eera
seyyAthu amaikalA vARu

The kindly ones, even in harder times are sure
to serve like a well in a dry river bed

ஒப்புரவி னால்வரும் கேடுஎனின் அஃதொருவன்
விற்றுக்கோள் தக்கது உடைத்து.   220

oppuravi nAlvarum kaeduenin aqthuoruvan
viRRukkOL thakkathu udaiththu

Even if it be loss encountered in service to
society, take it gladly in exchange for self

23. ஈகை
yeekai
CONTRIBUTION

(GIVING LIBERALLY AS A DUTY TO THE DESERVING ACCORDING
TO NEEDS AND MERIT IS A SOCIAL OBLIGATION)

வறியார்க்குஒன்று ஈவதே ஈகைமற்று எல்லாம்
குறியெதிர்ப்பை நீரது உடைத்து.　　　　221

*vaRiyArkkuonRu eevathae eekaimaRRu ellAm
kuRiethirppai n-eerathu udaiththu*

Help to the needy is contribution; other aids
are 'quid pro quo' stocks-in-trade

நல்லாறு எனினும் கொளல்தீது மேல்உலகம்
இல்எனினும் ஈதலே நன்று.　　　　222

*n-allARu eninum koLaltheethu maelulakam
ileninum eethalae n-anRu*

Accepting even good gratis is not nice; contribute
to the deserving even at the cost of elite society

இலன்என்னும் எவ்வம் உரையாமை ஈதல்
குலன்உடையான் கண்ணே உள.　　　　223

*ilanennum evvam uraiyAmai eethal
kulanudaiyAn kaNNae uLa*

Not mouthing the pain of want does exist only
in a society accustomed to benevolence

இன்னாது இரக்கப் படுதல் இரந்தவர்
இன்முகம் காணும் அளவு.　　　　224

*innAthu irakkap paduthal iran-thavar
inmukam kANum aLavu*

It is nice not to see a needy face in pain, give
till it blushes in joy with hands full of gain

ஆற்றுவார் ஆற்றல் பசிஆற்றல் அப்பசியை
மாற்றுவார் ஆற்றலின் பின்.　　　　225

*aatRRuvAr aatRal pasiaatRRal appasiyai
mAtRRuvAr atRalin pin*

The power to alleviate its causes is greater than the
capacity to quench the fire of hunger with food

அற்றார் அழிபசி தீர்த்தல் அஃதொருவன்
பெற்றான் பொருள்வைப் புழி.　　　　226

*atRRAr azipasi theerthal aqthuoruvan
petRRAn poruLvaip puzi*

Banishing hunger of the poor is the safest bet
to protect your gains and continue to serve

பாத்தூண் மறீஇ யவனைப் பசிஎன்னும்
தீப்பிணி தீண்டல் அரிது.　　　　227

*pAththUN mareei yavanaip pasiennum
theeppiNi theeNdal arithu*

Accustomed to share food and possessions with the
needy, one is free from the pain of suffering and want

ஈத்துஉவக்கும் இன்பம் அறியார்கொல் தாமுடைமை
வைத்துஇழக்கும் வன்க ணவர்.　　　　228

*eeththuuvakkum inpam aRiyArkol thAmudaimai
vaiththuizakkum vanka Navar*

The joy of contribution is unknown to aliens
who hoard and risk all their riches

இரத்தலின் இன்னாது மன்ற நிரப்பிய
தாமே தமியர் உணல்.　　　　229

*iraththalin innAthu manRa n-irappiya
thAmae thamiyar uNal*

The greed to monopolise hoarded riches, all
alone, is worse than the pain of seeking alms

சாதலின் இன்னாதது இல்லை இனிததூஉம்
ஈதல் இயையாக் கடை.　　　　230

*sAthalin innAthathu illai inithathUum
eethal iyaiyAk kadai*

Sensing of death is painful grief, even that
is sweeter than the dearth of helplessness

24. புகழ்
pukazh
GLORY (RENOWN)

(GLORY STAYS WITH THE NAME OF THOSE WHO THRIVE IN FAMILY
AND SOCIAL LIFE OF VIRTUES WITH HOSPITALITY AND GRATITUDE)

ஈதல் இசைபட வாழ்தல் அதுஅல்லது
ஊதியம் இல்லை உயிர்க்கு.   231

eethal isaipada vAzthal athuallathu
uuthiyam illai uyirkku

Contributing to the needy and living in harmony
with nature are gains in life's breath

உரைப்பார் உரைப்பவை எல்லாம் இரப்பார்க்குஒன்று
ஈவார்மேல் நிற்கும் புகழ்.   232

uraippAr uraippavai ellAm irappArkkuonRu
eevArmael n-iRkum pukazh

Worldly praise and sustained glory are for those
helping the ones in want, and seeking aid

ஒன்றா உலகத்து உயர்ந்த புகழ்அல்லால்
பொன்றாது நிற்பதுஒன்று இல்.   233

onRA ulakaththu uyarn-tha pukazallAl
ponRAthu n-iRapathuonRu il

Know one at the top of everlasting fame;
it is the one achieving glory in life

நிலவரை நீள்புகழ் ஆற்றின் புலவரைப்
போற்றாது புத்தேள் உலகு.   234

n-ilavarai n-eeLpukaz aatRRin pulavaraip
pOtRRAthu puththaeL ulaku

Gain and sustain glory as you live; the life ahead
renowns you on par with the learned

நத்தம்போல் கேடும் உளதாகும் சாக்காடும்
வித்தகர்க்கு அல்லால் அரிது.   235

n-aththampOl kaedum uLathAkum sAkkAdum
viththakarkku allAl arithu

Glory protected despite adversities, and fame outlasting
death, are sweet tricks of magic life

தோன்றின் புகழொடு தோன்றுக அஃதிலார்
தோன்றலின் தோன்றாமை நன்று.　　　　236

thOnRin pukazodu thOnRuka aqthuilAr
thOnRalin thOnRAmai n-anRu

Achieve fame and glory in whatever you touch;
or else leave worldly life totally untouched

புகழ்பட வாழாதார் தம்நோவார் தம்மை
இகழ்வாரை நோவது எவன்.　　　　237

pukazpada vAzAthAr thamnOvAr thammai
ikazvArai n-Ovathu evan

Remorseless life without any renown, has
no right to fault others' criticism

வசையென்ப வையத்தார்க் கெல்லாம் இசையென்னும்
எச்சம் பெறாஅ விடின்.　　　　238

vasaienpa vaiyaththArkku ellAm isaiennum
echcham peRAa vidin

It is a blemish on humanity that lives a life
without the savings of worthy renown

வசையிலா வண்பயன் குன்றும் இசையிலா
யாக்கை பொறுத்த நிலம்.　　　　239

vasaiilA vanpayan kunRum isaiilA
yAkkai poRuththa n-ilam

Life without glory is a body without instinct;
the world that bears its burden is barren

வசையொழிய வாழ்வாரே வாழ்வார் இசையொழிய
வாழ்வாரே வாழா தவர்.　　　　240

vasaioziya vAzvArae vAzvAr isaioziya
vAzvArae vAzA thavar

A life without glory of renown does not thrive;
a life without any blemish has its worth

25. அருளுடைமை
aruL udaimai
GRACE (COMPASSION)
(VIRTUE RIPENS KINDNESS FOR FRUITION OF GRACE)

அருள்செல்வம் செல்வத்துள் செல்வம் பொருள்செல்வம்
பூரியார் கண்ணும் உள. **241**

aruLselvam selvaththuL selvam poruLselvam
pUriyAr kaNNum uLa

Compassion is a wealth of grace; material
wealth even the basest can gain

நல்ஆற்றான் நாடி அருள்ஆள்க பல்ஆற்றால்
தேரினும் அஃதே துணை. **242**

n-allAtRRaan n-Adi aruLaaLka pallaatRRAl
thaerinum aqthae thuNai

Seek and preserve compassion by means fair and sound
in any reckoning, that is the best companion

அருள்சேர்ந்த நெஞ்சினார்க்கு இல்லை இருள்சேர்ந்த
இன்னா உலகம் புகல். **243**

aruLsaern-tha n-enjsinArkku illai iruLsaern-tha
innA ulakam pukal

The light of a graceful mind saves one
from the pain of ignorant darkness

மன்னுயிர் ஓம்பி அருள்ஆள்வார்க்கு இல்என்ப
தன்னுயிர் அஞ்சும் வினை. **244**

mannuyir oompi aruLaaLvArkku ilenpa
thannuyir anjsum vinai

Love all forms of lives with a mind of mercy;
fear not evil to self or surroundings

அல்லல் அருள்ஆள்வார்க்கு இல்லை வளிவழங்கும்
மல்லல்மா ஞாலம் கரி. **245**

allal aruLaaLvArkku illai vaLivazangkum
mallalmA njAlam kari

The grace of mercy saves the universe from being
tossed by swirling winds of mighty space

பொருள்நீங்கிப் பொச்சாந்தார் என்பர் அருள்நீங்கி

அல்லவை செய்துஒழுகு வார்.   246

*poruLn-eengkip pochchAn-thAr enpar aruLn-eengki
allavai seythuozuku vAr*

Those who forget compassion and indulge
in evil deeds forsake all wealth

அருள்இல்லார்க்கு அவ்வுலகம் இல்லை பொருள்இல்லார்க்கு

இவ்வுலகம் இல்லாகி யாங்கு.   247

*aruLillArkku avvulakam illai poruLillArkku
ivvulakam illAki yAngku*

Compassion and grace are basics of renunciation, a
social life has meaning only with material wealth

பொருள்அற்றார் பூப்பர் ஒருகால் அருள்அற்றார்

அற்றார்மற்று ஆதல் அரிது.   248

*poruLatRRAr pUppar orukAl aruLatRRAr
atRRArmatRRu aathal arithu*

Material possessions might be regained when lost; but
a mind without compassion cannot acquire grace

தெருளாதான் மெய்ப்பொருள் கண்டுஅற்றால் தேரின்

அருளாதான் செய்யும் அறம்.   249

*theruLAthAn meypporuL kaNduatRRAl thaerin
aruLAthAn seyyum aRam*

A vain mind seeking grace without mercy, is
like aspiring wisdom without knowledge

வலியாா்முன் தன்னை நினைக்கதான் தன்னின்

மெலியாா்மேல் செல்லும் இடத்து.   250

*valiyArmun thannai n-inakkathAn thannin
meliyArmael sellum idaththu*

Mind your feelings as you bow to the mighty, when you are
prone to act without compassion to the feeble

26. புலால் மறுத்தல்
pulAl maRuththal
ABJURING FLESH MEAT
(THIS WAS ADVOCATED AS A CODE OF INDIAN ETHICS OF NON-VIOLENCE NOT TO INFLICT PAINFUL HARM TO OTHER LIVING BEINGS)

தன்ஊன் பெருக்கற்குத் தான்பிறிது ஊன்உண்பான்
எங்ஙனம் ஆளும் அருள்.　　251

thanuun perukkaRkuth thAnpiRithu uunuNpAn
enganam aaLum aruL

Hardly any mercy is left in the minds of those, who
build their bodies with the flesh of other beings

பொருளாட்சி போற்றாதார்க்கு இல்லை அருள்ஆட்சி
ஆங்குஇல்லை ஊன்தின் பவர்க்கு.　　252

poruLaatchi pOtRAthArkku illai aruLaatchi
aangkuillai uunthin pavarkku

Wealth helps not those who do not patronize it;
mercy is missed by those who eat flesh meat

படைகொண்டார் நெஞ்சம்போல் நன்றுஊக்காது ஒன்றன்
உடல்சுவை உண்டார் மனம்.　　253

padaikoNdAr n-enjsampOl n-anRuUkkAthu onRan
udalsuvai uNdAr manam

Who take pleasure in killing to eat, have a mind of
steel impervious to mercy on the prey

அருள்அல்லது யாதுஎனின் கொல்லாமை கோறல்
பொருள்அல்லது அவ்வூன் தினல்.　　254

aruLallathu yAthuenin kollAmai kORal
poruLallathu avvUn thinal

Mercy demands not to kill; butchering is cruel,
and eating flesh meat is insensuous

உண்ணாமை உள்ளது உயிர்நிலை ஊன்உண்ண
அண்ணாத்தல் செய்யாது அளறு.　　255

uNNAmai uLLathu uyirn-ilai uunuNNa
aNNAththal seyyAthu aLaRu

Abstaining from meat is a way of saving lives; meateaters hardly get off from mental morbidity

தினல்பொருட்டால் கொல்லாது உலகுஎனின் யாரும்
விலைப்பொருட்டால் ஊன்தருவார் இல்.   256

thinalporuttaal kollAthu ulakuenin yArum
vilaiporuttAl uuntharuvAr il

If humanity abjures the habit of meat eating,
the ill reputed sale of it will not exist

உண்ணாமை வேண்டும் புலாஅல் பிறிதுஒன்றன்
புண்ணது உணர்வார்ப் பெறின்.   257

uNNAmai vaeNdum pulAal pirithuonRan
puNNathu uNarvArp peRin

Who realises the pain and wound of killing
will give up the habit of meat eating

செயிரின் தலைப்பிரிந்த காட்சியார் உண்ணார்
உயிரின் தலைப்பிரிந்த ஊன்.   258

saeyirin thalaippirin-tha kAtchiyAr uNNAr
uyirin thalaippirin-tha uun

Wisdom free from the painful mind of evil
will abstain from feeding on flesh

அவிசொரிந்து ஆயிரம் வேட்டலின் ஒன்றன்
உயிர்செகுத்து உண்ணாமை நன்று.   259

avisorin-thu aayiram vaettalin onRan
uyirsekuththu uNNAmai n-anRu

Abstaining from meat eating is good even in
hospitality with a rich fare of food in ghee

கொல்லான் புலாலை மறுத்தானைக் கைகூப்பி
எல்லா உயிரும் தொழும்.   260

kollAn pulAlai maRuththAnaik kaikUppi
ellA uyirum thozum

All life on earth will bow in gratefulness to those
who abstain from killing and meat eating

27. தவம்
thavam
PENANCE

(FORBEARING PAIN, HUNGER, STRESSES IN FAMILY LIFE IS
ENDURANCE AND IN RENUNCIATION IT IS PENANCE)

உற்றநோய் நோன்றல் உயிர்க்குஉறுகண் செய்யாமை
அற்றே தவத்திற்கு உரு.　　　　　　261

*utRRan-Oy n-OnRRal uyirkkuuRukaN seyyAmai
atRRae thavaththiRku uru*

Enduring pain, like fasting, and abjuring injury
to other lives are facets of penance

தவமும் தவமுடையார்க்கு ஆகும் அவம்அதனை
அஃதுஇலார் மேற்கொள் வது.　　　　　262

*thavamum thavamudaiyArkku aakum avamathanai
aqthuilAr maeRkoL vathu*

Mind control, politeness and compassion are
prerequisites for penance; otherwise it is a farce

துறந்தார்க்குத் துப்புரவு வேண்டி மறந்தார்கொல்
மற்றை யவர்கள் தவம்.　　　　　263

*thuRan-thArkkuth thuppuravu vaeNdi maRan-thArkol
matRRai yavarkaL thavam*

Intention to help renouncers is no alibi for
society to forget austerity and penance

ஒன்னார்த் தெறலும் உவந்தாரை ஆக்கலும்
எண்ணின் தவத்தான் வரும்.　　　　　264

*onnArth theralum uvan-thArai aakkalum
eNNin thavaththAn varum*

Winning foes and saving friends are possible
by the strength of a penitent mind

வேண்டிய வேண்டியாங்கு எய்தலால் செய்தவம்
ஈண்டு முயலப் படும்.　　　　　265

*vaeNdiya vaeNdiyAngku eythalAn seythavam
eeNdu muyalap padum*

Achievements on time and wish are possible in social
and family life itself, of austerity and penance

தவம்செய்வார் தங்கருமம் செய்வார்மற்று அல்லார்
அவம்செய்வார் ஆசையுள் பட்டு. **266**

*thavamseyvAr thamkarumam seyvArmaRRu allAr
avamseyvAr aasaiyuL pattu*

Doing one's social duties is a mission of penance
in life; or else it is mere pursuit of lust

சுடச்சுடரும் பொன்போல் ஒளிவிடும் துன்பம்
சுடச்சுட நோற்கிற் பவர்க்கு. **267**

*sudachchudarum ponpOl oLividum thunpam
sudachchuda n-OkkiR pavarkku*

Penance and forbearance to pain brightens
one like gold simmering on fire

தன்னுயிர் தான்அறப் பெற்றானை ஏனைய
மன்னுயிர் எல்லாம் தொழும். **268**

*thannuyir thAnaRap petRRAnai aenaiya
mannuyir ellAm thozum*

All life on earth bow in esteem to those who rise
above ego and control their mind in penance

கூற்றம் குதித்தலும் கைக்கூடும் நோற்றலின்
ஆற்றல் தலைப்பட் டவர்க்கு. **269**

*kUtRRam kuthiththalum kaikUdum n-ORRalin
aatRRAl thalaippat tavarkku*

Penance with sensual control on magnetism of life prolongs aging
(recycling energy of sexual vital fluids thro' yoga can control
sinking of life mechanism)

இலர்பல ராகிய காரணம் நோற்பார்
சிலர்பலர் நோலா தவர். **270**

*ilarpalar aakiya kAraNam n-OrppAr
silarpalar n-OlA thavar*

Many are poor and a few are rich, as the austere and
hardworking are sinking, while the idle multiply

28. கூடா ஒழுக்கம்
kuudA ozukkam
VILENESS AND IMPOSTURE
(CHEATING, CRIME, IMPOSTURE, SPITE ARE AGAINST DISCIPLINE)

வஞ்ச மனத்தான் படிற்றுஒழுக்கம் பூதங்கள்
ஐந்தும் அகத்தே நகும்.　　　　　　　　271

vanjsa manaththAn padiRRuozukkam pUthangkaL
ain-thum akaththae n-akum

The feigned postures of hypocrites are laughed at
by the five elements of their own self

வானுயர் தோற்றம் எவன்செய்யும் தன்நெஞ்சம்
தான்அறி குற்றப் படின்.　　　　　　　　272

vAnuyar thOtRRam evanseyyum thann-enjsam
thAnaRi kutRRap padin

The guilty conscience of skyhigh imposters
is invariably exposed by their deceit

வலியில நிலைமையான் வல்லுருவம் பெற்றம்
புலியின்தோல் போர்த்துமேய்ந்து அற்று.　　273

valiil n-ilaimayAn valluruvam petRRam
puliyinthOl pOrththumaeyn-thu atRRu

The weaklings posturing sainthood, is like a cow
grazing with the cover of a tiger's skin

தவமறைந்து அல்லவை செய்தல் புதல்மறைந்து
வேட்டுவன் புள்சிமிழ்த்து அற்று.　　　　274

thavamaRainthu allavai seythal puthalmaRain-thu
vaettuvan puLsimizththu atRRu

Wickedness in the garb of renouncers, is like a
fowler stealthily ambushing birds in a net

பற்றுஅற்றேம் என்பார் படிற்றொழுக்கம் எற்றெற்றென்று
ஏதம் பலவும் தரும்.　　　　　　　　275

patRRuatRRaem enpAr paditRRuozukkam etRRetRenRu
aetham palavum tharum

The venality of fake renouncers soaks them
in everlasting pain and grief to regret

நெஞ்சில் துறவார் துறந்தார்போல் வஞ்சித்து
வாழ்வாரின் வன்கணார் இல்.　　　　　**276**

*n-enjsil thuRavAr thuRan-thArpOl vanjsiththu
vAzvArin vankaNAr il*

Cheating by saintly postures, reluctant to renounce
evil from their minds, is the vilest of worldly life

புறம்குன்றி கண்டனைய ரேனும் அகம்குன்றி
மூக்கில் கரியார் உடைத்து.　　　　　**277**

*puRamkunRi kaNdanaiya raenum akamkunRi
mUkkil kariyAr udaiththu*

Beware of those with an external pose like a berry,
whose mind is stained dark like its nose

மனத்தது மாசாக மாண்டார்நீர் ஆடி
மறைந்துஒழுகு மாந்தர் பலர்.　　　　　**278**

*manaththathu mAsAka mANdArn-eer aadi
maRain-thuozuku mAn-thar palar*

A stained mind cannot be cleansed, bathing the body
in seas or rivers believed to be holy (such people
hide their wickedness in false exteriors)

கணைகொடிது யாழ்கோடு செவ்விதுஆங்கு அன்ன
வினைபடு பாலால் கொளல்.　　　　　**279**

*kaNaikodithu yAzkOdu sevvithuaangku anna
vinaipadu pAlAl koLal*

Weigh merit by behaviour, not by words; the straight
arrow can kill, the bent yazh has charm in its strings

மழித்தலும் நீட்டலும் வேண்டா உலகம்
பழித்தது ஒழித்து விடின்.　　　　　**280**

*maziththalum n-eettalum vaeNdA ulakam
paziththathu oziththu vidin*

Tonsuring head or tangling hair are of no avail, if
what is condemned as evil is not renounced

29. கள்ளாமை
kaLLAmai
ABSTAIN FROM FRAUD AND DECEIT
(THE MENTAL ATTITUDE TO CHEAT OR STEAL CAN ONLY END UP
IN LOSS, SHAME AND CRIME)

எள்ளாமை வேண்டுவான் என்பான் எனைத்துஒன்றும்
கள்ளாமை காக்கதன் நெஞ்சு.   281

*yeLLAmai vaeNduvAn enpAn enaiththuonrum
kaLLAmai kAkkathan n-enjsu*

**Keep your conscience free from the guilt of
fraud and guard against social reproach**

உள்ளத்தால் உள்ளலும் தீதே பிறன்பொருளைக்
கள்ளத்தால் கள்வேம் எனல்.   282

*uLLaththAl uLLalum theethae piRanporuLaik
kaLLaththAl kaLvaem enal*

**A stealthy mind scheming fraud, is a wicked
weapon destroying wealth and virtue**

களவினால் ஆகிய ஆக்கம் அளவிறந்து
ஆவது போலக் கெடும்.   283

*kaLavinAl aakiya aakkam aLaviRan-thu
aavathu pOlak kedum*

**Easy gains from fraud, may appear big, but
disappear soon the way they came**

களவின்கண் கன்றிய காதல் விளைவின்கண்
வீயா விழுமம் தரும்.   284

*kaLavinkaN kanRiya kAthal viLaivinkaN
veeyA vizumam tharum*

**The greed of fraudulent gains invariably
lead one to endless grief and pain**

அருள்கருதி அன்புடையர் ஆதல் பொருள்கருதிப்
பொச்சாப்புப் பார்ப்பார்கண் இல்.   285

*aruLkaruthi anpudaiyAr aathal poruLkaruthip
possAppup pArppArkaN il*

Love and compassion are alien virtues to those
who cheat and rob the unsuspecting weak

அளவின்கண் நின்றொழுகல் ஆற்றார் களவின்கண்
கன்றிய காத லவர்.   286

*aLavinkaN n-inRuozukal aatRRAr kaLavinkaN
kanRiya kAtha lavar*

Those who crave on covetous fraud do not
know any limits or the virtue of austerity

களவுஎன்னும் காரறி வாண்மை அளவுஎன்னும்
ஆற்றல் புரிந்தார்கண் இல்.   287

*kaLavuennum kAraRi vANmai aLavuennum
aatRRal purin-thArkaN il*

The wisdom of a contented mind has no
room for the dark mood of fraud

அளவுஅறிந்தார் நெஞ்சத்து அறம்போல நிற்கும்
களவுஅறிந்தார் நெஞ்சில் கரவு.   288

*aLavuaRin-thAr n-enjsaththu aRampOla n-iRkum
kaLavuaRin-thAr n-enjsil karavu*

Virtue is sustained by a mind tempered by values,
as deceit persists with the habit of fraud

அளவுஅல்ல செய்துஆங்கே வீவர் களவுஅல்ல
மற்றைய தேற்றா தவர்.   289

*aLavualla seythuaangkae veevar kaLavualla
matRRaiya thaetRRA :havar*

One who is sea deep in fraud, and acts
out of bounds, perishes in perfidity

கள்வார்க்குத் தள்ளும் உயிர்நிலை கள்ளார்க்குத்
தள்ளாது புத்தேள் உலகு.   290

*kaLvArkkuth thaLLum uyirn-ilai kaLLArkkuth
thaLLAthu puththaeL ulaku*

The fraudulent experience death as they live; a mind
free from treachery reaches a brave new world

30. வாய்மை
vAymai
VERACITY

(VERACITY REFERS TO HARMLESS TRUTH SPOKEN FROM THE
GOODNESS OF MIND. WORDS MEANT TO CONVEY
CONSCIENTIOUS VIRTUES ARE SYNONYMOUS TO TRUTH)

வாய்மை எனப்படுவது யாதுளெனின் யாதுஒன்றும்
தீமை இலாத சொலல்.   291

vAymai enappaduvathu yAthuenin yAthuonRum
theemai ilAtha solal

Harmless truth is the best to speak, guarding
against the consequences of evil

பொய்ம்மையும் வாய்மை இடத்த புரைதீர்ந்த
நன்மை பயக்கும் எனின்.   292

poymmaiyum vAymai idaththa puraitheern-tha
n-anmai payakkum enin

Words spoken in pursuit of goodness pure
are verily sure norms to truth serene

தன்நெஞ்சு அறிவது பொய்யற்க பொய்த்தபின்
தன்நெஞ்சே தன்னைச் சுடும்.   293

thann-enjsu aRivathu poyyaRka poyththapin
thann-enjsae thannaich sudum

Always speak true to your conscience, deliberate
falsehood scorches your senses sure

உள்ளத்தால் பொய்யாது ஒழுகின் உலகத்தார்
உள்ளத்துள் எல்லாம் உளன்.   294

uLLaththAl poyyAthu ozukin ulakaththAr
uLLaththuL ellAm uLan

Truthful and conscientious behaviour gains
love from the minds of the worthy

மனத்தொடு வாய்மை மொழியின் தவத்தொடு
தானஞ்செய் வாரின் தலை.   295

manaththodu vAymai moziyin thavaththodu
thAnamsey vArin thalai

Truth spoken in sincerity is munificence in penance,
and hospitality extended while fasting

பொய்யாமை அன்ன புகழில்லை எய்யாமை
எல்லா அறமும் தரும்.   296

poyyAmai anna pukazillai eyyAmai
ellA aRamum tharum

Virtue in its course is guarded best by truth;
fame is nurtured by abstinence from lies

பொய்யாமை பொய்யாமை ஆற்றின் அறம்பிற
செய்யாமை செய்யாமை நன்று.   297

poyyAmai poyyAmai aatRin aRampiRa
seyyaamai seyyAmai n-andRu

Sincerity to truth is a natural virtue, abjuring
vices despised by society is discipline

புறந்தூய்மை நீரான் அமையும் அகந்தூய்மை
வாய்மையால் காணப் படும்.   298

puRaththUymai n-eerAn amaiyum akaththUymai
vAymaiyAl kANap padum

Pure water purifies the body outer; truth
is the medicine that purifies the mind

எல்லா விளக்கும் விளக்குஅல்ல சான்றோர்க்குப்
பொய்யா விளக்கே விளக்கு.   299

ellA viLakkum viLakkualla sAnROrkkup
poyyA viLakkae viLakku

Truth is a powerful light, like the Sun, banishing
dark ignorance from the mind

யாம்மெய்யாக் கண்டவற்றுள் இல்லை எனைத்துஒன்றும்
வாய்மையின் நல்ல பிற.   300

yAmmeyyAk kaNdavatRRuL illai enaiththuonRum
vAymaiyin n-alla piRa

Of all things one ponders on and discovers
nothing surpasses truth serene

31. வெகுளாமை
vekuLaamai
BANISHING ANGER
(DO NOT GIVE ROOM FOR ANGER AND FRUSTRATION. THEY GENERATE HATRED, HARD WORDS AND VIOLENCE)

செல்லிடத்துக் காப்பான் சினம்காப்பான் அல்லிடத்துக்
காக்கின்என் காவாக்கால் என்.   301

*selidaththuk kAppAn sinamkAppAn allidaththuk
kAkkinen kAvAkkAl en*

**Restraining anger where you have cause
and option is valour; it is futile elsewhere**

செல்லா இடத்துச் சினம்தீது செல்லிடத்தும்
இல்அதனின் தீய பிற.   302

*sellA idaththuch sinamtheethu selidaththum
ilathanin theeya piRa*

**Anger is harmful, and safe to guard it against the
strong; it is harmful even against the weak**

மறத்தல் வெகுளியை யார்மாட்டும் தீய
பிறத்தல் அதனான் வரும்.   303

*maRaththal vekuLiyai yArmAttum theeya
piRaththal athanAn varum*

**Get rid of futile anger; in any case, it is a
dangerous source of evil and pain**

நகையும் உவகையும் கொல்லும் சினத்தின்
பகையும் உளவோ பிற.   304

*n-akaiyum uvakaiyum kollum sinaththin
pakaiyum uLavO piRa*

**There is no greater foe than ireful wrath
that kills a smile and a cheer in you**

தன்னைத்தான் காக்கின் சினம்காக்க காவாக்கால்
தன்னையே கொல்லும் சினம்.   305

*thannaiththAn kAkkin sinamkAkka kAvAkkAl
thannaiyae kollum sinam*

**Woeful anger devours your mind and body;
banish it fast from mind in self-defence**

சினம்என்னும் சேர்ந்தாரைக் கொல்லி இனம்என்னும்
ஏமப் புணையைச் சுடும்.   **306**

*sinamennum saern-thAraik kolli inamennum
aemap puNaiyaich sudum*

**Anger is fatal to friendship; it burns out
the life saving boat of kith and kin**

சினத்தைப் பொருளென்று கொண்டவன் கேடு
நிலத்துஅறைந்தான் கைபிழையாது அற்று.   **307**

*sinaththaip poruLenRu koNdavan kaedu
n-ilaththuaRain-thAn kaipizaiyAthu atRRu*

**The might of wrath is sure to destroy one, like
damage to a hand that dashes the ground**

இணர்எரி தோய்வன்ன இன்னா செயினும்
புணரின் வெகுளாமை நன்று.   **308**

*iNareri thOyvanna innA seyinum
puNarin vekuLAmai n-anRu*

**Even a torture like in fire shall not kindle your ire
on the wrongdoer, who seeks you in need**

உள்ளியது எல்லாம் உடன்எய்தும் உள்ளத்தால்
உள்ளான் வெகுளி எனின்.   **309**

*uLLiyathu ellAm udaneythum uLLaththAl
uLLAn vekuLi enin*

**It takes mental firmness to restrain anger; when
that is deployed to good, wishes turn to gains**

இறந்தார் இறந்தார் அனையர் சினத்தைத்
துறந்தார் துறந்தார் துணை.   **310**

*iRan-thAr iRan-thAr anaiyar sinaththaith
thuRan-thAr thuRan-thAr thuNai*

**Losing mental balance in wrath destroys; banishing
anger is the success of self renouncers**

32. இன்னா செய்யாமை
innA seyyAmai
ABJURING VIOLENCE AND HARM
(IT IS WISDOM AND GOOD GRACE NOT TO INFLICT PAIN AND INJURY TO OTHERS; AS SUCH ACTS BOOMERANG ON THE DOER)

சிறப்புஈனும் செல்வம் பெறினும் பிறர்க்குஇன்னா
செய்யாமை மாசுஅற்றார் கோள்.　　　　311

siRappueenum selvam peRinum piRarkkuinnA
seyyAmai mAsuatRRAr kOL

The code of non-violence is enlightenment; abide
by it even at the cost of wealth and fame

கறுத்துஇன்னா செய்தவக் கண்ணும் மறுத்துஇன்னா
செய்யாமை மாசுஅற்றார் கோள்.　　　　312

kaRuththuinnA seythavak kaNNum maRuththuinnA
seyyAmai mAsuatRRAr kOL

A mind not stained by malice and harm, gains
grace when it abstains from revenge

செய்யாமல் செற்றார்க்கும் இன்னாத செய்தபின்
உய்யா விழுமம் தரும்.　　　　313

seyyAmal setRRArkkum innAtha seythapin
uyyA vizumam tharum

A sense of revenge, even on a causeless hater
may rebound to cause baneful pain

இன்னா செய்தாரை ஒறுத்தல் அவர்நாண
நன்னயம் செய்து விடல்.　　　　314

innAsey thArai oRuththal avarn-ANa
n-annayam seythu vidal

The best punishment of violent harm is to put
the doer in pain of shame, in good turns

அறிவினான் ஆகுவது உண்டோ பிறிதின்நோய்
தந்நோய்போல் போற்றாக் கடை.　　　　315

aRivinAn aakuvathu uNdO piRithinn-Oy
thann-OypOl pORRAk kadai

Of what avail one's wisdom is, who cannot share
other's pain as his own and seek redress

இன்னா எனத்தான் உணர்ந்தவை துன்னாமை
வேண்டும் பிறன்கண் செயல்.　　　　　316

*innA enaththAn uNarn-thavai thunnAmai
vaeNdum piRankaN seyal*

What you realise painful to yourself, shall not
colour your thoughts and acts on others

எனைத்தானும் எஞ்ஞான்றும் யார்க்கும் மனத்தானாம்
மாணாசெய் யாமை தலை.　　　　　317

*enaiththAnum enjnAnRum yArkkum manaththAnAm
mANAsey yAmai thalai*

A noble mind does not entertain the intent
to harm anyone anywhere any time

தன்னுயிர்க்கு இன்னாமை தானறிவான் என்கொலோ
மன்னுயிர்க்கு இன்னா செயல்.　　　　　318

*thanuyirkku innAmai thAnaRivAn enkolO
mannuyirkku innA seyal*

One should not harm other living beings
by things known to be injurious to self

பிறர்க்குஇன்னா முற்பகல் செய்யின் தமக்குஇன்னா
பிற்பகல் தாமே வரும்.　　　　　319

*piRarkkuinnA muRpakal seyyin thamakkuinnA
piRpakal thAmae varum*

Nemesis is always alert to repay you promptly
in the aft, a harm done to others in forenoon

நோய்எல்லாம் நோய்செய்தார் மேலவாம் நோய்செய்யார்
நோயின்மை வேண்டு பவர்.　　　　　320

*n-OyellAm n-OyseythAr maelavAm n-OyseyyAr
n-Oyinmai vaeNdu pavar*

Sickness of pain rebounds on the giver; those
wary of pain to self dare not harm others

33. கொல்லாமை
kollAmai
ABSTAIN FROM KILLING

(PURSUING THE CODE OF HARMLESSNESS & NON-VIOLENCE, KILLING
INNOCENT LIVES IN A CRUDE MANNER LIKE HUNTING FOR THE HECK
OF IT AND GORING FLESH ARE TO BE ABJURED AS VILE)

அறவினை யாதுஎனில் கொல்லாமை கோறல்
பிறவினை எல்லாம் தரும்.   321

aRavinai yAthuenil kollAmai kORal
piRavinai ellAm tharum

Virtue thrives in abstinence from killing; a mind
prone to gore, is a storehouse of vices

பகுத்துண்டு பல்லுயிர் ஓம்புதல் நூலோர்
தொகுத்தவற்றுள் எல்லாம் தலை.   322

pakuthuthuNdu paluyir oomputhal n-UlOr
thokuththavatRRuL ellAm thalai

The compassion to share with and patronize lives
is a primary virtue praised by many scriptures

ஒன்றாக நல்லது கொல்லாமை மற்றுஅதன்
பின்சாரப் பொய்யாமை நன்று.   323

onRAka n-allathu kollAmai matRRuathan
pinsArap poyyAmai n-anRu

The resolve not to kill other lives is a unique
virtue; close to it will follow veracity

நல்லாறு எனப்படுவது யாதுஎனின் யாதுஒன்றும்
கொல்லாமை சூழும் நெறி.   324

n-allARu enappaduvathu yAthuenin yAthuonRum
kollAmai sUzum n-eRi

The righteous path is the enlightened code
not to slay and destroy other lives

நிலைஅஞ்சி நீத்தாருள் எல்லாம் கொலைஅஞ்சிக்
கொல்லாமை சூழ்வான் தலை.   325

n-ilaianjsi n-eeththAruL ellAm kolaianjsik
kollAmai sUzvAn thalai

Those who disdain killing are far ahead in virtues
of those who renounce weary of worldly chorus

கொல்லாமை மேற்கொண்டு ஒழுகுவான் வாழ்நாள்மேல்
செல்லாது உயிருண்ணும் கூற்று.   326

kollAmai maeRkoNdu ozukuvAn vAzn-ALmael
sellAthu uyiruNNum kUtRRu

Death stays away from those who have refined
their mind and cultivated a life of non-violence

தன்னுயிர் நீப்பினும் செய்யற்க தான்பிறிது
இன்னுயிர் நீக்கும் வினை.   327

thannuyir n-eeppinum seyyaRka thAnpiRithu
innuyir n-eekkum vinai

Even at the risk of self, refrain from acts that cause
the harmless beings, pain of losing their lives

நன்றாகும் ஆக்கம் பெரிதுஎனினும் சான்றோர்க்குக்
கொன்றுஆகும் ஆக்கம் கடை.   328

n-anRuaakum aakkam perithueninum sAnROrkkuk
konRuaakum aakkam kadai

Gains, though in plenty, if at the cost of other lives,
are abhorred by people of sublime virtues

கொலைவினையர் ஆகிய மாக்கள் புலைவினையர்
புன்மை தெரிவார் அகத்து.   329

kolaivinaiyar aakiya mAkkaL pulaivinaiyar
punmai therivAr akaththu

People who indulge in killing without any sense of
virtue, have a life of unmitigated suffering

உயிர்உடம்பின் நீக்கியார் என்ப செயிர்உடம்பின்
செல்லாத்தீ வாழ்க்கை யவர்.   330

uyirudampin n-eekkiyAr enpa seyirudampin
sellAththee vAzkkai yavar

The awful stain of killers blood sickens the
mind and makes their life miserable

34. நிலையாமை
n-ilaiyAmai
INSTABILITY (TRANSIENCE, DELUSION)
(IN THE FAST CYCLE OF TIME NATURE CHANGES PERPETUALLY)

நில்லாத வற்றை நிலையின என்றுஉணரும்
புல்லறி வாண்மை கடை.

331

n-illAtha vatRRai n-ilaiyina enRuuNarum
pullaRi vANmai kadai

It is a grave folly in life to misjudge, and
suffer fleeting things as lasting ones

கூத்தாட்டு அவைக்குழாத்து அற்றே பெருஞ்செல்வம்
போக்கும் அதுவிளிந்து அற்று.

332

kUththuaattu avaikkuzAththu atRRae perunjselvam
pOkkum athuviLin-thu atRRu

Like a theatre crowd at a passing show, wealth
gathers slowly and melts away fast

அற்கா இயல்பிற்றுச் செல்வம் அதுபெற்றால்
அற்குப ஆங்கே செயல்.

333

aRkA iyalpiRRuch selvam athupetRRAl
aRkupa aangkae seyal

Material wealth is unstable; use it fast to develop
enduring things of social benefit

நாளென ஒன்றுபோல் காட்டி உயிர்ஈரும்
வாளது உணர்வார்ப் பெறின்.

334

n-ALena onRupOl kAtti uyireerum
vALathu uNarvArp peRin

A day in the span of time fleets like
a saw, filing off life bit by bit

நாச்செற்று விக்குள்மேல் வாராமுன் நல்வினை
மேற்சென்று செய்யப் படும்.

335

n-AchchetRRu vikkuLmael varAmun n-alvinai
maeRsenRu seyyap padum

The tongue benumbs and spasms hiccup to signal life's
throb waning; take note and rise early to achieve good

நெருநல் உளன்ஒருவன் இன்றுஇல்லை என்னும்
பெருமை உடைத்துஇவ் வுலகு.   336

n-erun-al uLanoruvan inRuillai ennum
perumai udaiththuiv vulaku

Yesterday was his day, not today, the world
prides in its mysteries and poise, this way

ஒருபொழுதும் வாழ்வது அறியார் கருதுப
கோடியும் அல்ல பல.   337

orupozuthum vAzvathu aRiyAr karuthupa
kOdiyum alla pala

One who knows not in life what is in store
brims with wishes galore in crores

குடம்பை தனித்துஒழியப் புள்பறந் தற்றே
உடம்பொடு உயிரிடை நட்பு.   338

kudampai thaniththuoziya puLpaRan-thu atRRae
udampodu uyiridai n-atpu

Life's throb can fail the body anytime; as the
shell discarded by the chick flying off, dusts

உறங்கு வதுபோலும் சாக்காடு உறங்கி
விழிப்பது போலும் பிறப்பு.   339

uRangku vathupOlum sAkkAdu uRangki
vizippathu pOlum piRappu

Slumber and death, waking and birth, have apparent
resemblances in the fast cycle of life

புக்கில் அமைந்தின்று கொல்லோ உடம்பினுள்
துச்சில் இருந்த உயிர்க்கு.   340

pukkil amain-thinRu kollO udampinuL
thuchchil irun-tha uyirkku

Life's control centered in a corner of the brain activates
the body, but has no existence outside it

35. துறவு
thuRavu
RENUNCIATION

(RENUNCIATION IS SUBLIMATION OF MIND AND SPIRIT
BY SEEKING WISDOM OF TRUTH IN GRACE, AND ABDICATION OF
DESIRES IN PENANCE)

யாதனின் யாதனின் நீங்கியான் நோதல்
அதனின் அதனின் இலன்.   341

yAthanin yAthanin n-eengiyAn n-Othal
athanin athanin ilan

Whatever desires we are able to get rid of
liberate us from their torment and pain

வேண்டின்டன் டாகத் துறக்க துறந்தபின்
ஈண்டுஇயற் பால பல.   342

vaeNdinuN dAkath thuRakka thuRan-thapin
eeNduiyaR pAla pala

Competence to steadfastly renounce while possessing
wealth, is the way to achieve real happiness

அடல்வேண்டும் ஐந்தன் புலத்தை விடல்வேண்டும்
வேண்டிய எல்லாம் ஒருங்கு.   343

adalvaeNdum ain-than pulaththai vidalvaeNdum
vaeNdiya ellAm orungku

Winning over aspirations of our five senses with the
sixth and total renunciation are saintly feats

இயல்பாகும் நோன்பிற்குஒன்று இன்மை உடைமை
மயலாகும் மற்றும் பெயர்த்து.   344

iyalpuaakum n-OnpiRkuonRu inmai uNmai
mayalaakum matRRum peyarththu

Freedom from affinity is natural for renouncers, even
a least vacillation deceives and drowns in distress

மற்றும் தொடர்ப்பாடு எவன்கொல் பிறப்பறுக்கல்
உற்றார்க்கு உடம்பும் மிகை.   345

matRRum thodarppAdu evankol piRappaRukkal
utRRArkku udampum mikai

Saints who renounce and cut off active social
life, wary of pains, feel the body itself a burden

யான்எனது என்னும் செருக்குஅறுப்பான் வானோர்க்கு
உயர்ந்த உலகம் புகும்.   346

*yAnenathu ennum serukkuaRuppAn vAnOrkku
uyarn-tha ulakam pukum*

One with the will to banish 'I and mine' is endowed
with worldly fame, higher than heaven

பற்றி விடாஅ இடும்பைகள் பற்றினைப்
பற்றி விடாஅ தவர்க்கு.   347

*patRRi vidAa idumpaikaL patRRinaip
patRRi vidAa thavarkku*

Grief and suffering cling on to those, who
cannot get rid of bonds and desires

தலைப்பட்டார் தீரத் துறந்தார் மயங்கி
வலைப்பட்டார் மற்றை யவர்.   348

*thalaippattAr theerath thuRan-thAr mayangki
valaippattAr matRRai yavar*

Who can truly renounce are great, who are reluctant
are caught in the net of desires and suffer

பற்றுஅற்ற கண்ணே பிறப்புஅறுக்கும் மற்று
நிலையாமை காணப் படும்.   349

*patRRuatRRa kaNNae piRappuaRukkum matRRu
n-ilaiyAmai kANap padum*

Freedom from bondage of desires mitigates mundane
sufferings; till then it will be vacillation in vagueness

பற்றுக பற்றுஅற்றான் பற்றினை அப்பற்றைப்
பற்றுக பற்று விடற்கு.   350

*patRRuka patRRuaRRAn patRRinai appatRRai
patRRuka patRRu vidaRku*

Seek the company of saints free from bondage, that
is the strength to renounce worldly desires

36. மெய்யுணர்தல்
mey uNarthal
CONSCIOUSNESS OF TRUTH
(WISDOM OF REALISING THE TRUE CONTENT AND IMPORT OF MATTER AND ITS ELEMENTS)

பொருளல்ல வற்றைப் பொருளென்று உணரும்
மருளானாம் மாணாப் பிறப்பு.　　　351

poruLalla vatRRaip poruLenRu uNarum
maruLAnaam mANAp piRappu

The confused ones deem vain things worthy
and find life meritless and miserable

இருள்நீங்கி இன்பம் பயக்கும் மருள்நீங்கி
மாசறு காட்சி யவர்க்கு.　　　352

iruLn-eengki inpam payakkum maruLn-eengki
mAsaRu kAtchi yavarkku

Life blooms happy to those who overcome vacillation
and ignorance, to see things in clear perspective

ஐயத்தின் நீங்கித் தெளிந்தார்க்கு வையத்தின்
வானம் நணியது உடைத்து.　　　353

aiyaththin n-eengkith theLin-thArkku vaiyaththin
vAnam n-aNiyathu udaiththu

The insight to judge good and bad enables one to
identify ingredients of a life high in virtues

ஐயுணர்வு எய்தியக் கண்ணும் பயமின்றே
மெய்யுணர்வு இல்லா தவர்க்கு!　　　354

aiyuNarvu eythiyak kaNNum payaminRae
meyuNarvu illA thavarkku

Physical senses without the mental acumen to see
the world in proper perspective, are of no use

எப்பொருள் எத்தன்மைத்து ஆயினும் அப்பொருள்
மெய்ப்பொருள் காண்பது அறிவு.　　　355

epporuL eththanmaiththu aayinum apporuL
meypporuL kANpathu aRivu

What is knowledge is to research the inner qualities
and not to conclude by exterior of words, deeds, etc.

கற்றுஈண்டு மெய்ப்பொருள் கண்டார் தலைப்படுவர்
மற்றுஈண்டு வாரா நெறி.   356

*katRRuiiNdu meypporuL kaNdAr thalaippaduvar
matRRuiiNdu vArA n-eRi*

Who have studied and discovered different facets of Nature
enlighten fresh truths and codes, not known so far

ஓர்த்துஉள்ளம் உள்ளது உணரின் ஒருதலையாப்
பேர்த்துஉள்ள வேண்டா பிறப்பு.   357

*oorn-thuuLLam uLLathu uNarin oruthalaiyAp
paern-thuuLLa vaeNdA piRappu*

Contemplation and understanding body and life mechanism
enables one to chart his path without impediments

பிறப்புஎன்னும் பேதைமை நீங்கச் சிறப்புஎன்னும்
செம்பொருள் காண்பது அறிவு.   358

*piRappuennum paethaimai n-eengkach chiRappuennum
semporuL kANpathu aRivu*

Overcome misconception of pain in worldly chorus
by realizing the nature and goals of life

சார்புஉணர்ந்து சார்பு கெடஒழுகின் மற்றுஅழித்துச்
சார்தரா சார்தரு நோய்.   359

*sArpuuNarn-thu sArpu kedaozukin matRRuaziththuch
sArtharA sArtharu n-Oy*

The best remedy to the sickness of pain in life is
to go to the basics and eliminate their causes

காமம் வெகுளி மயக்கம் இவைமூன்றன்
நாமம் கெடக்கெடும் நோய்.   360

*kAmam vekuLi mayakkam ivaimUnRan
n-Amam kedakkedum n-Oy*

All of life's pain can be overcome as and when we
banish vices like lust, wrath and folly

37. அவா அறுத்தல்
avaa aRuththal
CURBING GREED

(UNJUST AND UNRESTRAINED DESIRES BREED GREED AND LEAD
TO GRIEF AND PAIN; IT IS BEST TO CURB AND CUT OFF DESIRES)

அவாஎன்ப எல்லா உயிர்க்கும்எஞ் ஞான்றும்
தவாஅப் பிறப்புஈனும் வித்து.　　　　　361

avAenpa ellA uyirkkumenj gnAnRum
thavAap piRappuiinum viththu

Desires and aspirations are but natural, like the life
instinct encased in a seed, seeking to sprout

வேண்டுங்கால் வேண்டும் பிறவாமை மற்றுஅது
வேண்டாமை வேண்ட வரும்.　　　　　362

vaeNdungkAl vaeNdum piRavAmai matRRuathu
vaeNdAmai vaeNda varum

A life without grief and pain is a modest ambition;
it is achieved by banishing undue desires and lust

வேண்டாமை அன்ன விழுச்செல்வம் ஈண்டுஇல்லை
யாண்டும் அஃதொப்பது இல்.　　　　　363

vaeNdAmai anna vizuchchelvam eeNduillai
yANdum aqthuoppathu il

Freedom from needless desires is peerless wealth to cherish,
here or anywhere, in family life or in renunciation

தூஉய்மை என்பது அவாஇன்மை மற்றது
வாஅய்மை வேண்ட வரும்.　　　　　364

thUuymai enpathu avAinmai maRRuathu
vAaymai vaeNda varum

Purify the mind from the dirt of lust, this is achieved
by adherence to veracity in words and deeds

அற்றவர் என்பார் அவாஅற்றார் மற்றையார்
அற்றாக அற்றது இலர்.　　　　　365

atRRavar enpAr avAatRRAr matRaiyAr
atRRAka atRRathu ilar

Renunciation is freedom from undue desires, those
in the bond of longing desires cannot renounce

அஞ்சுவது ஓரும் அறனே ஒருவனை
வஞ்சிப்பது ஓரும் அவா.   **366**

anjsuvathu oorum aRanae oruvanai
vanjsippathu oorum avA

Dreading the bond of desires is a step to virtue; be not
a slave to desires that surround to deceive

அவாவினை ஆற்ற அறுப்பின் தவாவினை
தான்வேண்டும் ஆற்றான் வரும்.   **367**

avAvinai aatRRa aRuppin thavAvinai
thAnvaeNdum aatRRAn varum

Banish all greedy desires outright; then life's
path is clear to aspire worthy deeds

அவாஇல்லார்க்கு இல்லாகும் துன்பம் அஃதுஉண்டேல்
தவாஅது மேன்மேல் வரும்.   **368**

avAillArkku ilAkum thunpam aqthuuNdael
thavAathu maenmael varum

Extinguish the wild fire of desires, with it goes pain;
till then grief comes in waves to torment

இன்பம் இடையறாது ஈண்டும் அவாஎன்னும்
துன்பத்துள் துன்பம் கெடின்.   **369**

inpam idaiaRAthu iiNdum avAennum
thunpaththuL thunpam kedin

Destruction of the woeful pain of desires allows
enjoyment of the mirth of serene happiness

ஆரா இயற்கை அவாநீப்பின் அந்நிலையே
பேரா இயற்கை தரும்.   **370**

aarA iyaRkai avAn-iippin an-n-ilaiyae
paerA iyaRkai tharum

Get rid of burden of desires insatiable and gain
a stable and natural state of happiness

38. ஊழ்
uuzh
POWER AND LAWS OF NATURE
(THE UNIVERSE CONSISTS OF MATTER AND ITS ELEMENTS ARE
MANIFESTED IN NATURE; HUMANITY IS PART OF IT AND IS
PREVAILED BY OMNIPOTENT NATURE)

ஆகூழால் தோன்றும் அசைவின்மை கைப்பொருள்
போகூழால் தோன்றும் மடி.　　　　371

aakUzAl thOnRum asaivuinmai kaipporuL
pOkUzAl thOnRum madi

Strength of mind and persistent efforts create favourable
surroundings; idle sloth loses wealth

பேதைப் படுக்கும் இழவூழ் அறிவுஅகற்றும்
ஆகலூழ் உற்றக் கடை.　　　　372

paethaip paduththum izavUz aRivuakatRRum
aakalUz utRRak kadai

Folly brings on adverse situations of loss and
despair, wisdom gains prosperity

நுண்ணிய நூல்பல கற்பினும் மற்றுந்தன்
உண்மை அறிவே மிகும்.　　　　373

n-uNNiya n-Ulpala kaRpinum maRRun-than
uNmai aRivae mikum

Study acquires subtle knowledge of theory,
robust innate wisdom alone can prevail

இருவேறு உலகத்து இயற்கை திருவேறு
தெள்ளியர் ஆதலும் வேறு.　　　　374

iruvaeRu ulakaththu iyaRkai thiruvaeRu
theLLiyar aathalum vaeRu

Worldly life has many facets and qualities, very
rarely material wealth and wisdom co-exist

நல்லவை எல்லாம் தீயவாம் தீயவும்
நல்லவாம் செல்வம் செயற்கு.　　　　375

n-allavai ellAm theeyavAm theeyavum
n-allavAm selvam seyaRku

In trying to earn wealth, seeming advantages turn
adverse and vice-versa, in the fast cycle of nature

பரியினும் ஆகாவாம் பாலல்ல உய்த்துச்
சொரியினும் போகா தம. 376

*pariyinum aakAvAm pAlalla uyththuch
soriyinum pOkA thama*

Things we do not deserve on merit are hard to gain;
wealth that is ours does'nt shrink in munificence

வகுத்தான் வகுத்த வகையல்லால் கோடி
தொகுத்தார்க்கும் துய்த்தல் அரிது. 377

*vakuththAn vakuththa vakaiallAl kOdi
thokuththArkkum thuyththal arithu*

Millions amassed outside the dictates of law
are of no avail to the wrongful gainers

துறப்பார்மன் துப்புரவு இல்லார் உறற்பால
ஊட்டா கழியும் எனின். 378

*thuRappArman thuppuravu illAr uRaRpAla
uuttA kaziyum enin*

Destitutes unable to acquire the wherewithal
of life are prone to quit life than honour

நன்றுஆங்கால் நல்லவாக் காண்பவர் அன்றுஆங்கால்
அல்லல் படுவது எவன். 379

*nanRuaangkaal nallavai kaaNbavar anRuaangkaal
allal paduvathu evan*

Those who perceive good in happiness should cultivate
an equanimous temper to face adversities in life

ஊழிற் பெருவலி யாவுள மற்றுஒன்று
சூழினும் தான்முந் துறும். 380

*uuziR peruvali yAvuLa matRRuonRu
sUzinum thAnmun- thuRum*

Human spirit endeavours to mould congenial surroundings;
but Nature's omnipotence dispenses its moods

திருவள்ளுவ மாலை

பாலெல்லாம் நல்லாவின்
    பாலாமோ ? பாரிலுள்ள
நூலெல்லாம் வள்ளுவர் செய்
    நூலாமோ ?

              - உரைச் சிறப்புப்பாயிரம்

வள்ளுவர்செய் திருக்குறளை
    மறுவறநன்கு உணர்ந்தோர்கள்
உள்ளுவரோ மனுவாதி
    ஒருகுலத்துக்கு ஒருநீதி ?

              - பேராசிரியர் சுந்தரம் பிள்ளை

மக்களுக்கு மாநிலத்தில் வாழ்க்கை வழிகளெல்லாம்
சிக்கலறக் காட்டிநலம் செய்நூராலாம் - மிக்கபுகழ்ச்
செந்தமிழ்ச் செல்வத் திருக்குறளை நெஞ்சமே
சிந்தனை செய்வாய் தினம்.

              - கவிமணி தேசிகவிநாயகம் பிள்ளை

எல்லாப் பொருளும் இதன்பால் உளஇதன்பால்
இல்லாத எப்பொருளும் இல்லையாம் - சொல்லாற்
பரந்தபா வால்என் பயன்வள் ளுவனார்
கரந்தபா வையத் துணை

              - மதுரைத் தமிழ் நாகனார்

'திறமைகொண்ட தீமையற்ற தொழில்புரிந்து யாவரும்
தேர்ந்தகல்வி ஞானமெய்தி வாழ்வம் இந்த நாட்டிலே'

- பாரதியார்

thiramaikoNda theemaiyatRa thozhilpurinthu yaavarum
thaernthakalvi njanamaethi vaazhvam intha n-aattilae

- paarathiyaar

பகுதி 2 – பொருட்பால்
pakuthi 2 - porutpaal
Part II - WEALTH

Efficient and harmless efforts guided by perceptive
learning and wisdom afford graceful life.

*- **Subramaniya Bharathiar.***

PART 2: WEALTH

Foreword

'ThirukkuRaL imparts knowledge to humanity to lead a humane life of compassion and love'

Ki. Aa. Po. Viswanathan, Thamizh scholar

Economics, the field dealing with production, preservation and utilisation of wealth, is meant to meet the needs and be useful for all species. The components of wealth are natural resources, food, clothing, accommodation, other accessories and facilities of life including education, entertainment and fine arts.

As an edict of socio-political thought, *KuRaL* 247 says wealth is fundamental for life on earth. Its objective is to aid an enlightened society to make its benefits available to everyone.

The economic management of wealth for prosperity of the land is to be judiciously cultivated (252). The task of wealth is to provide opportunities for everyone to part-take and grow in agriculture, industry, trade in goods and services; to get rid of poverty, famine and shortages of essential inputs; in which all toiling humans participate and enjoy their benefits fairly. It is the duty of responsible governance to aid the production, growth, protection and equitable distribution of wealth (385)

GOOD GOVERNANCE

For a country to prosper, various essentials, besides good governance, are:

LAND: Good Earth made rich (sans deserts, bushes, marshy saline) which unfailingly yields bounty of crops, by making use of surface and subsoil water, even in seasons of drought (406, 731, 1040)

'Our life prospers by bounty of water and crops' *NatRinai* 45

WATER: From rain, snow, rivers, fountains preserved in dams, lakes and ponds (737) and sea water (that has the wealth of minerals like salts, pearls, fish etc). Water that flows from higher levels is source of hydro-electric power.

HILLS & DALES: Are the repositories of water sources and flora and fauna that constitute wealth of nature to benefit humans; like minerals, oil, woods, fruits and honey, spices, ivory and skins. The use of iron, steel, gold and copper were known to our forbears 20 centuries ago. (155, 267, 759, 773, 931, 887, 931).

HUMAN POWER: People who are fit and respect work culture, and are skilled to produce and protect wealth can build up a flourishing society (731)

PRODUCE: Natural yields from forests and seas, cultivated products like grains, pulses, vegetables, fruits: the products of agro-related cultures, the highest esteem of labour and service. KuRaL praises agriculture as the foremost of selfless, prestigious occupations; the axis on/around which the world rotates and revolves (1025, 1031, 1032). All people have to depend on and go after it (1033-1036). The products of agriculture are not only food for humans and animals, but raw materials as inputs for industry to produce other goods. Thriving agriculture and growing industries are the two arms that strengthen society and build a land sought after (732, 738).

MATERIAL WEALTH: Richness in resources and produce is the wealth that affords security and abundance. Wealth in the possession of the mighty entrepreneurs works as capital for improving industry and trade; and wealth in the hands of the gracious and benevolent, benefits the needy as water in a community pond (215), like fruit trees in the village (216), like medicinal plants to relieve pain and suffering (217).

Wealth has to be continuously rotating among many, without being dormant and stagnating with a few. As investment capital it should be motivating growth of industry and multiply itself in the forms of inputs, capital, producer and consumer goods.

The three main inputs for wealth are - natural resources, capital and labour. It grows according to the efficiency of their utilisation. The misery of hard pursuit of scarce materials is debilitating; a country that can make such a situation rare is the best (732)

MERIT OF GOOD GOVERNANCE: The socio-economic policy of a good government aims at security of its land and people, protecting citizens' rights, meeting their needs according to merits, rendering just rule; increase wealth and prosperity, by constructing and maintaining dams, canals, lakes and ponds, roads, health and educational facilities. The normal sources of revenue of the government are: land and water tax, customs and excise duties, tax on income and wealth etc. It should be capable of facing natural disasters like earthquakes, volcanos, storms and floods, droughts and man-made occurrences like wars and feuds, theft and terrorism, environmental pollution etc.

It is the duty and responsibility of citizens to help and participate in the welfare activities of governance and to establish local bodies rule (733). The aim of a sound country is not just self sufficiency, but produce in abundance and security in its strength, to be self-reliant in any situation (738, 739).

Group 4: Chapters 39-63: Politics and Governance

In the olden days of 1st century BC, at the time of ThirukkuRaL, Thamizh country was ruled by monarchies of *Chera, Sozha, Paandia* regimes, and by sub-rulers under them. The method of elections for local self government was by drawing lots (*kudavOlai*) on names of contestants for a five member village council, eight member revenue board, judicial bodies, regents of the king, a council (*maasanam*) and ministers in the court of the king. But the principles and procedures of administration, and the qualifications of people employed therein as enunciated in KuRaL, are valid and applicable for good governance even today, with minor modifications of the form to suit current democratic concepts.

Those in positions of power should be people of integrity with proper education, experience, skills and alertness; guarding themselves against follies and contacts of the vice; seeking advice, aid and company of the worthy, encompassing kith and kin; to perform their duties judiciously at the proper time, place and with necessary means, acting with foresight and humanism, guarding against harshness and cruelty.

> 'To be born and deployed in the royal fold is painful
> responsibility; in no way worshipful adoration'

Silappathikaaram

Chapters 39, 55, 56 & 57 deal with the qualities of dignity and greatness of the ruler, duties & responsibilities and method of governance, and the consequences of despotism.

Chapters 40-43 elucidate the importance of education, listening to wisdom and being knowledgeable. The worth and vitality of knowledge & wisdom and ethical rationalism as the basis of all activity are stressed in as many as 93 couplets at different places. Those who black out wisdom and indulge in misrule are wily characters. In the process of evolution, good knowledge is acquired by our senses, processed by the mind, freed from follies, and refined by experience. The concept of an analytical mind is rationalistic by nature. Its findings are truth and love.

> 'Our body is the car, senses are the horses, mind
> is the reins and knowledge is the charioteer'

Vivekanandar

The mystics and the learned wise have adopted discipline in tune with internal and external nature, and achieved a haughty life of greatness and sublimity.

To listen to with interest and grasp the intricacies and wisdom of the disciplined best is an aspect of information systems and communication skills.

Chapter 44: Besides ego, anger, meanness, greed, glory sans honour, miserliness (parsimony) has been classified as crimes. This is a significant indicator of the norms of socialism advocated by kuRaL.

Chapters 45-54: The norms to be adopted by the ruler in the discharge of his functions and responsibilities include taking wise counsel of the learned great and advice of ministers, to maintain cordial relations with those who surround him and take their assistance; disdain insouciance, complacency, follies and crimes, respect the glorious traditions and qualities of the society, to analyse pros and cons of matters before him, decide with clarity and act swiftly and firmly, with determination and due regard to proper strength, time and place. Success of governance depends on the care and attention given to select suitable people after due tests and verification, find out their aptitudes, delegate responsibilities, encourage, guide and superintend their actions. These aspects of governance apply equally to modern day scientific management practices as well.

Chapter 53: Fostering traditional relationships, contacts and friendship, like the crow that calls and shares without concealing, looking to their legitimate needs on merits and moving on in harmony with them will strengthen the hands of the ruler. These aspects are forerunners to the study of behavioural patterns in human relations development.

Chapters 58, 60-63: Emphasize the primary importance of humanism, courtesy and foresight in public relations; motivation and diligence in planning, freedom from sloth and indolence; persistent and pervasive efforts, overcoming obstacles and mishaps.

LAW AND JUSTICE

Owing to paucity of documented records as to the prevalence and implementation of the legal system in ancient times, save for some references in literature and inscriptions on stones and copper plates, a format has to be constructed from what we see in kuRaL and other treatises. The fundamental principles of justice are apparent - good governance is the symbol of justice, that does not fail or bend, and dispensed with firmness and caution (543,546, 547).

For virtues, discipline, manners and social harmony to thrive, a legal system to prevent crimes is essential (388, 541).

That should be based on robust common sense, respected by the people and capable of proper implementation. Justice should be based on equity and uprightness, and balanced without lenience, slipping or let up, and protect all the people without discrimination (111,112). One who practices and enforces equity in thought and actions is the cardinal of justice (119). Confidence should prevail that those who function outside the codes of governance and justice cannot thrive (377). It is the duty of the ruler to frame and implement due process of law (388, 541).

Banishing crime and protecting community (548)
Putting down terror and cruelty by the hardest punishment (550)
Investigating fully and punishing to prevent recurrence (561)
Censure follies and mistakes sternly and punish lightly (562)

These are norms for constructive approach in dispensing justice. If the rulers fail in their duties the country will be ruined along with them (533-560).

A significant aspect of the codes of justice in kuRaL is the concept that what we do by folly, which can be corrected and saved from recurrence are termed as mistakes; which are done deliberately, repeatedly and which cannot be remedied are termed as felony or crimes, deserving inescapable hard punishment. In couplets 314, 549, and 550 the terminology used is 'punishment' (*oRuththal*) only; there is no thought or expression about ' pardon' for crimes.

Pain rebounds on those who inflict it on others (319, 320); there is no escape from its consequences. Those who suffer may forbear them, but that can be no excuse for the criminals.

The system of justice now prevailing mainly fails in implementation and bias of individual convictions, rather than the spirit of equity and law; people are losing faith in it due to its delay and ineffectiveness. The edict that 'justice delayed is justice denied' is lost sight of. Perhaps the religious belief of rebirth, that the consequences of actions continues in successive generations, has lulled the system of justice into a leisurely attitude.

HUMAN RESOURCES DEVELOPMENT, MANAGEMENT SCIENCES, INFORMATION SYSTEMS AND COMMUNICATION SKILLS

With the vast array of fast developments in the fields of science and technology, economics and human attitudes in recent times that have radically changed our life styles beyond recognition, it will be interesting and useful to reflect on and compare the values, ethical codes and systems that prevailed in ancient times, where refined civilizations thrived. That will help to know our bearings and traditions, strengthen our moral values and enhance the quality of our life, reducing stresses and strains, balancing thinking and working, with rest and recreation in sports and fine arts.

With this purpose in mind, we can delve deep into the treasure trove of ThirukkuRaL, like a prism throwing varied spectrums in different angles, to find wide and new dimensions, which have stood the test of time and prevailed, flexible to changes; and take guidance from them. Though the system of governance and nature of occupations were different in those times, the basic ingredients of human thought and actions were same.

The stunning level of knowledge acquired and practised in the fields of astronomy, atomic structure of the universe and the behavioural patterns of the elements of nature, by the bare eyed scientists of BC centuries, known in Thamizhnaadu as 'kaNiyarkaL', the codes evolved by them in education, human sciences, psychology, philosophy and management systems seem equally valid and useful even today.

Human Resources Development: Economic progress is basic for development of society and advancement of culture and civilization. Contributory to this are human resources, besides capital and technology. Developed countries like USA, Japan, Europe, China, Korea, Thaiwan and Singapore have deployed them to great success. For integrated growth, human resources properly cultivated and organised are of primary importance to make efficient use of capital and technology. The building blocks for HRD are purity of environment, health of body and mind, adequate care and involvement in rearing children from embryo stage; education based on discipline, innovative spirit and application; sense and deeds of equitable and cohesive social order. Growth of a child's brain is maximum from embryo to 6 years of age, when parental interest and efforts contribute more. In acquiring knowledge, besides a well founded cultural tradition and social background, the importance of technology, skills and craftiness and their continuous growth and upgrading should be inculcated. The system of education should be perfected with the involvement of dedicated teachers.

In the selection of people for various avocations, thorough and scientific based, capability and aptitude tests should be conducted, with due regard for psychological aspects. Proper placement, delegation of powers and assignment of duties, encouragement and support in execution and adequate incentives and retraining for keeping abreast of latest developments and improving efficiency are necessary.

The following KuraL couplets are worth referring to:

Analysing consequences of actions (469) testing for character, qualities and suitability for jobs on hand (501-510); Choosing by aptitudes and skills, knowing their perceptions, knowledge and capabilities encouraging, guiding and evaluating outcome (511-520}

PUBLIC RELATIONS

One's natural qualities, origin of thoughts and feelings, behaviour, purity of mind and action and their positive achievements, security, fame and glory, and benefits ahead are the outcome of the social background and environment in which one is born and brought up. People of character are moulded by and are part of an enlightened and progressive society. They analyse the implications and nature of their actions and perform them methodically with courage and skills (451-460).

While choosing people to be deployed in public relations duties, their perception of virtues, wealth, happiness and attitude towards life; depth of knowledge, outstanding qualities in upholding values of society; shunning shame and blame, guarding against complacency and indifference, acting with vigilance and foresight; their ways of performing duties and usefulness for the purpose on hand should be examined (501-505, 531-540).

Idle sloth, forgetting, dozing and lacking are harmful (605)

Patronising and assisting traditional relationships, contacts with friends and relations, soft and sweet approach, social demeanour, encompassing and getting on with people and benevolence to help, constitute special qualifications for public work (521-530).

To enhance the quality of human life and to succeed in achieving objectives, mental sophistication, foresight and deep perception and a humane approach are essential. A pleasing appearance, soft outlook and commitment to duties impress ones personality. To cultivate and upgrade our faculties, a healthy mind of noble thoughts, motivation and firmness in performance are required.

Magnanimity of service depends on excellence of efforts (613).

The maturity of mind to feel happy even in adversity (630).

THE SCIENCE OF MANAGEMENT

With the help of modern developments in science and technology, prospecting nature and utilising resources in its elements like heat, light, air, water and land; increasing productivity and wealth contribute to upgrade the quality of life in industry and trade, education and health, politics and governance etc. To organise and direct these activities efficiently, management systems play an important role. Such an approach can only match the fast changes and demands to succeed in economic growth and in the fields of scientific and psychological competency.

For those who take up responsibilities in management, the lore of learning, depth of knowledge and a subtle mind, ways and means of performing, purity of mind and sharp intelligence clarity of tongue, humility & self control, awareness and courage are essential ingredients (636, 670, 694, 715).

In these fields it is worth knowing what were the codes of conduct, systems and procedures adopted, as reflected in KuRaL, and how they could be related to and made use of in the present day context. The doctrines on management appear in *KurRaL* at various places in the following chapters:

1. Basic tenets of governance, justice, welfare (39-45,54-57)
2. Action after deliberations and decision (47)
3. Strengths, time and place (48-50)
4. Test and trust, evaluate and entrust (51, 52)
5. Humanism and foresight, motivation, alertness, pervading effort, overcoming hurdles (58, 60-63)
6. Planning and execution (64, 65, 59, 69, 70)
7. Purity, firmness and mode of actions (66-68)

The basics for success in management, as in other fields of life, are kindness, softness in words, harmlessness, gratefulness, equity, humility, discipline, integrity, forbearance, social responsibility, benevolence, glory in virtues, grace, veracity, education, knowledge and wisdom. Functional aspects of significance are amiable disposition, patience to bear with bitter truth, guarding against harm, abjuring vices, vanity and self-adulation; seeking advice of elders, selecting and treating people who surround, realising the importance of capital and inter dependence, purity of surroundings, of mind and firmness of action, evaluating possibilities, analysing costs and benefits, deliberating and deciding, respecting manners, and working with courage and conviction, but without ostentation inviting ridicule, and achieving goals in silence (385-500).

In any venture, its good and risky aspects and usefulness have to be examined, and proper planning should precede action. When time and place are opportune, grasp the chance and execute it to perfection; that alone can gain glory and a bright future. Persistent and ceaseless efforts widen the scope and content of progress. Those who pursue a mission of duty with a graceful mind have precedence for all the beauties of the world. The following merit specific attention:

An enterprise sans capital, lacks a toehold or profits (449)

Analyse the costs, yields and profits of a proposition (461)

Do not risk capital in expectation of doubtful gains (463)

Do not court disgrace, by involvement without clarity (464)

Indulge in a mission after due deliberations (467)

Take care of ways and means to back up efforts (468)

Nothing is beyond those who evaluate possibilities and stand by the best in executing assignments (472)

Out-go is to be planned suiting resources and fair means (478)

A chance rare and ripe in time is the best to dare (489)

Wait silently in patience and strike firmly at the right time, like the peck of the stork (490)

Beware of a wrong step at a wrong place (500)

The quality of ones deeds is the touch stone of their mind (505)

Select a person with competence to tackle a job and entrust (517)

Changing times and contacts do not dim the tradition of love (521)

Will power is the motivation to energise activity (592)

A job done in full is a job done well (612)

Ceaseless striving with confidence is the strength to succeed (620)

People of perseverance make mishaps to miss-out (625).

INFORMATION SYSTEMS AND COMMUNICATION SKILLS

We are living in a period of time where all that are seen and spoken in the world and beyond it in planets of the universe, are brought into our households by news papers, magazines, radio, telephone, cinema, communication satellites, internet web, television and computers up to tele-conference; many of these were not even in the realm of imagination a century or two back. This is an era of digital media growing very fast, shrinking distance and time. Very powerful and sophisticated communication systems for vivid pictures of subtle details, surveillance from high flying aircraft and satellites beyond the reach of radar. In olden days exchange of information was primarily thro' personal contacts supplemented by occasional written communicated thro' messengers or flown thro' trained doves. These required mental faculties, sign languages of the eyes, face and body movements of a high and refined level to convey/receive and understand messages; eloquence and craftiness of ministers, poets, envoys, spies and invigilators. Not only in politics, trade and social life, but in love and family life as well, communications thro' signs and signals play a vital role.

Chapters on kindness of words (10), listening (42), eloquence (65), intelligence/embassy (59, 69), judging by looks and signs (71), assessing the audience, facing councils of the learned (72,73), conveying / receiving messages in love life (110, 128) deal with various aspects of effective communication.

There are three basic types of communication:

1. Semantic, direct conveyance by signs
2. Phonetic, by spoken words
3. Suggestive, by indications.

'Subtleness, brevity, elite and thoughtful are words that portray intended matter'

Tholkaappiyam, poruL, 8.170

To 'say it with flowers', kind words with a smiling face, spoken softly but firmly, communicate thoughts effectively, attract and convince the listeners, and others to seek (91-100). Gift of good listening to gain knowledge and wisdom (411-420). Eloquence and effectiveness of expression, choosing words of beauty, conveying ideas and thoughts in a way to impress (641-650). The specialised skills and unique qualities of emissaries and envoys to port messages and building up cordial relations (701-710). Public speaking is a carefully cultivated art to keep the audience spell-bound and mesmerised. It requires real good stuff and courage to convince a council of the wise. Great care is needed to sustain credibility and honesty in successful communication skills (711-730).

Brilliance and eloquence for the enlightened,
simplicity and clarity for others (715)

The talent to choose flawless words and effective delivery (717)
The logic and substance of good speaking in an assembly (726)
Her brow-painted eyes have dual intend in looks (1091)
Secret symptoms in the bosom of her broad lips (1274)

In ministering and administering, two qualities are marked as of primary importance.

First is healthy functioning of the tongue. It is the medium of expression of thoughts; words determine the life path of people. Chapters 10, 13, 65, 72 and 73 deal with this. It is significant to note that our tongue is placed in a safe position, kept cool and moist to protect its functions. One mouth and two eyes and two years in the body notify the need for more hearing and seeing than speaking. *Silappathikaaram* speaks about the disasters of a wrangling tongue, *KuNdalakaesi* tells 'the tongue is more powerful in achieving victories', poet Barathi said 'the pleasure of words should be like the spell of hymns'

Second is the power to think, reason out and act. It is one of the unique qualities of human race; the faculty to understand/ express feelings by signs of the face, eyes and limbs. Chapters 58, 70, 110, 128 deal with its aspects in personal and social life. Face reflects the mind. Eyes gauge the feelings of the subtle mind. Intelligence refined by education and manners yield utility and glory.

WINDOW TO THE TEXT

Chapters 64-73: Cabinet and Governance

In olden times when kings ruled with moral codes of virtue and their conscience as guiding principles, ministers of the king's court occupied responsible positions, advised about politics and administration, and diligently handled their duties. Those selected as ministers were people of eminent wisdom; honest, straight forward, well mannered and discharged their functions with kindness and firmness in defence, external relations, prosperity of the land, welfare of its people and in dispensing justice without let or hindrance.

Chapters 64-68 deal with the faculties, eloquence, purity, firmness and methods of action required of them.

Learning, knowledge, firmness, mastery and protection (632)
A minister is duty bound to warn of facts and situations (638)
Weigh and employ words that can perform (645)
The power to drive in a message without fear or flaw (647)

KuRaL lays great stress on the purity, firmness and methods of ones actions, esp. of those in positions of power and responsibilities to society, and implies the code that 'ends cannot justify means'.

Clarity and strength of mind save us from demeaning acts (654)
Fair means, though halting, lead to enduring gains (659)
Total involvement in a task and the will power to perform (666)
It is wise to act in a manner feasible in time and method (673)

Chapters 59 & 69: Intelligence and emissary are vital for efficient and successful functioning of governance, avoiding wars, establishing goodwill and cordial relationships; promoting trade and culture. The qualifications, qualities, skills, duties and modes of performance of the personnel handling these assignments are: social stature, sound traditions, loveable personality, friendliness, wisdom, cultivated eloquence, pleasant, positive, firm and winsome ways of performance, and a rare sense of time and place. For this, one needs purity in thought and action, flawless courage, depth of perception, veracity, concise words and courting assistance. Those who commend virtuous ways to others should take care to avoid faulty steps, inept or harsh, and be fearless in their ventures.

To survive and thrive, take cognisance on intelligence (583)
The wise among the learned are apt to lie abroad (683)

Chapter 70: Besides ministers, envoys and intelligence agents, others who surround and work for the king in administration, personal services etc. have also to play a cautious role with tact and understanding; being always alert, unostentatious, unobstrucive; be wary of default, mistrust and inquisitiveness; respect what is there in light and might, without misusing positions of power. Such people have also to be adept at communication skills in understanding/expressing signs and words, and judging circumstances.

Unworthy acts under the trust of traditional
kinship, lead to ruinous woes (700)

From what we could gather on historical events of the early centuries BC & AD, kings and monarchs were eminent leaders bound by ethical codes and guidelines enunciated in great works like ThirukkuRaL, to protect their land and citizens and work for their welfare. But in the later centuries after 6th AD, due to interference of external influences, and the foot hold of religions, the system of governance was made subservient to priestly order (*Raja GurukkaL*) in the king's courts, who in the garb of spiritualism diverted attention of kings from their primary duties and caused deceit, hatred, dissent, wars and devastation, which resulted in the weakening of states, disintegration and submission to the Mohammedan and Europeans invaders. The fields of education, basic agriculture, crafts and skills were neglected and sidelined. Those engaged in those services were treated as inferior classes, subservient to the brahminical and privileged classes. Ancient achievements in sciences, fine arts, indigenous medicine etc. were ignored and left undocumented. KurRaL has forewarned against the manipulators in couplets like 274-278, 520, 553, 560 and 639.

As an aftermath and hangover of this deterioration, even in the current 'democratic' set up, conventional and conservative self interests are dominating to the detriment of targeted growth.

Politicians of the day have no qualms or norms, take advantage of situations and live for the day. Perhaps they take to the political tactics in KuRaL couplets 633 and 875, sans its virtues.

They do not seem to bother in the least to the warning in *Silappathikaaram* that 'the force of virtue will finish off those who fault political norms', and make politics a means of livelihood. It is imperative for the citizens to be alert, forewarned, actively participate in their social duties, be sharp in putting down wrongs, select people of integrity and character to political power and constantly monitor and supervise their activities and demand results to ensure progress.

PROSPERITY AND SECURITY OF THE COUNTRY

Chapters 74,76: The first component of community living of people is government of the state. A closer study of the codes of governance in KuRaL will reveal the objects of organising, enhancing and changing continuously the quality and standards of civilised life.

For the stability of a state, besides good governance, wealth of produce, material prosperity, fosterage and protection of society is responsible governance. This is achieved by an able army, equipment, secure fortress, ministers with foresight and a vigilant ruler, well supported by citizens, with a creed of liberty for all, with each one being a willing servant of the state - a concept which underlays the hight of genius.

Citizens of a shining land aid the ruler and help him
bear the pressing burden of state (733)

Health, wealth, bountiful yields, delight and defence
are jewels adorning a beautiful land (738)

Wealth is a wheel that rotates life. Its importance in gaining and maintaining liberty, safety and prosperity of a country is vital. It has to be cultivated and protected as an ever shining lamp driving the darkness of want.

Graciousness is the off spring of love, nourished by
the foster-mother of cherished wealth (757)

Virtue and happiness meet in rare unity where wealth
in abundance comes in shining grace (760)

Chapters 75,77& 78:

'Let us root out from the world feuds and wars
and build a new world of peace and prosperity'

Poet Bharathidasan

The importance of forts and their natural strength and
settings, the glory of defence and the pride of warriors are detailed.

A fort of facility, strength and safety is glory built (749)
Valour, honour, a folklore of glory and clarity (766)
The finer edge of valour is mercy to those in distress (773)

It is a noteworthy feature that, unlike many other literary
works of the Thamizh Sangam ages like Tholkaappiyam,
PuRanaanuuRu, KalingaththupparaNi, elaborating the procedures,
glorifying wars and the feats of kings and warriors, the joyous
life styles with liquor, ThirukkuRaL has departed from
conventions, opposed them and charted a new path of virtues,
in love, kindness, honour, grace and sublimity.

A society sans the disasters of war-mongering:

Though defence forces, fortresses, valour of citizens and
wealth are essential for security from the forces of evil (381),
more important are cordial relations with neighbours, internal
peace and prosperity of society and families in a life of friendship,
honesty and humane behaviour which are stressed by KuRaL.
Besides the references to needs of strength, skills and
commitment to defence, emphasis is laid on fostering ancient
traditions of kinship, efficient governance in pursuit of common
good of the populace.

With rare foresight, kuRaL advocates the need of and benefits
in establishing a social order free from feuds and wars, curbing
and erasing the evil spirit of discordance and defiance,
overcoming enmity by courteous manners and converting foes
into friends by dignified attitudes; therein lies the beauty,
greatness, eminence and excellence of leaders and nations.

Though the codes and ethics of chapters 86-88 on the above aspects may, prima face, seem to contradict the stance in chapters 59, 77 & 78 on security of the state, a deeper reflection brings out the correlated objects and the concept of non-violence of these codes and edicts. ThiruvaLLuvar has underlined this view by the following:

Mark your feelings before the mighty, and show
compassion in your acts to the feeble (250)
Choose to face foes of matching strength, there is
no honour or nobility in battling the weak (861)
Abhor and avoid enmity that breeds ill feelings (871)
People with grace win-over foes to friendship and
make this world all the more a pleasant place (874)
In distress and grief of foes keep off and avoid meddling (876)
Just pride resides in courtesy even to the foe (995)

Radically changing the mind-set of glorifying victory in wars as the height of valour, KuRaL pictures the ruler as leader of a peace loving and progressive social order.

The foundation for happiness is love and kindness either in a family or in a society. The acute diseases of defiance and enmity caused by anger, envy, insouciance, shallowness and foolishness of mind have to be eradicated to aim at a fine, calm, happy and stable life.

Be gracious to an ignorant foe and take the pain afflicting innocents as your own, are supreme values to be exhibited by compassion to a battered foe in distress. However this should not be misread to mean any lenience in keeping off characters raged blind to reason or mad in lust, deceits (of enmity within) who pretend as friends. For survival in safety, defying foes have to be destroyed early, like rooting out thorny shrubs when they are young (879).

The intricacies of a correct and positive approach to win over potential foes as friends, to ensure better safety and lasting peace, as adumbrated in kuRal have to be appreciated in proper perspective.

CHAPTERS 79 - 94: FRIENDSHIP

ThirukkuRaL has subtly analysed and qualified different types and stages in fostering friendship; its special aspects, traditions and ways of preserving them.

Love generates the seed of aspirations and the seedling of desires to seek acquaintances, that sprouts as friendship, grows as relationship, buds as intimacy, flowers as a rightful duty, ripens and yields as long standing traditions (*pazaimai*). The passion of love in people of gentle and courteous manners kindles affection to seek worthy contacts rare to gain. Knowledge, virtues, love, friendship, refinement, sociability, community life, sense of shame, honour, just pride, worthiness and sublimity are links of a chain, each supports and shines with others.

Love generates aspirations and springs natural friendship (74)
Friendship binds and motivates like life in the body (1122)
Life's throb sustains body; love sustains friendship (338)
Like rain that merges with and takes the colour and quality of the earth it falls to, the spirit of love unites people

KuRunthokai 40

The virtuous sing the praise of those who sustain the life of friendship, un-shaken by convulsions of the earth

PuRanAnURu 34

If our body is a temple, god is life therein,
When the body goes, with it life ends

Thirumanthiram 3.13

Genuine friendship of noble souls refines as it grows and sustains. The attachments between KarNan and Dhuriyothanan, Gukan and Raman in Indian epics Mahabaratha and Ramayana are examples of selfless mannerism.

It is the unity of senses that flower earnest friendships. Personal acquaintance or contacts are not essential basics for true friendship. This is brought out by Thamizh history about king Koupperunjchouzhan and poet Piciraanthaiyaar and the fellowship of the bard king Paari and poet Kabilar, stand testifying the grief and pain of separation of real friends.

Sensual union flowers fellowship in friends; physical proximity or intimacy are not its prerequisites (786)

The greatness of long-standing and ever growing friendship is to sustain ancient and traditional qualities of fellowship (801). The quality of friendship that has matured into privileged relations, takes in its stride anything done by fellows in good faith as a matter of right, without let or hindrance. (803, 805).

The grace of natural friendship is mental happiness, canalised smoothly, safeguarding from harm, part-taking in grief and forthcoming to relieve pain (787-789). Friendship of the worthy grows like a waxing moon (781) and to those who have delved deep into it there is no relaxation or redemption (791). An apt simile to the strength and honour of pure friendship of diligence and power of the disciplined great who do not conceal but take pleasure in sharing, is found in PuRanaaNURu -190.

The ferocious tiger does not turn, even in hunger,
to the meat of a wild boar dead on left, but seeks
to kill a bull to lie on right and feeds on it.

Evaluation for prospecting friendships acceptable qualities to be probed for honest friendship are:

Friends moral duty is to caution and correct from faults (784)
Unwavering friendship on firm ground, seeping deep roots (789)
Probe temperament, tradition and strains of kinship (793)
Descent from noble traits, shunning shame (794)
Condemning to tears, dinning wisdom, preventing wrong (795)
Comradeship of the unblemished is worthy of embrace (800)
Cherished bonds, not shaken in adversities (806)

Preserving Friendship: Real friendship has the natural quality of gratitude sans recompense (106, 107), is part of wealth of the ruler (381), affords safeguards against woes (781), the wise and the great respect and safeguard it (802).

Chapters 82-83 urge to guard against the association of fools and idiots, pretenders in winning smiles and cunning guiles, the devious, aliens to community and social order, whose antecedents have not been probed properly, who desert in distress, incompatible in character, lacking manners, who befriend for profit and devourers of gains, unfaithful, spoilers of goodness, whose deeds and words have no relationship, who praise in private and revile in public, with false tears lurking in harm and those who do not stick to norms . KuRal 822 when referring to those who lack good manners, compares them to the 'fickle, like the mind of ladies'. True though, no one has delved the depths of feelings to successfully solve the riddles and puzzles of their minds, this reference has to be taken to mean the usual stresses and strains they are subjected to in family life which challenge their strength of mind.

Chapters 84-85 deal with ignorance and shallowness of mind and their various manifestations, and effects of folly, smallness, and grief.

Chapters 86-89 analyse the different dimensions of enmity, such as pungent hatred, discordance, crookedness, inflexibility, negative attitudes, internal enmity and such others; explains the concept of honour and nobility in dealing with potential foes, avoiding enmity and bringing them round to friendship, all the same to be wary of internal and concealed enmity defying solutions and to deal with them firmly.

Chapters 90-94 highlight the harmful and inter-linked deceptions to be wary of, for peace and prosperity of family and social life.

Not to antagonise the great in might and right (893)
Not to surrender to female infatuation (903)
To keep away from women of immoral ways (912)
Not to drown in liquor and lose honour (924)
Resist the lure of luck in, and affliction to gambling (931)

POSITION OF WOMEN IN SOCIETY

Some researchers and literary critics have expressed views that though KuRaL has endowed a honourable place to women in family, their status and participation in social life had not been bright and not brought out clearly save for some stray cases of poetesses like Avvayaar and Kaakkaippaadiniar and epic characters like KaNNaki, MaNimaekalai. Especially chapters 91 and 92 of kuRaL are cited as showing women in poor light. While applying our thoughts to this aspect it is necessary to look into the available information on the social history of Thamiznadu in the period before and around the time of ThirukkuRaL.

In ancient times of civilization men and women worked together outside for sustenance of life, which slowly evolved into families. Towards end of the era of slavery and the beginning of the era of landed gentry, in some stories of the epic Mahabaaratham those about Pandavas-Dhrowpathy, Sudharsan-Oovathi (polyandry), Kavuthamar-Kavuthami (free society of tolerance to trafficing) and Jamathakkini-Renuka (monogamy or chastity - strict adherence to morals in family life) a process of evolution of a close-nit exclusive family system is seen where male domination was gaining an upper hand, by superiority of economic and physical power.

In the Thamizh sangam periods before Christian era, when ThirukkuRaL was born, what was the status of women in India? Religious cults like Buddham, SamaNam, Aaryan Brahminism (*sanathanam*) were invading South India (ancient Thamiznadu of Dravidian civilization). These religions disdained worldly pleasures and intimacy or equality of ladies. But Thamizh culture was totally different, living life fully for its beauties, including romanticism and family life. This is reflected fully in Thamizh literature of those times:

In the conventional traditions of romantic love and chaste wedlock, there is parting and reunion in Thamizh culture. It is real life not mysticism or delusion; Is there such a medicine in your mystic systems?

KuRunthokai

The sanadhanic system is primarily concerned with mysticism and instability of life; it hates romantic pleasures.

Passion of love is the lifeline of nature; it is no stupor or delusion. To understand and enjoy life fully, with proper knowledge of education, Thamizh civilization has evolved and refined a unique tradition of love life (akam) and social life (puram) with grammatical definitions. Part 3 of ThirukkuRaL is an educative treatise on happiness in love life.

In Manu's codes of the North Indian brahminic style, there is no humanism, due respect and recognition is denied to women; they are treated in slavery as subservient to father, husband, son and other male members and treated as domesticated animals. Though endowed with six senses, having the unique gift of begetting children; though superior to men in love, kindness, courtesy, considerateness, patience and dedication to service, they have been, and still continue to be treated in conservative societies retarding the path of progress, as servants carrying out the errands of males. The customs of beating, selling, deserting, widowing and destituting women and totally denying them independence is ingrained in Manu's codes. Provoked by this poet Barathi said:

'Let us clap our hands that we have cut off those
who insist on bringing into the house, the sordid
habit of beating, torturing and tying up cows
in the shed, to subjugate and subdue women'

Chapter 91: The usually misunderstood one, is on the character of men driven by lust and passion, losing their independent functionality, merging in stupor and subservient commands of ladies; this is in no way a reflection on women; on the contrary urging men to maintain their individuality. There is nowhere any reference that women are of a lower category, their relationship itself is bad or that men should not have any contact with them, as Manu has ordained.

Seeking desires, inferiority and inability, fear, executing errands on command of women, governed by the wink of damsels are described as the qualities of men surrendering to women.

These words and phrases have to be understood in their proper context.

1. Falling in love's lust (*vizaythal -veezthal*) - seeking in lust and stupor in passion, infatuation. In chapter 120 and other places 'falling' has been used to refer to kindness, friendship, desire and romantic love.

2. Losing self, lowering status (*thaazntha iyalbinmai*) - inferiority complex, getting inactive and not cultivating the natural qualities and duties of men

3. Fearing (*anjuthal*) - Forgetting that wife is a companion to be loved, obeying her as a manager in command.

4. Fancy errands (*yeaval*) - to carry out commands and instigations as humble slaves

5. Governed by the wink (*pettaangu ozhukal*) - to follow directions as a duty, without concern for good or bad, virtue or folly.

6. Foolishness of doting women *(peNsaernthaam paethaimai)* - abject dependence on women without the sensibility and faculty to think and act.

What thirukkuRaL strongly advises against is the slave mentality of humility and obedience to women, without rhyme or reason.

Chapter 92 warns men against their weaknesses and susceptibility to the lure of harlots, and its ill consequences spoiling mind, body and wealth. KuRaL 1311 castigates men as:

'you have not known chastity; your bosom is exposed to all women to gaze'

Chapter 95: Food and Medicine

KuRaL has postulated the theory that proper food is the best of medicines. Various aspects of health, diseases, therapy and medication are referred to at innumerable places in ThirukkuRaL, which have been brought out and highlighted by medical researchers, who consider kuRaL as a valuable guide to biological sciences and nature.

In the interest of healthy living, it is essential to be aware of the functioning of every part of our body, diseases and medication for them. Pure water, air, environment, immunity in the body, alertness and balance of mind to resist infective diseases, selected food and proper habits of intake are necessary. To preserve and rejuvenate stability of the body and mind, deep sleep, body rest in dreamy stage and in wakefulness are essential. To combat minor illness, without the aid of antibiotics, we should use compatible indigenous herbs and spices with medicinal qualities, combined with proper work, food, rest and recreation, for requisite relief, in a simple way.

GENETICS: The very first KuRaL says that for all the micro and macro organisms, primordial matter in the form of Nature is the origin. Body is the microcosm version of the macrocosm universe.

All lives on earth are equal in origin (972)

What we have come to know is the size of an atom, and what we are yet to know is like the universe in space; as we grow in knowledge, we engress and shrink the sea of ignorance (1110). The ultimate limit of knowledge is primordial matter (2); fullness of knowledge is pure discipline (6).

It is an innovative angle to go beyond spiritual approaches and find meanings to the couplets in chapter 36 about realisation of self, by means of physiological and psychological studies.

That which exists (*maei*) is the body, which has five apparent sensors. It is necessary to use the sixth sense of subtle reasoning to experience the functioning of life in the body (*mey yuNarvu-* 354, 355). With the help of education and experience, scholars of human sciences investigate and enlighten freshly, truths and codes not brought out so far (356).

Ancestral traditions (1043) of home and family, patrimony, progeny, clan, community, citizenship, society, friendship, comradeship, munificence, glory etc. (72, 107, 112,113, 793, 794, 996) are moulded by combination of environment with them; but things like education, refinement of discipline, prestige, honour, shyness to shame, mannerism and behaviour patterns acquired therein (409, 973, 993, 1012, 1013) are qualities beyond the realm of genetic descendence.

Genetic atoms of matter, which constitute the body structure, alone are capable of being transferred and imprinted genealogically. Verbal functions like throbbing, thinking, feeling, actions which are not atoms of matter but only energy forces in operation of the body, are not transferable genetically. These are evolved by environment, opportunities and habits formed naturally. No one is born a genius.

Genetic diseases: Afflicting the body such as diabetics, eyesight, asthma, blood hypertension, heart attacks, epilepsy, skin psoriasis could be transferred genetically. If their basic origins are investigated and proper remedial measures are taken it is possible to eradicate their causes (kuRaL 359). Recent DNA type tests, spectrum analysis and cloning of tissues by harvesting of embryo stem cells for therapy, have confirmed this possibility. The diseases afflicting living organisms can be diagnosed and classified as those of the body, of the mind and those affecting both inter-alia.

As indicated by the pulse, flex, bile and phlegm
in excess or short, cause disease (941)

Diseases of the Body: Deterioration by aging, immobilisation, Parkinson's disease, trauma due to accidents, paralysis, heart problems, allergy, pain of limbs, gastroenteritis, venereal diseases, infectious diseases like diarrhoea, smallpox, deadly ones like cancer and aids etc.

Diseases of the Mind: Caused by mental attitudes like passion, greed, envy, deceit, coveting, causing pain/injury, instability, lunacy, insomnia, Alzheimer's etc.

Diseases of Body & Mind: Intoxication, lure of luck, madness, musk-rutting, pallor and sallowness, pain of eve in separation etc. The grief and pains caused by hunger, malnutrition, poverty, shame of begging, indigence, loss of honour and dignity.

Medication for illness: Pure air and water in natural form are the elixir of life. Roots, bark, stems and leaves, flowers and seeds of plants and trees are rare herbal medicines. Avoiding harm and pain to others, precautions to guard against evil, to analyse the nature and root causes of sickness, ways of treatment and applying appropriate remedies are some of the steps in treatment. Doctors of medical and life sciences have to thoroughly examine the nature and gravity of illness, fitness and immunity level of the patient's body, seriousness of the ailment and employ suitable treatment with pain relievers, minimum of antibiotics, and medicines/nutrients to strengthen immunity, supported by proper equipment and nursing (947-949).

Diagnose the disease, its causes, ascertain the means and applies remedies appropriate to the illness. (948)

The primary duty of a doctor should be to cure the illness and improve the standard of life, but not to simply prolong life in a vegetable state (950). Mercy killing is no crime in extreme cases where it is demanded. These aspects have been stressed by the famous heart surgeon Dr. Christian Barnard in his lecture tours of India. For sickness of the mind, rational sense is the cure. (1091,1102). Even in sexual life, fulfilling of desires (1257), exertion to swell the salt of sweated brows (1328) and enjoying the pleasures of union (1330) are essential for mental happiness and physical health in family life.

Food as medicine: Intake of a litre of water (or very light tea) first thing in the morning and full fasting a session a day or a day in a week are medication to cleanse the digestion system. Observing time and discipline in taking a balanced and nutritious diet, just adequate in quantities, qualities and calories for the body's needs of work and growth, when the urge is felt to satisfy appetite; avoiding foods allergic to body and too rich in fats, will work as self medication to the body. Food has to be ground/ chewed in the mouth for proper mixing with saliva (which is the initial process of digestion) instead of just gulping and stuffing into the elastic stomach (942-947).

Know thy digestive system, discipline time and enjoy agreeable food, to the level of your appetite (944)

Environmental protection: It is important to identify and be aware of elements that affect healthy life, and the imperatives of a clean surrounding. Rain water helps a lot in purifying dust in the atmosphere and dirt on earth (11-20). External purity is achieved by use of water; the impure, the stained are stuck in a mire of mud (241, 835, 919). Purity of the mind is getting rid of greed, undue desires, laziness; lifting the darkness of ignorance, clear perception and cultivation of manners (352, 364, 601, 688, 721). Moving with the seasons is guarding of wealth (482); peace of mind is stability (370); incompatibility is like life with a serpent in its hole (890); the eve of pallid mist, spreading paleness heralds deluding darkness for lovers (1223, 29, 30)

Wealth of a Nation: To be free from droughts, floods, storms, earthquakes, wars, feuds, plagues, hunger and pain of poverty (732, 734, 738, 769) and to be ready with measures to prevent and cure illness afflicting the land (442).

Natural Medication: It is essential to organise, categorise and systematize all the indigenous systems of medication such as Siddha, Ayurveda in India, Unani in the Middle East, Homeopathy in Europe, and Acupuncture in China, on the lines of the allopathic system of the West. The qualities, character and potential values of medicines from herbs, elements and metals should be made known to the consumers. Doctors as well as patients should be aware of the curative capacity and side effects of all medicines they prescribe and use.

All indigenous medicines should be analysed and evaluated, measured and classified as to which element in it cures which illness and how. When these are subjected to microbiological tests, the methods of their functioning can be explained in relation to basic scientific knowledge. For example the essence 'L Dopa' from seeds of silk-cotton, when applied to the brain, converts to Dopamine and rectifies the defects in the nervous system of cerebellum, and cures Parkinson's disease.

To prevent side effects, strengths of medicines should be assessed, marked and applied on specialist advice. To neutralise the poisonous qualities of some mineral salts and metals like mercury, in the indigenous system of medicine, they are treated with a multitude of herbs and distilled, to bring out their usable medicinal qualities. The research to gain knowledge as to what herb helps to cure what harm in a particular DNA molecule will help bring it to prominence. Information about the basic ingredients and formulations of indigeneous medicines should be categorised, tabulated and documented for education and application.

Chapters 96-108: Merits & Miscellany

If bravery, fervour, skills, sense of security, coexistence, toiling, diligence, habit of saving, sharing and such other qualities are taken to have been acquired by observing other species, human race is unique in having innovated with the help of reasoning, and improved by experience the ways of family and social living, agriculture, industry, arts and crafts and cultivated civilizations.

Chapter 96: The nobility of Social life stems from qualities of discipline, veracity, happiness, munificence, comradeship, kind words, equity, sense of shame, safeguarding from meanness, blame and instability.

Chapter 103: Devotion to social causes imply sense of duty, freedom from insolence and inferiority complex, prestige, greatness, motivation and enterprise, refined wisdom, perseverance, firmness, forbearance, encompassing relationships, managing families, and capacity to perform.

Chapter 104: The farming culture of cultivation is a basic service rendered as a natural duty to the society without expectation of recompense. The ploughing of land by hard toil is the highest of occupations; it has the prestige of munificence refusing alms. It is a useful way of life in harmony with nature.

The Western history of science records Copernicus as the first to find in 1545 AD that the world rotates and revolves around the sun in the solar system. It is interesting to note that even prior to first century BC, the traditional scientists of India were aware of the fact that the world rotates on its own axis and simultaneously revolves around the sun, as quoted in kuRaL couplets 1031 and 1025.

Chapter 97: The unique quality of dignity and honour (*maanam*, for which there appear no single equivalent word in any other language) has evolved thro' long traditions of culture and civilisation advancement of Thamizh land. The word seems to have been derived from *kavarimaan*, a variety of deer that ends its life when it senses its body's hair starts falling. A very intricate sense of honour is implied in it that life is not worth living when the body is unfit for it. This is on the higher side of human values.

Chapter 102: Next to dignity and honour, Thamizh's culture gives importance to the sense of shame (1012), one of the qualities that distinguish humans from other species. KuRaL classifies the sense of shame into two categories. The one concerns shame of inability to do ones duties and to do wrongful things. The second metaphor is on the special qualities of womanhood - which are dealt with in part 3, on happiness in life. The things to shy away are: blame (433, 506), crime and stain (502), inability and inferiority (903), straying from equanimity (172). This is a part of citizenship (951), worthiness (983), healthy mannerism (960).

Chapters 98-100: Protection of prestige, worthiness and refined manners are qualities of social life. Prestige is distinguished and separated from vanity and smallness. KuRal couplet 972 is significant in stressing the fact that 'all lives are born equal; qualities vary according to avocations'. This is a basic code that discrimination on the count of castes, creed, descendance, professions etc are artificial and selfish. This refutes the theory of Aariyan race of North India, enunciated by Manu and referred to in Gita, that god created the arbitrary racial system of four castes -Brahmins, Warriors, Traders and Others (branded as the 'lower' castes untouchable). This has been alien to Thamizh culture and Dravidian civilization.

The Aaryan epic *RamaayaNa* by sage Vaalmeeki states that drums, rustics, lower castes and women are fit to be beaten like animals. Kavudilya's Arthasaastra says that harlots who refuse to extend pleasure to the commandeers of the king are to be punished by whipping thousand times. According to the Aaryan cults only those born in between the Himalayas in the North and the Vindhya mountains to the South are eligible for attainment of 'salvation at the feet of God'. People of other lands are not fit to practise vedic rituals.

Conflicts started when other religions like Buddhism, Jainism in the North refuted and challenged the audacious attitude of the brahmin, and started encompassing people spreading the concepts of equality and abolishing differences on the basis of birth and castes. It is history that brahmins connived and conspired with the ruling clans, suppressed and drove out Buddhism from India and contained Jainism by cruel force. Sanadhanic Brahminism which invaded South India, owing to pressures and strains in the North, did considerable damage, dissection and degradation to the cultural values and cohesiveness of Dravidian Culture. This persisted for a major part of the middle ages, and the invasion of Mohammedans and Europeans brought in further changes. It was only in the later parts of 19th and the 20th century AD that renaissance and rationalist movements started in Thamizh Nadu to retrieve the glory of language and cultural values of the past; a mission at social engineering.

In the forefront of these movements were poets Barathi and Barathidaasan, rationalist Ee.Vee.Raa., Thamizh scholars Thiru Vee.Kaa., Maraimalai Adhikal, Ki.Aa.Po.Viswanathan and others. Poet Barathi, though born in a brahmin family, was a scholar in Thamizh and Sanskrit languages and had revolutionary approach to social equality, nationalism and equality of women.

'There are no castes, it is a sin to classify
and discriminate people on the basis of birth;
there is no justice separate for the idyllist
brahmins and for the down trodden; if any codes
prescribe these, they are invalid treacheries'

Barathi

There have been many legends and epics
to breed foolishness and perpetuate feuds
on the basis of castes to blind the eyes of society;
to destroy the fountain of rational knowledge;
Philosophy of the owls, caste differences,
religious divisions, faltering justice, faulty codes,
blind habits all are to be driven out by hard efforts

Barathidaasan

Chapter 99: All good things are the duty of the worthy. Kindness, shame, social concerns, compassion and veracity of truth are the pillars of sublimity. Humility, not to blame others, doing good, firmness, stability and forbearance are brought out as the qualities of the worthy.

Chapter 100: Sophistication, sense of duty, social compatibility, traditional values, dignity in dealing with foes, sustenance of the world, pleasant disposition are the qualities of good mannerism.

Chapters 101, 108: Wealth that is wasted without being used to help the distressed, and cowardice demeaning human values are categorised as crimes on society.

People hoarding avariciously to hide from the needy
are unworthy of their burden to the earth (1003)
No care or concerns bother the low (1072)
The base resemble the divine in callousness (1073)
Fear is the rod that drives the low to behave (1075)

These imply the truth that religious beliefs based on fear, and the stories based on them bind people in ignorance. The 'divine residents of heaven' are described as stewing in fear unable to win the giants, enjoying pleasures without toiling and drowning in liquor etc; in short they are defined as cowards.

Chapters 105-107: Indigence, seeking and dreading of alms are aspects of poverty caused by negligence of farming and other services, hoarding of wealth and actions of cowards.

Existence of poor by seeking alms is degrading humanity-kuRunthokai

It may appear that KuRaL ethics advocating hospitality and munificence to patronise society for attaining glory, as in chapters 22,23,and 24 are contradicted by the edicts in chapters 105-107 that it is demeaning to seek alms and better to die with honour than to live by seeking alms. Needs to examine in what context these have been weighed and evaluated, to gain clarity.

While stressing that life is sweet and rare sustainer, motivator, deserves to be cherished and fruitfully enjoyed, loved in the face of grief and pains, KuRaL has not omitted to state in what circumstances life has to be given up; they are-falsification for sustenance (183), insensitivity to social obligations (214), inability to protect the needy (230), poverty lacking the basics of life (378, 1050), drought of glory (966), loss of honour (969), to protect from shame (1017), sense of cruelty in seeking alms (1070).

It is better to die than trying to live in beggery (1062)
If death is in glory it is worth seeking (780)
Do not seek those who have no qualms in hiding (1067)

However in circumstances extraordinary, as an unavoidable duty to society to protect the handicapped, destitute children, the weak aged who are not in a position to earn their living, instead of escaping from responsibilities, it is no harm to seek aid and help them"

'The blind, the deaf and dumb, the handicapped, the destitute, the sick, the fasting, the ones burning in the fire of hunger' deserve help

MaNimaekalai

To the exception of material wealth, seeking and gaining wealth like education add to glory (395). It will be wrong to conclude that the emphasis laid on munificence could encourage the tendency to enjoy without labour to earn livelihood. This is conditioned by the following qualifications:

Giving out in measure to the deserving needy (477)
Accepting even good gratis is bad (222)
Good earth blushes and shames at the able bodied
idling in sloth and lurking in poverty (1040)
Be it gruel, it is sweet, earned by toil and efforts (1065)

These definitely are to enhance the imperative of hard labour, and the importance of help by merit.

39. இறைமாட்சி
iRai maatchi
MAKINGS OF A RULER
(FACULTIES AND QUALITIES ESSENTIAL FOR AN ABLE RULER)

படைகுடி கூழ்அமைச்சு நட்புஅரண் ஆறும்
உடையான் அரசருள் ஏறு.　　　　　　　381

padaikudi kUzamaichchu n-atpuaraN aaRum
udaiyAn arasuruL aeRu

Warriors, worthy citizens, wise council, warm friends, wealth
and vantage forts are makings of a leader among rulers

அஞ்சாமை ஈகை அறிவுஊக்கம் இந்நான்கும்
எஞ்சாமை வேந்தர்க் கியல்பு.　　　　　382

anjsAmai eekai aRivu-uukkam inn-Ankum
enjsAmai vaen-thaRk kiyalpu

Courage, munificence, wisdom and zeal in fullness
are natural attributes of a leader among rulers

தூங்காமை கல்வி துணிவுடைமை இம்மூன்றும்
நீங்கா நிலனாள் பவர்க்கு.　　　　　383

thUngkAmai kalvi thuNivudaimai immUnRum
n-eengkA n-ilanAL pavarkku

Adherence to alacrity, knowledge and bravery
are essential accomplishments of a ruler

அறன்இழுக்காது அல்லவை நீக்கி மறன்இழுக்கா
மானம் உடையது அரசு.　　　　　384

aRanizukkAthu allavai n-eekki maRanizukkA
mAnam udaiyathu arasu

Unblemished virtue, free from vices, and enterprising
valour add dignity to governance

இயற்றலும் ஈட்டலும் காத்தலும் காத்த
வகுத்தலும் வல்லது அரசு.　　　　　385

iyatRRalum eettalum kAththalum kAththa
vakuththalum vallathu arasu

Producing, saving, protecting, regulating and equitably distributing are salient features in governing wealth

காட்சிக்கு எளியன் கடுஞ்சொல்லன் அல்லனேல்
மீக்கூறும் மன்னன் நிலம். 386

*kAtchikku eLiyan kadunjsollan allanael
meekkURum mannan n-ilam*

An amiable disposition and courteous approach of a ruler earns fame and prosperity for the land

இன்சொலால் ஈத்தளிக்க வல்லார்க்குத் தன்சொலால்
தான்கண்டு அனைத்துஇவ் வுலகு. 387

*insolAl een-thaLikka vallArkku thansolAl
thAnkaNdu anaiththuiv vulaku*

Kindness in words and grace in dispensation enable the ruler to shape up the land ideally

முறைசெய்து காப்பாற்றும் மன்னவன் மக்கட்கு
இறைஎன்று வைக்கப் படும். 388

*muRaiseythu kAppAtRRum mannan makkatku
iRaienRu vaikkap padum*

Sound and humane justice in governance, protecting the citizens, raises the ruler in esteem to a statesman

செவிகைப்பச் சொல்பொறுக்கும் பண்புடை வேந்தன்
கவிகைக்கீழ்த் தங்கும் உலகு. 389

*sevikaippach solpoRukkum paNpudaiya vaen-than
kavikaikkeez thangkum ulaku*

The patience to bear with bitter truth and bold advice, is the umbrella protecting citizens of a wise ruler

கொடை அளி செங்கோல் குடியோம்பல் நான்கும்
உடையானாம் வேந்தர்க்கு ஒளி. 390

*kodaiaLi sengkOl kudioompal n-Ankum
udaiyAnAm vaen-tharkku oLi*

Bountiful grace, justice, care and protection of society are qualities of a leading light among rulers

40. கல்வி (அகழ்ந்தெடுத்தல்)
kalvi (akazthal)
EDUCATION

(THE BENEFITS OF READING, STUDY, LEARNING AND ACQUIRING
KNOWLEDGE AND GAINING WISDOM FOR ATTAINING VIRTUES)

கற்க கசடுஅறக் கற்பவை கற்றபின்
நிற்க அதற்குத் தக.　　　　　　　　　　391

kaRka kasaduaRak kaRpavai katRRapin
n-iRka athaRkuth thaka

Study and learn with clarity what is worthy of learning
and stand firm by their norms of virtue

எண்என்ப ஏனை எழுத்துஎன்ப இவ்விரண்டும்
கண்என்ப வாழும் உயிர்க்கு.　　　　　　392

eNenpa aenai ezuththuenpa ivviraNdum
kaNenpa vAzum uyirkku

Learning the arts and sciences by letters and numbers
opens our eyes to live a life of fullness

கண்ணுடையர் என்பவர் கற்றோர் முகத்துஇரண்டு
புண்ணுடையர் கல்லா தவர்.　　　　　　393

kaNudaiyar enpavar katRROr mukaththuiraNdu
puNudaiyar kallA thavar

Knowledge by learning gives eyes to the mind to see
the truth; vision of the ignorant is a blind sore

உவப்பத் தலைக்கூடி உள்ளப் பிரிதல்
அனைத்தே புலவர் தொழில்.　　　　　　394

uvappath thalaikkUdi uLLap pirithal
anaiththae pulavar thozil

The art of joying in confabulations and cherishing in
contemplation is the gift of the learned

உடையார்முன் இல்லார்போல் ஏக்கற்றும் கற்றார்
கடையரே கல்லா தவர்.　　　　　　395

udaiyArmun illArpOl aekkatRRum katRRAr
kadaiyarae kallA thavar

The devotion and dedication to yearn for knowledge
from the learned, is alien to the ignorant

தொட்டனைது ஊறும் மணற்கேணி மாந்தர்க்குக்

கற்றனைத்து ஊறும் அறிவு. 396

thottanaiththu uuRum maNaRkaeNi mAn-tharkkuk
katRRanaiththu uuRum aRivu

Deeper you dig the sand the higher a spring flows; the
ardour you devote to learning, the fuller is knowledge

யாதானும் நாடாமால் ஊராமால் என்னொருவன்

சாந்துணையும் கல்லாத வாறு. 397

yAthAnum n-AdaamAl uuraamAl ennoruvan
sAn-thuNaiyum kallAtha vARu

All lands and places are familiar fields for the learned
to tread; yet why neglect learning and waste life

ஒருமைக்கண் தான்கற்ற கல்வி ஒருவற்கு

எழுமையும் ஏமாப்பு உடைத்து. 398

orumaikkaN thAnkatRRa kalvi oruvaRku
ezumaiyum aemAppu udaiththu

Single minded devotion to learning stands one in
good stead, in the life ahead and to posterity

தாம்இன் புறுவது உலகுஇன் புறக்கண்டு

காமுறுவர் கற்றறிந் தார். 399

thAmin puRuvathu ulakuin puRakkaNdu
kAmuRuvar katRRuaRin- thAr

The wealth of worldly knowledge multiplies in exchange;
the wise love to pursue it with delight

கேடில் விழுச்செல்வம் கல்வி ஒருவற்கு

மாடுஅல்ல மற்றை யவை. 400

kaeduil vizuchchelvam kalvi oruvRku
mAdualla matRRai yavai

Knowledge is serene and indestructible wealth;
there is nothing else in benefits to compare

41. கல்லாமை (கல்வியறிவு பெறாமை)
kallAmai (kalviyaRivu peRAmai)
LACK OF EDUCATION

(EDUCATION MAY BE ACQUIRED BY STUDY OR LEARNING FROM
HEARING, SOCIAL UPBRINGING AND ASSOCIATION WITH THE WISE)

அரங்கின்றி வட்டாடி யற்றே நிரம்பிய
நூலின்றிக் கோட்டி கொளல்.　　　　　　　　　401

arangkuinRi vattAdi atRRae n-iRampiya
n-UlinRik kOtti koLal

The uneducated venturing a debate with the wise is
like playing chess without squares on the board

கல்லாதான் சொற்கா முறுதல் முலைஇரண்டும்
இல்லாதாள் பெண்காமுற்று அற்று.　　　　　　402

kallAthAn solkA muRuthal mulaiiraNdum
illAthAL peNkAmutRRu atRRu

Passion of the uneducated to preach and lending ears
to it, is like the shapeless immature craving in love's lust

கல்லா தவரும் நனிநல்லர் கற்றார்முன்
சொல்லாது இருக்கப் பெறின்.　　　　　　　403

kallA thavarum n-anin-allar katRRarmun
sollAthu irukkap peRin

Being polite and calm benefits the uneducated,
in an assembly of deliberations among the wise

கல்லாதான் ஒட்பம் கழியநன்று ஆயினும்
கொள்ளார் அறிவுடை யார்.　　　　　　　404

kallAthAn otpam kaziyan-anRu aayinum
koLLar aRivudai yAr

An exalted position or status of the uneducated snobs
is not recognised by the wise as knowledgeable

கல்லா ஒருவன் தகைமை தலைப்பெய்து
சொல்லாடச் சோர்வு படும்.　　　　　　　405

kallA oruvan thakaimai thalaippeythu
sollAdach sOrvu padum

The uneducated posing as knowledgeable
persons, fail in their dialogue with the wise

உளரென்னும் மாத்திரையர் அல்லால் பயவாக்

களரனையர் கல்லா தவர்.   406

uLarennum mAththiraiyar allAl payavAk
kaLaranaiyar kallA thavar

People who do not gain by learning have spent their
lives in vain, like a land barren without produce

நுண்மாண் நுழைபுலம் இல்லான் எழில்நலம்

மண்மாண் புனைபாவை அற்று.   407

n-uNmAN n-uzaipulam illAn eziln-alam
maNmAN punaipAvai atRRu

Beauty and stature of the one, without mental acumen
of learning, is like a terracotta doll painted bright

நல்லார்கண் பட்ட வறுமையின் இன்னாதே

கல்லார்கண் பட்ட திரு.   408

n-allArkaN patta vaRumaiyin innAthae
kallArkaN patta thiru

Penury of an honest person is far less harmful
than wealth in the hands of the uneducated

மேற்பிறந்தார் ஆயினும் கல்லாதார் கீழ்ப்பிறந்தும்

கற்றார் அனைத்துஇலர் பாடு.   409

maeRpiRan-thAr aayinum kallAthAr keezppiRan-thum
kaRRAr anaiththuilar pAdu

The social origin of birth is not relevant, as the wise
gain fame, the uneducated stagnate in any strata

விலங்கொடு மக்கள் அனையர் இலங்குநூல்

கற்றாரோடு ஏனை யவர்.   410

vilangkodu makkaL anaiyar ilangkun-Ul
katRRArOdu eenai yavar

Skill of the sixth sense distinguishes humans from animals;
who gain knowledge by good learning shine

42. கேள்வி
kaeLvi
LISTENING TO INSTRUCTION
(SHARPENING YOUR EARS)
(SHARPENING EARS TO LISTEN TO GOOD THINGS FROM THE WISE AND IMPROVE KNOWLEDGE)

செல்வத்துள் செல்வம் செவிச்செல்வம் அச்செல்வம்
செல்வத்துள் எல்லாம் தலை.

411

selvaththuL selvam sevichchelvam achchelvam
selvaththuL ellAm thalai

The gift of good listening is a basic wealth that affords
other forms of wealth, and hence the best of wealth

செவிக்குஉணவு இல்லாத போழ்து சிறிது
வயிற்றுக்கும் ஈயப் படும்.

412

sevikkuuNavu illAtha pOzthu siRithu
vayitRRukkum eeyap padum

When there is a respite for the ears, the stomach is fed
to survive in good spirits for useful listening

செவியுணவின் கேள்வி யுடையார் அவியுணவின்
ஆன்றாரோடு ஒப்பர் நிலத்து.

413

seviuNavin kaeLvi udaiyAr aviuNavin
aanRArOdu oppar n-ilaththu

It was a stepup in civilization to cook food for good life
like feeding the mind thro' good listening for knowledge

கற்றிலன் ஆயினும் கேட்க அஃதுஒருவற்கு
ஒற்கத்தின் ஊற்றுஆம் துணை.

414

katRRilan aayinum kaetka aqthuoruvaRku
ooRkaththin uutRRuaam thuNai

Even if you miss education, listen to and heed the wise,
that will be a saving and service staff in times of need

இழுக்கல் உடையுழி ஊற்றுக்கோல் அற்றே
ஒழுக்கம் உடையார்வாய்ச் சொல்.

415

izukkal udaiyuzi uutRRukkOl atRRae
ozukkam udaiyArvAys sol

Turn your ears to the wisdom of the virtuous voices;
that will be a strong staff on a slippery ground

எனைத்தானும் நல்லவை கேட்க அனைத்தானும்
ஆன்ற பெருமை தரும்.   416

*enaiththAnum n-allavai kaetka anaiththAnum
aanRa perumai tharum*

Listen to and grasp the good, that useful habit
affords an exalted life to lead in fame

பிழைத்துணர்ந்தும் பேதைமை சொல்லார் இழைத்துணர்ந்து
ஈண்டிய கேள்வி யவர்.   417

*pizaiththuNarn-thum paethaimai sollAr izaiththuNarn-thu
iiNdiya kaeLvi yavar*

Those who listen to sharply and grasp to enlighten
their minds do not slip out to talk foolishly

கேட்பினுங் கேளாத் தகையவே கேள்வியால்
தோட்கப் படாத செவி.   418

*kaetpinum kaeLAth thakaiyavae kaeLviyAl
thOdkap padAtha sevi*

Ears that are not pierced by words of wisdom are
deaf and of no avail, listening to dull sounds

நுணங்கிய கேள்வியர் அல்லார் வணங்கிய
வாயினர் ஆதல் அரிது.   419

*n-uNangkiya kaeLviyar allAr vaNangkiya
vAyinar aathal arithu*

Those who do not turn their ears sharply to wise counsel
cannot learn to speak politely and sensibly

செவியின் சுவையுணரா வாயுணர்வின் மாக்கள்
அவியினும் வாழினும் என்.   420

*seviyin suvaiuNarA vAyuNarvin mAkkaL
aviyinum vAzinum en*

Who miss the pleasure of sweet words, to the taste
of the tongue, live or perish, doesn't matter

43. அறிவுடைமை
aRivu udaimai
VIRTUE OF WISDOM

(BESIDES LEARNING AND LISTENING, EXPERIENCE IN LIFE AND
MENTAL ACUMEN ADD TO KNOWLEDGE. MENTAL FACULTIES
SAVE HUMANITY. THEY ARE ACQUIRED BY RATIONAL THINKING)

அறிவுஅற்றம் காக்கும் கருவி செறுவார்க்கும்
உள்ளழிக்கல் ஆகா அரண்.   421

aRivuatRRam kAkkum karuvi seRuvArkkum
uLazikkal aakA araN

**Wisdom is a more flexible and reliable weapon of the
mind than the fortress or armour, against the foe**

சென்ற இடத்தால் செலவிடாது தீதுஒரீஇ
நன்றின்பால் உய்ப்பது அறிவு.   422

senRa idaththAl selavidAthu theethuorIi
n-anRinpAl uyppathu aRivu

**Wisdom is the reins that control the horses of senses;
it can keep away evils and impel goodness**

எப்பொருள் யார்யார்வாய்க் கேட்பினும் அப்பொருள்
மெய்ப்பொருள் காண்பது அறிவு.   423

epporuL yAryArvAyk kaetpinum apporuL
meypporuL kANpathu aRivu

**To identify and grasp the truth from whatever you
hear, from wherever, is the virtue of wisdom**

எண்பொருள வாகச் செலச்சொல்லித் தான்பிறர்வாய்
நுண்பொருள் காண்பது அறிவு.   424

eNporuLa vAkach selachchollith thAnpiRarvAy
n-uNporuL kANpathu aRivu

**Impressing with clear exposition of thoughts and compre-
hending subtle senses is the quintessence of wisdom**

உலகம் தழீஇயது ஒட்பம் மலர்தலும்
கூம்பலும் இல்லது அறிவு.   425

ulakam thazeeiyathu otpam malarthalum
kUmpalum illathu aRivu

The learned stand at the altar of worldly wisdom
with a balanced mind, be it bloom or gloom

எவ்வது உறைவது உலகம் உலகத்தோடு
அவ்வது உறைவது அறிவு.   426

evvathu uRaivathu ulakam ulakaththOdu
avvathu uRaivathu aRivu

Move on with the sanguine wisdom of the world
in strides with its changing times and ways

அறிவுடையார் ஆவ தறிவார் அறிவிலார்
அஃதுஅறி கல்லா தவர்.   427

aRivudaiyAr aavathu aRivAr aRivilAr
aqthuaRi kallA thavar

The learned use their senses to judge and foresee causes
and effects; the uninitiated lack that knowledge

அஞ்சுவது அஞ்சாமை பேதைமை அஞ்சுவது
அஞ்சல் அறிவார் தொழில்.   428

anjsuvathu anjsamai paethaimai anjsuvathu
anjsal aRivAr thozil

Be wise to avoid frightful evil; not to fear their
dreadful effects is, folly of the weak

எதிரதாக் காக்கும் அறிவினார்க்கு இல்லை
அதிர வருவதோர் நோய்.   429

ethirathAk kAkkum aRivinArkku illai
athira varuvathoor n-Oy

Those who are wise to foresee the pain of evil
guard themselves against surprise shocks

அறிவுடையார் எல்லாம் உடையார் அறிவிலார்
என்னுடைய ரேனும் இலர்.   430

aRivudaiyAr ellAm udaiyAr aRivilAr
ennudaiya raenum ilar

Those who are wise have the senses to guard their possessions;
the dull are unaware even how they lose

44. குற்றங்கடிதல்
kutRAm kadithal
ESCHEWING CRIME (DETESTING PENALTY)
(DETESTING PENALTY- PROTECTING ONESELF FROM
INVOLVEMENT IN AND PREVENTING CRIME; MISERLY AVARICE,
INFLICTING PAIN, MEANNESS, REPROACH, SLANDER, STAIN,
DISREPUTE ARE ASPECTS OF CRIMINAL TENDENCY)

செருக்கும் சினமும் சிறுமையும் இல்லார்
பெருக்கம் பெருமித நீர்த்து.   431

serukkum sinamum siRumaiyum illAr
perukkam perumitha n-eerththu

Free from the follies of ego, anger and meanness
one is entitled to prosperity with modest pride

இவறலும் மாண்புஇறந்த மானமும் மாணா
உவகையும் ஏதம் இறைக்கு.   432

ivaRalum mANpuiRan-tha mAnamum mANA
uvakaiyum aetham iRaikku

Mean pleasure, honour without glory and miserly
avarice are blemishes a leader has to shun

தினைத்துணையாம் குற்றம் வரினும் பனைத்துணையாக்
கொள்வர் பழிநாணு வார்.   433

thinaiththuNaiyAm kutRRam varinum panaiththuNaiyAk
koLvar pazin-ANu vAr

A crime may look a millet in size, but those who
detest disgrace will fear it like a big palm

குற்றமே காக்க பொருளாகக் குற்றமே
அற்றம் தரூஉம் பகை.   434

kutRRAmE kAkka poruLAkak kutRRamae
atRRam tharUum pakai

Things are to be watched carefully for potent crime;
in default they develop as foes of destruction

வருமுன்னர்க் காவாதான் வாழ்க்கை எரிமுன்னர்
வைத்தூறு போலக் கெடும்.   435

varumunnark kAvAthAn vAzkkai erimunnar
vaiththURu pOlak kedum

Lives of those who care not to guard against fatal
flaws in advance, burn out as straw on fire

தன்குற்றம் நீக்கிப் பிறர்குற்றம் காண்கிற்பின்
என்குற்றம் ஆகும் இறைக்கு.   436

thankutRRam n-eekkip piRarkutRRam kAnkiRpin
enkutRRam aakum iRaikku

A leader who is aware of, and cures first his own flaws,
is entitled to scan and scout others' blemishes

செயற்பால செய்யாது இவறியான் செல்வம்
உயற்பாலது அன்றிக் கெடும்.   437

seyaRpAla seyyAthu ivaRiyAn selvam
uyaRpAlathu anRik kedum

Wealth not spent for a good cause, is a miser's
hoard, prone to be lost without a trace

பற்றுள்ளம் என்னும் இவறன்மை எற்றுள்ளும்
எண்ணப் படுவதுஒன் றன்று.   438

patRRuLLam ennum ivaRanmai etRRuLLum
eNNap paduvathuon RanRu

A miser's mind that grips wealth in greed
is a sore crime spot, that stands apart

வியவற்க எஞ்ஞான்றும் தன்னை நயவற்க
நன்றி பயவா வினை.   439

viyavaRka enjnjAnRum thannai n-ayavaRka
n-anRi payavA vinai

Boast not of self-esteem in any mood, any time;
nor aspire deeds that do no good

காதல காதல் அறியாமை உய்க்கிற்பின்
ஏதில ஏதிலார் நூல்.   440

kAthala kAthal aRiyAmai uykkiRpin
aethila aethilAr n-Ul

A leader with the skills to achieve, not revealing
his mind, is safe from the designs of the foe

45. பெரியாரைத் துணைக்கோடல்
periyAraith thuNaikkOdal
SEEKING GUIDANCE OF THE WORTHY
(IT IS WISE TO TAKE THE ADVICE AND GUIDANCE OF ELDERS KNOWLEDGABLE, CAPABLE AND WELL MANNERED)

அறனறிந்து மூத்த அறிவுடையார் கேண்மை
திறனறிந்து தேர்ந்து கொளல்.   441

aRanaRin-thu mUththa aRivudaiyAr kaeNmai
thiRanaRin-thu thaern-thu koLal

Seek good company of the worthy and avail
the virtues of their mature wisdom

உற்றநோய் நீக்கி உறாஅமை முற்காக்கும்
பெற்றியார்ப் பேணிக் கொளல்.   442

utRRan-Oy n-iikki uRAamai muRkAkkum
petRRiyarp paeNik koLal

Help from the proficient to ward off and guard
against ills, is to be cherished in friendship

அரியவற்றுள் எல்லாம் அரிதே பெரியாரைப்
பேணித் தமராக் கொளல்.   443

ariyavatRRuL ellAm arithae periyAraip
paeNith thamarAk koLal

The rarest of rare things to achieve is to
cultivate relationship of the worthy

தம்மின் பெரியார் தமரா ஒழுகுதல்
வன்மையுள் எல்லாம் தலை.   444

thammin periyAr thamarA ozukuthal
vanmaiyuL ellAm thalai

To develop and cultivate friendship of the worthy, and
to follow their noble path is strength of strengths

சூழ்வார்கண் ணாக ஒழுகலான் மன்னவன்
சூழ்வாரைச் சூழ்ந்து கொளல்.   445

sUzvArkaN NAka ozukalAn mannavan
sUzvAraich sUzn-thu koLal

The wise and the virtuous are eyes to the ruler,
who is diligent to choose people to surround

தக்கார் இனத்தனாய்த் தானொழுக வல்லானைச்
செற்றார் செயக்கிடந்தது இல்.   446

thakkAr inaththanAith thAnozuka vallAnaich
seRRAr seyakkidan-thathu il

The leader who moves with noble kin and upholds
sure discipline, has no harm from foes to fear

இடிக்கும் துணையாரை ஆள்வாரை யாரே
கெடுக்கும் தகைமை யவர்.   447

idikkum thuNaiyArai aaLvArai yArae
kedukkum thakaimai yavar

Advisors with the courage to warn of ills, keep
their leader safe from foes who foil

இடிப்பாரை இல்லாத ஏமரா மன்னன்
கெடுப்பார் இலானும் கெடும்.   448

idippArai illAtha eemarA mannan
keduppAr ilAnum kedum

The leader who has no regard for advice of the
wise to play safe, leads his own way to ruin

முதலிலார்க்கு ஊதியம் இல்லை மதலையாம்
சார்புஇலார்க்கு இல்லை நிலை.   449

muthalilArkku uuthiyam illai mathalaiyAm
sArpuilArkku illai n-ilai

An enterprise sans capital lacks profits; a ruler sans
comrades lacks a secure toe-hold to stay

பல்லார் பகைகொளலின் பத்துஅடுத்த தீமைத்தே
நல்லார் தொடர்கை விடல்.   450

pallAr pakaikoLalin paththu-aduththa theemaiththae
n-allAr thodarkai vidal

To give up links of trusted friendship is ten of tens
worse than encountering foes all-round

46. சிற்றினம் சேராமை
sitRinam sErAmai
DISTANCING BAD SOCIETY
(CHERISHING GOOD COMPANY)
(WHILE CHERISHING GOOD COMPANY, IT IS NECESSARY TO KEEP
OFF THOSE IMPURE AND LACKING GOODWILL IN COMMUNITY
AND SOCIETY)

சிற்றினம் அஞ்சும் பெருமை சிறுமைதான்
சுற்றமாச் சூழ்ந்து விடும்.   451

sitRRinam anjsum perumai siRumaithAn
sutRRamAch sUzn-thu vidum

The great of honourable society dread the ignoble,
the mean gather among as kinsmen dear

நிலத்தியல்பால் நீர்திரிந்து அற்றாகும் மாந்தர்க்கு
இனத்தியல்பது ஆகும் அறிவு.   452

n-ilaththuiyalpAl n-eerthirin-thu atRRAkum mAn-tharkku
inaththuiyalpathu aakum aRivu

As rain water takes the colour and quality of soil it falls
on, wisdom is moulded by quality of one's company

மனத்தான்ஆம் மாந்தர்க்கு உணர்ச்சி இனத்தானாம்
இன்னான் எனப்படும் சொல்.   453

manaththAnaam mAn-tharkku uNarchchi inaththAnaam
innAn enappadum sol

Senses are shaped by the mind; the worth of people
is judged by quality of their friendship

மனத்துளது போலக் காட்டி ஒருவற்கு
இனத்துளது ஆகும் அறிவு.   454

manaththuLathu pOlak kAtti oruvaRku
inaththuLathu aakum aRivu

Knowledge is apparent on mental faculties, which
are gained from tradition and habits of society

மனந்தூய்மை செய்வினை தூய்மை இரண்டும்
இனந்தூய்மை தூவா வரும்.   455

manaththUymai seyvinaith thUymai iraNdum
inaththUymai thUvA varum

Purity of thought and action has its origin in the integrity
and merits of the society one moves with and lives in

மனம்தூயார்க்கு எச்சம்நன் றாகும் இனம்தூயார்க்கு
இல்லைநன்று ஆகா வினை.   456

manamthUyArkku echchamn-an Raakum inamthUyArkku
illain-anRu aakA vinai

Honesty of the mind leaves a legacy of fame;
victory is in good reach of a flawless society

மனநலம் மன்னுயிர்க்கு ஆக்கம் இனநலம்
எல்லாப் புகழும் தரும்.   457

manan-alam mannuyirkku aakkam inan-alam
ellAp pukazum tharum

Kindness of the mind aids and motives thriving of life;
company of worthy society aids to foster fame

மனநலம் நன்குடைய ராயின் சான்றோர்க்கு
இனநலம் ஏமாப்பு உடைத்து.   458

manan-alam n-ankuudaiya rAyin sAnROrkku
inan-alam aemAppu udaiththu

Facility of a sublime mind is secured and strengthened
by contacts and association with a fertile society

மனநலத்தின் ஆகும் மறுமைமற்று அஃதும்
இனநலத்தின் ஏமாப்பு உடைத்து.   459

manan-alaththin aakum maRumaimatRRu aqthum
inan-alaththin aemAppu udaiththu

Goodness of mind adds strength to compassion and
penance; these are secured by good company

நல்லினத்தின் ஊங்கும் துணையில்லை தீயினத்தின்
அல்லல் படுப்பதூஉம் இல்.   460

n-allinaththin uungkum thuNaiillai theeyinaththin
allal paduppathUum il

Good company is the best of help in society;
bad company brings in pain and anguish

47. தெரிந்து செயல்வகை
therin-thu seyalvakai
ACTION AFTER DELIBERATIONS
(IN GOVERNANCE, MANAGEMENT AND BUSINESS, AS IN SOCIAL LIFE
IT IS ESSENTIAL TO EXAMINE ALL PROS AND CONS BEFORE DECISION)

அழிவதூஉம் ஆவதூஉம் ஆகி வழிபயக்கும்
ஊதியமும் சூழ்ந்து செயல்.　　　　461

azivathUum aavathUm aaki vazipayakkum
uuthiyamum sUzn-thu seyal

Analyse the costs involved, yields and profits
achievable before acting on a proposition

தெரிந்த இனத்தொடு தேர்ந்தெண்ணிச் செய்வார்க்கு
அரும்பொருள் யாதொன்றும் இல்.　　　　462

therin-tha inaththodu thaerntheNNich seyvArkku
arumporuL yAthuonRum il

It is not hard to achieve objectives if one acts with
resolve, weighing the facts, on wise counsel

ஆக்கம் கருதி முதலிழக்கும் செய்வினை
ஊக்கார் அறிவுடை யார்.　　　　463

aakkam karuthi muthalizakkum seyvinai
uukkAr aRivudai yAr

The wise do not venture to risk their capital
in anticipation of doubtful gains

தெளிவு இலதனைத் தொடங்கார் இளிவென்னும்
ஏதப்பாடு அஞ்சு பவர்.　　　　464

theLivu ilathanaith thodangkAr iLivennum
aeethappAdu anjsu pavar

Those who scorn the pain of disgrace will not involve
in anything whose implications they are not aware

வகையறச் சூழாது எழுதல் பகைவரைப்
பாத்திப் படுப்பதோர் ஆறு.　　　　465

vakaiyaRach sUzAthu ezuthal pakaivaraip
pAththip paduppathOr aaRu

Acting without due forethought or viable plans
throws the field open, fertile for the foes

செய்தக்க அல்ல செயக்கெடும் செய்தக்க
செய்யாமை யானும் கெடும். 466

seythakka alla seyakkedum seythakka
seyAmai yAnum kedum

Taking upon acts that do not benefit one, or failing
to perform bounden duties both lead to ruin

எண்ணித் துணிக கருமம் துணிந்தபின்
எண்ணுவம் என்பது இழுக்கு. 467

eNNith thuNika karumam thuNin-thapin
eNNuvam enpathu izukku

Indulge in a mission after due deliberations; hesitation
after commitment leads to painful disgrace

ஆற்றின் வருந்தா வருத்தம் பலர்நின்று
போற்றினும் பொத்துப் படும். 468

aatRin varun-thA varuththam palarn-inRu
pOtRRinum poththup padum

Blind efforts, unmindful of ways and means are bound
to fail, even if backed up by folks around

நன்றுஆற்றல் உள்ளும் தவறுஉண்டு அவரவர்
பண்புஅறிந்து ஆற்றாக் கடை . 469

n-anRuaatRRal uLLum thavaRuuNdu avaravar
paNpuaRin-thu aatRRAk kadai

Well meant deeds may even end up harmful
without due deliberations on demeanour

எள்ளாத எண்ணிச் செயல்வேண்டும் தம்மொடு
கொள்ளாத கொள்ளாது உலகு. 470

eLLAtha eNNich seyalvaeNdum thammodu
koLLAtha koLLAthu ulaku

Move cautiously without exposure to ridicule, the world
does not take kindly to unbecoming adventures

48. வலியறிதல்
vali aRithal
ASSESSING STRENGTH

(AS IN WAR EVEN IN MANAGEMENT AND GOVERNANCE IT IS
ESSENTIAL TO PROPERLY ASSESS THE NATURE OF JOBS,
STRENGTH OF SELF AND SUPPORT AND THE PROBLEMS TO BE
TACKLED)

வினைவலியும் தன்வலியும் மாற்றான் வலியும்
துணைவலியும் தூக்கிச் செயல்.   471

*vinaivaliyum thanvaliyum mAtRRAn valiyum
thuNaivaliyum thUkkich seyal*

Weigh judiciously nature of the task, strength of
foes, allies and self before launching action

ஒல்வது அறிவது அறிந்துஅதன் கண்தங்கிச்
செல்வார்க்குச் செல்லாதது இல்.   472

*olvathu aRivathu arin-thuathan kaNthangkich
selvArkkuch sellAthathu il*

Nothing is beyond those who evaluate possibilities and
stand by the best, in executing an assignment

உடைத்தம் வலியறியார் ஊக்கத்தின் ஊக்கி
இடைக்கண் முறிந்தார் பலர்.   473

*udaiththam valiaRiyAr uukkaththin uukki
idaikkaN murin-thAr palar*

Those who do not assess their might, but overshoot
on ambition, invariably fall out on the way

அமைந்தாங்கு ஒழுகான் அளவுஅறியான் தன்னை
வியந்தான் விரைந்து கெடும்.   474

*amain-thAngku ozukAn aLavuaRiyAn thannai
viyan-thAn virain-thu kedum*

Boasting pride, disregarding limitations and inadapt-
ability are sure norms leading fast to destruction

பீலிபெய் சாகாடும் அச்சுஇறும் அப்பண்டம்
சால மிகுத்துப் பெயின்.   475

*peelipey sAkAdum achchuiRum appaNdam
sAla mikuththup peyin*

Be it the feathery light peacock's flume, an excess
load breaks axle of the cart carrying it

நுனிக்கொம்பர் ஏறினார் அஃதுஇறந்து ஊக்கின்
உயிர்க்குஇறுதி யாகி விடும். 476

*n-unikkompar aeRinAr aqthuiRan-thu uukkin
uyirkkuiRuthi yaaki vidum*

Skipping beyond the branches' tip of a tree
is sure to slip life out of your body

ஆற்றின் அளவுஅறிந்து ஈக அதுபொருள்
போற்றி வழங்கும் நெறி. 477

*aatRRin aLavuaRin-thu eeka athuporuL
pOtRRi vazangkum n-eRi*

Suiting limits of resources and giving out in measures
to the needy is the best way to treasure wealth

ஆகாறு அளவிட்டிது ஆயினும் கேடில்லை
போகாறு அகலாக் கடை… 478

*aakARu aLavittithu aayinum kaedillai
pOkARu akalAk kadai*

Outgo is to be planned in tune with resources, seeking
income by any means to bridge largesse is ruinous

அளவுஅறிந்து வாழாதான் வாழ்க்கை உளபோல
இல்லாகித் தோன்றாக் கெடும். 479

*aLavuaRin-thu vAzAthAn vAzkkai uLapOla
illAkith thOnRAk kedum*

A lavish life style out of all bounds, though appearing
gorgeous, fades off fast without a trace

உளவரை தூக்காத ஒப்புர வாண்மை
வளவரை வல்லைக் கெடும். 480

*uLavarai thUkkAtha oppura vANmai
vaLavarai vallaik kedum*

Socializing at a level beyond one's means
dries up wealth fast, and ruins its resources

49. காலம் அறிதல்
kAlam aRithal
CHOOSING TIME

(CHOOSING PROPER AND APPROPRIATE TIME IS IMPORTANT FOR
SUCCESSFUL ACCOMPLISHMENT OF DEEDS WITH SPEED AND
PATIENCE, IN TUNE WITH THE ENVIRONMENT)

பகல்வெல்லும் கூகையைக் காக்கை இகல்வெல்லும்
வேந்தர்க்கு வேண்டும் பொழுது.   481

pakalvellum kUkaiyaik kAkkai ikalvellum
vaen-thaRkku vaeNdum pozuathu

The crow overpowers the owl during daytime, in spite
of its strength; time is important to win over foes

பருவத்தோடு ஒட்ட ஒழுகல் திருவினைத்
தீராமை ஆர்க்கும் கயிறு.   482

paruvaththOdu otta ozukal thiruvinaith
theerAmai aarkkum kayiRu

Moving in unison with the seasons is not only privy to
gains; it is the cord that binds wealth from slipping

அருவினை என்ப உளவோ கருவியான்
காலம் அறிந்து செயின்.   483

aruvinai enpa uLavO karuviyAn
kAlam aRin-thu seyin

Knowing to act with proper means, at an appropriate
time makes even a tougher job easy to rein

ஞாலம் கருதினும் கைகூடும் காலம்
கருதி இடத்தால் செயின்.   484

njAlam karuthinum kaikUdum kAlam
karuthi idaththAl seyin

There is nothing impossible in the universe to achieve
by perseverance, choosing proper time and place

காலம் கருதி இருப்பர் கலங்காது
ஞாலம் கருது பவர்.   485

kAlam karuthi iruppar kalangkAthu
njAlam karuthu pavar

Those who aim at achievements beyond the world
wait in patience for the best of time to move

ஊக்கம் உடையான் ஒடுக்கம் பொருதகர்
தாக்கற்குப் பேரும் தகைத்து.   486

uukkam udaiyAn odukkam poruthakar
thAkkaRkup paerum thakaiththu

Strength of the able waits in silence, like the ram
backing its feet, to strike from a vantage position

பொள்ளென ஆங்கே புறம்வேரார் காலம்பார்த்து
உள்வேர்ப்பர் ஒள்ளி யவர்.   487

poLena aangkae puRamvaerAr kAlampArththu
uLvaerppar oLLi yavar

The wise do not sweat out in rattle, but wait with
mental fervour to act firm at an appropriate time

செறுநரைக் காணின் சுமக்க இறு(தி)வரை
காணின் கிழக்காம் தலை.   488

seRun-araik kAnin sumakka iRu(thi)varai
kANin kizakkAm thalai

When you encounter foes with mindless hostility, bear
with them till they rush in haste to downfall

எய்தற்கு அரியது இயைந்தக்கால் அந்நிலையே
செய்தற்கு அரிய செயல்.   489

eythaRku ariyathu iyain-thakkAl an-n-ilaiyae
seythaRku ariya seyal

A chance rare and ripe in time is the best
to dare on things hard to wrest

கொக்கொக்க கூம்பும் பருவத்து மற்றுஅதன்
குத்துஒக்க சீர்த்த இடத்து.   490

kokkuokka kUmpum paruvaththu matRRuathan
kuththuokka seerththa idaththu

Learn from the stork patience to wait in silence and
strike firmly like its peck, at the right moment

50. இடன் அறிதல்
idan aRithal
JUDGING PLACE
(AS IMPORTANT AS TIME IS A PLACE SUITED FOR THE DEED ON HAND)

தொடங்கற்க எவ்வினையும் எள்ளற்க முற்றும்
இடங்கண்ட பின்அல் லது.   **491**

thodangkaRka evvinaiyum eLLaRka mutRRum
idamkaNda pinal lathu

Until you choose a place proper, do not begin
to act, or underestimate the task ahead

முரண்சேர்ந்த மொய்ம்பி னவர்க்கும் அரண்சேர்ந்தாம்
ஆக்கம் பலவும் தரும்.   **492**

muraNsaern-tha moyppi navarkkum araNsaern-thAm
aakkam palavum tharum

Security to a place of safety like a fort adds
strength to the will to act and achieve

ஆற்றாரும் ஆற்றி அடுப இடன்அறிந்து
போற்றார்கண் போற்றிச் செயின்.   **493**

aatRRArum aatRRi adupa idanaRin-thu
pOtRRArkaN pORRich seyin

The weak can also fight to win, if the field chosen
is proper, and aim at the foe with determination

எண்ணியார் எண்ணம் இழப்பர் இடன்அறிந்து
துன்னியார் துன்னிச் செயின்.   **494**

eNNiyAr eNNam izappar idanaRin-thu
thunniyAr thunnich seyin

If you stay with courage at a position of vantage
the foe cannot but give up plans of attack

நெடும்புனலுள் வெல்லும் முதலை அடும்புனலின்
நீங்கின் அதனைப் பிற.   **495**

n-edumpunaluL vellum muthalai adumpunalin
n-eengkin athanaip piRa

The crocodile dominates in deep waters; once
out of water, it is an easy prey to its foes

கடலோடா கால்வல் நெடுந்தேர் கடலோடும்
நாவாயும் ஓடா நிலத்து.   496

*kadalOdA kAlval n-edun-thEr kadalOdum
n-AvAyum OdA n-ilaththu*

A tall temple car does not sail in the sea; nor a ship
runs on land; there is a proper place for everything

அஞ்சாமை அல்லால் துணைவேண்டா எஞ்சாமை
எண்ணி இடத்தாற் செயின்.   497

*anjsAmai allAl thuNaivaeNdA enjsAmai
eNNi idaththAR seyin*

Courage is companion in aid to the one who
acts firm, from a chosen field, using brain

சிறுபடையான் செல்லிடம் சேரின் உறுபடையான்
ஊக்கம் அழிந்து விடும்.   498

*siRupadaiyAn sellidam saerin uRupadaiyAn
uukkam azin-thu vidum*

Though small in the strength of forces, a chieftain, in
the security of his land, can spoil the will of a foe

சிறைநலனும் சீரும் இலர்எனினும் மாந்தர்
உறைநிலத்தோடு ஒட்டல் அரிது.   499

*siRain-alanum seerum ilareninum mAn-thar
uRain-ilaththOdu ottal arithu*

Even when weak in security and form, people on
their native soil cannot be subjugated for long

காலாழ் களரில் நரியடும் கண்அஞ்சா
வேலாள் முகத்த களிறு.   500

*kAlaazh kaLaril n-ariadum kaNanjsA
vaelaaL mukaththa kaLiRu*

A fearless tusker caught in a quagmire may even be
prey to a fox; beware of a wrong step at a wrong place

51. தெரிந்து தெளிதல்
therin-thu theLithal
TEST AND TRUST

(CHOOSE A PERSON EMINENTLY SUITED FOR THE JOB ON HAND
AFTER FULLY ANALYSING THE CAPABILITIES, CHARACTER AND
APTITUDES)

அறம்பொருள் இன்பம் உயிரச்சம் நான்கின்
திறண்தெரிந்து தேறப் படும்.　　　　　501

*aRamporuL inpam uyirachcham n-Ankin
thiRantherin-thu thaerap padum*

**Test people by their attitudes to life in virtue,
wealth, love and survival before you trust**

குடிப்பிறந்து குற்றத்தின் நீங்கி வடுப்பரியும்
நாண்டஉடையான் கட்டே தெளிவு.　　　　　502

*kudippiRan-thu kutRRaththin n-eengki vaduppariyum
n-ANudaiyAn kattae theLivu*

**Noble heritage, freedom from vices and shame
of blame are some norms to choose the worthy**

அரியகற்று ஆகுஅற்றார் கண்ணும் தெரியுங்கால்
இன்மை அரிதே வெளிறு.　　　　　503

*ariyakatRRu aasuatRRAr kaNNum theriyungkAl
inmai arithae veLiRu*

**Even among scholars who have overcome folly, it is
hard to find a few, fully free from ignorance**

குணம்நாடிக் குற்றமும் நாடி அவற்றுள்
மிகைநாடி மிக்க கொளல்.　　　　　504

*kuNamn-Adik kutRRamum n-Adi avaRRuL
mikain-Adi mikka koLal*

**Weigh with care the good and bad traits of people
and choose them by virtues that prevail**

பெருமைக்கும் ஏனைச் சிறுமைக்கும் தத்தம்
கருமமே கட்டளைக் கல்.　　　　　505

*perumaikkum aenaich siRumaikkum thaththam
karumamae kattaLaik kal.*

The quality of one's deeds is the touchstone to
see through their greatness or meanness of mind

அற்றாரைத் தேறுதல் ஓம்புக மற்றுஅவர்
பற்றிலர் நாணார் பழி.   **506**

*atRRAraith thaeRuthal Ompuka matRRuavar
patRRilar n-ANAr pazi*

A person disregarding virtues and lacking the
shame of blame, is not to be trusted upon

காதன்மை கந்தா அறிவுஅறியார்த் தேறுதல்
பேதைமை எல்லாம் தரும்.   **507**

*kAthanmai kan-thA aRivuaRiyArth thaeRuthal
paethaimai ellAm tharum*

A choice out of affinity, as favour to people
devoid of knowledge, entails folly to suffer

தேரான் பிறனைத் தெளிந்தான் வழிமுறை
தீரா இடும்பை தரும்.   **508**

*thaeran piRanaith theLin-thAn vazimuRai
theerA idumpai tharum*

Trust on an untested stranger brings about
endless troubles to one and to kin as well

தேறற்க யாரையும் தேராது தேர்ந்தபின்
தேறுக தேறும் பொருள்.   **509**

*thaeRaRka yAraiyum thaerAthu thaern-thapin
thaeRuka thaeRum poruL*

Select no one without adequate tests; on satisfactory
assessment, trust them with work to suit them

தேரான் தெளிவும் தெளிந்தான்கண் ஐயுறவும்
தீரா இடும்பை தரும்.   **510**

*thaerAn theLivum therin-thAnkan aiyuRavum
theerA idumpai tharum*

Do not repose trust without tests; nor lurk in
doubt after the choice - both are harmful

52. தெரிந்து வினையாடல்
therin-thu vinaiyAdal
EVALUATE AND ENTRUST

(IT IS A VITAL TASK IN HRD AND SUCCESSFUL MANAGEMENT
NOT ONLY TO SELECT PERSONS SUITED, BUT TO ASSIGN THEM
DUTIES ACCORDING TO APTITUDES AND SKILLS AND TO
DELEGATE POWERS AND RESPONSIBILITIES)

நன்மையும் தீமையும் நாடி நலம்புரிந்த
தன்மையான் ஆளப் படும்.　　　511

*n-anmaiyum theemaiyum n-Adi n-alampurin-tha
thanmaiyAn aaLap padum*

The wise who can discern good and bad of things
and perform right, are the best to choose

வாரி பெருக்கி வளம்படுத்து உற்றவை
ஆராய்வான் செய்க வினை.　　　512

*vAri perukki vaLampaduththu utRRavai
aarAyvAn saeyka vinai*

Entrust a job to one competent to augment revenue
and foster wealth, crossing all hurdles on the way

அன்புஅறிவு தேற்றம் அவாஇன்மை இந்நான்கும்
நன்குடையான் கட்டே தெளிவு.　　　513

*anpuaRivu thaetRRam avAinmai in-n-Ankum
n-ankudaiyAn kattae theLivu*

Select those who have gained clear perception by
wisdom, love, discerning wit and freedom from lust

எனைவகையான் தேறியக் கண்ணும் வினைவகையான்
வேறாகும் மாந்தர் பலர்.　　　514

*enaivakaiyAn thaeriyak kaNNum vinaivakaiyAn
vaeRAkum mAn-thar palar*

However much one is tested and tried, each one
has his own perception and ways to perform

அறிந்துஆற்றிச் செய்கிற்பாற்கு அல்லால் வினைதான்
சிறந்தான்என்று ஏவற்பாற்று அன்று.　　　515

aRin-thuaatRRich seykkiRpARku allAl vinaithAn
siRan-thAnenRu yaevaRpAtRRu anRu

Assess persons' knowledge and ability to turn a job
to success before yassigning them responsibility

செய்வானை நாடி வினைநாடிக் காலத்தோடு
எய்த உணர்ந்து செயல்.   516

seyvAnai n-Adi vinain-Adik kAlaththOdu
eytha uNarn-thu seyal

Choose a useful person proper for a job and
cause it to be done at an appropriate time

இதனை இதனால் இவன்முடிக்கும் என்றுஆய்ந்து
அதனை அவன்கண் விடல்.   517

ithanai ithanAl ivanmudikkum enRuaayn-thu
athanai avankaN vidal

Select a person with appropriate means to tackle the
kind of job, and entrust it for efficient management

வினைக்குஉரிமை நாடிய பின்றை அவனை
அதற்குஉரியன் ஆகச் செயல்.   518

vinaikku-urimai n-Adiya pinRai avanai
athaRkuuriyan aakach seyal

Scan well and determine fitness for a job and
leave that to be done to the best of ability

வினைக்கண் வினையுடையான் கேண்மைவே றாக
நினைப்பானை நீங்கும் திரு.   519

vinaikkaN vinaiyudaiyAn kaeNmaivE RAka
n-inaippAnai n-eengkum thiru'

Doubting determination of 'doers for duty sake'
leads to quick departure of one's wealth

நாள்தோறும் நாடுக மன்னன் வினைசெய்வான்
கோடாமை கோடாது உலகு.   520

n-ALthORum n-Aduka mannan vinaiseyvAn
kOdAmai kOdAthu ulaku

Always keep dear in mind the interest of workers
whose steady hands keep the world on stride

53. சுற்றம் தழூஉல்
sutRam thazAl
CHERISHING KITH AND KIN

(IN ANY ENDEAVOUR OF GOVERNANCE, BUSINESS OR SERVICE IT
IS USEFUL TO ENLIST KITH AND KIN WHO CAN STAND TOGETHER
IN THICK AND THIN)

பற்றுஅற்ற கண்ணும் பழைமைபா ராட்டுதல்
சுற்றத்தார் கண்ணே உள.   521

patRRuatRa kaNNum pazamaipA rAttuthal
sutRRaththAr kaNNE uLa

Changing times and contacts do not dim the
tradition of love and affection of kinship

விருப்புஅறாச் சுற்றம் இயையின் அருப்பறா
ஆக்கம் பலவும் தரும்.   522

viruppuaRAch sutRRam iyaiyin aruppaRA
aakkam palavum tharum

The links of love in kinship are like buds blossoming
into flowers to spread fragrance of kindness

அளவளாவு இல்லாதான் வாழ்க்கை குளவளாக்
கோடுஇன்றி நீர்நிறைந்து அற்று.   523

aLavaLAvu illAthAn vAzkkai kuLavaLAk
kOduinRi n-eern-iRain-thu atRRu

A life bereft of comradory in kinship is like a pond
losing its waters without proper bunds

சுற்றத்தால் சுற்றப் படஒழுகல் செல்வந்தான்
பெற்றத்தால் பெற்ற பயன்.   524

sutRRaththAl sutRRap padaozukal selvamthAn
petRRaththAl petRRa payan

The joy and happiness of kin surrounding in
support is the purpose and fruits of wealth

கொடுத்தலும் இன்சொலும் ஆற்றின் அடுக்கிய
சுற்றத்தால் சுற்றப் படும்.   525

koduththalum insolum aaRRin adukkiya
sutRRaththAl sutRRap padum

A liberal hand that extends along with the kindness
of words, encircles kith and kin thick in love

பெரும்கொடையான் பேணான் வெகுளி அவனின்
மருங்குஉடையார் மாநிலத்து இல்.   526

perumkodaiyAn paeNAn vekuLi avanin
marungkuudaiyAr mAn-ilaththu il

One with the glory of munificence, abjuring wrath
commands kinship of countless numbers on earth

காக்கை கரவா கரைந்துஉண்ணும் ஆக்கமும்
அன்னநீ ரார்க்கே உள.   527

kAkkai karavA karain-thuuNNum aakkam
annan-ee rArkkae uLa

Welfare abides a mind that takes the crow's habit of
calling kith and kin, to share food without concealing

பொதுநோக்கான் வேந்தன் வரிசையா நோக்கின்
அதுநோக்கி வாழ்வார் பலர்.   528

pothun-OkkAn vaen-than varisaiyA n-Okkin
athun-Okki vAzvAr palar

The ruler is common in public gaze; yet who perceives
by merit, is bound to help citizens according to needs

தமராகித் தன்துறந்தார் சுற்றம் அமராமைக்
காரணம் இன்றி வரும்.   529

thamaraakith than-thuRan-thAr sutRRam amarAmaik
kAraNam inRi varum

Alleviating causes of discord with kin makes them
revive forsaken friendship to stay firm

உழைப்பிரிந்து காரணத்தின் வந்தானை வேந்தன்
இழைத்திருந்து எண்ணிக் கொளல்.   530

uzaippirin-thu kAraNaththin van-thAnai vaen-than
izaiththirun-thu eNNik koLal

Those who have left in circumstances adverse and return on
purpose, the leader should test, judge and receive

54. பொச்சாவாமை (விழிப்புணர்வு)
pochchAvAmai(vizippuNarvu)
GUARDING AGAINST COMPLACENCY
(FORGETFULNESS, INSOUCIANCE, INDIFFERENCE)
(NOT TO GIVE ANY ROOM FOR SLOTH, FORGETFULNESS, INSOUCIANCE, INDIFFERENCE WHICH ARE HARMFUL TO GRACE, HONOUR AND FAME)

இறந்த வெகுளியின் தீதே சிறந்த
உவகை மகிழ்ச்சியில் சோர்வு.   531

iRan-tha vekuLiyin theethae siRan-tha
uvakai makizhchchiyil sOrvu

Sloth in a 'happy-go-joy' mood is more
harmful than uncontrolled wrath

பொச்சாப்புக் கொல்லும் புகழை அறிவினை
நிச்ச நிரப்புக்கொன் றாங்கு.   532

pochchAppuk kollum pukazai aRivinai
n-ichcha n-iRappukkon RAngku

Persistent menace of penury destroys wisdom;
forgetful complacency kills renown

பொச்சாப்பார்க்கு இல்லை புகழ்மை அதுவுலகத்து
எப்பால்நூ லோர்க்கும் துணிவு.   533

pochchAppArkku illai pukazhmai athu-ulakaththu
eppAl n-UlOrkkum thuNivu

Fame is alien to the insoucient; enlightened
codes of all schools of thought concur

அச்சம் உடையார்க்கு அரணில்லை ஆங்குஇல்லை
பொச்சாப்பு உடையார்க்கு நன்கு.   534

achcham udaiyArkku araNillai aangkuillai
pochchAppu udaiyArkku n-anku

A mind in fear holds no fortress dear; complacent
indifference never finds goodness in a chance

முன்னுறக் காவாது இழுக்கியான் தன்பிழை
பின்னூறு இரங்கி விடும்.   535

munnuRak kAvAthu izukkiyAn thanpizai
pinnURu irangki vidum

Lacking safety or foresight in sloth, the unwary
rue their follies in times that follow

இழுக்காமை யார்மாட்டும் என்றும் வழுக்காமை
வாயின் அதுவொப்பது இல்.　　　　536

izukkAmai yArmAttun enRum vazukkAmai
vAyin athuvoppathu il

Slip not from wakefulness and miss no gains;
there is no strength than alertness to compare

அரியன்று ஆகாத இல்லைபொச் சாவாக்
கருவியால் போற்றிச் செயின்.　　　　537

ariyaenRu aakAtha illaipoch sAvAk
karuviyAl pOtRRich saeyin

There is rarely anything impossible for those,
who persist with alacrity and zeal to achieve

புகழ்ந்தவை போற்றிச் செயல்வேண்டும் செய்யாது
இகழ்ந்தார்க்கு எழுமையும் இல்.　　　　538

pukazn-thavai pOtRRich saeyalvaeNdum seyyAthu
ikazn-thArkku ezumaiyum il

Worthy deeds demand ceaseless efforts; in neglect
and indifference there is no life to commend

இகழ்ச்சியின் கெட்டாரை உள்ளுக தாம்தம்
மகிழ்ச்சியின் மைந்துஊறும் போழ்து.　　　　539

ikazchchiyin kettArai uLLuka thAmtham
makizchchiyin main-thuURum pOzthu

Forget not to think of those who fail by negligence,
even as you may revel in deluding joy

உள்ளியது எய்தல் எளிதுமன் மற்றுந்தான்
உள்ளியது உள்ளப் பெறின்.　　　　540

uLLiyathu aeythal eLithuman matRRunthAn
uLLiyathu uLLap peRin

Set the mind firm on an objective and act; that
makes the goal more easier to achieve

55. செங்கோன்மை
sengkOnmai
GOOD GOVERNANCE
(THE CODE OF CONDUCT FOR RULERS IN A WELFARE STATE ADMINISTRATION AND JUSTICE)

ஓர்ந்துகண் ஒடாது இறைபுரிந்து யார்மாட்டும்
தேர்ந்துசெய் வஃதே முறை.   **541**

Orn-thukaN OdAthu iRaipurin-thu yArmAttum
thaern-thusey vaqthae muRai

Considered action on wise counsel, even on pros and
cons, without lenience leads to just governance

வாந்நோக்கி வாழும் உலகுஎல்லாம் மன்னவன்
கோல்நோக்கி வாழும் குடி.   **542**

vAnn-Okki vAzum ulakuellAm mannavan
kOln-Okki vAzum kudi

Life on earth thrives on rain and celestial knowledge;
society looks upon good governance to thrive

அந்தணர் நூற்கும் அறத்திற்கும் ஆதியாய்
நின்றது மன்னவன் கோல்.   **543**

an-thaNar n-URkum aRaththiRkum aathiyAy
n-inRathu mannavan kOl

Scriptures of wisdom and virtues spring and thrive
in glory, in the grace of good governance

குடிதழீஇக் கோலோச்சும் மாநில மன்னன்
அடிதழீஇ நிற்கும் உலகு.   **544**

kudithazeeik kOlOchchum mAn-ila mannan
adithazeei n-iRkum ulaku

The ruler who upholds and protects the interests
of citizens, is assured of their strength of support

இயல்புளிக் கோலோச்சும் மன்னவன் நாட்ட
பெயலும் விளையுளும் தொக்கு.   **545**

iyalpuLik kOlOchchum mannavan n-Atta
peyalum viLaiyuLum thokku

Just and fair the governance in tune with nature, the
land is enriched like with copious rains and produce

வேல்அன்று வென்றி தருவது மன்னவன்
கோல்அதூஉம் கோடாது எனின்.   546

vaelanRu venRi tharuvathu mannavan
kOlathuvum kOdAthu enin

It is not armour that sustains success of a ruler,
so much as virtues and just governance

இறைகாக்கும் வையக மெல்லாம் அவனை
முறைகாக்கும் முட்டாச் செயின்.   547

iRaikAkkum vaiyakam ellAm avanai
muRaikAkkum mutAch seyin

Rulers duty is to protect wealths of land; benevolence
and good governance protect the ruler

எண்பதத்தான் ஓரா முறைசெய்யா மன்னவன்
தண்பதத்தான் தானே கெடும்.   548

eNpathaththAn oorA muRaiseyyA mannavan
thaNpathaththAn thAnae kedum

An unjust ruler, hard in mind and face, disregards
advice, and in weakness works towards ruin

குடிபுறம் காத்தோம்பிக் குற்றம் கடிதல்
வடுஅன்று வேந்தன் தொழில்.   549

kudipuRam kAththuoompik kutRRam kadithal
vaduanRu vaen-than thozil

A fearless ruler is duty bound to protect society from
external harm and internal crime, with a strong arm

கொலையில் கொடியாரை வேர்த்துஒறுத்தல் பைங்கூழ்
களைகட் டதனொடு நேர்.   550

kolaiyil kodiyArai vaen-thuoRuththal paingkUz
kaLaikat tathanodu n-aer

Protecting crops by de-weeding the fields to yield,
the ruler has to banish terror by hard punishments

56. கொடுங்கோன்மை
kodungkOnmai
TYRANNY OF RULE (CRUEL GOVERNANCE)
(CRUELTY IN GOVERNANCE ENDS UP IN MISERY OF THE PEOPLE AND RUIN OF THE REGIME)

கொலைமேற்கொண் டாரிற் கொடிதே அலைமேற்கொண்டு
அல்லவை செய்தொழுகும் வேந்து.   551

kolaimaeRkoN dArin kodithae alaimaeRkoNdu
allai seythozukum vaen-thu

Oppressive and unjust misrule of a tyrant
is worse than cruelty of murderers

வேலொடு நின்றான் இடுஎன் றதுபோலும்
கோலொடு நின்றான் இரவு.   552

vaelodu n-inRAn iduen RathupOlum
kOlodu n-inRAn iravu

A ruler misusing powers to extort in the guise of gift
is like a dacoit with a spear waylaying to rob

நாள்தொறும் நாடி முறைசெய்யா மன்னவன்
நாள்தொறும் நாடு கெடும்.   553

n-ALthoRum n-Adi muRaisaeyyA mannavan
n-ALthoRum n-Adu kedum

A ruler who fails to feel the pulse of people to redress
their grievances, ruins his realm day by day

கூழும் குடியும் ஒருங்குஇழக்கும் கோல்கோடிச்
சூழாது செய்யும் அரசு.   554

kUzum kudiyum orungkuizakkum kOlkOdich
sUzAthu seyyum arasu

Ignoring wise council and abusing governance
causes the ruler to lose prosperity and citizens

அல்லல்பட்டு ஆற்றாது அழுதகண் ணீரன்றே
செல்வத்தைத் தேய்க்கும் படை.   555

allalpattu aatRRAthu azuthakaN NIranRae
selvaththaith thaeykkum padai

Tears of hapless citizens, groaning under tyranny,
with none to console, floods to erode wealth

மன்னர்க்கு மன்னுதல் செங்கோன்மை அஃதுஇன்றேல்
மன்னாவாம் மன்னர்க்கு ஒளி.   556

mannarkku mannuthal sengkOnmai aqthuinRael
mannAvAm mannarkku oLi

Just governance sustains glory of the ruler; without
it, one wanes out of light and fame

துளியின்மை ஞாலத்திற்கு எற்றுஅற்றே வேந்தன்
அளியின்மை வாழும் உயிர்க்கு.   557

thuLiinmai njAlaththiRku etRRuatRRae vaen-than
aLiinmai vAzum uyirkku

All life and prosperity on earth withers without rains;
grace of benevolence in rule is essential for living

இன்மையின் இன்னாது உடைமை முறைசெய்யா
மன்னவன் கோல்கீழ்ப் படின்.   558

inmaiyin innAthu udaimai muRaisaeyyA
mannavan kOlkeezp padin

To suffer useless wealth possessed, under the
rule of a tyrant, is worse than pain in penury

முறைகோடி மன்னவன் செய்யின் உறைகோடி
ஒல்லாது வானம் பெயல்.   559

muRaikOdi mannavan saeyyin uRaikOdi
ollAthu vAnam peyal

When an unjust ruler misbehaves, barren lands fail
to attract rains and decayed reservoirs fail crops

ஆபயன் குன்றும் அறுதொழிலோர் நூல்மறப்பர்
காவலன் காவான் எனின்.   560

aapayan kunRum aRuthozilOr n-UlmaRappar
kAvalan kAvAn enin

Entrepreneurs lose their skills, accrual of wealth dims
when the ruler fails to protect the land and wealth

57. வெருவந்த செய்யாமை
veruvan-tha seyyAmai
REFRAIN FROM TERRORISM
(MINDLESS TREPIDATION)

(MINDLESS TREPIDATION AND CRUEL REIN TERRIFIES THE
PEOPLE AND RUINS THE SAFETY AND WEALTH OF THE LAND)

தக்காங்கு நாடித் தலைச்செல்லா வண்ணத்தால்
ஒத்தாங்கு ஒறுப்பது வேந்து.   561

thakkAngku n-Adith thalaichsellA vaNNaththAl
oththAngku oRuppathu vaen-thu

A probing inquiry and due punishment adequate to
deter recurrence of crime is the rule of justice

கடிதோச்சி மெல்ல எறிக நெடிதுஆக்கம்
நீங்காமை வேண்டு பவர்.   562

kadithuochchi mella eRika n-edithuaakkam
n-eengkAmai vaeNdu pavar

It is in long term interest of a successful ruler
to reprimand firmly and punish lightly

வெருவந்த செய்தொழுகும் வெங்கோல நாயின்
ஒருவந்தம் ஒல்லைக் கெடும்.   563

veruvan-tha saeythuozukum vengkOla naayin
oruvan-tham ollaik kedum

Senseless and cruel regime of a terrifying ruler
lands the country in ruins sure and fast

இறைகடியன் என்றுஉரைக்கும் இன்னாச்சொல் வேந்தன்
உறைகடுகி ஒல்லைக் கெடும்.   564

iRaikadiyan enRuuraikkum innAchchol vaen-than
uRaikaduki ollaik kedum

A tyrant's rule, hard in words and deeds, shortens
life and destroys the land and people

அருஞ்செவ்வி இன்னா முகத்தான் பெருஞ்செல்வம்
பேஎய்கண் டன்னது உடைத்து.   565

arunjsevvi innA mukaththAn perunjselvam
paeykaN dannathu udaiththu

The vastness of wealth of a ruler, with a cross face
and scaring to the people, instills terror in them

கடுஞ்சொல்லன் கண்ணிலன் ஆயின் நெடுஞ்செல்வம்
நீடின்றி ஆங்கே கெடும். 566

kadunjsollan kaNNilan aayin n-edunjselvam
n-eedinRi aangke kedum

A mind devoid of compassion and a tongue harsh in
words, prevent growth and erode traditional wealth

கடுமொழியும் கையிகந்த தண்டமும் வேந்தன்
அடுமுரண் தேய்க்கும் அரம். 567

kadumoziyum kaiyikan-tha thaNdamum vaen-than
adumuraN thaeykkum aram

Rough and rude out of bounds, are the acts
that file off and erode the armour of a ruler

இனத்தாற்றி எண்ணாத வேந்தன் சினத்தாற்றிச்
சீரின் சிறுகும் திரு. 568

inaththAtRRi eNNAtha vaen-than sinaththAtRRich
seeRin siRukum thiru

Wrath in wild rage ignoring wisdom of kin and
council, shrinks the ruler in wealth and fame

செருவந்த போழ்தில் சிறைசெய்யா வேந்தன்
வெருவந்து வெய்து கெடும். 569

seruvan-tha pOzthil siRaisaeyyA vaenthan
veruvan-thu veythu kedum

A tepid ruler, who cares no precautions, fails to build
in protection against foes, and loses in fear and fits

கல்லார்ப் பிணிக்கும் கடுங்கோல் அதுஅல்லது
இல்லை நிலக்குப் பொறை. 570

kallArp piNikkum kadungkOl athuallathu
illai n-ilakkup poRai

Tyrants seeking the company of fools are
the greatest of burdens on this earth

58. கண்ணோட்டம்
kaNNOttam
SYMPATHY - FORESIGHT
(HUMANE CONSIDERATENESS)
(A GRACEFUL MIND OF SYMPATHY AND FORESIGHT, A SOFT SIGHT AND A BENIGN ATTITUDE AND AN EQUANIMOUS DISPOSITION TO OTHERS)

கண்ணோட்டம் என்னும் கழிபெரும் காரிகை
உண்மையான் உண்டிவ் வுலகு.   **571**

kaNNOttam ennum kaziperum kArikai
uNmaiyAl uNduiv vulaku

A considerate mind shows its bounteous beauty through
soft eyes; the strength on which the world thrives

கண்ணோட்டத் துள்ளது உலகியல் அஃதுஇலார்
உண்மை நிலக்குப் பொறை.   **572**

kaNNOttaththu uLLathu ulakiyal aqthuilAr
uNmai n-ilakkup poRai

Worldly life moves around benign eyes; those
who lack them are mere burdens on earth

பண்என்னாம் பாடற்கு இயைபுஇன்றேல் கண்என்னாம்
கண்ணோட்டம் இல்லாத கண்.   **573**

paNennAm pAdaRku iyaipuinRael kaNennAm
kaNNOttam illAtha kaN

Music not in tune with the burden of a song, and
barren looks without grace of mind are of no avail

உளபோல் முகத்துஎவன் செய்யும் அளவினால்
கண்ணோட்டம் இல்லாத கண்.   **574**

uLapOl mukaththu-evan saeyyum aLavinaal
kaNNOttam illAtha kaN

Our face mirrors the mind; eyes have no purpose when
one lacks a mind of measured feelings to reflect

கண்ணிற்கு அணிகலன் கண்ணோட்டம் அஃதுஇன்றேல்
புண்ணென்று உணரப் படும்.   **575**

kaNNiRku aNikalan kaNNOttam aqthuinRael
puNenRu uNarap padum

Kinder looks add beauty to the eyes; without
feelings to reflect, they are sore spots of pain

மண்ணோடு இயைந்த மரத்துஅனையர் கண்ணோடு
இயைந்துகண் ஓடா தவர்.   576

maNNOdu iyan-tha maraththuanaiyar kaNNOdu
iyain-thukaN oodA thavar

When eyes freeze in the chillness of the mind, they are
no different from a tree standing inert on earth

கண்ணோட்டம் இல்லவர் கண்ணிலர் கண்ணுடையார்
கண்ணோட்டம் இன்மையும் இல்.   577

kaNNOttam illavar kaNilar kaNNudaiyAr
kaNNOttam inmaiyum il

Without the soft light of mind the eyes are dimmed;
the eyes that perceive, move the mind

கரும் சிதையாமல் கண்ணோட வல்லார்க்கு
உரிமை உடைத்துஇவ் வுலகு.   578

karumam sithaiyAmal kaNNOda vallArkku
urimai udaiththuiv vulaku

Those who pursue a mission of duty with a graceful
mind, have a right for all beauties of the world

ஒறுத்து ஆற்றும் பண்பினார் கண்ணும்கண் ணோடிப்
பொறுத்து ஆற்றும் பண்பே தலை.   579

oRuththuaatRRum paNpinAr kaNNumkaN oodip
poRuththuaatRRum paNpae thalai

Being considerate and bearing with those who grieve
us on a vexed mind, is the mark of high manners

பெயக்கண்டும் நஞ்சுஉண்டு அமைவர் நயத்தக்க
நாகரிகம் வேண்டு பவர்.   580

peyakkaNdum n-anjsuuNdu amaivar n-ayaththakka
n-Akarikam vaeNdu pavar

People of humane tradition with equanimous disposition
will consume even poison cheerfully, if offered kindly

59. ஒற்றாடல் (உளவு அறிதல்)
otRAdal (uLavu aRithal)
SCOUTING INTELLIGENCE (ESPIONAGE)
(ESPIONAGE IS ONE OF THE VITAL LINKS FOR THE SECURITY AND
GOVERNANCE OF A STATE FROM EXTERNAL THREATS AND
INTERNAL DISCORD)

ஒற்றும் உரைசான்ற நூலும் இவைஇரண்டும்
தெற்றுஎன்க மன்னவன் கண்.   581

otRRum uraisAnRa n-Ulum ivaiiraNdum
thetRRuenka mannavan kaN

A code of governance and intelligent spying are
like eyes to the ruler who acts with clarity

எல்லார்க்கும் எல்லாம் நிகழ்பவை எஞ்ஞான்றும்
வல்லறிதல் வேந்தன் தொழில்.   582

ellArkkum ellAm n-ikazpavai enjnjAnRum
vallaRithal vaen-than thozil

All that happens in society, in course and off course,
the ruler should always know fully and act promptly

ஒற்றினான் ஒற்றிப் பொருள்தெரியா மன்னவன்
கொற்றம் கொளக்கிடந்தது இல்.   583

otRRinAn otRRip poruLtheriyA mannavan
kotRRam koLakkidan-thathu il

There is no way for a ruler to survive and thrive, who
cannot take cognizance and act on intelligence

வினைசெய்வார் தம்சுற்றம் வேண்டாதார் என்றுஆங்கு
அனைவரையும் ஆராய்வது ஒற்று.   584

vinaiseyvAr thamsutRRam vaeNdAthAr enRuaangku
anaivaraiyum aarAyvathu otRRu

Be they kin, aids, friends or foes in a society; an intelligent
spy does not spare them from watchful eyes

கடாஉ உருவொடு கண்அஞ்சாது யாண்டும்
உகாஅமை வல்லதே ஒற்று.   585

kadAa uruvodu kaNanjsAthu yANdum
ukAmai vallathae otRRu

Unsuspected pose and guise, fearless face and resolve
to guard secrets, bring success to an able spy

துறந்தார் படிவத்த ராகி இறந்துஆராய்ந்து
என்செயினும் சோர்வுஇலது ஒற்று.   586

thuRan-thAr padivaththa raaki iRan-thuarayn-thu
ensaeyinum sOrvuilathu otRRu

Deep probing, an air of detachment and the resolve to
face alertly come what may, are attributes of a spy

மறைந்தவை கேட்கவற்று ஆகி அறிந்தவை
ஐயப்பாடு இல்லதே ஒற்று.   587

maRain-thavai kaetkavaRRu aaki aRin-thavai
aiyappAdu illathae otRRu

The ability to unravel truth about nocturnal operators,
through contacts, and to ascertain facts, is essential

ஒற்றுஒற்றித் தந்த பொருளையும் மற்றுமோர்
ஒற்றினால் ஒற்றிக் கொளல்.   588

otRRuotRRith than-tha poruLaiyum matRRumOur
otRRinAl otRRik koLal

A successful ruler cross-checks the intelligence
reports of a spy through another spy to satisfy

ஒற்றுஒற்று உணராமை ஆள்க உடன்மூவர்
சொல்தொக்க தேறப் படும்.   589

otRRuotRRu uNarAmai aaLka udanmUvar
solthokka thaeRap padum

Employ spies alone, keep them apart unawares, and
weigh the reports of at least three, to concur on facts

சிறப்பறிய ஒற்றின்கண் செய்யற்க செய்யின்
புறப்படுத்தான் ஆகும் மறை.   590

siRappaRiya oRRinkaN saeyyaRka seyyin
puRappaduththAn aakum maRai

Encomiums in public to those in secret service
can render their jobs difficult to perform

---

60. ஊக்கம் உடைமை
uukkam udaimai
MOTIVATION
(DILIGENCE, WILLPOWER AND INITIATIVE TO PERFORM ARE
BASICS FOR SUCCESS IN ANY WALK OF LIFE)

உடையர் எனப்படுவது ஊக்கம் அஃதில்லார்
உடையது உடையரோ மற்று.   591

udaiyar enappaduvathu uukkam aqthilAr
udaiyathu udaiyarO matRRu

Motivation is a pride to possess, sans it other possessions
are unsafe, if not guarded against lethargy

உள்ளம் உடைமை உடைமை பொருளுடைமை
நில்லாது நீங்கி விடும்.   592

uLLam udaimai udaimai poruLudaimai
n-illAthu n-eengki vidum

Will-power is the motivation to energise activity;
in its absence, worldly wealth departs

ஆக்கம் இழந்தேம்என்று அல்லாவார் ஊக்கம்
ஒருவந்தம் கைத்துஉடை யார்.   593

aakkam izan-thaemenRu allAvAr uukkam
oruvan-tham kaiththuudai yAr

Motivation as a trusted aid of strength, one does
not lose hope to bemoan slipping of gains

ஆக்கம் அதர்வினாய்ச் செல்லும் அசைவிலா
ஊக்க முடையான் உழை.   594

aakkam atharvinAych sellum asaivilA
uukkam udayAn uzai

Wealth and gains go with a boom in search of
those who strive tirelessly, with a firm resolve

வெள்ளத்து அனைய மலர்நீட்டம் மாந்தர்தம்
உள்ளத்து அனையது உயர்வு.   595

veLLaththu anaiya malarn-eettam mAn-thartham
uLLaththu anaiyathu uyarvu

The deeper the water the lilly/lotus stem in and float
firmer the mental strength, the higher people rise

உள்ளுவது எல்லாம் உயர்வுள்ளல் மற்றுஅது
தள்ளினும் தள்ளாமை நீர்த்து.   596

uLLuvathu ellAm uyarvuLLal maRRuathu
thaLLinum thaLLAmai n-Irththu

Higher and firmer the objectives aimed, safer and
surer the goals reached, overcoming hurdles

சிதைவிடத்து ஒல்கார் உரவோர் புதையம்பில்
பட்டுப்பாடு ஊன்றும் களிறு.   597

sithaividaththu olkAr uravOr puthaiampil
pattuppAdu uunRum kaLiRu

An elephant fights to its reputation, unmindful of
arrows; the courageous relent not in adversities

உள்ளம் இலாதவர் எய்தார் உலகத்து
வள்ளியம் என்னும் செருக்கு.   598

uLLam ilAthavar eythAr ulakaththu
vaLLiyam ennum saerukku

A mind devoid of the strength of diligent benevolence
cannot take pride of munificence to the world

பரியது கூர்ங்கோட்டது ஆயினும் யானை
வெரூஉம் புலிதாக் குறின்.   599

pariyathu kUrngkOttathu aayinum yAnai
verUum pulithAk kuRin

An elephant of size, sharp in tusks relents and panics
when attacked by a tiger with ferocity

உரம்ஒருவற்கு உள்ள வெறுக்கை அஃதுஇல்லார்
மரம்மக்கள் ஆதலே வேறு.   600

uramoruvaRku uLLa veRukkai aqthuilAr
marammakkaL aathalae vaeRu

Mental courage is the strength in people who
perform; without it they stand still like trees

61. மடி இன்மை (சோம்பல் படாமை)
madi inmai
FREEDOM FROM SLOTH
(AVOIDING LAZINESS, INDOLENCE)

(AVOIDING LAZINESS, INDOLENCE WHICH DIM AND FADE OUT
ENTERPRISE AND DESTROYS EFFORTS)

குடிஎன்னும் குன்றா விளக்கம் மடிஎன்னும்
மாசுஊர மாய்ந்து கெடும்.   601

kudiennum kunRA viLakkam madiennum
mAsuuura mAyn-thu kedum

Where the dirt and stain of sloth seep in, the everlasting
light of social glitter dims and fades out

மடியை மடியா ஒழுகல் குடியைக்
குடியாக வேண்டு பவர்.   602

madiyai madiyA ozukal kudiyaik
kudiyAka vaeNdu pavar

The endeavour to foster social values should
keep out sloth as a despised evil

மடிமடிக் கொண்டொழுகும் பேதை பிறந்த
குடிமடியும் தன்னினும் முந்து.   603

madimadik koNdozukum paethai piRan-tha
kudimadiyum thanninum mun-thu

The ignorant who carry the burden of sloth cause
downfall of their society before they perish

குடிமடிந்து குற்றம் பெருகும் மடிமடிந்து
மாண்ட உளுற்றி லவர்க்கு.   604

kudimadin-thu kutRRam perukum madimadin-thu
mANda unjatRi lavarkku

The society whose people stew in sloth, without
striving to rise up decays and steeps in crime

நெடுநீர் மறவி மடிதுயில் நான்கும்
கெடுநீரார் காமக் கலன்.   605

n-edun-eer maRavi madithuyil n-Ankum
kedun-eerAr kAmak kalan

Idle, sloth, forgetfulness, dozing off and lackadaisical
attitude are attributes the sluggish are fond of

படியுடையார் பற்றுஅமைந்தக் கண்ணும் மடியுடையார்
மாண்பயன் எய்தல் அரிது.   606

padiudaiyAr patRRuamain-thak kaNNum madiyudaiyAr
mANpayan eythal arithu

The slothful cannot gain anything worthy from
the munificence and support of the wealthy

இடிபுரிந்து எள்ளும்சொல் கேட்பர் மடிபுரிந்து
மாண்ட உஞற்றி லவர்.   607

idipurin-thu eLLumsol kaetpar madipurin-thu
mANda unjatRi lavar

Those lacking noble efforts, and under the duress of
sloth will be objects of scornful ridicule in society

மடிமை குடிமைக்கண் தங்கின்தன் ஒன்னார்க்கு
அடிமை புகுத்தி விடும்.   608

madimai kudimaikkaN thangkin-than onnArkku
adimai pukuththi vidum

Sloth that invades a thriving society damages
and enslaves it to the foes

குடியாண்மை உள்வந்த குற்றம் ஒருவன்
மடியாண்மை மாற்றக் கெடும்.   609

kudiyANmai uLvan-tha kutRRam oruvan
madiyANmai mARRak kedum

A ruler caught in the crime of sluggishness can
redress the society only by banishing sloth

மடியிலா மன்னவன் எய்தும் அடிஅளந்(து)தான்
தாஅயது எல்லாம் ஒருங்கு.   610

madiyilA mannavan eythum adiaLan-(thu)thAn
thAayathu ellAm orungku

A ruler to whom sloth is alien, encompasses all
the space and wealth he treads and strives

62. ஆள்வினை உடைமை
aaLvinai udaimai
PERVADING EFFORT

(DEEP INVOLVEMENT IN THE TASKS ON HAND AND SUSTAINED
ACTION IN EXECUTING THEM TO PERFECTION)

அருமை உடைத்துஎன்று அசாவாமை வேண்டும்
பெருமை முயற்சி தரும். 611

arumaiudaiththu endRu asAvAmai vaeNdum
perumai muyaRchi tharum

All pervasive efforts attain fame; nothing can
frustrate people from their goals, striven hard

வினைக்கண் வினைகெடல் ஓம்பல் வினைக்குறை
தீர்ந்தாரின் தீர்ந்தன்று உலகு. 612

vinaikkaN vinaikedal oompal vinaikkuRai
theerththArin theerththanRu ulaku

A job done in full is a job done well; the world
has no place for those who shirk and sulk

தாளாண்மை என்னும் தகைமைக்கண் தங்கிற்றே
வேளாண்மை என்னும் செருக்கு. 613

thALANmai ennum thakaimaikkaN thangkitRae
vaeLANmai ennum serukku

Magnanimity of service to society depends
on the industrious excellence of efforts

தாளாண்மை இல்லாதான் வேளாண்மை பேடிகை
வாளாண்மை போலக் கெடும். 614

thALANmai illAthAn vaeLANmai paedikai
vALANmai pOlak kedum

The mission of service in the hands of those who disdain
efforts, is like a sword with a coward in battle

இன்பம் விழையான் வினைவிழைவான் தன்கேளிர்
துன்பம் துடைத்துஊன்றும் தூண். 615

inpam vizaiyAn vinaivizaivAn thankaeLir
thunpam thudaiththu-uunRum thUN

Who strives hard at work, not running after pleasures,
is a pillar alleviating the grief of comrades

முயற்சி திருவினை ஆக்கும் முயற்றின்மை
இன்மை புகுத்தி விடும்.   616

muyaRchi thiruvinai aakkum muyaRRinmai
inmai pukuththi vidum

Sensible efforts and studious industry build
prosperity; indolence breeds poverty

மடிஉளாள் மாமுகடி என்ப மடிஇலான்
தாள்உளாள் தாமரையி னாள்.   617

madiuLAL mAmukadi enpa madiilAn
thALuLAL thAmaraiyi nAL

Where sloth resides total darkness prevails; where
industry thrives, brightness radiates like a lotus

பொறியின்மை யார்க்கும் பழியன்று அறிவுஅறிந்து
ஆள்வினை இன்மை பழி.   618

poRiyinmai yArkkum paziyanRu aRivuaRin-thu
aaLvinai inmai pazi

Defect of limbs, equipment or opportunity is no handicap
to one who understands and strives hard at work

தெய்வத்தான் ஆகாது எனினும் முயற்சிதன்
மெய்வருத்தக் கூலி தரும்.   619

theyvaththAn aakAthu eninum muyaRchithan
meyvaruththak kUli tharum

Though hope on human or divine guidance may fail;
sincere and hard labour always has its reward

ஊழழயும் உப்பக்கம் காண்பர் உலைவின்றித்
தாழாது உளுற்று பவர்.   620

uuzaiyum uppakkam kANpar ulaivinRith
thAzAthu unjatRu pavar

Ceaseless striving with confidence is, in essence, the
strength that moulds one's environment to success

63. இடுக்கண் அழியாமை
idukkaN aziyAmai
OVERCOMING OBSTACLES (MISHAPS)
(ADVERSITIES AND MISHAPS IN LIFE ARE TO BE TAKEN IN THE
STRIDE AND FACED WITH BOLD RESOLVE)

இடுக்கண் வருங்கால் நகுக அதனை
அடுத்தூர்வது அஃதுஒப்பது இல்.　　　621

idukkaN varungkAl n-akuka athanai
aduththUrvathu aqthuoppathu il

One should learn to laugh at adversities and do well
to know, the ones that follow cannot be harder

வெள்ளத்து அனைய இடும்பை அறிவுடையான்
உள்ளத்தின் உள்ளக் கெடும்.　　　622

veLLaththu anaiya idumpai aRivudaiyAn
uLLaththin uLLak kedum

A mind that has the wisdom to face sorrows in
floods, has the power to overcome mishaps

இடும்பைக்கு இடும்பை படுப்பர் இடும்பைக்கு
இடும்பை படாஅ தவர்.　　　623

idupaikku idumpai paduppar idumpaikku
idumpai padAa thavar

The one who is not easily suffocated by pain,
makes pain suffer in course, its own woes

மடுத்தவாய் எல்லாம் பகுடுஅன்னான் உற்ற
இடுக்கண் இடர்ப்பாடு உடைத்து.　　　624

maduththavAy ellAm pakaduannAn utRRa
idukkan idarppAdu udaiththu

Like a cart ceaselessly negotiating a rough track,
people of perseverance make mishaps miss out

அடுக்கி வரினும் அழிவுஇலான் உற்ற
இடுக்கண் இடுக்கட் படும்.　　　625

adukki varinum azivuilAn utRRa
idukkaN idukkat padum

Mishaps in multitudes that cannot daunt a
resolute person, perish in their own form

அற்றேமென்று அல்லற் படுபவோ பெற்றேம்என்று
ஒம்புதல் தேற்றா தவர்.   626

*atRRaemenRu allal padupavO petRRaemenru
oomputhal thaetRRA thavar*

People who do not care to cherish and patronize
wealth, are unlikely to mind when they lose

இலக்கம் உடம்புஇடும்பைக்கு என்று கலக்கத்தைக்
கையாராக் கொள்ளாதாம் மேல்.   627

*ilakkam udampuidumpaikku enRu kalakkaththaik
kaiyARAk koLLAthAm mael*

Pain and suffering are part of the game that
is life; the wise are not unduly worried

இன்பம் விழையான் இடும்பை இயல்புஎன்பான்
துன்பம் உறுதல் இலன்.   628

*inpam vizaiyAn idumpai iyalpuenpAn
thunpam uRuthal ilan*

Those who do not seek after pleasures and take
pain in their stride, do not suffer its woes

இன்பத்துள் இன்பம் விழையாதான் துன்பத்துள்
துன்பம் உறுதல் இலன்.   629

*inpaththuL inpam vizaiyAn thunpaththuL
thunpam uRuthal ilan*

One who does not go after and overjoy
in happiness, grieves not in sorrow

இன்னாமை இன்பம் எனக்கொளின் ஆகும்தன்
ஒன்னார் விழையும் சிறப்பு.   630

*innAmai inpam enakkoLin aakumthan
onnAr vizaiyum siRappu*

The maturity of mind to feel happy, even in
adversity, gains the esteem of adversaries

64. அமைச்சு
amaichchu
MINISTERING (COUNCIL IN STATE)
(THE QUALITIES, FACULTIES, CHARACTER AND SKILLS REQUIRED OF MINISTERS OF COUNCIL IN STATE)

கருவியும் காலமும் செய்(வ)கையும் செய்யும்
அருவினையும் மாண்டது அமைச்சு.   631

karuviyum kAlamum sey(va)kaiyum seyyum
aruvinaiyum mANdathu amaichchu

**Right choice of time, means and modes for a worthy
cause is an attribute of an able minister**

வன்கண் குடிகாத்தல் கற்றுஅறிதல் ஆள்வினையோடு
ஐந்துடன் மாண்டது அமைச்சு.   632

vankaN kudikAththal katRu-aRithal aaLvinayoudu
ain-thudan mANdathu amaichchu

**Learning, knowledge, firmness, mastery over tasks
and protection to society add fame to a minister**

பிரித்தலும் பேணிக் கொளலும் பிரிந்தார்ப்
பொருத்தலும் வல்லது அமைச்சு.   633

piriththalum paeNik koLalum piriththArp
poruththalum vallathu amaichchu

**A shrewd minister drives a wedge among foes, cherishes
friends and attracts the parted ones to blend**

தெரிதலும் தேர்ந்து செயலும் ஒருதலையாச்
சொல்லலும் வல்லது அமைச்சு.   634

therithalum thaern-thu seyalum oruthalaiyAch
sollalum vallathu amaichchu

**A minister is capable who analyses and chooses the
best means to act, and speaks sure of the facts**

அறன்அறிந்து ஆன்றுஅமைந்த சொல்லான்எஞ் ஞான்றும்
திறன்அறிந்தான் தேர்ச்சித் துணை.   635

aRanaRin-thu aanRuamain-tha sollAnenj njAnRum
thiRanaRin-thAn thaerchith thuNai

Choose for support an efficient person with the gift of
virtuous thought and words of wisdom, as minister

மதிநுட்பம் நூலோடு உடையார்க்கு அதிநுட்பம்

யாஎள முன்னிற் பவை.   636

mathin-utpam n-UlOdu udaiyArkku athin-utpam
yAuLa munn-iR pavai

The lore of learning combined with a subtle mind
stands firm against any scheming designs of foes

செயற்கை அறிந்தக் கடைத்தும் உலகத்து

இயற்கை அறிந்து செயல்.   637

seyaRkai aRin-thak kadaiththum ulakaththu
iyaRkai aRin-thu seyal

Knowing the best method to act, learn to do things
in good nature, the way the mighty world moves

அறிகொன்று அறியான் எனினும் உறுதி

உழைஇருந்தான் கூறல் கடன்.   638

aRikonRu aRiyAn eninum uRuthi
uzaiirun-thAn kURal kadan

A minister is duty bound to warn of facts and situations,
though the ruler, in ignorance, may refute wisdom

பழுதுஎண்ணும் மந்திரியின் பக்கத்துள் தெவ்வோர்

எழுபது கோடி உறும்.   639

pazuthueNNum man-thiriyin pakkaththuL thevvour
ezupathu kOdi uRum

Foes in multi-crores are no match to a minister
who is bitter and moves sinister to damage

முறைப்படச் சூழ்ந்தும் முடிவுஇலவே செய்வர்

திறப்பாடு இலாஅ தவர்.   640

muRaippadach sUzn-thum mudivuilavae seyvar
thiRappAdu illAa thavar

The inefficient lot lack the capacity to perform
to fruition, even intelligently laid out designs

65. சொல்வன்மை
solvanmai
ELOQUENCE (COMMUNICATION SKILLS)
(SOFT AND BOLD, SWEET AND GOOD, COGENT AND IMPRESSIVE
DELIVERY THAT SPELLBINDS THE AUDIENCE AND ATTRACTS
STRANGERS ARE THE BEST AMONG COMMUNICATION SKILLS)

நாநலம் என்னும் நலன்உடைமை அந்நலம்
யாநலத்து உள்ளதூஉம் அன்று.

641

*n-An-alam ennum n-alanudaimai an-n-alam
yAn-alaththu uLLathuum il*

The quality of goodness in speech is a wealth
unmatched by any other wealth for gains

ஆக்கமும் கேடும் அதனால் வருதலால்
காத்துஓம்பல் சொல்லின்கண் சோர்வு.

642

*aakkamum kaedum athanAl varuthalaal
kAththuommpal sollinkaN sOrvu*

Softness of tongue gains fame and wealth; a foul mouth
leads to disaster; guard against sloth and folly in words

கேட்டார்ப் பிணிக்கும் தகையவாய்க் கேளாரும்
வேட்ப மொழிவதாம் சொல்.

643

*kaettArp piNikkum thakaiyavAyk kaeLArum
vaetpa mozivathAm sol*

A speech is outstanding that binds the audience
and attracts the disinterested as well, to listen

திறன்அறிந்து சொல்லுக சொல்லை அறனும்
பொருளும் அதனின்ஊங்கு இல்.

644

*thiRanaRin-thu solluka sollai aRanum
poruLum athaninuungku il*

Weigh and employ words that can perform; there is
no stronger tool to achieve virtue and wealth

சொல்லுக சொல்லைப் பிறிதுஓர்சொல் அச்சொல்லை
வெல்லும்சொல் இன்மை அறிந்து.

645

solluka sollaip piRithuoorsol achchollai
vellumsol inmai aRin-thu

Select and employ words that can win over; and
no other words can refute their strength

வேட்பத்தாம் சொல்லிப் பிறர்சொல் பயன்கோடல்
மாட்சியின் மாசுஅற்றார் கோள்.   646

vaetpaththAm sollip piRarsol payankOdal
mAtchiyin mAsuatRRAr kOL

It is enlightening to impress the listener with meaningful
words, and grasp the essence of wisdom from others

சொலல்வல்லன் சோர்விலன் அஞ்சான் அவனை
இகல்வெல்லல் யார்க்கும் அரிது.   647

solalvallAn sOrvilAn anjsAn avanai
ikalvellal yArkkum arithu

The power to drive in a message without fear or flaw
gives the rare strength to keep the foes at bay

விரைந்து தொழில்கேட்கும் ஞாலம் நிரந்தினிது
சொல்லுதல் வல்லாற்ப் பெறின்.   648

virain-thu thozilkaetkum njAlam n-iran-thinithu
solluthal vallArp peRin

The attribute of sweet and cogent speech binds
the world, to act at one's will and command

பலசொல்லக் காழுறுவர் மன்ற மாசற்ற
சிலசொல்லல் தேற்றா தவர்.   649

palasollak kAmuRuvar manRa mAsatRRa
silasollal thaetRRA thavar

One who can speak to impress with clarity, without
flaw, does not go after a pile of empty words

இணர்ஊழ்த்தும் நாறா மலர்அனையர் கற்றது
உணர விரித்துஉரையா தார்.   650

iNaruuzn-thum n-ARA malaranaiyar katRRathu
uNara viriththuuraiyA thAr

As a bunch of flowers with beauty, without fragrance,
inability to disseminate knowledge, does not adore

66. வினைத்தூய்மை
vinaith thUymai
PURITY OF ACTION

(IN PURSUING AN OBJECT , IN EXECUTING A MISSION, PURITY OF
MEANS IS AS IMPORTANT AS THE GOALS. THIS IS A CONCEPT UNIQUE,
EMPHASISED BY THE ETHICS OF ANCIENT THAMIZH CULTURE)

துணைநலம் ஆக்கம் தருஉம் வினைநலம்
வேண்டிய எல்லாம் தரும்.　　　　651

thuNain-alam aakkam tharUum vinain-alam
vaeNdiya ellAm tharum

Good companionship aids creativity; purity of action
for worthy ends, fulfills desires in good measure

என்றும் ஒருவுதல் வேண்டும் புகழொடு
நன்றி பயவா வினை.　　　　652

enRum oruvuthal vaeNdum pukazodu
n-anRi payavA vinai

Actions that do not gain fame or good achievements
should be always despised at any cost

ஓஓதல் வேண்டும் ஒளிமாழ்கும் செய்வினை
ஆஅதும் என்று மவர்.　　　　653

Ooothal vaeNdum oLimAzkum seyvinai
Aaathum ennu mavar

One who aspires to grow up in worldly esteem
should disdain actions that dim one's fame

இடுக்கண் படினும் இளிவந்த செய்யார்
நடுக்குஅற்ற காட்சி யவர்.　　　　654

idukkaN padinum iLivan-tha seyyAr
n-adukkuatRRa kAtchi avar

Clarity and unwavering strength of mind save us from
demeaning acts, whatever the obstacles or mishaps

எற்றுஎன்று இரங்குவ செய்யற்க செய்வானேல்
மற்றுஅன்ன செய்யாமை நன்று.　　　　655

etRRuenRu irangkuva seyyaRka seyvAnael
matRRuanna seyyAmai n-anRu

Be cautious to avoid hasty acts to regret later; if
helpless, safeguard against their recurrence

ஈன்றாள் பசிகாண்பான் ஆயினும் செய்யற்க

சான்றோர் பழிக்கும் வினை.　　　　　　　**656**

eenRAL pasikANpAn aayinum seyaRka
sAnROr pazikkum vinai

Even in the face of painful hunger of one's own mother,
the virtuous do not act in ways despised by society

பழிமலைந்து எய்திய ஆக்கத்தின் சான்றோர்

கழிநல் குரவே தலை.　　　　　　　**657**

pazimalin-thu eythiya aakkaththin sAnROr
kazin-al kuravae thalai

Hoarded gains on a pile of vices are worse
than pinching poverty, to the virtuous wise

கடிந்த கடிந்துஒழார் செய்தார்க்கு அவைதாம்

முடிந்தாலும் பீழை தரும்.　　　　　　　**658**

kadin-tha kadin-thuorAr seythArkku avaithAm
mudin-thAlum peezai tharum

Keep off from forbidden and unworthy deeds;
their fleeting gains lead to lasting regrets

அழக்கொண்ட எல்லாம் அழப்போம் இழப்பினும்

பிற்பயக்கும் நற்பா லவை.　　　　　　　**659**

azakkoNda ellAm azappOm izappinum
piRpayakkum n-aRpA lavai

Gains extracted from tears go down the drain weeping;
fair means, though halting, lead to enduring virtues

சலத்தால் பொருள்செய்தே மார்த்தல் பசுமண்

கலத்துள்நீர் பெய்துஇரீஇ யற்று.　　　　　　　**660**

salaththAl poruLseythae mArththal pasumaN
kalaththuLn-eer peythuirIi yatRRu

A guilty conscience on a devious path to gather wealth
is as vain as water in a raw clay pot, to preserve

15

67. வினைத்திட்பம்
vinaith thitpam
FIRMNESS OF ACTION
(STRENGTH OF DEEDS)
(RESOLUTE, DETERMINED AND BOLD STEPS
ARE THE STRENGTH OF DEEDS)

வினைத்திட்பம் என்பது ஒருவன் மனத்திட்பம்
மற்றைய எல்லாம் பிற. 　　　　　661

vinaiththitpam enpathu oruvan manaththitpam
matRRaiya ellAm piRa

**Strength of mind has the power to succeed; in its
absence all other strengths falter and fail**

ஊறுஒரால் உற்றபின் ஒல்காமை இவ்விரண்டின்
ஆறுஎன்பர் ஆய்ந்தவர் கோள். 　　　　　662

uuRuorAl uRRapin olkAmai ivviraNdin
aaRuenpar aayn-thavar kOL

**Guard against adversities and cross obstacles with
firmness; the wise abide by these cardinal principles**

கடைக்கொட்கச் செய்தக்கது ஆண்மை இடைக்கொட்கின்
எற்றா விழுமம் தரும். 　　　　　663

kadaikkotkach seythakkathu aaNmai idaikkotkin
etRRA vizumam tharum

**Strength of mind fulfills an act to perfection; work
delayed or exposed midway ends in peril**

சொல்லுதல் யார்க்கும் எளிய அரியவாம்
சொல்லிய வண்ணம் செயல். 　　　　　664

solluthal yArkkum eLiya ariyavAm
soliya vaNNam seyal

**It is easily said how best to do a job; the responsibility
to perform well and fulfill, is hard all the way**

வீறுஎய்தி மாண்டார் வினைத்திட்பம் வேந்தன்கண்
ஊறுஎய்தி உள்ளப் படும். 　　　　　665

veeRueythi mANdAr vinaththitpam vaen-thankaN
uuRueythi uLLap padum

The ruler has all the praise for the valour of those
who act and succeed in heroic deeds

எண்ணிய எண்ணியாங்கு எய்துப எண்ணியார்
திண்ணியர் ஆகப் பெறின்.   666

eNNiya eNNiyAngku eythuvar eNNiyAr
thiNNiyar aakap peRin

Total involvement in a task and the will-power to
perform leads to success the way one targets

உருவுகண்டு எள்ளாமை வேண்டும் உருள்பெருந்தேர்க்கு
அச்சாணி அன்னார் உடைத்து.   667

uruvukaNdu eLLAmai veNdum uruLperun-thaerkku
achchANi annAr udaiththu

Do not ridicule the figure or form of a person; linch-pins
keep in position the big temple car wheels on the move

கலங்காது கண்ட வினைக்கண் துளங்காது
தூக்கம் கடிந்து செயல்.   668

kalangkAthu kaNda vinaikkaN thuLangkAthu
thUkkam kadin-thu seyal

Clarity of thought sans confusion or hesitation,
gives strength to an act to succeed well

துன்பம் உறவரினும் செய்க துணிவுஆற்றி
இன்பம் பயக்கும் வினை.   669

thunpam uRavarinum seyka thuNivuaatRRi
inpam payakkum vinai

Though beset with pains, good acts performed with the
strength of courage, can lead to enduring gains

எனைத்திட்பம் எய்தியக் கண்ணும் வினைத்திட்பம்
வேண்டாரை வேண்டாது உலகு.   ·670

enaiththitpam eythiyak kaNNum vinaiththitpam
vaeNdArai vaeNdAthu ulaku

The world cares not those who lack will-power to act;
even in the face of other strengths at their command

68. வினைசெயல்வகை
vinai seyalvakai
MODE OF ACTION (WAYS TO PERFORM)
(WAYS TO PERFORM DUTIES AND AVOCATIONS)

சூழ்ச்சி முடிவு துணிவுஎய்தல் அத்துணிவு
தாழ்ச்சியுள் தங்குதல் தீது.

*sUzhchchi mudivu thuNivueythal aththuNivu
thAzhchchiyuL thangkuthal theethu*

**Due deliberations and wise counsel lead to strong
resolve; delays in action thereafter entail harm**

671

தூங்குக தூங்கிச் செயற்பால தூங்கற்க
தூங்காது செய்யும் வினை.

*thUngkuka thUngkich seyaRpAla thUngkaRka
thUngkAthu seyyum vinai*

**Delay does not matter on acts that have to proceed
cautiously; hurry up tasks that demand quick action**

672

ஒல்லும்வாய் எல்லாம் வினைநன்றே ஒல்லாக்கால்
செல்லும்வாய் நோக்கிச் செயல்.

*ollumvAy ellAm vinain-anRae ollAkkAl
sellumvAy n-Okich seyal*

**It is wise to act in a manner feasible in time and
method; or else seek viable alternatives**

673

வினைபகை என்றுஇரண்டின் எச்சம் நினையுங்கால்
தீயெச்சம் போலத் தெறும்.

*vinaipakai enRuiraNdin echcham n-inaiungkAl
thee-echcham pOlath theRum*

**A fire not put out fully may flare up any time; a deed or
a foe not done to completion, are potential harmers**

674

பொருள்கருவி காலம் வினைஇடனென்று ஐந்தும்
இருள்தீர எண்ணிச் செயல்.

*poruLkaruvi kAlam vinaiidanodu ain-thum
iruLtheera eNNich seyal*

675

While pursuing a task, be clear on its nature, dimension, the place, time and means to achieve gains

முடிவும் இடையூறும் முற்றியாங்கு எய்தும்
படுபயனும் பார்த்துச் செயல்.   676

mudivum idaiyURum mutRRiyAngku eythum
padupayanum pArththuch seyal

Judge well the ultimate objective, likely hindrance and benefits on completion, before venturing on a task

செய்வினை செய்வான் செயல்முறை அவ்வினை
உள்ளறிவான் உள்ளம் கொளல்.   677

seyvinai seyvAn seyalmuRai avvinai
uLLaRivAn uLLam koLal

Learn from experts on the job the intricacies of it and be sure of the ways to push it to fruition

வினையால் வினையாக்கிக் கோடல் நனைகவுள்
யானையால் யானையாத் தற்று.   678

vinaiyAl vinaiyAkik kOdal n-anaikavuL
yAnaiyAl yAnayAth thatRRu

Catch a tusker by employing a trained tusker; achieve a deed by purposefully manoeuvring the tasks

நட்டார்க்கு நல்ல செயலின் விரைந்ததே
ஒட்டாரை ஒட்டிக் கொளல்.   679

n-attArkku n-alla seyalin virain-thae
ottArai ottik koLal

It is important to befriend a potential foe first and foremost, faster than helping a friend in need

உறைசிறியார் உள்நடுங்கல் அஞ்சிக் குறைபெறின்
கொள்வர் பெரியார்ப் பணிந்து.   680

uRaisiRiyar uLn-adungkal anjsik kuRaipeRin
koLvar periyArp paNin-thu

When you are weak against a prospective foe, it is wise to join a capable and dependable ally to match

69. தூது
thuuthu
EMBASSY (ENVOY, EMISSARY)
(AN ENVOY OR EMISSARY WHO PORTS THE MESSAGES AND
EDICTS OF HIS STATE TO AN ALIEN STATE IN AN IMPRESSIVE
AND CONVINCING MANNER TO WIN LAURELS ON BOTH SIDES)

அன்புடைமை ஆன்ற குடிப்பிறத்தல் வேந்தவாம்
பண்புடைமை தூதுரைப்பான் பண்பு.　　681

*anpudaimai aanRa kudippiRaththal vaen-thavAm
paNpudaimai thUthuraippAn paNpu*

Lovable, worthy social stature, and courteous to impress
the rulers are essential traits of a true ambassador

அன்புஅறிவு ஆராய்ந்த சொல்வன்மை தூதுஉரைப்பார்க்கு
இன்றி அமையாத மூன்று.　　682

*anpuaRivu arAyn-tha solvanmai thUthu-uraippArkku
inRi amaiyAtha mUnRu*

Friendliness, knowledge and cultivated eloquence are
prerequisites for the success of any envoy

நூலாருள் நூல்வல்லன் ஆகுதல் வேலாருள்
வென்றி வினைஉரைப்பான் பண்பு.　　683

*n-UlAruL n-Ulvallan aakuthal vaelAruL
venRi vinaiuraippAn paNpu*

The wise among the learned are apt to lie abroad
as successful ambassadors for their country

அறிவுஉரு ஆராய்ந்த கல்விஇம் மூன்றன்
செறிவுஉடையான் செல்க வினைக்கு.　　684

*aRivu-uRu aarAyn-tha kalviim mUnRan
seRivu-udaiyAn selka vinaikku*

Good form, purposeful learning and knowledge with
depth of perception make fit to shoulder a tough task

தொகச்சொல்லித் தூவாத நீக்கி நகச்சொல்லி
நன்றி பயப்பதாம் தூது.　　685

thokachcholli thUvAtha n-eekki n-akachcholli
n-anRi payappathAm thUthu

An ambassador's winsome ways impress by pleasant and
concise words taking care to avoid the inept and harsh

கற்றுக்கண் அஞ்சான் செலச்சொல்லிக் காலத்தால்
தக்கது அறிவதாம் தூது. 686

katRRukkaN anjsAn selachchollik kAlaththAl
thakkathu aRivathAm thUthu

Bold and convincing ways to put across facts and ideas
with a sense of time and place, are feats laudable

கடன்அறிந்து காலம் கருதி இடன்அறிந்து
எண்ணி உரைப்பான் தலை. 687

kadanaRin-thu kAlam karuthi idanaRin-thu
eNNi uraippAn thalai

Awareness about duty of mission, opportune time and
place enable an emissary to excel in expositions

தூய்மை துணைமை துணிவுஉடைமை இம்மூன்றின்
வாய்மை வழிஉரைப்பான் பண்பு. 688

thUymai thuNaimai thuNivu-udaimai immUnRin
vAymai vaziuraippAn paNpu

Boldness, purity of thought and a helpful disposition
are desirable faculties and attributes of an envoy

விடுமாற்றம் வேந்தர்க்கு உரைப்பான் வடுமாற்றம்
வாய்சோரா வன்க ணவன். 689

vidumAtRRam vEn-tharkku uraippAn vadumAtRRam
vAysOrA vanka Navan

An envoy who acts with flawless courage and conviction
is the best to port a ruler's message to other lands

இறுதி பயப்பினும் எஞ்சாது இறைவற்கு
உறுதி பயப்பதாம் தூது. 690

iRuthi payappinum enjsAthu iRavaRku
uRuthi payappathAm thUthu

The bold envoy braves his life with determination
to safeguard the ruler's interests at any cost

70. மன்னரைச் சேர்ந்து ஒழுகல்
mannaraich chaern-thu ozukal
COMPANY OF THE RULER
(HUMAN RELATIONS - INTERACTING WITH PEOPLE)
(HUMAN RELATIONS ASPECTS OF INTERACTION AMONG PEOPLE;
ESP. PRECAUTIONS ESSENTIAL FOR THOSE WHO HAVE TO MOVE
WITH THOSE IN POWER)

அகலாது அணுகாது தீக்காய்வார் போல்க
இகல்வேந்தர்ச் சேர்ந்துஒழுகு வார்.　　　691

akalAthu aNukAthu theekkAyvAr pOlka
ikalvaen-tharch saern-thuozuku vAr

Neither be too close or too far to a fire place in the
cold; same caution is essential to work for a ruler

மன்னர் விழைப விழையாமை மன்னரான்
மன்னிய ஆக்கம் தரும்.　　　692

mannar vizaipa vizaiyAmai mannarAn
manniya akkam tharum

For lasting favours and position, do not go after things
that are the ruler's favourite and fond ones

போற்றின் அரியவை போற்றல் கடுத்தபின்
தேற்றுதல் யார்க்கும் அரிது.　　　693

pOtRRin ariyavai pOtRRal kaduththapin
thaetRuthal yArkkum arithu

Be wary of even small defaults, and safeguard
against mistrust that will be hard to erase

செவிச்சொல்லும் சேர்ந்த நகையும் அவித்துஒழுகல்
ஆன்ற பெரியார் அகத்து.　　　694

sevichchollum saern-tha n-akaiyum aviththuozukal
aanRa periyAr akaththu

Eagerness to be close to ears, and smiling in chorus are
to be avoided while moving with people of eminence

எப்பொருளும் ஓரார் தொடரார்மற்று அப்பொருளை
விட்டக்கால் கேட்க மறை.　　　695

epporuLUm oorAr thodarArmatRRu apporuLai
vittakkAl kaetka maRai

Peeping from behind inquisitively to probe secrets is
bad; wait in patience for due disclosures by ruler

குறிப்புஅறிந்து காலம் கருதி வெறுப்புஇல
வேண்டுப வேட்பச் சொல்.   696

kuRippuaRin-thu kAlam karuthi veRuppuila
vaeNdupa vaetpach solal

Discerning moods and choosing time, tell the ruler in a
pleasant way, what he is keen on, avoiding dislikes

வேட்பன சொல்லி வினையில எஞ்ஞான்றும்
கேட்பினும் சொல்லா விடல்.   697

vaetpana solli vinaiyila enjnjAnRum
kaetpinum sollA vidal

Speak on matters important, the ruler is anxious to
know, skillfully keeping off things that are futile

இளையர் இ(ன்)னமுறையர் என்றுஇகழார் நின்ற
ஒளியோடு ஒழுகப் படும்.   698

iLaiyar i(n)namuRaiyar enRuikazAr n-inRa
oLiyOdu ozukap padum

Do not slight the ruler as an youngster or as kin; learn
to respect what is there, in light and might

கொளப்பட்டேம் என்றுஎண்ணிக் கொள்ளாத செய்யார்
துளக்குஅற்ற காட்சி யவர்.   699

koLappattaem endRueNNik koLLAtha seyyAr
thuLakkuatRRa kAtchi yavar

The enlightened and unblemished in positions of power
dare not misuse their privileges to baser ends

பழயம் எனக்கருதிப் பண்புஅல்ல செய்யும்
கெழுதகைமை கேடு தரும்.   700

pazayam enakkaruthip paNpualla seyyum
kezuthakaimai kaedu tharum

Unworthy acts under the privilege of traditional
friendship, besmirch and lead to ruinous woes

71. குறிப்பறிதல்
kuRippu aRithal
JUDGING BY LOOKS (READING THE MIND)
(READING AND EXPRESSING THE MIND THRO' SYMPTOMS OF THE FACE AND OTHER PARTS)

கூறாமை நோக்கிக் குறிப்புஅறிவான் எஞ்ஞான்றும்
மாறாநீர் வையக்கு அணி.　　　　　　**701**

kURAmai n-Okkik kuRippuaRivAn enjnjAnRum
mARAn-eer vaiyakku aNi

When words are silent the skill to read the
mind by looks, adores this noble world

ஐயப் படாஅது அகத்தது உணர்வானைத்
தெய்வத்தோடு ஒப்பக் கொளல்.　　　　　　**702**

aiyap padAathu akaththathu uNarvAnaith
theyvaththOdu oppak koLal

The power to picturise feelings of the mind through the
eyes, with clarity, is a rare divine like prowess

குறிப்பிற் குறிப்புஉணர் வாரை உறுப்பினுள்
யாது கொடுத்தும் கொளல்.　　　　　　**703**

kuRippin kuRippu-uNar vArai uRuppinuL
yaathu koduththum koLal

One who senses others' mind with his eyes deserves
a place of importance to match his skills

குறித்தது கூறாமைக் கொள்வாரோடு ஏனை
உறுப்போர் அனையரால் வேறு.　　　　　　**704**

kuRiththathu kURAmai koLvArOdu eenai
uRuppOr anaiyarAl vaeRu

The wisdom of those who scan the depth of
other's mind is far ahead of ordinary humans

குறிப்பிற் குறிப்புணரா ஆயின் உறுப்பினுள்
என்ன பயத்தவோ கண்.　　　　　　**705**

.kuRippiR kuRippuNarA aayin uRuppinuL
enna payaththavO kaN

Of what avail are the eyes among senses if they
cannot read a mind through symptoms on the face

அடுத்தது காட்டும் பளிங்குபோல் நெஞ்சம்
கடுத்தது காட்டும் முகம். 706

*aduththathu kAttum paLingkupOl n-enjsam
kaduththathu kAttum mukam*

The marble is a mirror of times yore to reflect images;
face is better than a mirror in reflecting the mind

முகத்தின் முதுக்குஎ றைந்தது உண்டோ உவப்பினும்
காயினும் தான்முந் துறும். 707

*mukaththin muthukku-uRain-thathu uNdO uvappinum
kAyinum thAnmun- thuRum*

The face is a master craftsman, as the first to
exhibit joys and sorrows throbbing the mind

முகம்நோக்கி நிற்க அமையும் அகம்நோக்கி
உற்றது உணர்வார்ப் பெறின். 708

*mukamn-Okki n-iRka amaiyum akamn-Okki
uRRathu unarvArp peRin*

Just a facial appearance is enough to judge, for
those endowed with the powers of mind reading

பகைமையும் கேண்மையும் கண்ணுரைக்கும் கண்ணின்
வகைமை உணர்வார்ப் பெறின். 709

*pakaimaiyum kaeNmaiyum kaNNuraikkum kaNNin
vakaimai uNarvArp peRin*

Those conversant with the language of facial signs
easily gauge the likes and dislikes of other's mind

நுண்ணியம் என்பார் அளக்கும்கோல் காணுங்கால்
கண்ணல்லது இல்லை பிற. 710

*n-uNNiyAr enpAr aLakkumkOl kANungkAl
kaNNallathu illai piRa*

The eyes are precision measuring instruments of
the subtler ones who can gauge other's mind

72. அவை அறிதல்
avai aRithal
ASSESSING THE AUDIENCE
(COMPREHENSION OF AN ASSEMBLY)

(COMPREHENDING THE QUALITY OF AN ASSEMBLY, ITS ENVIRONMENT,
AND THE SUBJECTS ON HAND WHILE VENTURING TO SPEAK)

அவைஅறிந்து ஆராய்ந்து சொல்லுக சொல்லின்
தொகைஅறிந்த தூய்மை யவர்.   711

avaiaRin-thu aarAyn-thu solluka sollin
thokaiaRin-tha thUymai yavar

Those pure in thoughts weigh the effect of their words
and present them in a way to suit the audience

இடைதெரிந்து நன்குணர்ந்து சொல்லுக சொல்லின்
நடைதெரிந்த நன்மை யவர்.   712

idaitherin-thu n-ankuuNarn-thu solluka sollin
n-adaitherin-tha n-anmai yavar

The art of good speaking demands from the knowledgeable
judgement of words to suit time and place

அவைஅறியார் சொல்லல்மேற் கொள்பவர் சொல்லின்
வகைஅறியார் வல்லதூஉம் இல்.   713

avaiaRiyAr sollalmaeR koLpavar sollin
vakaiaRiyAr vallathUum il

Neither sensing audience, nor knowing mode of effective
delivery, speaking at length serves no purpose

ஒளியார்முன் ஒள்ளியர் ஆதல் வெளியார்முன்
வான்சுதை வண்ணம் கொளல்.   714

oLiyArmun oLLiyar aathal veLiyArmun
vAnsuthai vaNNam koLal

Brilliance and eloquence will be apt in an assembly of
the enlightened; simplicity and clarity for others

நன்றென்ற வற்றுள்ளும் நன்றே முதுவருள்
முந்து கிளவாச் செறிவு.   715

n-anRenRa vatRRuLLum n-anRae muthuvaruL
mun-thu kiLavAch serivu

The strength of mind and restraint from speaking out
ensure calm of goodness, before the elderly wise

ஆற்றின் நிலைதளர்ந்து அற்றே வியன்புலம்
ஏற்றுணர்வார் முன்னர் இழுக்கு.   716

*aatRRin n-ilaithaLarn-thu atRRae viyanpulam
eetRRuNarvAr munnar izukku*

A faltering tongue in an assembly of discerning
talent is slipping astray from a righteous path

கற்றுஅறிந்தார் கல்வி விளங்கும் கசடுஅறச்
சொல்தெரிதல் வல்லார் அகத்து.   717

*kaRRuaRin-thAr kalvi viLangkum kasaduaRach
soltherithal vallAr akaththu*

The talent to choose flawless words for effective
delivery, is the hallmark of scholarly minds

உணர்வது உடையார்முன் சொல்லல் வளர்வதன்
பாத்தியுள் நீர்சொரிந்து அற்று.   718

*uNarvathu udaiyArmun sollal vaLarvathan
pAththiyuL n-eersorin-thu atRRu*

Speaking to a receptive and understanding audience
is like watering for the growth of healthy plants

புல்அவையுள் பொச்சாந்தும் சொல்லற்க நல்அவையுள்
நன்கு செலச்சொல்லு வார்.   719

*pullavaiyuL pochchAn-thum sollaRka n-allavaiyuL
n-anku selachchollu vAr*

Those who can impress a knowledgeable audience
do not come forward to speak to a motely crowd

அங்கணத்துள் உக்க அமிழ்துஅற்றால் தங்கணத்தர்
அல்லார்முன் கோட்டி கொளல்.   720

*angkaNaththuL ukka amizthuatRRAl thangkaNaththar
allArmun kOtti koLal*

The attempt to argue in a situation not congenial for
reason or sense, is like spilling nectar on the floor

73. அவை அஞ்சாமை
avai anjsAmai
FEARLESSNESS BEFORE AN ASSEMBLY
(WEIGHING THE IMPACT WORDS AND EXPRESSING THEM WITHOUT
FEAR OR FAVOUR IN AN IMPRESSIVE AND CONVINCING MANNER)

வகைஅறிந்து வல்லவை வாய்ச்சோரார் சொல்லின்
தொகைஅறிந்த தூய்மை யவர்.   **721**

vakaiaRin-thu vallavai vAysOrAr sollin
thokaiaRin-tha thUymai yavar

Strength of pure knowledge fails not the power of words,
and a mode of delivery to suit the mood of council

கற்றாருள் கற்றார் எனப்படுவர் கற்றார்முன்
கற்ற செலச்சொல்லு வார்.   **722**

katRAruL katRAr enappaduvar katRArmun
katRRa selachchollu vAr

The best among scholars are those who are capable of
holding to attention an assembly of the learned

பகையகத்துச் சாவார் எளியர் அரியர்
அவையகத்து அஞ்சா தவர்.   **723**

pakaiyakaththuch sAvAr eLiyar ariyar
avaiyakaththu anjsA thavar

Heroes brave death in battle; those who fearlessly
succeed in facing wise council are rare

கற்றார்முன் கற்ற செலச்சொல்லித் தாம்கற்ற
மிக்காருள் மிக்க கொளல்.   **724**

katRRArmun katRRa selachchollith thAmkatRRa
mikkAruL mikka koLal

Scholars who gain acceptance in wise councils have
the acumen to grasp the mature wisdom of savants

ஆற்றின் அளவுஅறிந்து கற்க அவையஞ்சா
மாற்றம் கொடுத்தல் பொருட்டு.   **725**

aatRRin aLavuaRin-thu kaRka avaianjsA
mAtRRam koduththal poruttu

Learn the logic and substance of good speaking, to
counter and convince an assembly by arguments

வாளொடுஎன் வன்கண்ணர் அல்லார்க்கு நூலொடுஎன்
நுண்ணவை அஞ்சு பவர்க்கு.   726

*vALoduen vankaNNar allArkku n-Uloduen
n-uNNavai anjsu pavarkku*

A sword is a toy in the hands of the weak, books of
knowledge are burden to one who shys a subtle assembly

பகையகத்துப் பேடிகை ஒள்வாள் அவையகத்து
அஞ்சும் அவன்கற்ற நூல்.   727

*pakaiyakaththup paedikai oLvAL avaiyakaththu
anjsum avankatRRa n-Ul*

A coward with a sword on the field and a scholar
shying on assembly of the wise, are futile

பல்லவை கற்றும் பயமிலரே நல்லவையுள்
நன்கு செலச்சொல்லா தார்.   728

*pallavai katRRum payamilarae n-allavaiyuL
n-anku selachchollA thAr*

Knowledge deep and wise is of no avail to those
who cannot impress an assembly of the learned

கல்லா தவரின் கடையென்ப கற்றுஅறிந்தும்
நல்லார் அவையஞ்சு வார்.   729

*kallA thavarin kadaienpa katRRuaRin-thum
n-allAr avaianjsu vAr*

The learned who dread to face a sensible assembly
are lowest in the esteem of the unlettered

உளர்எனினும் இல்லாரொடு ஒப்பர் களன்அஞ்சிக்
கற்ற செலச்சொல்லா தார்.   730

*uLareninum illArodu oppar kaLananjsik
katRRa selachchollA thAr*

Those who dare not assert boldly in a debate what
they know for sure, breathe but stay still like the dead

74. நாடு (நாட்டு வளம்)
n-Adu (n-Attu vaLam)
COUNTRY (AND ITS PEOPLE)

(A LAND ENDOWED WITH NATURAL RESOURCES AND ITS
ENTREPRENEURIAL PEOPLE MAKE IT STRONG AND RICH
WITHOUT NEED TO LOOK FOR AID FROM OUTSIDE)

தள்ளா விளையுளும் தக்காரும் தாழ்விலாச்
செல்வரும் சேர்வது நாடு.　　　　　　　　731

thaLLA viLaiyuLum thakkArum thAzvilAch
selvarum saervathu n-Adu

Lands of unfailing yields, worthy society and growing
wealth unite to make a country strong and stable

பெரும்பொருளால் பெட்டக்கது ஆகி அருங்கேட்டான்
ஆற்ற விளைவது நாடு.　　　　　　　　732

perumporuLAl pettakkathu aaki arungkaettAn
aatRRa viLaivathu n-Adu

A country with a treasure of wealth and bountiful crops
lures and keeps its people, free from the pain of want

பொறைஒருங்கு மேல்வருங்கால் தாங்கி இறைவற்கு
இறைஒருங்கு நேர்வது நாடு.　　　　　　　733

poRaiorungku maelvarungkAl thAngki iRaivaRku
iRaiorungku n-aervathu n-Adu

Citizens of a shining land aid the ruler with taxes, materials
and help to bear pressing burdens of State

உறுபசியும் ஓவாப் பிணியும் செறுபகையும்
சேராது இயல்வது நாடு.　　　　　　　734

uRupasiyum oovAp piNiyum seRupakaiyum
saerAthu iyalvathu n-Adu

A country marches on, which is not affected by
famines, plagues and fury of the foes

பல்குழுவும் பாழ்செய்யும் உட்பகையும் வேந்துஅலைக்கும்
கொல்குறும்பும் இல்லது நாடு.　　　　　　735

palkuzuvum pAzseyyum utpakaiym vaen-thualaikkum
kolkuRumpum illathu n-Adu

The tranquility of a country is safe, when there are no
dissenting sects, ruinous traitors or terrorist tormentors

கேடுஅறியாக் கெட்ட இடத்தும் வளம்குன்றா
நாடுஎன்ப நாட்டின் தலை.   736

kaeduaRiyAk ketta idaththum vaLamkunRA
n-Aduenpa n-Attin thalai

A country stands tall which has inherent strength to contain
calamities, and rebuild with growing strength

இருபுனலும் வாய்ந்த மலையும் வருபுனலும்
வல்லரணும் நாட்டிற்கு உறுப்பு.   737

irupunalum vAyntha malaiyum varupunalum
vallaraNum n-AttiRku uRuppu

Where hills and dales, streams and springs adorn and
strong forts guard, the country prospers in peace

பிணிஇன்மை செல்வம் விளைவுஇன்பம் ஏமம்
அணியென்ப நாட்டிற்குஇவ் வைந்து.   738

piNiinmai selvam viLaivu-inpam aemam
aNienpa n-AttiRkuiv vain-thu

Health, wealth, bountiful yields, delight and defence
are five jewels adorning a beautiful land

நாடுஎன்ப நாடா வளத்தன நாடுஅல்ல
நாட வளம்தரு நாடு.   739

n-Aduenpa n-AdA vaLaththana n-Adualla
n-Ada vaLamtharu n-Adu

A country relying on internal strength without undue
exertion or outside dependence grows in respect

ஆங்குஅமைவு எய்தியக் கண்ணும் பயமின்றே
வேந்துஅமைவு இல்லாத நாடு.   740

aangkuamaivu eythiyak kaNNum payaminRae
vaen-thuamaivu illAtha n-Adu

Endowed with all other attributes in full, but without
a capable ruler, a country languishes in peril

75. அரண்
araN
FORTRESS OF SAFETY
(IS SET IN NATURAL SURROUNDINGS GUARDED BY MOUNTAINS,
FORESTS, CANALS AND STREAMS AND CUSTOM BUILT IN STRENGTH)

ஆற்று பவர்க்கும் அரண்பொருள் அஞ்சித்தற்
போற்று பவர்க்கும் பொருள்.　　741

aatRRu pavarkkum araNporuL anjsiththaR
pOtRRu pavarkkum poruL

A fortress is a place of safety to those who operate
on offensive on the foe, or retreat in defence

மணிநீரும் மண்ணும் மலையும் அணிநிழல்
காடும் உடையது அரண்.　　742

maNin-eerum maNNum malaiyum aNin-izal
kAdum udaiyathu araN

A fort paramount is set among mountains, contained
by streams and canals and covered by thick forests

உயர்வுஅகலம் திண்மை அருமைஇந் நான்கின்
அமைவுஅரண் என்றுஉரைக்கும் நூல்.　　743

uyarvuakalam thiNmai arumaiin n-Ankin
amaivuaraN enRuuraikkum n-Ul

High, wide and strong, hard to penetrate, stands
a fort, ideally set to builders code of construction

சிறுகாப்பின் பேரிடத்தது ஆகி உறுபகை
ஊக்கம் அழிப்பது அரண்.　　744

siRukAppin paeridaththathu aaki uRupakai
uukkam azippathu araN

Easy to hold, ample in space, a fort of impregnable
strength spoils the might of a determined foe

கொளற்குஅரிதாய்க் கொண்டகூழ்த்து ஆகி அகத்தார்
நிலைக்குஎளிதாம் நீரது அரண்.　　745

koLaRkuarithAyk koNdakUzthu aaki akaththAr
n-ilaikkueLithAm n-eerathu araN

Hard of access, ample in food stores, facile for the forces
to operate from within, sustain fame of a fort

எல்லாப் பொருளும் உடைத்தாய் இடத்துஉதவும்
நல்ஆள் உடையது அரண். **746**

*ellAp poruLum udaiththAy idaththu-uthavum
n-allAL udaiyathu araN*

A fort built-in safety, where there are adequate
provisions and arms for the army and alert inmates

முற்றியும் முற்றாது எறிந்தும் அறைப்படுத்தும்
பற்றற்கு அரியது அரண். **747**

*mutRRiyum mutRRAthu eRin-thum aRaippaduththum
patRRaRku ariyathu araN*

Besiege, dart in strength or in treachery, a real
fort holds on in undaunted strength

முற்றாற்றி முற்றி யவரையும் பற்றாற்றிப்
பற்றியார் வெல்வது அரண். **748**

*mutRRARRi mutRRi yavaraiyum patRRARRip
patRRiyAr velvathu araN*

A fort of inherent strength, with arms and army,
frustrates encircling foes in wait, and wins them

முனைமுகத்து மாற்றலர் சாய வினைமுகத்து
வீறுஎய்தி மாண்டது அரண். **749**

*munaimukaththu mAtRRalar sAya vinaimukaththu
veeRueythi mANdathu araN*

A fort of facility for its forces to operate on the field
from strength of its safety, to foil foes, is glory built

எனைமாட்சித்து ஆகியக் கண்ணும் வினைமாட்சி
இல்லார்கண் இல்லது அரண். **750**

*enaimAtchiththu aakiyak kaNNUm vinaimAtchi
illArkaN illathu araN*

Howsoever grand in name and fame, a fort is not safe
if the people inside are inefficient

76. பொருள் செயல்வகை
poruL seyalvakai
MEANS OF WEALTH

(WEALTH IS A WHEEL THAT ROTATES. THE WAYS AND MEANS OF
MAKING, PROTECTING AND USING WEALTH ARE IMPORTANT. LOVE IS
THE CHILD OF GRACE, NURSED BY THE NANNY OF WEALTH)

பொருளால் லவரைப் பொருளாகச் செய்யும்
பொருளல்லது இல்லை பொருள்.　　　　751

poruLal lavaraip poruLakach seyyum
poruLallathu illai poruL

Wealth, sought and cultivated, that alone makes
and builds the worthless into worthy stuff

இல்லாரை எல்லாரும் எள்ளுவர் செல்வரை
எல்லாரும் செய்வர் சிறப்பு.　　　　752

illArai ellArum eLLUvar selvarai
ellArum saeyvar siRappu

The world has no respect of the multitude of
have-nots; the wealthy rise to be held in praise

பொருள்என்னும் பொய்யா விளக்கம் இருள்அறுக்கும்
எண்ணிய தேயத்துச் சென்று.　　　　753

poruLennum poyyA viLakkam iruLaRukkum
eNNiya theeyaththuch senRu

Wealth is held as an unfailing light to guide and
reach places, by lifting the darkness of want

அறன்ஈனும் இன்பமும் ஈனும் திறன்அறிந்து
தீதுஇன்றி வந்த பொருள்.　　　　754

aRaneenum inpamum eenum thiRanaRin-thu
theethuinRi van-tha poruL

Wealth acquired in thrift by fair means, goes
to build virtue and bliss in goodness

அருளொடும் அன்பொடும் வாராப் பொருளாக்கம்
புல்லார் புரள விடல்.　　　　755

aruLodum anpodum vArAp poruLaakkam
pullAr puraLa vidal

Riches gained ignoring fond love, virtuous
grace are to be despised as disgrace

உறுபொருளும் உல்கு பொருளும்தன் ஒன்னார்த்
தெறுபொருளும் வேந்தன் பொருள்.   756

uRupoRuLum ulku poruLumthan onnArth
theRuporuLum vaen-than poruL

Compensation for war damages, duties and levies are
sources of funds for the ruler to administer the State

அருள்என்னும் அன்புஈன் குழவி பொருள்என்னும்
செல்வச் செவிலியால் உண்டு.   757

aruLennum anpuiin kuzavi poruLennum
selvach seviliyAl uNdu

Graciousness is the off-spring of kind love nourished
by the foster mother of cherished wealth

குன்றுஎறி யானைப்போர் கண்டுஅற்றால் தன்கைத்துஒன்று
உண்டாகச் செய்வான் வினை.   758

kunRuaeRi yAnaippOr kaNduatRRAl thankaiththuonRu
uNdAkach seyvAn vinai

Endeavouring a task with earned fund support is like
witnessing from hilltop, jungle tuskers locking horns

செய்க பொருளைச் செறுநர் செருக்குஅறுக்கும்
எஃகுஅதனின் கூரியது இல்.   759

seyka poruLaich seRun-ar serukkuaRukkum
eqkuathanin kUriyathu il

Make wealth in plenty, that is the spear sharp
to quell the pride of a hostile foe

ஒண்பொருள் காழ்ப்ப இயற்றியார்க்கு எண்பொருள்
ஏனை இரண்டும் ஒருங்கு.   760

oNporuL kAzppa iyatRRiyArkku eNporuL
aenai iraNdum orungku

Virtue and happiness meet in rare unity where
wealth in abundance, comes in shining grace

77. படைமாட்சி
padai mAtchi
GLORY OF DEFENCE
(CHARACTER AND VALOUR OF THE PERSONNEL AND THE IMPORTANCE OF DISCIPLINE AND COHERANCE)

உறுப்புஅமைந்து ஊறுஅஞ்சா வெல்படை வேந்தன்
வெறுக்கையுள் எல்லாம் தலை.   761

*uRuppuamain-thu uuRuanjsA velpadai vaen-than
veRukkaiyuL ellAm thalai*

**An army built in winning strength, to dare impediments
is a source of supreme confidence to the ruler**

உலைவிடத்து ஊறுஅஞ்சா வன்கண் தொலைவிடத்துத்
தொல்படைக்கு அல்லால் அரிது.   762

*ulaividaththu uuRuanjsA vankaN tholaividaththuth
tholpadaikku allAl arithu*

**Daring strength to face setbacks in distress and the
will to win, are natural pride to an army of tradition**

ஒலித்தக்கால் என்னாம் உவரி எலிப்பகை
நாகம் உயிர்ப்பக் கெடும்.   763

*oliththakkAl ennAm uvari elippakai
n-Akam uyirppak kedum*

**Rat like foes in numbers roaring like waves, melt
in the face of a cobra whiff, from a mighty force**

அழிவுஇன்று அறைபோகா தாகி வழிவந்த
வன்க ணதுவே படை.   764

*azivuinRu aRaipOkA thAki vazivan-tha
vanka Nathuvae padai*

**A force with the fame of its might and courage cannot
be destroyed by the strength or stealth of a foe**

கூற்றுஉடன்று மேல்வரினும் கூடி எதிர்நிற்கும்
ஆற்றல் அதுவே படை.   765

*kUtRRuudanRu maelvarinum kUdi ethirn-iRkum
aatRRal athuvae padai*

An army rallying its forces in the strength of unity and purpose, is hardly affected by deadly attacks of a foe

மறம்மானம் மாண்ட வழிச்செலவு தேற்றம்
எனநான்கே ஏமம் படைக்கு.   **766**

maRam-mAnam mANda vazichchelavu thaetRRam
enan-Ankae aemam padaikku

Valour, honour, a folk-lore of glory and strength of leadership are safeguarding merits of a force

தார்தாங்கிச் செல்வது தானை தலைவந்த
போர்தாங்கும் தன்மை யறிந்து.   **767**

thArthAngkich selvathu thAnai thalaivan-tha
pOrthAngkum thanmai yaRin-thu

Knowing the strategy and strength of the foe, attacking in defence fetches winning laurels to an army

அடல்தகையும் ஆற்றலும் இல்னெனினும் தானை
படைத்தகையால் பாடு பெறும்.   **768**

adalthakaiyum aatRRalum ileninum thAnai
padaiththakaiyAl pAdu peRum

Though lacking in capability or performance, an army gains face and force in its formations and display

சிறுமையும் செல்லாத் துனியும் வறுமையும்
இல்லாயின் வெல்லும் படை.   **769**

siRumaiyum sellAth thuniyum vaRumaiyum
illAyin veḷḷum padai

An army that can overcome weakness in discipline and strength, sans aversion and shortages, gains will to win

நிலைமக்கள் சால உடைத்துஎனினும் தானை
தலைமக்கள் இல்வழி இல்.   **770**

n-ilaimakkaL sAla udaiththhueninum thAnai
thalaimakkaL ilvazi il

Troops with valour and stability are ineffective in the absence of a chief in command, leading to success

78. படைச்செருக்கு

(படைவீரர் ஆற்றலும் பெருமிதமும்)

padaich cherukku

PRIDE OF WARRIORS

(THE PREDOMINANCE AND EXCELLENCE OF LEADERSHIP OF
DEFENCE AND THEIR SENSE OF HEROISM AND SACRIFICE)

என்னைமுன் நில்லன்மின் தெவ்விர் பலர்என்னை
முன்நின்று கல்நின் றவர்.　　　　　　　771

ennaimun n-illanmin thevvir palarennai
munn-inRu kaln-in Ravar

Stand not against my leader, many were those
who persisted and stand in stones

கான முயல்எய்த அம்பினில் யானை
பிழைத்தவேல் ஏந்தல் இனிது.　　　　　　772

kAna muyaleytha ampinil yAnai
pizaiththavael aen-thal inithu

Darting a lance that aims at a mighty tusker is sweeter
in pride than shooting an arrow at a hare

பேராண்மை என்ப தறுகண்ஒன்று உற்றக்கால்
ஊராண்மை மற்றுஅதன் எஃகு.　　　　　773

paerANmai enpa thaRukaNonRu utRRakkAl
uuRaaNmai matRRuathan eqku

Courage is fighting with valour; its finer edge
is steely firmness to manage in distress

கைவேல் களிற்றொடு போக்கி வருபவன்
மெய்வேல் பறியா நகும்.　　　　　　774

kaivael kaLiRRodu pOkki varupavan
meyvael paRiyA n-akum

Driving a tusker on the war front flinging his lance, the
one on his chest cheers him with another chance

விழித்தகண் வேல்கொண்டு எறிய அழித்துஇமைப்பின்
ஓட்டுஅன்றோ வன்க ணவர்க்கு.　　　　　775

viziththakaN vaelkoNdu eRiya aziththuimaippin
ottuanRO vanka Navarkku

Ferocious eyes on the foe do not wink at a lance
on attack, lest they bear a blemish on valour

விழுப்புண் படாதநாள் எல்லாம் வழுக்கினுள்
வைக்கும்தன் நாளை எடுத்து.   776

vizuppuN padAthan-AL ellAm vazukkinuL
vaikkumthan n-ALai eduththu

The brave love to sustain battle wounds in a row, and
do not like to miss a day in their valiant ventures

சுழலும் இசைவேண்டி வேண்டா உயிரார்
கழல்யாப்புக் காரிகை நீர்த்து.   777

suzalum isaivaeNdi vaeNdA uyirAr
kazalyAppuk kArikai n-eerththu

The valiant who sacrifice their lives, to sustain beaming
fame, have their anklets jingling beauty in their name

உறின்உயிர் அஞ்சா மறவர் இறைவன்
செறினும்சீர் குன்றல் இலர்.   778

uRinuyir anjsA maRavar iRaivan
seRinumseer kunRal ilar

A frown from the ruler, they do not mind; heroes opt
for glory by sacrificing their lives in strife

இழைத்தது இகவாமைச் சாவாரை யாரே
பிழைத்தது ஒறுக்கிற் பவர்.   779

izaiththathu ikavAmai sAvArai yArae
pizaiththathu oRukkiR pavar

Vow to win and perish in fight; none dare to
blame, but salute their heroism in battle.

புரந்தார்கண் நீர்மல்கச் சாகிற்பின் சாக்காடு
இரந்துகோள் தக்கது உடைத்து.   780

puran-thArkaN n-eermalkach sAkiRpin sAkkAdu
iran-thukOL thakkathu udaiththu

If death is in glory to draw tears from the ruler
and foster, it is even worth seeking in alms

79. நட்பு (நட்பின் தன்மையும், சிறப்பும்)
natpu
QUALITY OF FRIENDSHIP
(THE FINER ASPECTS AND BENEFITS OF REAL AND HONEST FRIENDSHIP)

செயற்குஅரிய யாவுள நட்பின் அதுபோல்
வினைக்குஅரிய யாவுள காப்பு.   781

seyaRkuariya yAvuLa n-atpin athupOl
vinaikkuariya yAvuLa kAppu

True friendship is rare and hard to gain; once achieved
that safeguards against unpredictable woes

நிறைநீர் நீரவர் கேண்மை பிறைமதிப்
பின்நீர பேதையார் நட்பு.   782

n-iRain-eera n-eeravar kaeNmai piRaimathip
pinneera paethaiyAr n-atpu

Good friendship waxes thick and shines like a full moon;
the bad one of fools withers like a waning moon

நவில்தொறும் நூல்நயம் போலும் பயில்தொறும்
பண்புடை யாளர் தொடர்பு.   783

n-avilthoRum n-Uln-ayam pOlum payilthoRum
paNpudai yALar thodarpu

Treasure of good literature reveals riches each time
we probe; friendship grows with new dimensions of ecstasy

நகுதற் பொருட்டுஅன்று நட்டல் மிகுதிக்கண்
மேற்சென்று இடித்தற் பொருட்டு.   784

n-akuthaR poruttuanRu n-attal mikuthikkaN
maeRsenRu idiththal poruttu

Friendship is not only for pleasure and play; its moral
duty is more to caution and correct faults

புணர்ச்சி பழகுதல் வேண்டா உணர்ச்சிதான்
நட்பாம் கிழமை தரும்.   785

puNarchchi pazakuthal vaeNdA uNarchchithAn
n-atpAm kizamai tharum

Unison in sentiments flowers fellowship in friends; physical proximity or intimacy is not its prerequisite

முகம்நக நட்பது நட்புஅன்று நெஞ்சத்து
அகம்நக நட்பது நட்பு.   786

mukamn-aka n-atpathu n-atpanRu n-enjsaththu
akamn-aka n-atpathu n-atpu

A smile on the face is not always a mark of friendship; sentiment of mind is real repository of lasting ties

அழிவின் அவைநீக்கி ஆறுய்த்து அழிவின்கண்
அல்லல் உழப்பதாம் நட்பு.   787

azivin avain-eekki aaRuyththu azivinkaN
allal uzappathAm n-atpu

Saving the ship of friendship from harmful seas, piloting it to safety, sharing loads of pain are friends' duties

உடுக்கை இழந்தவன் கைபோல ஆங்கே
இடுக்கண் களைவதாம் நட்பு.   788

udukkai izan-thavan kaipOla aangkae
idukkaN kaLaivathAm n-atpu

Like the hands clasping a slipping robe by instinct, true friendship hastens to relieve distress

நட்பிற்கு வீற்றிருக்கை யாதெனில் கொட்பின்றி
ஒல்லும்வாய் ஊன்றும் நிலை.   789

n-atpiRku veetRRirukkai yAthenil kotpinRi
ollumvAy uunRum n-ilai

Real friendship sits high on firm ground, seeping its roots deep, unmindful of adversities

இனையர் இவர்எமக்கு இன்னம்யாம் என்று
புனையினும் புல்என்னும் நட்பு.   790

inaiyar ivaremakku innamyAm enRu
punaiyinum pullennum n-atpu

Boasting the nature of self and relationships mars the purity and sanctity of true friendship

80. நட்பு ஆராய்தல் (நட்புகொள்ளத் தகுதி ஆய்தல்)

n-atpu aarAythal

PROBING FOR FRIENDSHIP

(PROSPECTING, EVALUATING AND NOURISHING FRIENDSHIP TO KINSHIP AND CAMARADERIE)

நாடாது நட்டலிற் கேடுஇல்லை நட்டபின்
வீடுஇல்லை நட்புஆள் பவர்க்கு. 791

n-AdAthu n-attalin kaeduillai n-attapin
veeduillai n-atpuaaL pavarkku

Courting friendship without searching evaluation is a bad risk; redemption is scarce once friendship is held

ஆய்ந்துஆய்ந்து கொள்ளாதான் கேண்மை கடைமுறை
தான்சாம் துயரம் தரும். 792

aayn-thuaayn-thu koLLAthAn kaeNmai kadaimuRai
thAnsAm thuyaram tharum

Camaraderie accepted without deep prospecting runs the risk of grief and pain, till the end to death

குணனும் குடிமையும் குற்றமும் குன்றா
இனனும் அறிந்துயாக்க நட்பு. 793

kuNanum kudimaiyum kutRRamum kundRA
inanum aRin-thuyAkka n-atpu

Nourish companionship, having evaluated temperament, tradition, defects and strains of kinship held

குடிப்பிறந்து தன்கண் பழிநாணு வானைக்
கொடுத்தும் கொளல்வேண்டும் நட்பு. 794

kudippiRan-thu thankaN pazin-ANu vAnaik
koduththum koLalvaeNdum n-atpu

Descent from a family of noble traits, shyness to shame are qualities of friendship, worth seeking at any price

அழச்சொல்லி அல்லது இடித்து வழக்கறிய
வல்லார்நட்பு ஆய்ந்து கொளல். 795

azachcholli allathu idiththu vazakkuaRiya
vallArn-atpu aayn-thu koLal

Condemning to tears, preventing wrong deeds and
dinning in wisdom, are traits eligible for friendship

கேட்டினும் உண்டுஒர் உறுதி கிளைஞரை
நீட்டி அளப்பதோர் கோல்.   796

kaettinum uNduoor uRuthi kiLainjarai
n-eeti aLappathOr kOl

The scale to measure the depth and width of faithful
kinship, is the behaviour in a situation of crisis

ஊதியம் என்பது ஒருவற்குப் பேதையார்
கேண்மை ஒரீஇ விடல்.   797

uuthiyam enpathu oruvaRkup paethaiyar
kaeNmai oreei vidal

There are no better gains to aim than wriggling out from
companionship of fools, to save oneself from shame

உள்ளற்க உள்ளம் சிறுகுவ கொள்ளற்க
அல்லற்கண் ஆற்றுஅறுப்பார் நட்பு.   798

uLLaRka uLLam siRukuva koLLaRka
allaRkaN aatRRuaRuppAr n-atpu

Banish from the mind thoughts that degrade; depart
from friendship that deserts while drowning

கெடுங்காலைக் கைவிடுவார் கேண்மை அடுங்காலை
உள்ளினும் உள்ளம் சுடும்.   799

kedungkAlaik kaividuvAr kaeNmai adungkAlai
uLLinum uLLam sudum

Companionship of feigning friends, who betray in pain
and ruin, burns the mind even at the brink of death

மருவுக மாசற்றார் கேண்மைஒன்று ஈத்தும்
ஒருவுக ஒப்பிலார் நட்பு.   800

maruvuka mAatRRAr kaeNmaionRu yeen-thum
oruvuka oppilAr n-atpu

Camaraderie of unblemished friends is worth embracing;
unequals of baser motives are worth parting at a cost

81. பழைமை (பழமையான பாரம்பரிய நட்பு)
pazaimai
INTIMACY OF FRIENDSHIP
(AMITY OF GOOD FRIENDSHIP RIPENS INTO TRADITIONAL
INTIMACY THAT HOLDS FAST AND IS CHERISHED FOR EVER)

பழைமை எனப்படுவது யாதுஎனின் யாதும்
கிழைமையைக் கீழ்ந்திடா நட்பு.   801

pazamai enappaduvathu yAthuenin yAthum
kizamaiyaik keezn-thidA n-atpu

Ripened friendship shines in good amity, that
neither restrains nor denigrates intimacy

நட்பிற்கு உறுப்புக் கெழுதகைமை மற்றுஅதற்கு
உப்புஆதல் சான்றோர் கடன்.   802

n-atpiRku uRuppuk kezuthakaimai matRRuathaRku
utpuaathal sAnROr kadan

Merit of intimacy is a vital part of friendship; the
great and the wise respect and safeguard it

பழகிய நட்புஎவன் செய்யும் கெழுதகைமை
செய்தாங்கு அமையாக் கடை.   803

pazhakiya n-atpuevan seyyum kezuthakaimai
seythAngku amaiyAk kadai

Traditional intimacy will lose meaning, when we fail
to treat righteous acts of comrades as our own

விழைதகையான் வேண்டி யிருப்பர் கெழுதகையால்
கேளாது நட்டார் செயின்.   804

vizaithakaiyAn vaeNdi iruppar kezuthakaiyAl
kaeLAthu n-attAr seyin

Acts of loving friends, done in good faith as a
matter of right, shall win accolades of the wise

பேதைமை ஒன்றோ பெருங்கிழமை என்றுஉணர்க
நோதக்க நட்டார் செயின்.   805

paethaimai onRO perumkizamai enRuuNarka
n-Othakka n-attAr seyin

Well intended acts of friends may fault and offend,
but will be deemed by the great as folly of intimacy

எல்லைக்கண் நின்றார் துறவார் தொலைவிடத்தும்
தொல்லைக்கண் நின்றார் தொடர்பு.

ellaikkaN n-inRAr thuRavAr tholaividaththum
thollaikkaN n-inRAr thodarpu

806

Who have cherished the bonds of traditional intimacy
will not forsake friendship in situations adverse

அழிவந்த செய்யினும் அன்புஅறார் அன்பின்
வழிவந்த கேண்மை யவர்.

azivan-tha seyyinun anpuaRAr anpin
vazivan-tha kaeNmai yavar

807

Comradeship flourishing out of noble love does not
waver or break bonds even in the face of ruin

கேள்இழுக்கம் கேளாக் கெழுதகைமை வல்லார்க்கு
நாள்இழுக்கம் நட்டார் செயின்.

kaeLizukkam kaeLAk kezuthakaimai vallArkku
n-ALizukkam n-attAr seyin

808

A day bosom friends have done wrong is taken well in
stride by comrades, who like not listen to tales ill

கெடாஅ வழிவந்த கேண்மையார் கேண்மை
விடாஅர் விழையும் உலகு.

kedAa vazivan-tha kaeNmaiyAr kaeNmai
vidAr vizaiyum ulaku

809

Comradeship growing in unbroken ties, from times
of yore, is cherished by the world in love

விழையார் விழையப் படுப பழையார்கண்
பண்பின் தலைப்பிரியா தார்.

vizaiyAr vizaiyap padupa pazaiyArkaN
paNpin thalaippiriyA thAr

810

The great who cherish and sustain traditional friendship
in courtesy, are admired even by adversaries

82. தீநட்பு (தீங்கு செய்யும் தீயவரின் நட்பு)
thIn-atpu
HARMFUL FRIENDSHIP
(IT IS WISE TO PART WITH OPPORTUNISTIC AND MEAN
CHARACTERS WHO COURT FOR GAINS AND DESERT IN DEARTH,
FOOLS AND PRETENDERS)

பருகுவார் போலினும் பண்பிலார் கேண்மை
பெருகலின் குன்றல் இனிது.   811

parukuvAr pOlinum paNpilAr kaeNmai
perukalin kunRal inithu

It is better to shrink than shine, comradeship of people
without character, who swallow in fake love

உறின்நட்டு அறின்ஒருஉம் ஒப்பிலார் கேண்மை
பெறினும் இழப்பினும் என்.   812

uRinn-attu aRinorUum oppilAr kaeNmai
peRinum izappinum en

Friendship will harm and forlorn will save, of cheats
who court for gains and desert in dearth

உறுவது சீர்தூக்கும் நட்பும் பெறுவது
கொள்வாரும் கள்வரும் நேர்.   813

uRuvathu seerthUkkum n-atpum peRuvathu
koLvArum kaLvarum n-aer

Friends for profit, thieves and devourers of gains
are no different in their intent and acts

அமரகத்து ஆற்றுஅறுக்கும் கல்லாமா அன்னார்
தமரின் தனிமை தலை.   814

amarakaththu aatRuaRukkum kallAmA annAr
thamarin thanimai thalai

To remain aloof is better than trusting opportunistic
friends who dump like a faithless horse in a battle

செய்துஏமம் சாராச் சிறியவர் புன்கேண்மை
எய்தலின் எய்தாமை நன்று.   815

seythuaemam sArAch siRiyavar punkaeNmai
eythalin eythAmai n-anRu

It is good not to aim for unsafe friendship, and better
go without it, of people low and mean in mind

பேதை பெருங்கெழீஇ நட்பின் அறிவுடையார்
ஏதுஇன்மை கோடி உறும்.   **816**

*paethai perungkezeei n-atpin aRivudaiyAr
aethuinmai kOdi uRum*

Saving hatred of the wise, is a million times better than
intimacy of fools, who are more dangerous to deal

நகைவகைய ராகிய நட்பின் பகைவரால்
பத்தடுத்த கோடி உறும்.   **817**

*n-akaivakaiyar aakiya n-atpin pakaivarAl
paththaduththa kOdi uRum*

Those who laugh outwardly and pretend as friends are
harmful ten of million times, than foes with open hostility

ஒல்லும் கருமம் உடற்று பவர்கேண்மை
சொல்லாடார் சோர விடல்.   **818**

*ollum karumam udatRRu pavarkaeNmai
sollAdAr sOra vidal*

Eschew friendship of those with intent to spoil deeds,
that are normally capable of good success

கனவினும் இன்னாது மன்னோ வினைவேறு
சொல்வேறு பட்டார் தொடர்பு.   **819**

*kanavinum innAthu mannO vinaivaeRu
solvaeRu pattAr thodarpu*

Even in dreams their memory torments, whose words
have no relationship to their deliberate deeds

எனைத்தும் குறுகுதல் ஓம்பல் மனைக்கெழீஇ
மன்றில் பழிப்பார் தொடர்பு.   **820**

*enaiththum kuRukuthal Ompal manaikkezeei
manRil pazippAr thodarpu*

Try to cut down and cut off friendship of those
who praise in private and revile in public

83. கூடா நட்பு
kUdA n-atpu
FALSE FRIENDSHIP

(GUARD AGAINST ASSOCIATION OR CONTACTS WITH FAKES, DUPES,
ENVIOUS, SPITEFUL, WORTHLESS AND INCOMPATIBLE IN SOCIETY)

சீரிடம் காணின் எறிதற்குப் பட்டடை
நேரா நிரந்தவர் நட்பு.   **821**

seeridam kANin eRithaRkup pattadai
n-aerA n-iRanthavar n-atpu

Pretence of friendship with enmity in mind, is like an
anvil of the smith, which strikes down when ripe

இனம்போன்று இனமல்லார் கேண்மை மகளிர்
மனம்போல வேறு படும்.   **822**

inampOnRu inamallAr kaenmai makaLir
manampOla vaeRu padum

False companionship of those unworthy of a commune
is like the fickleness of a lady in household strife

பலநல்ல கற்றக் கடைத்தும் மனந்நல்லர்
ஆகுதல் மாணார்க்கு அரிது.   **823**

palan-alla katRRak kadaiththum manamn-allar
aakuthai mANArkku arithu

Though knowledgeable in good learning, it is rare for a
spiteful mind, to stand by honourable friendship

முகத்தின் இனிய நகாஅ அகத்துஇன்னா
வஞ்சரை அஞ்சப் படும்.   **824**

mukaththin iniya n-akAa akaththuinnA
vanjsarai anjsap padum

Fear and caution are essential when dealing with false
friends, posing winning smiles in cunning guile

மனத்தின் அமையா தவரை எனைத்துஒன்றும்
சொல்லினால் தேறற்பாற்று அன்று.   **825**

manaththin amaiyA thavarai enaiththuonRum
sollinAl thaeRaRpARRu anRu

When friendship cannot unite in mental attitudes,
do not opt to assess on the face value of words

நட்டார்போல் நல்லவை சொல்லினும் ஒட்டார்சொல்
ஒல்லை உணரப் படும். 826

*n-attArpOl n-allavai sollinum ottArsol
ollai uNarap padum*

Kindness in words, like bosom friends, should not
deceive one from identifying incompatibility

சொல்வணக்கம் ஒன்னார்கண் கொள்ளற்க வில்வணக்கம்
தீங்கு குறித்தமை யான். 827

*solvaNakkam onnArkaN koLLaRka vilvaNakkam
theengku kuRiththamai yAn*

The bow bends to dart arrows; humility and politeness
of foes posing as friends, conceal evil intents

தொழுதகை யுள்ளும் படையொடுங்கும் ஒன்னார்
அழுதகண் ணீரும் அனைத்து. 828

*thozuthakai uLLum padaiodungkum onnAr
azuthakaN Neerum anaiththu*

The hands that rise folded in reverence can conceal
deadly arms, like the false tears of foes lurking harm

மிகச்செய்து தம்ள்ளு வாரை நகச்செய்து
நட்பினுள் சாப்புல்லல் பாற்று. 829

*mikachcheythu thameLLu vArai n-akachcheythu
n-atpinuL sAppullal pAtRRu*

Do not believe those who shower praise in words, but
despise in mind; dump them in friendly guise

பகைநட்பாம் காலம் வருங்கால் முகம்நட்டு
அகநட்பு ஒரீஇ விடல். 830

*pakain-atpAm kAlam varungkAl mukamn-attu
akan-atpu oreei vidal*

In circumstances where you have to play a friend to
foes with a pleasant look, keep distant in mind

84. பேதைமை
paethaimai
FOOLISHNESS (IMPROPER UNDERSTANDING)
(FOLLY AND IMPROPER UNDERSTANDING LEAD TO SUFFERING
AND SHAME)

பேதைமை என்பதுஒன்று யாதுஎனின் ஏதம்கொண்டு
ஊதியம் போக விடல்.   831

paethaimai enpathuonRu yAthuenin aethamkoNdu
uuthiyam pOka vidal

Foolishness stands out in glare, when one opts to
forgo gains and to take on loss and grief

பேதைமையுள் எல்லாம் பேதைமை காதன்மை
கையல்ல தன்கண் செயல்.   832

paethaimaiyuL ellAm paethaimai kAthanmai
kaiyalla thankaN seyal

It is the height of foolishness to aspire lewdly
things beyond one's reach, and suffer

நாணாமை நாடாமை நாரின்மை யாதுஒன்றும்
பேணாமை பேதை தொழில்.   833

n-ANAmai n-AdAmai n-Arinmai yAthuonRum
paeNAmai paethai thozil

Shameless to evil, aimless in life, listless in mind and
callous to surroundings are hallmarks of a fool's trade

ஓதிஉணர்ந்தும் பிறர்க்குஉரைத்தும் தான் அடங்காப்
பேதையிற் பேதையார் இல்.   834

oothi uNarn-thum piRarkku-uraiththum thAnadangkAp
paethaiyiR paethaiyar il

Studies and learns, preaches to others, cares not to
abide by discipline, no fool can excel the ignorant

ஒருமைச் செயலாற்றும் பேதை எழுமையும்
தான்புக்கு அழுந்தும் அளறு.   835

orumaich cheyalaaRRum paethai ezumaiyum
thAnpukku azun-thum aLaRu

The callous acts of self-laudatory fools drown them
in a mire of grief and pain, beyond retribution

பொய்படும் ஒன்றோ புனைபூணும் கையறியாப்
பேதை வினைமேற் கொளின்.　　　　836

poypadum onRO punaipUNum kaiyaRiyAp
paethai vinaimaeR koLin

Daring a deed ignorant of its dimensions and implications, fools fail hopelessly and invite fetters

ஏதிலார் ஆரத் தமர்பசிப்பர் பேதை
பெருஞ்செல்வம் உற்றக் கடை.　　　　837

aethilAr aarath thamarpasippar paethai
perunjselvam utRRak kadai

A vast wealth falling into the hands of fools, feeds
strangers to benefit and causes kinship to suffer

மையல் ஒருவன் களித்துஅற்றால் பேதைதன்
கையொன்று உடைமை பெறின்.　　　　838

maiyal oruvan kaLiththuatRRAl paethaithan
kaionRu udaimai peRin

When fools come to possess something worthy, they
are dazed like the stupids exuberant in drunkenness

பெரிதுஇனிது பேதையார் கேண்மை பிரிவின்கண்
பீழை தருவதுஒன்று இல்.　　　　839

perithuinithu paethaiyar kaeNmai pirivinkaN
peezai tharuvathuonRu il

Freedom from the company of fools is sweet to
cherish, it entails no regrets or after-effects

கழாஅக்கால் பள்ளியுள் வைத்தற்றால் சான்றோர்
குழாஅத்துப் பேதை புகல்.　　　　840

kazAakkAl paLLiyuL vaiththatRRAl sAnROr
kuzAaththup paethai pukal

Fools intruding into assemblies of the learned savants
is like imprints of dirty feet in a clean abode

85. புல்லறிவாண்மை
pullaRivANmai
SHALLOWNESS OF SENSES
(PETTY CONCEIT)
(LACK OF WISDOM, DUNCE, SMALLNESS PETTY CONCEIT)

அறிவுஇன்மை இன்மையுள் இன்மை பிறிதுஇன்மை
இன்மையா வையாது உலகு.　　　**841**

aRivuinmai inmaiyuL inmai pirithuinmai
inmaiyA vaiyAthu ulaku

Lack of wisdom is famine in poverty; lack of wealth can
be recouped, and hence not deemed as dire need

அறிவிலான் நெஞ்சுஅவந்து ஈதல் பிறிதுயாதும்
இல்லை பெறுவான் தவம்.　　　**842**

aRivuilAn n-enjsuuvan-thu eethal piRithuyAthum
illai peRuvan thavam

The power of penance bestows on the receiver,
ability to make the ignorant gift with glee

அறிவிலார் தாம்தம்மைப் பீழிக்கும் பீழை
செறுவார்க்கும் செய்தல் அரிது.　　　**843**

aRivuilAr thAmthammaip peezikkum peezai
seRuvArkkum seythal arithu

Endless torments the ignorant bring on themselves, which
they are not capable of inflicting on their foes

வெண்மை எனப்படுவது யாதுஎனின் ஒண்மை
உடையம்யாம் என்னும் செருக்கு.　　　**844**

veNmai enappaduvathu yAthuenin oNmai
udaiyamyAm ennum serukku

It is petty conceit of fools to pride that
they too repose the light of sagacity

கல்லாத மேற்கொண்டு ஒழுகல் கசடற
வல்லதூஉம் ஐயம் தரும்.　　　**845**

kallAtha maeRkoNdu ozukal kasadaRa
vallathUum aiyam tharum

The vain feign knowledge and pretend, leading to
suspicion on what little they know for sure

அற்றம் மறைத்தலோ புல்லறிவு தம்வயின்

குற்றம் மறையா வழி.   846

atRRam maRaiththalO pullaRivu thamvaiyin
kutRRam maRaiyA vazi

Fools care not to realise and eliminate glaring faults,
even as they would conceal nakedness

அருமறை சோரும் அறிவிலான் செய்யும்

பெருமிறை தானே தனக்கு.   847

arumaRai sOrum aRivilAn seyyum
perumiRai thAnae thanakku

The shallow who are lazy to listen to wise counsel,
are prone to inflict on themselves grave harm

ஏவவும் செய்கலான் தான்தேறான் அவ்வுயிர்

போஒம் அளவும்ஓர் நோய்.   848

aevavum seykalAn thAn-thaerAn avvuyir
pOom aLavumoor n-Oy

The pain of ignorance lasts the full life of those, who do
not take guidance, nor care to know themselves

காணாதான் காட்டுவான் தான்காணான் காணாதான்

கண்டானாம் தான்கண்ட வாறு.   849

kANAthAn kAttuvAn thAnkANAn kANAthAn
kaNdAnAm thAnkaNda vARu

Fools think what they know is knowledge serene, and
pretend; who try to enlighten them and none the wiser

உலகத்தார் உண்டுஎன்பது இல்லென்பான் வையத்து

அலகையா வைக்கப் படும்.   850

ulakaththAr uNduenpathu ilenpAn vaiyaththu
alakaiyA vaikkap padum

What people of worldly knowledge deem by experience
as true, fools in vain ignore and expose their evil spirits

86. இகல் (மாறுபாடு)
ikal (mARupAdu)
SPIRIT OF DEFIANCE
(HARMFUL FEELINGS OF ENMITY, HATRED AND DISCORDANCE)

இகல்என்ப எல்லா உயிர்க்கும் பகல்என்னும்
பண்புஇன்மை பாரிக்கும் நோய்.　　　851

ikalenpa ellA uyirkkum pakalennum
paNpuinmai pArikkum n-Oy

Enmity breeds the disease of hatred that
spreads to destroy grace in living beings

பகல்கருதிப் பற்றா செயினும் இகல்கருதி
இன்னாசெய் யாமை தலை.　　　852

pakalkaruthip patRRA seyinum ikalkaruthi
innAsey yAmai thalai

Desisting from unkind deeds even to foes is far
better than unfriendly acts born of enmity

இகல்என்னும் எவ்வநோய் நீக்கின் தவல்இல்லாத்
தாவில் விளக்கம் தரும்.　　　853

ikalennum evvan-Oy n-eekkin thavalillA
thAvil viLakkam tharum

Liberty from the painful disease of hatred
ensures everlasting fame without fail

இன்பத்துள் இன்பம் பயக்கும் இகல்என்னும்
துன்பத்துள் துன்பம் கெடின்.　　　854

inpaththuL inpam payakkum ikalennum
thunpaththuL thunpam kedin

When we overcome hatred, the woe of pain and
grief, its relief heralds the pleasure of joy

இகல்எதிர் சாய்ந்துஒழுக வல்லாரை யாரே
மிகல்ஊக்கும் தன்மை யவர்.　　　855

ikalethir sAyn-thuozuka vallArai yArae
mikaluukkum thanmai yavar

One who has the skill to skip the foe of hatred
cannot be won by anyone, in glory

இகலின் மிகல்இனிது என்பவன் வாழ்க்கை
தவலும் கெடலும் நணித்து.   856

ikalin mikalinithu enpavan vAzkkai
thavalum kedalum n-aNiththu

Those who believe in accentuating hatred, to win in
enmity, are more likely to slip and fall in ruins

மிகல்மேவல் மெய்ப்பொருள் காணார் இகல்மேவல்
இன்னா அறிவி னவர்.   857

mikalmaeval meypporuL kANAr ikalmaeval
innA aRivi navar

Harmful thoughts breed hatred and cloud the eyes of
those, who cannot see the wisdom of winning ways

இகலிற்கு எதிர்சாய்தல் ஆக்கம் அதனை
மிகல்ஊக்கின் ஊக்குமாம் கேடு.   858

ikaliRku ethirsAythal aakkam athanai
mikaluukkin uukkumAm kaedu

To bow out of enmity and hatred is creative gain;
to be goaded by those evils hastens ruin

இகல்காணான் ஆக்கம் வருங்கால் அதனை
மிகல்காணும் கேடு தரற்கு.   859

ikalkANAn aakkam varungkAl athanai
mikalkANum kaedu tharaRku

Enmity subsides in circumstances favourable for
good; enhancing hatred breeds disaster

இகலான்ஆம் இன்னாத எல்லாம் நகலான்ஆம்
நன்னயம் என்னும் செருக்கு.   860

ikalAnaam innAtha ellAm n-akalAnaam
n-ann-ayam ennum serukku

The feeling of enmity encourages evil; the
spirit of congeniality grows from amity

87. பகைமாட்சி (பகையிலும் மாண்புடைமை)
pakai maatchi
NOBILITY IN HOSTILITY

(TRUE WARRIORS FACE FOES OF NO INFERIORITY AND
STRENGTHEN THEIR POSITION BY GAINING FRIENDS, ARMS, AIDS
AND WEALTH TO MATCH)

வலியார்க்கு மாறுஏற்றல் ஒம்புக ஒம்பா
மெலியார்மேல் மே(வு)க பகை.   861

valiyArkku mARuaetRal oompuka, oompA
meliyArmael mae(vu)ka pakai

Noble warriors choose to face foes of matching strength;
there is no honour, save tact, in battling the weak

அன்புஇலன் ஆன்ற துணைஇலன் தான்துவ்வான்
என்பரியும் ஏதிலான் துப்பு.   862

anpuilan aanRa thuNaiilan thAnthuvvAn
enpariyum aethilAn thuppu

Sans loving friends, helping aids, strength of arms and
wealth, one cannot hope to withstand mighty foes

அஞ்சும் அறியான் அமைவிலன் ஈகலான்
தஞ்சம் எளியன் பகைக்கு.   863

anjsum aRiyAn amaivilan eekalAn
thanjsam eLiyAr pakaikku

Timid, unversed, unfit and uncharitable; these are
the ones apt to meekly surrender to foes

நீங்கான் வெகுளி நிறைஇலன் எஞ்ஞான்றும்
யாங்கணும் யார்க்கும் எளிது.   864

n-eengkAn vekuLi n-iRaiilan enjnjAnRum
yAngkaNum yArkkum eLithu

Consumed by anger, lacking mental balance and control,
people are easy prey to anyone, anytime, anywhere

வழிநோக்கான் வாய்ப்பன செய்யான் பழிநோக்கான்
பண்புஇலன் பற்றார்க்கு இனிது.   865

vazin-OkkAn vAyppana seyyAn pazin-OkkAn
paNpuilan patRRArkku inithu

Not caring decent ways, lacking tact on opportunities,
unmindful and ill-mannered, are easy targets to foes

காணாச் சினத்தான் கழிபெரும் காமத்தான்
பேணாமை பேணப் படும்.   866

*kANAch chinaththAn kaziperum kAmaththAn
paeNAmai paeNap padum*

Rage blind to reason, mad in lust beyond measure,
it is best to leave them at a deliberate distance

கொடுத்தும் கொளல்வேண்டும் மன்ற அடுத்திருந்து
மாணாத செய்வான் பகை.   867

*koduththum koLalvaeNdum manRa aduththirun-thu
mANAtha seyvAn pakai*

Such enmity is worth a price, of those who
surround as friends, but cheat in deceit

குணன்இலனாய்க் குற்றம் பலவாயின் மாற்றார்க்கு
இனன்இலனாம் ஏமாப்பு உடைத்து.   868

*kuNanilanAyk kutRRam palavAyin mAtRRArkku
inanilanAm aemAppu udaiththu*

Knows not any values, vices have no dearth, loses
society to fall safe in the hands of vile foes

செறுவார்க்குச் சேண்இகவா இன்பம் அறிவிலா
அஞ்சும் பகைவர்ப் பெறின்.   869

*seruvArkkuch chaeNikavA inpam aRivilA
anjsum pakaivarp peRin*

Opponents in blissful ignorance and timidity
are joyful targets for the foes to win

கல்லான் வெகுளும் சிறுபொருள் எஞ்ஞான்றும்
ஒல்லானை ஒல்லாது ஒளி.   870

*kallAn vekuLum siRuporuL enjnjAnRum
ollAnai ollAthu oLi*

The light of fame is not seen by those, who
cannot overcome the ignorant weaklings

88. பகைத்திறம் தெரிதல்
pakaiththiRam therithal
APPRAISING ENEMY'S SKILLS
(BETTER THAN KNOWING, ENDEAVOUR TO OVERCOME AND BEFRIEND, BUILD SAFEGUARDS, BUT NOT HESITATE TO DESTROY DEFYING FOES)

பகையென்னும் பண்பி லதனை ஒருவன்
நகையேயும் வேண்டற்பாற்று அன்று.   871

pakaiennum panpi lathanai oruvan
n-akaiyaeyum vaeNdaRpAtRRu anRu

Enmity that breeds bad manners is to be abhorred
and avoided, even as a matter of fun

வில்லேர் உழவர் பகைகொளினும் கொள்ளற்க
சொல்லேர் உழவர் பகை.   872

vilaer uzavar pakaikoLinum koLLaRka
solaer uzavar pakai

Hostility to the wise in command of their tongue is more
dangerous to guard against than that of expert archers

ஏமுற் றவரினும் ஏழை தமியனாய்ப்
பல்லார் பகைகொள் பவன்.   873

aemuR Ravarinum aezai thamiyanAyp
pallAr pakaikoL pavan

The forlorn ignorance of courting enmity of
many, is worse than affliction of insanity

பகைநட்பாக் கொண்டுஒழுகும் பண்புடை யாளன்
தகைமைக்கண் தங்கிற்று உலகு.   874

pakain-atpAk koNduozukum paNpudai yALan
thakaimaikkaN thangkitRRu ulaku

People with grace who can win over foes to friendship
make this world, all the more a pleasant place

தன்துணை இன்றால் பகைஇரண்டால் தான்ஒருவன்
இன்துணையாக் கொள்கஅவற்றின் ஒன்று.   875

than-thuNai inRAl pakai-iraNdAl thAnoruvan
inthuNaiyAk koLka-avaRRin onRu

Confronted alone by two foes, and helpless, the wise
contrive to ally with one of them, to save the situation

தேறினும் தேறா விடினும் அழிவின்கண்
தேறான் பகாஅன் விடல்.   876

thaeRinum thaeRA vidinum azivinkaN
thaeRAn pakAan vidal

Evaluated or otherwise, during distress and grief,
keep aloof and avoid meddling with foes

நோவற்க நொந்தது அறியார்க்கு மேவற்க
மென்மை பகைவ ரகத்து.   877

n-OvaRka n-on-thathu aRiyArkku maevaRka
menmai pakaiva rakaththu

Do not venture to bemoan your woes to those not
aware; guard against exposing weakness to foes

வகையறிந்து தற்செய்து தற்காப்ப மாயும்
பகைவர்கண் பட்ட செருக்கு.   878

vakaiaRin-thu thaRseythu thaRkAppa mAyum
pakaivarkaN patta serukku

Learn well the ways to proceed, gain strength and
safeguards, to keep the pride of foes at bay

இளைதாக முள்மரம் கொல்க களையுநர்
கைகொல்லும் காழ்த்த இடத்து.   879

iLaithAka muLmaram kolka kaLaiyun-ar
kaikollum kAzaththa idaththu

Destroy thorny shrubs from their roots young; when
they grow into trees, are sure to harm and injure

உயிர்ப்ப உளரல்லர் மன்ற செயிர்ப்பவர்
செம்மல் சிதைக்கலா தார்.   880

uyirppa uLarallar manRa seyirppavar
semmal sithaikkalA thAr

Those who hesitate to destroy defying foes promptly,
may not last to breathe and survive a battle

89. உட்பகை (மறைந்து நிற்கும் பகைமை)
utpakai
ENMITY WITHIN

(BE WARY OF SPITE AND ENMITY HIDDEN OR CONCEALED WITHIN
ONESELF AND AMONG KITH AND KIN, FRIENDS AND SOCIETY)

நிழல்நீரும் இன்னாத இன்னா தமர்நீரும்
இன்னாவாம் இன்னா செயின்.   881

n-izaln-eerum innAtha innA thamarn-eerum
innAvAm innA seyin

Kith and kin, like shade and water, are to protect; when
they embitter and harm, identify for what they are

வாள்போல் பகைவரை அஞ்சற்க அஞ்சுக
கேள்போல் பகைவர் தொடர்பு.   882

vALpOl pakaivarai anjsaRka anjsuka
kaeLpOl pakaivar thodarpu

Open enmity, like a sword, can be taken on fearlessly;
but apprehend cautiously, foes feigning friendship

உட்பகை அஞ்சித்தற் காக்க உலைவிடத்து
மட்பகையின் மாணத் தெறும்.   883

utpakai anjsiththaR kAkka ulaividaththu
matpakaiyin mANath theRum

Beware of secret foes and be cautious; in a crisis,
they are prone to cut off like a potter's knife

மனம்மாணா உட்பகை தோன்றின் இனம்மாணா
ஏதம் பலவும் தரும்.   884

manammANA utpakai thOnRin inammANA
aetham palavum tharum

Internal foes who rise with evil intent, cause
grief and distress to destroy social values

உறல்முறையான் உட்பகை தோன்றின் இறல்முறையான்
ஏதம் பலவும் தரும்.   885

uRalmuraiyAn utpakai thOnRin iRalmuRaiyAn
aetham palavum tharum

Treachery that springs foes within kinship,
causes endless trouble and pain that ruins

ஒன்றாமை ஒன்றியார் கண்படின் எஞ்ஞான்றும்
பொன்றாமை ஒன்றல் அரிது.   886

onRAmai onRiyAr kaNpadin enjnjAnRum
ponRAmai onRal arithu

Discordance in a family thriving in unison, causes
enmity and renders longevity of accord rarer

செப்பின் புணர்ச்சிபோல் கூடினும் கூடாதே
உட்பகை உற்ற குடி.   887

seppin puNarchchipOl kUdinum kUdAthae
utpakai utRRa kudi

A family or society afflicted by internal feuds may stay
together like metals joined, but not concur in attitudes

அரம்பொருத பொன்போலத் தேயும் உரம்பொருது
உட்பகை உற்ற குடி.   888

aramporutha ponpOlath thaeyum uramporuthu
utpakai utRRa kudi

A steel file wears out and weakens metals; secret
spite wears out a society and destroys its might

எள்பகவு அன்ன சிறுமைத்தே ஆயினும்
உட்பகை உள்ளதாம் கேடு.   889

eLpakavu anna siRumaiththae aayinum
utpakai uLLathAm kaedu

Though in size like a split sesame seed, enmity
lurks in secret foes, with intent to destroy

உடம்பாடு இலாதவர் வாழ்க்கை குடங்கருள்
பாம்போடு உடன்உறைந் தற்று.   890

udampAdu ilAthavar vAzkkai kudangkaruL
pAmpodu udanuRain-thu atRRu

Life in incompatible surroundings, is like
co-existence with a snake in its hold

90. பெரியாரைப் பிழையாமை
periyAraip pizaiyAmai
AVOIDING OFFENCE TO THE GREAT
(IT IS RESPECTFUL MANNERISM NOT TO SPITE THE ELDERLY
AND THE GREAT IN MIND AND STRENGTH)

ஆற்றுவார் ஆற்றல் இகழாமை போற்றுவார்
போற்றலுள் எல்லாம் தலை.　　　　　　891

aatRRuvAr aatRRal ikazAmai pOtRRuvAr
pOtRRaluL ellAm thalai

Not to spite the mighty who act to achieve, is a manner
of extending respect, and safeguarding one's interest

பெரியாரைப் பேணாது ஒழுகின் பெரியாரால்
பேரா இடும்பை தரும்.　　　　　　892

periyAraip paeNAthu ozukin periyArAl
paerA idumpai tharum

Failure to heed the ways and wisdom of the mighty
may attract their wrath and cause trouble

கெடல்வேண்டின் கேளாது செய்க அடல்வேண்டின்
ஆற்று பவர்கண் இழுக்கு.　　　　　893

kedalvaeNdin kaeLAthu seyka adalvaeNdin
aatRRu pavarkaN izukku

The great aiming at targets to achieve, do not
tolerate any nonsense of those inviting grief

கூற்றத்தைக் கையால் விளித்தற்றால் ஆற்றுவார்க்கு
ஆற்றாதார் இன்னா செயல்.　　　　894

kURRaththaik kaiyAl viLiththaRRAl aatRRuvArkku
aatRRAthAr innA seyal

The weak who attempt to insult or injure the mighty,
wilfully invite on themselves disaster and death

யாண்டுச்சென்று யாண்டும் உளராகார் வெந்துப்பின்
வேந்து செறப்பட்ட வர்.　　　　895

yANduchchenRu yANdum uLarAkAr ven-thuppin
vaen-thu seRappatta var

Escape or reprieve are hard to gain for those who
antagonise and invite the ire of a mighty ruler

எரியால் சுடப்படினும் உய்வுண்டாம் உய்யார்
பெரியார்ப் பிழைத்துஒழுகு வார்.   896

eriyAl sudappadinum uyvuuNdAm uyyAr
periyArp pizaiththuozuku vAr

Chances may be there to survive fire burns, but
who offend and insult the great surely perish

வகைமாண்ட வாழ்க்கையும் வான்பொருளும் என்னாம்
தகைமாண்ட தக்கார் செறின்.   897

vagaimAnda vAzhkaiyum vAnporulum yennAm
thakaimAnda thackkAr serin

Life of varied pleasures and wealth stacked high are
of no avail against the wrath of the mighty in society

குன்றுஅன்னார் குன்ற மதிப்பின் குடியொடு
நின்றுஅன்னார் மாய்வர் நிலத்து.   898

kunRuannAr kunRa mathippin kudiyodu
n-inRuannAr mAyvar n-ilaththu

The prosperous and prestigious in society vanish into
nothing, if they underestimate the mighty, like a hill

ஏந்திய கொள்கையார் சீறின் இடைமுரிந்து
வேந்தனும் வேந்து கெடும்.   899

aen-thiya koLkaiyAr seeRin idaimurin-thu
vaen-thanum vaen-thu kedum

The honest steadfast in their principles, when provoked,
should rise up like a volcano to burn out despots

இறந்துஅமைந்த சார்புஉடையர் ஆயினும் உய்யார்
சிறந்துஅமைந்த சீரார் செறின்.   900

iRan-thuamain-tha sArpudaiyar aayinum uyyAr
siRan-thuamain-tha sIrAr seRin

Even the mighty with inexhaustible support cannot
survive, if they enrage the sensitivity of seers

91. பெண்வழிச் சேறல்
peNvazich chaeRal
FEMALE INFATUATION

(GUARD AGAINST THE LURE OF PASSION, FOLLY OF LURKING BEHIND,
DOTING SUBMISSION IN FEAR AND MEEK SERVITUDE TO PURVEYING
WOMEN, SURRENDERING MANLINESS. THIS IN NO WAY IS A REFLECTION
ON WOMEN OF MODESTY WHO ARE HELD FAR HIGHER IN GLORY)

மனைவிழைவார் மாண்பயன் எய்தார் வினைவிழைவார்
வேண்டாப் பொருளும் அது.　　　　　901

manaivizaivAr mANpayan eythAr vinaivizaivAr
vaeNdAp poruLum athu

The lure of passion for women destroys glory and gains;
those caught in, fail in their duties to family and society

பேணாது பெண்விழைவான் ஆக்கம் பெரியதோர்
நாணாக நாணுத் தரும்.　　　　　902

paeNAthu peNvizaivAn aakkam periyathOr
n-ANAka n-ANuth tharum

One who lurks behind women, ignoring his responsibilities
brings on shame to his name

இல்லாள்கண் தாழ்ந்த இயல்புஇன்மை எஞ்ஞான்றும்
நல்லாருள் நாணுத் தரும்.　　　　　903

illALkaN thAzn-tha iyalpuinmai enjnjAnRum
n-allAruL n-ANuth tharum

Servitude to women, surrendering manliness, makes one
hang his head in shame, before a honourable society

மனையாளை அஞ்சும் மறுமை யிலாளன்
வினையாண்மை வீறுஎய்தல் இன்று.　　　　904

manaiyALai anjsum maRumai ilALan
vinaiyANmai veeRueythal inRu

One who deems his wife as boss and purveyor, loses
happiness in life, and the will to achieve glory

இல்லாளை அஞ்சுவான் அஞ்சும்மற்று எஞ்ஞான்றும்
நல்லார்க்கு நல்ல செயல்.　　　　905

illALai anjsuvAn anjsummatRRu enjnjAnRum
n-allArkku n-alla seyal

One who lacks compatibility in life and meekly submits
to his wife, in fear, fails in his duties to help the good

இமையாரின் வாழினும் பாடுஇலரே இல்லாள்
அமையார்தோள் அஞ்சு பவர்.   906

imaiyArin vAzinum pAduilarae illAL
amaiyArthOL anjsu pavar

People in high society look petty when they behave
in abject fear, in the drowsing arms of their wives

பெண்ஏவல் செய்துஒழுகும் ஆண்மையின் நாணுடைப்
பெண்ணே பெருமை உடைத்து.   907

peNaeval seythuozukum aaNmaiyin n-ANudaip
peNNae perumai udaiththu

Women of modesty are far higher in glory, than men who
fancy their errands, or acts that suit their delicate hands

நட்டார் குறைமுடியார் நன்றுஆற்றார் நன்னுதலாள்
பெட்டாங்கு ஒழுகு பவர்.   908

n-attAr kuRaimudiyAr n-anRuaatRRAr n-annuthalAL
pettAngku ozuku pavar

Governed by the wink of fairy-browed damsels, the
weak cannot help out friends, or do good to society

அறவினையும் ஆன்ற பொருளும் பிறவினையும்
பெண்ஏவல் செய்வார்கண் இல்.   909

aRavinaiyum aantRa poruLum piRavinaiyum
peNaeval seyvArkaN il

Neither virtue nor wealth nor happiness could reside
in people who submit in servitude to women

எண்சேர்ந்த நெஞ்சத்து இடனுடையார்க்கு எஞ்ஞான்றும்
பெண்சேர்ந்தாம் பேதைமை இல்.   910

eNsaern-tha n-enjsaththu idanudaiyArkku enjnjAnRum
peNsaern-thaam paethaimai il

Who have the strength of mind, to think and act
freely, do not suffer the folly of doting on women

92. வரைவின் மகளிர்
varaivin makaLir
HARLOTS
(WOMEN OUTSIDE THE VIRTUE OF FAMILY BONDS)
(TO KEEP AWAY FROM WOMEN OF BANAL PURSUITS, OUTSIDE
THE VIRTUE OF FAMILY BONDS, WHO LURE, CAJOLE AND TRADE
THEIR BODIES FOR MATERIAL GAINS)

அன்பின் விழையார் பொருள்விழையும் ஆய்தொடியார்
இன்சொல் இழுக்குத் தரும்.   911

anpin vizaiyAr poruLvizaiyum aaythodiyAr
insol izukkuth tharum

**Bangled damsels angling for material gains, do not
have the least of love, but cajole by tongue**

பயன்தூக்கிப் பண்புரைக்கும் பண்புஇல் மகளிர்
நயன்தூக்கி நள்ளா விடல்.   912

payanthUkkip paNpuraikkum paNpuil makaLir
n-ayanthUkki n-aLLA vidal

**Be wary of whores who feign love in deceit, but
have their eyes only on beneficial gains**

பொருட்பெண்டிர் பொய்ம்மை முயக்கம் இருட்டறையில்
ஏதில் பிணந்தழீஇ அற்று.   913

porutpeNdir poymai muyakkam iruttaraiyil
aethil piNamthazeei atRRu

**The unreal embrace of hired bellies, is like
the contact of alien corpse in darkness**

பொருட்பொருளார் புன்னலம் தோயார் அருட்பொருள்
ஆயும் அறிவி னவர்.   914

porutporuLAr punnalam thOyAr arutporuL
aayum aRivi navar

**Those who seek the grace of love, disdain the false
embrace of harlots, who aim at material gains**

பொதுநலத்தார் புன்னலம் தோயார் மதிநலத்தின்
மாண்ட அறிவி னவர்.   915

pothun-alaththAr punnalam thOyAr mathin-alaththin
mANda aRivi navar

The wisdom of a sound mind will never seek to covet
pleasures from women, who trade their body for gains

தந்நலம் பாரிப்பார் தோயார் தகைசெருக்கிப்
புன்னலம் பாரிப்பார் தோள்.   **916**

thannalam pArippAr thOyAr thakaiserukkip
punnalam pArippAr thOL

Those who wish to guard their health, wealth and fame
will never embrace vamps of banal pursuits

நிறைநெஞ்சம் இல்லவர் தோய்வர் பிறநெஞ்சில்
பேணிப் புணர்பவர் தோள்.   **917**

n-iRain-enjsam illavar thOyvar piRan-enjsil
paeNip puNarpavar thOL

Dissatisfied in family life, the unsteady in mind embrace
harlots whose interests focus elsewhere, lest love

ஆயும் அறிவினர் அல்லார்க்கு அணங்குளென்ப
மாய மகளிர் முயக்கு.   **918**

aayumaRivinar allArkku anangkuenpa
mAya makaLir muyakku

The ecstasy and luring embrace of damsels is mystic
to one, who lacks the wisdom of an analytical mind

வரைவிலா மாணிழையார் மென்தோள் புரையிலாப்
பூரியர்கள் ஆழும் அளறு.   **919**

varaivilA mANizaiyaar menthOL puraiilAp
pUriyarkaL aazum aLaRu

The bejewelled arms of bellies outside of family bonds
drown the demented in a mire of slush

இருமனப் பெண்டிரும் கள்ளும் கவறும்
திருநீக்கப் பட்டார் தொடர்பு.   **920**

irumanap peNdirum kaLLum kavarum
thirun-eekkap pattAr thodarpu

False pretentions of harlots, liquor and dice are luring
companions of those, whom wealth deserts

93. கள்ளுண்ணாமை
kaL uNNAmai
ABJURING LIQUOR
(AVOIDING DRUNKENNESS)
(AVOID DRUNKENNESS AND ADDICTION WHICH BENUMB SENSES AND LEAD TO VILENESS, PENURY, SHAME AND INSANITY)

உட்கப் படாஅர் ஒளியிழப்பர் எஞ்ஞான்றும்
கட்காதல் கொண்டுஒழுகு வார்.　　　　　　　921

utkap padAar oLiizappar enjnjAnRum
katkAthal koNduozuku vAr

Addicts to liquor lose their glory in daily doses,
and fall flat in the esteem of society

உண்ணற்க கள்ளை உணில்உண்க சான்றோரால்
எண்ணப் படவேண்டா தார்.　　　　　　　922

uNNaRka kaLLai uNiluNka sAnROrAl
eNNap padavaeNdA thAr

Do not be a slave to liquor; those who ignore this
edict do not count in the reckoning of the wise

ஈன்றாள் முகத்தேயும் இன்னாதால் என்மற்றுச்
சான்றோர் முகத்துக் களி.　　　　　　　923

eenRAL mukaththaeyum innAthAl enmatRRuch
sAnROr mukaththuk kaLi

Drunkards invite frowns in the pained faces of mothers;
what to say of their vile joy in the presence of elders!

நாணென்னும் நல்லாள் புறங்கொடுக்கும் கள்ளென்னும்
பேணாப் பெருங்குற்றத் தார்க்கு.　　　　　　　924

n-ANennum n-allAL puRangkodukkum kaLLennum
paeNAp perungkutRRath thArkku

The dame of modesty turns her face away in shame
from those condemned to the guilt of drunkenness

கையறி யாமை யுடைத்தே பொருள்கொடுத்து
மெய்யறி யாமை கொளல்.　　　　　　　925

kaiaRi yAmai udaiththae poruLkoduththu
meyaRi yAmai koLal

Ignorance of the mind leads to lose material wealth
and to drown in liquor, that benumbs their senses

துஞ்சினார் செத்தாரின் வேறுஅல்லர் எஞ்ஞான்றும்
நஞ்சுஉண்பார் கள்ளுண் பவர்.   926

thunjsinAr seththArin vaeRuallar enjnjAnRum
n-anjsu-uNpAr kaLLuN pavar

Losing senses in liquor and dozing off is akin to a body
dead; toddy in excess is a collective poison

உள்ஒற்றி உள்ளூர் நகப்படுவர் எஞ்ஞான்றும்
கள்ஒற்றிக் கண்சாய் பவர்.   927

uLotRRi uLLUr n-akappaduvar enjnjAnRum
kaLotRRik kaNsAy pavar

Longing to be in unison with liquor in secrecy, leads
one to be the laughing stock of the locals

களித்துஅறியேன் என்பது கைவிடுக நெஞ்சத்து
ஒளித்துதூஉம் ஆங்கே மிகும்.   928

kaLiththuaRiyaen enpathu kaividuka n-enjsaththu
oLiththathuvum aangkae mikum

The mental stability of drunkards is hard to take; slaved
to drinks, they give up secrets that are ought to be kept

களித்தானைக் காரணம் காட்டுதல் கீழ்நீர்க்
குளித்தானைத் தீத்துரீஇ யற்று.   929

kaLiththAnaik kAraNam kAttuthal keezn-eerk
kuLiththAnaith theeththureei yatRu

Trying to reason out to the drunken, is like giving light
from a torch to the one drowning in deep waters

கள்உண்ணாப் போழ்தில் களித்தானைக் காணுங்கால்
உள்ளான்கொல் உண்டதன் சோர்வு.   930

kaLuNNAp pOzthil kaLiththAnaik kANungkAl
uLLAnkol uNdathan sOrvu

In saner moments will not the drunkards ponder
over the sad plight of the drunken souls?

94. சூது (சூதாட்டம்)
sUthu (sUthAttam)
GAMBLING

(IT IS THE RESULT OF BLIND FAITH IN SO CALLED 'LUCK', A
BELIEF OF THOSE WHO DETEST HARD AND HONEST LABOUR
AND ATTEMPT SHORT CUTS TO END UP IN LOSS AND
FRUSTRATION)

வேண்டற்க வென்றிடினும் சூதினை வென்றதூஉம்
தூண்டிற்பொன் மீன்விழுங்கி யற்று.　　　931

vaeNdaRka venRidinum sUthinai venRathUum
thUNdiRpon meenvizungki yatRRu

Do not go after gambling wins; that is like the
fish falling to the hook, lusting for the bait

ஒன்றுஎய்தி நூறுஇழக்கும் சூதர்க்கும் உண்டாங்கொல்
நன்றுஎய்தி வாழ்வதோர் ஆறு.　　　932

onRueythi nuuRuizakkum sUtharkkum uNdAngkol
n-anRueythi vAzvathOr aaRu

A gambler who aims for a win, despite losing many
a score, has no redemption for a good life

உருள்ஆயம் ஓவாது கூரின் பொருள்ஆயம்
போஒய்ப் புறமே படும்.　　　933

uruLAyam oovAthu kURin poruLaayam
pOoyp puRamae padum

If one falls for rolling the dice ceaselessly, his
wealth and income role off unobstrusively

சிறுமை பலசெய்து சீரழிக்கும் சூதின்
வறுமை தருவதுஒன்று இல்.　　　934

siRumai palasaeythu seerazikkum sUthin
vaRumai tharuvathuonRu il

Nothing will make you pauper faster than gambling,
that piles on endless woes and ruins life

கவறும் கழகமும் கையும் தருக்கி
இவறியார் இல்லாகி யார்.　　　935

kavaRum kazakamum kaiyum tharukki
ivaRiyAr illAki yAr

Who inhabit gambling dens and hold on to dice, in the
blind confidence to win, come to grief in no time

அகடுஆரார் அல்லல் உழப்பர்சூது என்னும்
முகடியால் மூடப்பட் டார்.   936

akaduaaRAr allal uzapparsUthu ennum
mukadiyAl mUdappat tAr

People covered under the dark lid of gambling
forgo their food and stew in distress

பழகிய செல்வமும் பண்பும் கெடுக்கும்
கழகத்துக் காலை புகின்.   937

pazakiya selvamum paNpum kedukkum
kazakaththuk kAlai pukin

Traditional wealth and good manners are lost forever
to those who make gambling dens their abodes

பொருள்கெடுத்துப் பொய்மேற் கொளீஇ அருள்கெடுத்து
அல்லல் உழப்பிக்கும் சூது.   938

poruLkeduththup poymaeR koLeei aruLkeduththu
allal uzappikkum sUthu

Gambling deprives material wealth, forces one to lie,
spoils grace and drowns in a mire of wretchedness

உடைசெல்வம் ஊண்ஒளி கல்விஎன்று ஐந்தும்
அடையாவாம் ஆயம் கொளின்.   939

udaiselvam uuNoLi kalvienRu ain-thum
adaiyAvAm aayam koLin

The honour of dress, wealth, food, fame and learning
does not stay with those who stick to gambling dens

இழத்தொறூஉம் காதலிக்கும் சூதேபோல் துன்பம்
உழத்தொறூஉம் காதற்று உயிர்.   940

izaththoRUum kAthalikkum sUthaepOl thunpam
uzaththoRUum kAthaRRu uyir

The longing for life intensifies when sorrows surround;
the love for gambling is nonetheless in losing

95. மருந்து
marunthu
FOOD AS MEDICINE
(THE DIFFERENT KINDS AND CAUSES OF DISEASES, DIAGNOSIS
AND THE ANCIENT SYSTEM OF NATURAL MEDICATION)

மிகினும் குறையினும் நோய்செய்யும் நூலோர்
வளிமுதலா எண்ணிய மூன்று.   **941**

*mikinum kuRaiyinum n-Oyseyyum n-UlOr
vaLimuthalA eNNiya mUnRu*

Doctors of medicine deem that, as indicated by pulse,
flex, bile and phlegm, in excess or short, cause disease

மருந்தென வேண்டாவாம் யாக்கைக்கு அருந்தியது
அற்றது போற்றி உணின்.   **942**

*marun-thuena vaeNdAvAm yAkkaikku arun-thiyathu
atRRathu pOtRRi uNin*

One who knows his digestive system and feeds his body
just sufficient to needs, needs no other medicine

அற்றால் அளவுஅறிந்து உண்க அஃதுஉடம்பு
பெற்றான் நெடிதுய்க்கும் ஆறு.   **943**

*atRRAl aLavuaRin-thu uNka aqthu-udampu
petRRAr n-edithuykkum aaRu*

Make sure of digestion and cleaning, and eat in
measures, to ensure pleasure and longevity

அற்றது அறிந்து கடைப்பிடித்து மாறுஅல்ல
துய்க்க துவரப் பசித்து.   **944**

*atRRathu aRin-thu kadaippidiththu mARualla
thuykka thuvarap pasiththu*

Know your digestive capacity, discipline time and
enjoy agreeable food, to the level of your appetite

மாறுபாடு இல்லாத உண்டி மறுத்துஉண்ணின்
ஊறுபாடு இல்லை உயிர்க்கு.   **945**

*mARupAdu illAtha uNdi maRuththu-uNNin
uuRupAdu illai uyirkku*

Fasting to adjust the system and taking food that is not
allergic, cures ills of life, and makes you bright

இழிவுஅறிந்து உண்பான்கண் இன்பம்போல் நிற்கும்
கழிபே ரிரையான்கண் நோய்.   946

*izivuaRin-thu uNpAnkaN inpampOl n-iRkum
kazipaer iraiyAnkaN n-Oy*

Healthy and happy are those who eat with a clean
stomach; swallowing in lots makes a storehouse of ills

தீயள வன்றித் தெரியான் பெரிதுண்ணின்
நோயளவு இன்றிப் படும்.   947

*theeyaLa vanRith theriyAn perithuNNin
n-OyaLavu inRip padum*

Quench the fire of hunger by food just sufficient;
greedy glut breeds and abides in ill-health

நோய்நாடி நோய்முதல் நாடி அதுதணிக்கும்
வாய்நாடி வாய்ப்பச் செயல்.   948

*n-Oyn-Adi n-Oymuthal n-Adi athuthaNikkum
vAyn-Adi vAyppach seyal*

Diagnose the disease, its causes, ascertain means of
cure and apply remedies, appropriate to the patient

உற்றான் அளவும் பிணிஅளவும் காலமும்
கற்றான் கருதிச் செயல்.   949

*utRRAn aLavum piNiaLavum kAlamum
katRRAn karuthich seyal*

A doctor of skills makes sure to know the patient,
the sickness and the time best for treatment

உற்றவன் தீர்ப்பான் மருந்துஉழைச் செல்வானென்று
அப்பால்நாற் கூற்றே மருந்து.   950

*utRavan theerppAn marun-thu-uzaich selvAnenRu
appAln-Al kUtRRae marun-thu*

The fourfold components of treatment are the
patient, the curer, medicine and nursing

96. குடிமை (சமுதாயப் பண்பாடு)
kudimai (samuthAyap paNpAdu)
NOBILITY OF SOCIETY
(TRUTH, DISCIPLINE, MODESTY, EQUITY, KINDNESS,
MUNIFICENCE ETC. ARE QUALITIES OF ANCIENT SOCIETIES OF
TRADITIONAL VALUES. THEY ARE TO BE CHERISHED AND
SUSTAINED TO PRESERVE CIVILIZATIONS AND FLOURISH)

இல்பிறந்தார் கண்அல்லது இல்லை இயல்பாகச்
செப்பமும் நாணும் ஒருங்கு.   951

ilpiRan-thAr kaNallathu   illai iyalpAkach
seppamum n-ANum orungku

Equity and modesty naturally reside together
in a family of traditional honour and heritage

ஒழுக்கமும் வாய்மையும் நாணும்இம் மூன்றும்
இழுக்கார் குடிப்பிறந் தார்.   952

ozukkamum vAymaiyum n-ANumim mUnRum
izukkAr kudippiRan- thAr

Noble traditions of a family save from blemishes
the virtues of discipline, truth and modesty

நகைஈகை இன்சொல் இகழாமை நான்கும்
வகைஎன்ப வாய்மைக் குடிக்கு.   953

n-akaieekai insol ikazAmai n-Ankum
vakaienapa vAymaik kudikku

Pleasant looks, munificence, kind words and courtesy
mark the traits of a truly noble society

அடுக்கிய கோடி பெறினும் குடிப்பிறந்தார்
குன்றுவ செய்தல் இலர்.   954

adukkiya kOdi peRinum kudippiRan-thAr
kunRuva seythal ilar

People of good social traditions shun blemishes,
even in the face of a bait of many millions

வழங்குவ துள்வீழ்ந்தக் கண்ணும் பழங்குடி
பண்பில் தலைப்பிரிதல் இன்று.   955

vazangkuva thuLveezn-thak kaNNum pazangkudi
paNpil thalaippirithal inRu

The means of largesse may dwindle, but ancient
tradition adheres to courtesy and munificence

சலம்பற்றிச் சால்புஇல செய்யார்மாசு அற்ற
குலம்பற்றி வாழ்த்தும்என் பார்.   956

salampaRRich sAlpuila seyyArmAsu atRRa
kulampatRRi vAzthumen pAr

Who cherish purity and virtues of family life, do not
indulge in cunning deeds unworthy of honour

குடிப்பிறந்தார் கண்விளங்கும் குற்றம் விசும்பின்
மதிக்கண் மறுப்போல் உயர்ந்து.   957

kudippiRan-thAr kaNviLangkum kutRRam visumpin
mathikkaN maruppOl uyarn-thu

Defects in people of prestigious descent appear
prominently as the dark spots on the clear moon

நலத்தின்கண் நாரின்மை தோன்றின் அவனைக்
குலத்தின்கண் ஐயப் படும்.   958

n-alaththinkaN n-Arinmai thOnRin avanaik
kulaththinkaN aiyap padum

An attitude of indifference and callousness to good
manners, exposes one's family honour to doubts

நிலத்தில் கிடந்தமை கால்காட்டும் காட்டும்
குலத்திற் பிறந்தார்வாய்ச் சொல்.   959

n-ilaththil kidan-thamai kAlkAttum kAttum
kulaththil piRan-thArvAych sol

The health of plants exhibits richness of the soil; social
values ring in the positive quality of one's tongue

நலம்வேண்டின் நாணுடைமை வேண்டும் குலம்வேண்டின்
வேண்டுக யார்க்கும் பணிவு.   960

n-alamvaeNdin n-ANudaimai vaeNdum kulamvaeNdin
vaeNduka yArkkum paNivu

All good and gains spring from modesty of acts;
glory of a traditional society shines in humility

97. மானம் (தன் நிலையில் தாழாத பண்பு)
maanam
SENSITIVITY TO DIGNITY

(MAANAM IS A UNIQUE QUALITY, WITH NO DIRECT WORD IN
ENGLISH; VARIOUSLY DESCRIBED AS DIGNITY, HONOUR, SELF
RESPECT. IT IS HELD PRECIOUS THAN LIFE AND DENOTES NON
DETERIORATION IN ONE'S STATUS IN ANY ASPECT)

இன்றி அமையாச் சிறப்பின ஆயினும்
குன்ற வருப விடல்.　　　　　　　　　　　961

inRi amaiyAch siRappina aayinum
kunRa varupa vidal

Even if indispensable, of special advantage,
give up things affecting dignity and honour

சீரினும் சீரல்ல செய்யாரே சீரொடு
பேராண்மை வேண்டு பவர்.　　　　　　　962

seerinum seeralla seyyArae seerodu
paerANmai vaeNdu pavar

Those who pursue valour and fame, will not
indulge in deeds not befitting their dignity

பெருக்கத்து வேண்டும் பணிதல் சிறிய
சுருக்கத்து வேண்டும் உயர்வு.　　　　　963

perukkaththu vaeNdum paNithal siRiya
surukkaththu vaeNdum uyarvu

Humility is the 'sine qua non' in prosperity and
fame; even in adversities, uphold dignity

தலையின் இழிந்த மயிர்அனையர் மாந்தர்
நிலையின் இழிந்தக் கடை.　　　　　　964

thalaiyin izin-tha mayiranaiyar mAn-thar
n-ilaiyin izin-thak kadai

Decline of status in society mars dignity,
like the hair fallen from the head

குன்றின் அனையாரும் குன்றுவர் குன்றுவ
குன்றி அனைய செயின்.　　　　　　　965

kunRin anaiyArum kunRuvar kunRuva
kunRi anaiya seyin

A mean deed, though small like a berry seed
diminishes respect, for the mighty like a hill

புகழ்இன்றால் புத்தேள்நாட்டு உய்யாதால் என்மற்று
இகழ்வார்பின் சென்று நிலை.   966

pukazinRaal puththaeLn-Attu uyyAthAl enmatRRu
ikazvArpin senRu n-ilai

There is no sustained pleasure without fame; why then
toe and cringe behind those, who snub in scorn?

ஒட்டார்பின் சென்றுஒருவன் வாழ்தலின் அந்நிலையே
கெட்டான் எனப்படுதல் நன்று.   967

ottArpin senRu oruvan vAzthalin an-n-ilaiyae
kettAn enappaduthal n-anRu

It is far better to die in dignity, than compromising one's
honour, and hankering after those who disregard

மருந்தோமற்று ஊன்ஓம்பும் வாழ்க்கை பெருந்தகைமை
பீடழிய வந்த இடத்து.   968

marun-thO-matRRu uunOmpum vAzkkai perun-thakaimai
peeduaziya van-tha idaththu

When dignity and honour run the risk of forfeiture,
life as a medicine to nurse the body, is of no avail

மயிர்நீப்பின் வாழாக் கவரிமா அன்னார்
உயிர்நீப்பர் மானம் வரின்.   969

mayirn-eeppin vAzAk kavarimA annAr
uyirn-eeppar mAnam varin

A rare species of Deer seeks its end when its hairs
shed; people of dignity forfeit life to save honour

இளிவரின் வாழாத மானம் உடையார்
ஒளிதொழுது ஏத்தும் உலகு.   970

iLivarin vAzAtha mAnam udaiyAr
oLithozuthu aeththum ulaku

Those who will not live to see their honour sink, are
leading lights, whom the world adorns and hails

98. பெருமை
perumai
PRIDE IN GREATNESS
(LEGITIMATE PRIDE RESIDES SAFEGUARDED IN GREATNESS,
VIRTUES, VERACITY AND SKILLS, CONTRA DISTINCT FROM
VANITY, PETTINESS AND MEANNESS)

ஒளிஒருவற்கு உள்ள வெறுக்கை இளிஒருவற்கு
அஃதுஇறந்து வாழ்தும் எனல்.　　　　　971

*oLioruvaRku uLLa veRukkai iLioruvaRku
aqthuiRan-thu vAzthum enal*

Strength of a pure mind is the light of greatness;
a life devoid of justifiable pride is baneful

பிறப்புஒக்கும் எல்லா உயிர்க்கும் சிறப்புஒவ்வா
செய்தொழில் வேற்றுமை யான்.　　　　　972

*piRappuokkum ellA uyirkkum siRappuovvA
seythozil vaetRRumai yAn*

All life on earth is same in origin; but each one's merit
varies according to avocations and skills, not by birth

மேலிருந்தும் மேலல்லார் மேலல்லர் கீழிருந்தும்
கீழல்லார் கீழல் லவர்.　　　　　973

*maelirun-thum maelallar maelallar keezirun-thum
keezallar keezal lavar*

Wealth and position are not essential signs of greatness;
the honest retain virtues even in extreme privation

ஒருமை மகளிரே போலப் பெருமையும்
தன்னைத்தான் கொண்டுஒழுகின் உண்டு.　　　　　974

*orumai makaLirae pOlap perumaiyum
thannaiththAn koNduozukin uNdu*

Greatness, like chastity of humans, has to be safely
guarded by self-discipline and veracity

பெருமை உடையவர் ஆற்றுவார் ஆற்றின்
அருமை உடைய செயல்.　　　　　975

perumai udaiyavar aatRRuvAr aatRRin
arumai udaiya seyal

Great deeds are achieved by rare skills of people
who act with a mission and pride of fullfilment

சிறியார் உணர்ச்சியுள் இல்லை பெரியாரைப்
பேணிக்கொள் வேமென்னும் நோக்கு.   976

siRiyAr uNarchchiyuL illai periyAraip
paeNikkoL vaemennum n-Okku

The petty minded lack a sense of purpose and
care not to respect and seek the great

இறப்பே புரிந்த தொழிற்றுஆம் சிறப்புந்தான்
சீரல் லவர்கண் படின்.   977

iRappae purin-tha thoziRRuaam siRappun-thAn
seeral lavarkaN padin

The low, given to dubious ways, in power and pelf,
behave in contempt of decency and overshoot

பணியுமாம் என்றும் பெருமை சிறுமை
அணியுமாம் தன்னை வியந்து.   978

paNiyumAm enRum perumai siRumai
aNiyumAm thannai viyan-thu

Greatness always bows in dignified modesty;
meanness revels in self-acclaimed vanity

பெருமை பெருமிதம் இன்மை சிறுமை
பெருமிதம் ஊர்ந்து விடல்.   979

perumai perumitham inmai siRumai
perumitham uurn-thu vidal

Greatness, sans vanity, is just pride; pettiness
rides in boastful joy on offensive vanity

அற்றம் மறைக்கும் பெருமை சிறுமைதான்
குற்றமே கூறி விடும்.   980

atRRam maRaikkum perumai siRumaithAn
kutRRAmae kURi vidum

The pride of greatness doesn't expose weaknesses;
the vanity of smallness proclaims in vilification

99. சான்றாண்மை
sAnRANmai
WORTHINESS (SUBLIMITY)

(LOVE, MODESTY, BENIGNANCY, FOSTERING AND TRUTH SUSTAIN
SUBLIMITY. HUMILITY, DIGNITY TO BEAR REPULSES, KINDNESS
AND STEADFASTNESS ADD STRENGTH TO IT.)

கடன்என்ப நல்லவை எல்லாம் கடன்அறிந்து
சான்றாண்மை மேற்கொள் பவர்க்கு.　　　　　981

kadanenpa n-allavai ellAm kadanaRin-thu
sAnRANmai maeRkoL pavarkku

For those dedicated to deeds worthy of good
character, goodness is a duty cast on them

குணநலம் சான்றோர் நலனே பிறநலம்
எந்நலத்து உள்ளதூஉம் அன்று.　　　　　982

kuNan-alan sAnROr n-alanae piRan-alam
yen-n-alaththu uLLathUum anRu

Goodness reposes in character and adorns; there
is no greater fame that surpasses sublimity

அன்புநாண் ஒப்புரவு கண்ணோட்டம் வாய்மையொடு
ஐந்துசால்பு ஊன்றிய தூண்.　　　　　983

anpun-AN oppuravu kaNNOttam vAymaiyodu
ain-thusAlpu uunRiya thUN

Love, modesty, benignness, fostership and truth
are the five pillars sustaining sublimity

கொல்லா நலத்தது நோன்மை பிறர்தீமை
சொல்லா நலத்தது சால்பு.　　　　　984

kollA n-alaththathu n-Onmai piRartheemai
sollA n-alaththathu sAlpu

Penance conditions the mind to abstain from killing;
sublimity controls the tongue from slandering

ஆற்றுவார் ஆற்றல் பணிதல் அதுசான்றோர்
மாற்றாரை மாற்றும் படை.　　　　　985

aatRRuvAr aatRRal paNithal athusAnROr
mAtRRArai mAtRRum padai

Humility adds strength to valour; for the worthy,
that is a non-violent weapon to wean the foe

சால்பிற்குக் கட்டளை யாதுஎனில் தோல்வி
துலையல்லார் கண்ணும் கொளல்.   986

*sAlpiRkuk kattaLai yAthuenil 'thOlvi
thulaiallAr kaNNum koLal*

The dignity to bear repulses from unequals, is the
touch-stone of character, for the worthy

இன்னாசெய் தார்க்கும் இனியவே செய்யாக்கால்
என்ன பயத்ததோ சால்பு.   987

*innAsey thArkkum iniyavae seyyAkkAl
enna payaththathO sAlpu*

If one does not extend kindness to cure those
who inflict pain, sublimity has no meaning

இன்மை ஒருவற்கு இளிவுஅன்று சால்பென்னும்
திண்மைஉண் டாகப் பெறின்.   988

*inmai oruvaRku izivuanRu sAlpennum
thiNmaiuN dAkap peRin*

Steadfastness to good character, even in dire
needs, saves one from the pain of shame

ஊழி பெயரினும் தாம்பெயரார் சான்றாண்மைக்கு
ஆழி எனப்படு வார்.   989

*uuzi peyarinum thAmpeyarAr sAnRANmaikku
aazi enappadu vAr*

The great who sail firm in a sea of virtue, shake not
even when the mighty universe is in convulsions

சான்றவர் சான்றாண்மை குன்றின் இருநிலந்தான்
தாங்காது மன்னோ பொறை.   990

*sAnRavar sAnRANmai kunRin irun-ilanthAn
thAngkAthu mannO poRai*

When the sublime sink from virtue's worth
the burden of woes is hard on the earth

100. பண்புடைமை (குணநலம்)
paNpu udaimai
COURTEOUS MANNERS

(KINDNESS OF LOVE, SOFT BEHAVIOUR AND HUMANISM AID TO
THE CULTURE OF GOOD MANNERS)

எண்பதத்தால் எய்தல் எளிதுஎன்ப யார்மாட்டும்
பண்புடைமை என்னும் வழக்கு.
991

eNpathaththAl eythal eLithuenpa yArmAttum
paNpudaimai ennum vazakku

Courteousness is a natural way of life with the polite,
who are free for access and forthcoming

அன்புடைமை ஆன்ற குடிப்பிறத்தல் இவ்விரண்டும்
பண்புடைமை என்னும் வழக்கு.
992

anpudaimai aanRa kudippiRaththal ivviraNdum
paNpudaimai ennum vazakku

Worthy social background and the kindness
of love foster courtesy as an easy trait

உறுப்பொத்தல் மக்கள்ஒப்பு அன்றால் வெறுத்தக்க
பண்புஒத்தல் ஒப்பதாம் ஒப்பு.
993

uRuppoththal makkaLoppu anRAl veRuththakka
paNpoththal oppathAm oppu

Similarity of shapes does not make peoples' worth;
it is courteous manners unique in humankind

நயனொடு நன்றி புரிந்த பயனுடையார்
பண்புபா ராட்டும் உலகு.
994

n-ayanodu n-anRi purin-tha payanudaiyAr
paNpupA rAttum ulaku

Soft and benign in attitudes and duty bound,
the world acclaims the graciously helpful

நகைஉள்ளும் இன்னாது இகழ்ச்சி பகைஉள்ளும்
பண்புஉள பாடுஅறிவார் மாட்டு.
995

n-akaiuLLum innAthu ikazchchi pakaiuLLum
paNpu-uLa pAduaRivAr mAttu

Insult is harmful even in jest; just pride
resides in courtesy even to the foe

பண்புடையார்ப் பட்டுஉண்டு உலகம் அதுஇன்றேல்
மண்புக்கு மாய்வது மன்.   996

*paNpu-udaiyArp pattuuNdu ulakam athuinRael
maNpukku mAyvathu mun*

The world survives and thrives on benign best; history
is replete with civilizations losing bonds, buried in dust

அரம்போலும் கூர்மையர் ஏனும் மரம்போல்வர்
மக்கள்பண்பு இல்லா தவர்.   997

*arampOlum kUrmaiyar aenum marampOlvar
makkaLpaNpu illA thavar*

Though sharp in mind like a saw, lacking manners
and human kindness, the body is dead as wood

நண்புஆற்றா ராகி நயமில செய்வார்க்கும்
பண்புஆற்றார் ஆதல் கடை   998

*n-aNpuaatRRA raaki n-ayamila seyvArkkum
paNpuaaRRAr aathal kadai*

Discourtesy even to the unfriendly and unkind,
is mean behaviour to the mannered

நகல்வல்லர் அல்லார்க்கு மாயிரு ஞாலம்
பகலும்பாற் பட்டுஅன்று இருள்.   999

*n-akalvallAr allArkku mAiru njAlam
pakalumpAR pattuanRu iruL*

Bereft of courteous smiles, one sees only darkness
in the universe, unaware of its brighter side.

பண்புஇலான் பெற்ற பெருஞ்செல்வம் நன்பால்
கலம்தீமை யால்திரிந்து அற்று.   1000

*paNpuilAn petRRa perunjselvam n-anpAl
kalamtheemai yAlthirin-thu atRRu*

A defective container sours the milk it holds; the
ill-mannered pile up wealth to spoil in disuse

101. நன்றிஇல் செல்வம்
n-anRi il selvam
FUTILE (DORMANT) WEALTH

(HOARDED IN STRAIN BY MISERS, NOT RELISHED BY THEM OR MADE
AVAILABLE TO REDRESS OTHERS, ROTS AND FADES AWAY IN WASTE)

வைத்தான்வாய் சான்ற பெரும்பொருள் அஃதுஉண்ணான்
செத்தான் செயக்கிடந்தது இல்.   1001

*vaiththAnvAy sAnRa perumporuL aqthuuNNAn
seththAn seyakkidanthathu il*

Stacking wealth to the brim and fading off, without
relishing it, nothing is achieved in worth

பொருளான்ஆம் எல்லாமென்று ஈயாது இவறும்
மருளான்ஆம் மாணாப் பிறப்பு.   1002

*poruLAnaam ellAmenRu eeyAthu ivaRum
maruLAnaam mANAp piRappu*

Listless existence of a miser, who hankers on money
as everything worth in life, is quite dubious

ஈட்டம் இவறி இசைவேண்டா ஆடவர்
தோற்றம் நிலக்குப் பொறை.   1003

*eettam ivaRi- isaivaeNdA aadavar
thOtRRam n-ilakkup poRai*

People hoarding wealth avariciously, ignoring fame,
are unworthy of their burden to the earth

எச்சமென்று என்எண்ணுங் கொல்லோ ஒருவரால்
நச்சப் படாஅ தவன்.   1004

*echchamenRu eneNNung kollO oruvarAl
n-achchap padAa thavan*

What legacy they can leave behind, who are
despised by society as unhelpful misers

கொடுப்பதூஉம் துய்ப்பதூஉம் இல்லார்க்கு அடுக்கிய
கோடிஉண் டாயினும் இல்.   1005

*koduppathUum thuyppathUum illArku adukkiya
kOdiuN dAyinum il*

Of what avail are, countless millions stacked,
for those who would neither use nor gift?

ஏதம் பெருஞ்செல்வம் தான்துவ்வான் தக்கார்க்குஒன்று
ஈதல் இயல்பிலா தான்.   1006

aetham perunjselvam thAn thuvvAn thakkArkkuonRu
eethal iyalpilA thAn

Hugeness of wealth is a painful slur on those who
are not accustomed to enjoy it or help the needy

அற்றார்க்குஒன்று ஆற்றாதான் செல்வம் மிகநலம்
பெற்றாள் தமியள்மூத் தற்று.   1007

atRRArkkuonRu aatRRAthAn selvam mikan-alam
petRRAL thamiyaLmUth thaRRu

Wealth that loathes to redress pain of the poor,
is like spinsters in fine niche, aging in loneliness

நச்சப் படாதவன் செல்வம் நடுஊருள்
நச்சு மரம்பழுத்து அற்று.   1008

n-achchap padAthavan selvam n-adu-uuruL
n-achchu marampazuththu atRRu

Wealth with those, whom people cannot seek, is like
poisonous fruits of a tree, amidst a commune

அன்புஒளீஇத் தற்செற்று அறம்நோக்காது ஈட்டிய
ஒண்பொருள் கொள்வார் பிறர்.   1009

anpuoreeith thaRsetRRu aRamn-OkkAthu eettiya
oNporuL koLvAr piRar

Aliens pack off glittering gold, hoarded in strain
by misers, forsaking love and ignoring virtues

சீருடைச் செல்வர் சிறுதுனி மாரி
வறம்கூர்ந் தனையது உடைத்து.   1010

seerudaich selvar siRuthuni mAri
vaRamkUrn thanaiathu udaiththu

Momentary hardships of benign rich, of righteous
means, is like a drought in seasonal rains

102. நாணுடைமை
n-AN udaimai
SENSITIVITY TO SHAME (MODESTY)
(IS UNIQUE TO HUMANITY, FROM OTHER SPECIES. WORTHY
TRAITS ADORN MODESTY. SHAME OF BLAME GUARDS THE GREAT
WHO PATRONISE WORLDLY GOOD)

கருமத்தான் நாணுதல் நாணுத் திருநுதல்
நல்லவர் நாணும் பிற.　　　　　　　　　1011

*karumaththAn n-ANuthal n-ANuth thirun-uthal
n-allavar n-ANum piRa*

Sense of shame to do harmful acts and the blushing
of pretty faces in modesty, are not the same

ஊன்உடை எச்சம் உயிர்க்குஎல்லாம் வேறல்ல
நாணுடைமை மாந்தர் சிறப்பு.　　　　　1012

*uuNudai echcham uyirkkuellAm vaeRalla
n-ANudaimai mAn-thar siRappu*

Food, sense of security and the likes are no different
in lives; sensitivity of shame is unique to humanity

ஊனைக் குறித்த உயிரெல்லாம் நாண்என்னும்
நன்மை குறித்தது சால்பு.　　　　　　　1013

*uunaik kuRiththa uyirellAm n-ANennum
n-anmai kuRiththathu sAlpu*

There is no life without a body; all worthy traits
reside in the goodness of human modesty

அணிஅன்றோ நாணுடைமை சான்றோர்க்கு அஃதின்றேல்
பிணிஅன்றோ பீடு நடை.　　　　　　　1014

*aNianRO n-ANudaimai sAnROrkku aqthuinRael
piNianRO peedu n-adai*

Sense of shame and modesty adorn the worthy;
devoid of them, swaggering is painful vanity

பிறர்பழியும் தம்பழியும் நாணுவார் நாணுக்கு
உறைபதி என்னும் உலகு.　　　　　　　1015

piRarpaziyum thanpaziyum n-ANuvAr n-ANukku
uRaipathi ennum ulaku

Blameful acts, either of self or those around, induce
a shame in the worthy, where modesty resides

நாண்வேலி கொள்ளாது மன்னோ வியன்ஞாலம்
பேணலர் மேலா யவர்.   1016

n-ANvaeli koLLAthu mannO viyannjAlam
paeNalar maelA yavar

Modesty guards the great in society, who take on
the noble task of patronising worldly good

நாணால் உயிரைத் துறப்பர் உயிர்ப்பொருட்டால்
நாண்துறவார் நாண்ஆள் பவர்.   1017

n-ANAl uyiraith thuRappar uyirpporuttAl
n-ANthuRavAr n-ANaaL pavar

The guardians of modesty choose rather to give their
lives to save their pride, than to live in shame

பிறர்நாணத் தக்கது தான்நாணா நாயின்
அறம்நாணத் தக்கது உடைத்து.   1018

piRarn-ANath thakkathu thAnn-ANA naayin
aRamn-Anath thakkathu udaiththu

From those who are shameless to what the world
blames, dame virtue departs in shame

குலம்சுடும் கொள்கை பிழைப்பின் நலம்சுடும்
நாணின்மை நின்றக் கடை.   1019

kulamsudum koLkai pizaippin n-alamsudum
n-ANinmai n-inRak kadai

Lapses in codes of conduct erode social values;
blameful shame sticks to harm good grace

நாண்அகத்து இல்லார் இயக்கம் மரப்பாவை
நாணால் உயிர்மருட்டி யற்று.   1020

n-ANakaththu illAr iyakkam marappAvai
n-ANAl uyirmarutti yatRRu

Movement of duds without any sense of shame,
is like puppet shows manipulated by strings

103. குடிசெயல் வகை
kudiseyal vakai
DEVOTION TO SOCIAL CAUSES

(NATURE HELPS RESOLVE TO PERFORM DUTIES TO SOCIETY
GUIDED BY WISDOM WITHOUT AIM ON GAINS OR EXCUSES ON
SLOTH OR SEASONS. PEOPLE REVOLVE AROUND THEM LIKE THE
EARTH ROUND THE SUN)

கருமம் செயஒருவன் கைதூவேன் என்னும்
பெருமையின் பீடுடையது இல்.   1021

karumam seyaoruvan kaithUvaen ennum
perumaiyin peedu-udaiyathu il

No glory is greater than the resolve to perform
duties to one's society without slackening

ஆள்வினையும் ஆன்ற அறிவும் எனஇரண்டின்
நீள்வினையால் நீளும் குடி.   1022

aLvinaiyum aanRa aRivum enairaNdin
n-eeLvinaiyAl n-eeLum kudi

Deep devotion to duty, guided by ripe wisdom
and persistent efforts enrich society's welfare

குடிசெய்வல் என்னும் ஒருவற்குத் தெய்வம்
மடிதற்றுத் தான்முந் துறும்.   1023

kudiseyval ennum oruvaRkuth theyvam
madithatRRuth thAnmun thuRum

Mother Nature comes forth in strength to guide
those with the resolve to raise their race

சூழாமல் தானே முடிவுஎய்தும் தம்குடியைத்
தாழாது உழற்று பவர்க்கு.   1024

sUzAmal thAnae mudivueythum thamkudiyaith
thAzAthu unjaRRu pavarkku

Ceaseless toil, without wavering on gains, to upbring
society achieves success in its usual course

குற்றம் இலனாய்க் குடிசெய்து வாழ்வானைச்
சுற்றமாச் சுற்றும் உலகு.   1025

kutRRam ilanAyk kudiseythu vAzvAnaich
sutRRamAch sutRRum ulaku

People revolve, like the world around the Sun, as kith and
kin, who protect society to thrive without blemishes

நல்லாண்மை என்பது ஒருவற்குத் தான்பிறந்த
இல்லாண்மை ஆக்கிக் கொளல்.   1026

n-allANmai enpathu oruvaRkuth thAnpiRan-tha
illANmai aakkik koLal

Valour and might shine on the capability of those
who lead the family and society they belong to

அமரகத்து வன்கண்ணர் போலத் தமரகத்தும்
ஆற்றுவார் மேற்றே பொறை.   1027

amarakaththu vankaNNar pOlath thamarakaththum
aaRRuvAr maetRae poRai

Like bold heroes in battle, the burden of success rests
on the shoulders of those who perform in society

குடிசெய்வார்க்கு இல்லை பருவம் மடிசெய்து
மானம் கருதக் கெடும்.   1028

kudiseyvArkku illai paruvam madiseythu
mAnam karuthak kedum

To protect one's honour, to do good to society and
in time, sloth or seasons bear no excuse

இடும்பைக்கே கொள்கலள் கொல்லோ குடும்பத்தைக்
குற்றம் மறைப்பான் உடம்பு.   1029

idumpaikkae koLkalan kollO kudumpaththaik
kutRRam maRaippAn udampu

One who protects society from faults and mishaps, has
to gladly bear the burden of woes on his body

இடுக்கண்கால் கொன்றிட வீழும் அடுத்துஊன்றும்
நல்லாள் இலாத குடி.   1030

idukkaNkAl konRida veezum aduththu-uunRum
n-allAL illAtha kudi

A society lacking the strength of efficient people
to pop it up, falls apart when distress descends

104. உழவு
uzhavu
FARMING (PLOUGHING)

(THE CULTURE OF PLOUGHING AND CULTIVATING CROPS IS THE
HIGHEST SELFLESS SERVICE. GLORY AND PRESTIGE OF
AGRICULTURE IS IN TOIL LEADING AND HELPING OUT OTHERS.
DAME EARTH BLUSHES AT IDLERS IN SLOTH)

சுழன்றும்ஏர்ப் பின்னது உலகம் அதனால்
உழந்தும் உழவே தலை.   1031

suzanRumaerp pinnathu ulakam athanAl
uzan-thum uzavae thalai

Planet Earth rotates to remain firm; the culture of farming
in harness helps common good, and hence leads

உழுவார் உலகத்தார்க்கு ஆணிஅஃது ஆற்றாது
எழுவாரை எல்லாம் பொறுத்து.   1032

uzuvAr ulakththArkku aaNiaqthu aatRRAthu
ezuvArai ellAm poRuththu

Tillers of soil are linchpins to the vehicle of life, bearing
burden of all those opting out for vocations lighter

உழுதுஉண்டு வாழ்வாரே வாழ்வார்மற்று எல்லாம்
தொழுதுஉண்டு பின்செல் பவர்.   1033

uzuthuNdu vAzvArae vAzvArmatRRu ellAm
thozuthuNdu pinsel pavar

Agriculture has the unique prestige of self-reliance;
other professions have to bow and toe to eat

பலகுடை நீழலும் தங்குடைக்கீழ்க் காண்பர்
அலகுடை நீழ லவர்.   1034

palakudai n-eezalum thangkudaikkeezk kANpar
alakudai n-eezha lavar

Who rule the lands that have the shade of bountiful
crops, can protect others under their umbrellas

இரவார் இரப்பார்க்குஒன்று ஈவர் கரவாது
கைசெய்துஉண் மாலை யவர்.   1035

iravAr irappArkkuonru eevAr karavAthu
kaiseythuN mAlai yavar

Who proud of their toil on the soil, look not to others to
subsist, but willingly help out those seeking in need

உழவினார் கைம்மடங்கின் இல்லை விழைவதூஉம்
விட்டேமென் பார்க்கும் நிலை.   1036

uzavinAr kaimmadangkin illai vizaivathUum
vittaemen pArkkum n-ilai

Sages claiming renunciation cannot save their lives
when farmers shrink their hands and fail to perform

தொடிப்புழுதி கஃசா உணக்கின் பிடிஎருவும்
வேண்டாது சாலப் படும்.   1037

thodippuzuthi kaqsA uNakkin pidieruvum
vaeNdAthu sAlap padum

Ploughed and sun dried to dust, four fold in volume, the
soil yields in richness, sans even a handful of manure

ஏரினும் நன்றால் எருஇடுதல் கட்டபின்
நீரினும் நன்றுஅதன் காப்பு.   1038

aerinum n-anRAl eruiduthal kattapin
n-eerinum n-anRuathan kAppu

Manuring is as good as ploughing and watering; after
weeding, protecting crops from harm is of equal need

செல்லான் கிழவன் இருப்பின் நிலம்புலந்து
இல்லாளின் ஊடி விடும்.   1039

sellAn kizavan iruppin n-ilampulan-thu
illALin uudi vidum

When the farmer suitor fails to visit, court and
love, dame field longs, sulks and spouts

இலம்என்று அசைஇ இருப்பாரைக் காணின்
நிலம்என்னும் நல்லாள் நகும்.   1040

ilamenRu asaii iruppAraik kAnin
n-ilamennum n-allAL n-akum

Good earth blushes and laughs at the able
bodied idling in sloth and lurking in poverty

105. நல்குரவு
nalkuravu
POVERTY (INDIGENCE)
(INDIGENCE, DEPRIVATION, LACK OF WHEREWITHAL, CRAVING
WANT INDUCE FATIGUE, FALTERING, MISERIES; DESTROYS
VIRTUES AND RESPECT AND DRIVES TO RENOUNCE LIFE)

இன்மையின் இன்னாதது யாதுஎனின் இன்மையின்
இன்மையே இன்னா தது.　　　　　1041

*inmaiyin innAthathu yAthuenin inmaiyin
inmaiyae innA thathu*

There is no pain greater than poverty; deprivation
pinches and torments like nothing else

இன்மை எனஒரு பாவி மறுமையும்
இம்மையும் இன்றி வரும்.　　　　　1042

*inmai enaoru pAvi maRumaiyum
immaiyum inRi varum*

The cruel lack of wherewithal, in the guise of poverty,
spoils life to-day and expectations of tomorrow

தொல்வரவும் தோளும் கெடுக்கும் தொகையாக
நல்குரவு என்னும் நசை.　　　　　1043

*tholvaravum thOlum kedukkum thokaiyAka
n-alkuravu ennum n-asai*

Ancestral traditions and family bonds are severely
destroyed by the painful itch of poverty

இற்பிறந்தார் கண்ணேயும் இன்மை இளிவந்த
சொல்பிறக்கும் சோர்வு தரும்.　　　　　1044

*iRpiRan-thAr kaNNaeyum inmai iLivan-tha
solpirakkum sOrvu tharum*

Even in people from credible society, craving
want induces fatigue and foul mouth

நல்குரவு என்னும் இடும்பையுள் பல்குறைத்
துன்பங்கள் சென்று படும்.　　　　　1045

n-alkuravu ennum idumpaiuL palkuraith
thunpangkaL senRu padum

The chest of pain in poverty stores and breeds
a train of other miseries, in a row

நல்பொருள் நன்குஉணர்ந்து சொல்லினும் நல்கூர்ந்தார்
சொல்பொருள் சோர்வு படும்.   1046

n-alporuL n-ankuuNarn-thu sollinum n-alkUrn-thAr
solporuL sOrvu padum

Saner advice from consummate wisdom of the learned
poor fails to carry any conviction, and falters

அறம்சாரா நல்குரவு ஈன்றதா யானும்
பிறன்போல நோக்கப் படும்.   1047

aRamsArA n-alkuravu eenRathA yAnum
piRanpOla n-Okkap padum

Deprivation by acts inconsistent with the bonds of virtue
are looked upon strangely, even by a mother

இன்றும் வருவது கொல்லோ நெருநலும்
கொன்றது போலும் நிரப்பு.   1048

inRum varuvathu kollO n-erun-alum
konRathu pOlum n-irappu

The fiery want of hunger that benumbed me yesterday;
will it re-visit today to end my life?

நெருப்பினுள் துஞ்சலும் ஆகும் நிரப்பினுள்
யாதுஒன்றும் கண்பாடு அரிது.   1049

n-eruppinuL thunjsalum aakum n-irappinuL
yAthuonRum kaNpAdu arithu

The fire outside can envelop one to eternal sleep;
that inside, of hunger permits not a wink of the brow

துப்புரவு இல்லார் துவரத் துறவாமை
உப்பிற்கும் காடிக்கும் கூற்று.   1050

thuppuravu illAr thuvarath thuRavAmai
uppiRkum kAdikkum kUtRRu

The poor, who cannot muster the means of livelihood, should
renounce in full, instead of depleting salt and gruel

106. இரவு (பிறரிடம் பொருள் வேண்டிப் பெறல்)
iravu (piRaridam porul vaeNdip peRal)
SEEKING ALMS

(IT IS DISPARAGING TO HUMAN DIGNITY. AID WITH GRACE CONSCIOUS
OF DUTY TO CONTRIBUTE TO NEEDY AS AN EQUITY REDEEMS GRIEF OF
THE HAVE-NOTS AND ENHANCES GLORY OF THE GIVER)

இரக்க இரத்தக்கார்க் காணின் கரப்பின்
அவர்பழி தம்பழி யன்று.   1051

irakka iraththakkAr kANin karappin
avarpazi thampazi yanRu

**The needy seek those who can afford; blame sticks
to the one who declines and conceals**

இன்பம் ஒருவற்கு இரத்தல் இரந்தவை
துன்பம் உறாஅ வரின்.   1052

inpam oruvaRku iraththal iran-thavai
thunpam uRAa varin

**If aid comes in grace, without paining the seeker,
the beneficiary's joy is all the more greater**

கரப்பிலா நெஞ்சின் கடன்அறிவார் முன்நின்று
இரப்பும்ஓர் ஏர் உடைத்து.   1053

karappilA n-enjsin kadanaRivAr munn-inRu
irappumoor aer udaiththu

**One who is conscious of the duty to contribute
without constraints, charms the taker's pride**

இரத்தலும் ஈதலே போலும் கரத்தல்
கனவிலும் தேற்றாதார் மாட்டு.   1054

iraththalum iithalae pOlum karaththal
kanavilum thaetRRAthAr mAttu

**Deem giving and taking as a matter of equity, and
do not fancy even in dreams, ideas to hold back**

கரப்புஇலார் வையகத்து உண்மையான் கண்நின்று
இரப்பவர் மேற்கொள் வது.   1055

karappuilAr vaiyakaththu uNmaiyAl kaNn-inRu
irappavar maeRkoL vathu

As the world has goodness in people without mental
constraints, the hapless seek their munificence

கரப்புஇடும்பை இல்லாரைக் காணின் நிரப்புஇடும்பை
எல்லாம் ஒருங்கு கெடும்.   1056

karappuidumpai illAraik kANin n-irappuidumpai
ellAm orungku kedum

Free from the pain of concealing, the genial face
of the munificent redeems grief of the have-nots

இகழ்ந்துள்ளாது ஈவாரைக் காணின் மகிழ்ந்துஉஎஎள்ளம்
உள்ளுள் உவப்பது உடைத்து.   1057

ikazn-thueLLAthu iivAraik kANin makizn-thu-uLLam
uLLuL uvappathu udaiththu

The act of giving in dignity, without maligning in
derision, makes the mind rejoice in contemplation

இரப்பாரை இல்லாயின் ஈர்ங்கண்மா ஞாலம்
மரப்பாவை சென்றுவந்து அற்று.   1058

irappArai illAyin eerngkaNmA njAlam
marappAvai senRuvan-thu atRRu

When takers are scarce in this kind great world, lacking
the pleasures of giving, people move like puppets

ஈவார்கண் என்னுண்டாம் தோற்றம் இரந்துகோள்
மேவார் இலாஅக் கடை.   1059

eevArkaN enuNdAm thOtRRam iran-thukOL
maevAr ilAak kadai

Where does glory stand, when there are no takers
to offer mental satisfaction to the giver?

இரப்பான் வெகுளாமை வேண்டும் நிரப்புஇடும்பை
தானேயும் சாலும் கரி.   1060

irappAn vekuLAmai vaeNdum n-irappuidumpai
thAnaeyum sAlum kari

Seekers should disdain anger; the giver, even
with good intent, may also be in dire straits

107. இரவு அச்சம் (இரத்தலின் இழிவை அஞ்சுதல்)
iravu achcham
DREADING ALMS

(SEEKING ALMS FOR LIVELIHOOD IS DISPARAGING; SUCH A
SOCIAL ORDER HAS TO BE CHANGED. THE HONOUR AND
DIGNITY OF CEASELESS TOIL AND EFFORTS SHOULD BE UPHELD)

கரவாது உவந்துஈயும் கண்ணன்னார் கண்ணும்
இரவாமை கோடி யுறும்.　　1061

karavAthu uvan-thueeyum kaNNannAr kaNNum
iravAmai kOdi yurum

The code of not seeking alms, even from friends who
extend with benign mirth, is worth millions

இரந்தும் உயிர்வாழ்தல் வேண்டின் பரந்து
கெடுக உலகுஇயற்றி யான்.　　1062

iran-thum uyirvAzthal vaeNdin paran-thu
keduka ulakuiyaRRi yAn

Let the rulers who contrive situations where people
have to seek alms for living, shall loiter and rot

இன்மை இடும்பை இரந்துதீர் வாம்என்னும்
வன்மையின் வன்பாட்டது இல்.　　1063

inmai idumpai iran-thutheer vAmennum
vanmaiyin vanpAttathu il

There is nothing more disparaging than the de-meaning
act of seeking alms to alleviate the pain of poverty

இடமெல்லாம் கொள்ளாத் தகைத்தே இடமில்லாக்
காலும் இரவுஒல்லாச் சால்பு.　　1064

idamellAm koLLAth thakaiththae idamillAk
kAlum iravuollAch chAlpu

Worth of the great is greater than space, who do not
seek alms, even when there is no other way to live

தெண்ணீர் அடுபுற்கை ஆயினும் தாள்தந்தது
உண்ணலில் ஊங்குஇனியது இல்.　　1065

theNNeer adupuRkai aayinum thALthan-thathu
uNNalin uungkuiniyathu il

Be it thin watery gruel, it is sweet satisfaction, when earned
with one's own ceaseless toil and efforts

ஆவிற்கு நீரென்று இரப்பினும் நாவிற்கு
இரவின் இளிவந்தது இல்.　　　　　**1066**

aaviRku n-eerenRu iRappinum n-AviRku
iravin iLivan-thathu il

Begging is a mean word the tongue shall shun,
even for a good cause like water for the cow

இரப்பன் இரப்பாரை எல்லாம் இரப்பின்
கரப்பார் இரவன்மின் என்று.　　　　　**1067**

irappan irappArai ellAm irappin
karappAr iravanmin enRu

Besiege the seekers of alms, if they have to seek, not
to seek those who have no qualms in concealing

இரவென்னும் ஏமாப்பில் தோணி கரவென்னும்
பார்தாக்கப் பக்கு விடும்.　　　　　**1068**

iravuennum aemAppil thouNi karavuennum
pArthAkkap pakku vidum

The boat of life, sailing in the dark to seek alms, lacking
safety of mental strength, crashes on a rock of refusal

இரவுஉள்ள உள்ளம் உருகும் கரவுஉள்ள
உள்ளதூஉம் இன்றிக் கெடும்.　　　　　**1069**

iravuuLLa uLLam urukum karavu-uLLa
uLLathUum inRik kedum

The strength of mind melts at the thought of begging
pain; there is no life left to take on repulses

கரப்பவர்க்கு யாங்குஒளிக்கும் கொல்லோ இரப்பவர்
சொல்லாடப் போலும் உயிர்.　　　　　**1070**

karappavarkku yAngkuoLikkum kollO irappavar
sollAdap pOm uyir

A word of refusal kills the seeker of alms;
where does a niggard's life hide for safety?

108. கயமை (இழிவான எண்ணம், செயல், பழக்கம்)
kayamai
MEANNESS (COWARDICE)
(MEANNESS OF THOUGHTS, ACTIONS AND HABITS ARE THE
OUTCOME OF NEGLECTING TOIL AND SELF-HELP AND SEEKING
ALMS IGNORING DIGNITY AND HONOUR)

மக்களே போல்வர் கயவர் அவரன்ன
ஒப்பாரி யாம்கண்டது இல்.   **1071**

makkaLae pOlvar kayavar avaranna
oppAri yAmkaNdathu il

The mean seem human in form; it is very hard
to differentiate the sham by mere looks

நன்றறி வாரிற் கயவர் திருஉடையர்
நெஞ்சத்து அவலம் இலர்.   **1072**

n-anRaRi vAriR kayavar thiru-udaiyar
n-enjsaththu avalam ilar

No care or concern bothers the low; that way
cowards are better endowed than the wise

தேவர் அனையர் கயவர் அவரும்தாம்
மேவன செய்துஒழுக லான்.   **1073**

thaevar anaiyar kayavar avarumthAm
maevana seythuozuka lAn

The base resemble the divine, in supposed heaven,
in their callousness and pursuit of easy gains

அகப்பட்டி ஆவாரைக் காணின் அவரின்
மிகப்பட்டுச் செம்மாக்கும் கீழ்.   **1074**

akappatti aavAraik kAnin avarin
mikappattuch semmAkkum keez

The mean in the company of shameless
rakes, revel in vile and exult in smile

அச்சமே கீழ்களது ஆசாரம் எச்சம்
அவாஉண்டேல் உண்டாம் சிறிது.   **1075**

achchamae keezkaLathu aasAram echcham
avAuNdael uNdAm siRithu

Fear is the rod that drives the low to behave;
on occasions they pose discipline in desires

அறைபறை அன்னர் கயவர்தாம் கேட்ட
மறைபிறர்க்கு உய்த்துரைக்க லான்.   1076

aRaipaRai annar kayavarthAm kaetta
maRaipiRarkku uyththuraikka lAn

The base are keen to proclaim secrets to others, like
the drum beats announcing the diktats of law

ஈர்ங்கை விதிரார் கயவர் கொடிறுஉடைக்கும்
கூன்கைய ரல்லா தவர்க்கு.   1077

eerngkai vithirAr kayavar kodiRu-udaikkum
kUnkaiya rallA thavarkku

The low will not shake their damp hands or give in,
except to threats of clenched fists that break jaws

சொல்லப் பயன்படுவர் சான்றோர் கரும்புபோல்
கொல்லப் பயன்படும் கீழ்.   1078

sollap payanpaduvar sAnROr karumpupOl
kollap payanpadum keez

The worthy listen to words of wisdom and do good; the
mean yield juice like sugarcane crushed to pulp

உடுப்பதூஉம் உண்பதூஉம் காணின் பிறர்மேல்
வடுக்காண வற்றாகும் கீழ்.   1079

uduppathUum uNpathUum kANin piRarmael
vadukkANa vatRRAkum keez

The low cannot tolerate to see others relish food
and dress, but stoop to fault and blame

எற்றிற் குரியர் கயவர்ஒன்று உற்றக்கால்
விற்றற்கு உரியர் விரைந்து.   1080

etRiR kuriyar kayavaronRu utRakkAl
vitRaRku uriyar virain-thu

The mean are bereft of any manners; in a
crisis they easily barter themselves in haste

திருவள்ளுவ மாலை

எம்மதமும் எவ்வினமும் எந்நாளும்
சம்மதம் என்று ஏற்கும் தமிழ்வேதம்

- சுத்தானந்த பாரதியார்

ஆயிரத்து முந்நூற்று முப்ப தருங்குறளும்
பாயிரத்தி னோடு பகர்ந்ததற்பின் - போயொருத்தர்
வாய்க்கேக்க நூல்உளவோ மன்னு தமிழ்ப்புலவ
ராய்க்கேட்க வீற்றிருக்க லாம்.

- நத்தத்தனார்

மணற்கிளைக்க நீர்ஊறும் மைந்தர்கள் வாய்வைத்து
உணச்சுரக்கும் தாய்முலை ஒண்பால் - பிணக்கிலா
வாய்மொழி வள்ளுவர் முப்பால் மதிப்புலவோர்க்கு
ஆய்தொறும் ஊறும் அறிவு.

- உருத்திரசன்ம கண்ணர்

தானே முழுதுணர்ந்து தண்டமிழின் ஒண்குறளால்
ஆனா அறமதலா அந்நான்கும் - ஏனோருக்கு
ஊழின் உரைத்தாற்கும் ஒண்ணீர் முகிலுக்கும்
வாழிஉலகு என்னாற்று மற்று.

- நக்கீரர்

'புனலிடைமூழ்கிப் பொழிலிடையுலவிப் பொன்னார்இழையும்
துகிலும்பூண்டு
கனிமொழி பேசி இல்லறம் நாடும் காதல் மாந்தர் மகிழ்வுறும் நாடு'
                                                    - பாரதிதாசன்

'punalidaimUzkip pozilidaiulavip ponnArizaiyum thukilumpUNdu
kanimozi pEsi illaRam n–Adum kAthal mAn-thar makizvuRum n–Adu'
                                                    - pArathithAsan

---

பகுதி 3 – இன்பத்துப்பால்
pakuthi 3 - inbaththuppaal
Part III – LOVE LIFE

'Lovers' own country to swim the streams and stroll the dales
draped in silks, decked in jewels, sharing sweet thoughts.

                                                    - *Bharathidasan.*

PART 3: LOVE LIFE
Foreword

It is a special feature of ThiukkuRaL to balance life in three equal parts namely virtues, wealth and happiness; rather than lining them on priorities, stress is laid on harmonising and integrating them as vital parts, one complementing the other.

'Be a light unto thyself, seek not aid of external lights'

Buddha

Fullness of life is achieved by virtuously acquired wealth of education, knowledge, wisdom, self realisation combined with material prosperity and a healthy social order which is based on an exemplary life in family, promoting cultural values. Complete understanding, tolerance and cooperation, besides mental and physical compatibility between the husband and wife are essential in a family to foster relations, friends, hospitality, munificence for happiness and peaceful progress.

Ancient Thamizh literature like Tholkaappiyam, AkanAnuuRu, KuRunthokai deal elaborately on the glory of civilization and cultural refinement achieved by the people in social and family life, as in courting and romance in personal life. Peoples' lives were synchronised with Nature and organised in terms of Lands (hills, dales, farm lands, dry lands), Sea sides, Time (into six divisions) and Seasons (into four).

Personal life was divided into two stages, romance in love *(kaLaviyal)* and chaste wedlock *(kaRpiyal)* with well defined customs and procedures dealt with in literature. It is an exclusive merit of this part of KuRaL that it deals in an enchanting manner with the mental and psychological aspects and niceties of romance and personal life in the format of a monologue drama in the words of the lovers, with unmatched poetic excellence of the highest sophistication and imagination about seeing, meeting, confabulating, understanding, attachment of passion, uniting in marriage, separation on avocations, the pain and pallor of it, the pleasure of reunion, enhanced by feigned sulking and pouting preceding it. The option of monologue with only the lovers as solo players, as against the dialogue dramas in other popular literature in Thamizh and in other languages like Sanskrit and English, has special effects in vividly impressing the content. Instead of dealing elaborately on the customs of extra-marital lives of males, KuRaL just leaves them with hints in the passing.

It is rare to see any other literature, in any other language, dealing with all aspects of life in totality, with an integrated view in a single work. It is also significant, while dealing with the finer ecstatic aspects of sexual life implicitly, KuRaL has kept off from the erotic/esoteric aspects of sex (as dealt with by Vaathsyaayanar in Sanskrit and by KoKo and others in English).

Family life has been defined in traditional customs as the partnership for life (not a contract of marriage, or living together for convenience) by a male and female of suitable age who love each other, achieve a union of minds and when the male is capable of supporting a family, enter into wedlock. The male used to give gifts of cattle, sheep etc. to the girl's parents as compensation for taking her hand in marriage. This still continues to be a practice with some hill tribes.

'The hunters maids use to play in the forests and
the warriors love and take them in marriage'

Baarathidaasan

Though males were in the forefront of society, KuRaL evidences the fact that ladies were respected as partners in life, bearing responsibilities. In later periods in the middle ages this turned topsy- turvy by external invasion, whereby marriages are arranged by the families mainly with material gains as consideration, and the girls' parents are subjected to enormous strains and penury, to comply with compulsory gifts extracted from them by the boys' families. The girls are taken in only if they came in with a fortune. An Arab proverb says:

'The borders of all countries are readily opened
to the asses that bring in loads of gold'.

The cow has been considered from times yore as a property to the family (KuRaL also hints at this in couplets 400 and 524). Even today in brahmin families the daughter-in-law is called cow-girl (*maattup peN*) implying her usage as a source for extracting money from the in-laws. This is totally alien to traditional Thamizh culture, which deems and welcomes the bride as another daughter of the house united in the family (*marumakaL*).

'It will be a fantasy like the horn of a rabbit, until slavery

of ladies is eradicated, to expect the land to be free'

BaarathidAsan

ROMANCE IN LOVE

Chapters 109-115: Romance in Love. In a way of life attuned to nature, the youth coming of age indulge in courting and loving. This usually starts in secrecy; as the first step the boy and girl seeing and admiring each other is described as stealing the soul of the other (*kaLaviyal*). They enjoy love initially concealing their desires, without the other coming to know about it. The seed of desire sown in the field of soul, watered by love, sprouts in thoughts and flowers in the face thro' eyes. This is brought out beautifully in the following verses of poet Baarathidaasan.

'Love is the song of eyes in cosy Thamizh

Love is the language of face when the tongue is silent

Love is the natural manifestation of existence

Love sits like a soft flower on the shoulders of the dame;

When one falls for the other that stance is love

Like the flower that waffles in the gentle wind

Love bristles the figure of the beloved belle

Like juice from the honeycomb, like water of tender coconut

Love is sweet and comes in floods of streams;

The pearls smile at white lily flowers to signal love.

Young mango trees branch out in clusters of thick groves

Wide fields of flowers embraced by gentle breeze

The sea and sky merge in fantasy of rainbow colours

like the mind and eyes filled with pleasant scenes;

The peacock dancing in ecstasy of the rain clouds

The cuckoos float the dales singing sweet melodies

Green fields of paddy with golden cobs and purple canes

Trees of fruits that taste and stick like nectar

Streams in moon shine that twist and crawl stealthy;

Like the full moon piercing bright thro' the clouds

The damsel emerges from the pond in wet robes;

Waist a blitz, lips the cherry fruits, the fountain of honey;

The creeper of flowers with a shaking smile,

that the bees surround to suck for honey.

The lover seeks to drown in it; the pretty parrot flies.

As a flood merging with another, one in mind

and soul, the lovers united as tune in strings.

As they stroll in dales and groves he played the

mischief and kissed her all of a sudden; she sought

an embrace but he vanished from her eyes,

and in stealth rode into her soul to reside.

Grace of this poetry and sweetness of words surpasses any description of the ways of the lovers in romance. Love has stood young through the long passage of time to sustain life beyond the boudaries of lands, language, castes, religions and customs, with micro changes in methods and practices. The kindness of love when overcome by passion leads to sexual lust.

In personal life, Thamizh community had classified its different stages in the context of nature as:

Contacts in secrecy (kaLavu)	*KuRinji* (Hills)
Forbearance in separation	*Mullai* (Forest)
Sulking caused by separation	*Marutham* (Fields)
Separation for learning, avocations	*Paalai* (Dry Lands)
Sorrowing pain in separation	*Neithal* (Coastal)

Chapter 114: MADAL: The love-lorn male, suffering in pain, rides a dummy horse made of palmyra tree hands and leaves, surrounded by his friends and goes round the village to attract attention and to receive sympathy of folks, to gain the hands of the beloved. Even now people witness a street dance in Kerala (adjoining Thamizh Naadu) depicting this concept of ancient times (*Oolaik kuthirai aattam*).

CHASTE WEDLOCK (*KaRpiyal*)

It is a concomitant result of romance in love fruiting into a sustaining relationship for living in a family surrounded by relations and friends. Chastity has been deemed wrongly for a long time as a label attached only to women in family life. Reflecting family customs and the prevailing social order, KuRaL has also referred to this as the quality exclusive to them (54, 57, 974).

While sense of shame has been cited as common to males and females, a society dominated by males has branded women should be chaste. The deplorable situation that men can marry many women, widowers can re-marry, and men can maintain extra-marital relationships, but women are forbidden from these have been reinforced by some religious codes as well. This unilateral discrimination should have no place in a civilized society.

KuRaL while praising the uniqe qualities of women as paramount, has criticised the waywardness of men going out of bounds of family life (ch. 92), losing themselves in slavery to lust (ch. 91) and in particular specifies that reasoned wisdom has to keep away from harlots (917); those who mind their health should stay off from the contact of women outside virtues (916).

Of the 18 chapters in *KaRpiyal* those dealing with separation for amassing wealth (1230, 1263), to take up assignments from the ruler (690, 1268), for other reasons of discordance (1130, 1155, 1255), sensing the eve of separation, taking it in the stride, variously feeling and bemoaning the pain of it, the expressions are mostly of the loved one, the female.

While couplet 1196 says that one sided infatuation is sour; out of 180 couplets 18 alone are spoken by the male, while 160 are by the female; only two by the maid; so as to stress that the grief and pain of separation is primarily on the female bearing its burden. In romance it is the male who is more forthcoming, 51 out of 70 times. Perhaps kuRaL also stands witness to the practice that after marriage, the male loses his voice in the family; language itself is termed as 'mother tongue' as the father has less opportunities to speak out.

Reference to a recently reported anecdote about the behaviour of doves in love-life is interesting. From a pair, the female was separated and left off 1000 miles away. It flew back fearlessly , un-mindful of fatigue, to get back and rejoin its mate. But on a similar trial, the male chose to halt many times on its way where it established new contacts, and returned after a long time. When we look deep, it tells us that the male species even in humanity has not come off from such habits, save in one aspect. The female dove goes out in search of the male pair and finds it out at its camp, while the human female waits in patience for the leisurely return of the male.

Wedlock: Chapters 116-133: These detail the various stages of separation of the lovers and the pains caused by it. 116. The mental status of lovers on the eve of separation. 117. In the thoughts of the lover the beloved's body fatigues and leans. 118. The love blames her eyes for her grief. 119. Her body is dominated by pallor and pimples. 120. Withering in loneliness 121. Bemoaning separation. 122. Scenes in the dreams of the love 123. Pain inflicted by the pallid eve. 124. Body losing its glamour and charm. 125. The lady seeking solace from her soul 126. Compose of the mind disturbed. 127. Throbbing to meet the lover. 128. Hinting at her physical/mental strains to others 129. Throbbing for re-union. 130. Sulking with her soul. All these are presented as the expressions of the lady love addressing her lover, maid, to the features of nature and to her soul, to give vent to her grief, trying to bear the pain and the inability to succeed in that.

Noteworthy features of this situation are - though in suspicion and suspense of her lover's interest in her and the chance of reunion, the lady in distress is anxious that he should be in good health and spirits wherever he is; folks around should not fault him for desertion; and expresses sympathy to the plight of those suffering like her in one-sided passion, separation, desertion, destitution and widow-hood.

Chapters 131-133: On return of the lover, he takes to console her grief, she spouts in feigned sulking, he tries to overcome it and both enjoy the pleasures of intimacy; the delicacy of these are graphically presented.

In couplet 1187 ' I turned a nonce from his close embrace, as if waiting for the chance, pallor seized me in a trance' describes the closeness of lovers and the solidness of life in wedlock. In couplet 1197, the reference to Cupid is a metaphor for the passion of love.

Sugar-cane, the bow of cupid, has interesting resemblances to love - sweetness increases from top to bottom, beginning to the end (1110); sucrose chewed with the pulp and saliva is more sweet and healthy; love laced with sulking multiplies pleasure; like sugar contained in the juice of pulp covered by a thick skin, passion in love is conditioned and protected by the norms of wedlock.

There is humour galore in the comparison of intoxicating toddy with the passion of love – a fool in possession of a precious gift is exhilarated like a drunkard (838); the lure of liquor leads to disgrace, blurs the sense of shame and is despised by the worthy and even by the mother; it destroys health and wealth, induces fatigue and insanity (ch. 92, 93).

Couplets 1090, 1145, 1201, 1281 and 1288 bring out the superiority of love. Liquor intoxicates only those who drink it, but love affects senses of feeling and thinking; it lures at sight and brings in pleasure and lasting happiness.

109. தகையணங்குறுத்தல்
thakaiaNangku uRuththal
LOVE THAT BEAUTY DARTS
(THE PERSONALITY, SOFT MOVEMENTS AND GLANCES OF DAMSELS BAFFLE AND BEGUILE SENSES)

அணங்குகொல் ஆய்மயில் கொல்லோ கனங்குழை
மாதர்கொல் மாலும்என் நெஞ்சு.   1081

aNangkukol aaymayil kollO kanangkuzai
mAtharkol mAlumen n-enjsu

A mystic angel, a pretty peacock or a damsel with jingling
ear-lobes; my heart craves and sighs for her

நோக்கினாள் நோக்குஎதிர் நோக்குதல் தாக்கணங்கு
தானைக்கொண் டன்னது உடைத்து.   1082

n-OkkinAL n-Okkuethir n-Okkuthal thAkkaNangku
thAnaikkoN dannathu udaiththu

As I see her, the dame's counter glances are real
lances of light darting at me from her eyes

பண்டுஅறியேன் கூற்றுஎன் பதனை இனிஅறிந்தேன்
பெண்தகையால் பேரமர்க் கட்டு.   1083

paNduaRiyaen kUtRRuen pathanai iniaRin-thaen
peNthakaiyAl paeramark kattu

I had not known the harbinger of death; now I see it is
a field warrior with battling eyes, in feminine form

கண்டார் உயிருண்ணும் தோற்றத்தால் பெண்தகைப்
பேதைக்கு அமர்த்தன கண்.   1084

kaNdAr uyiruNNum thORRaththAl peNthakaip
paethaikku amarn-thana kaN

This humble artless dame surprises me with her magnetic
eyes that suck life out of me unawares

கூற்றமோ கண்ணோ பிணையோ மடவரல்
நோக்கம்இம் மூன்றும் உடைத்து.   1085

kUtRRamO kaNNO piNaiyO madavaral
n-Okkamim mUnRum udaiththu

The form of demise, mesmerizing eyes, dazzling doe; or
all at once, in her winsome looks that confuse me

கொடும்புருவம் கோடா மறைப்பின் நடுங்கஞர்
செய்யல மன்இவள் கண்.

1086

kodumpuruvam kOdA maRaippin n-adungkanjar
seyyala manivaL kaN

Why not the brows stay firm and screen her eyes
that dart lances at me, trembling in pain?

கடாஅக் களிற்றின்மேல் கட்படாம் மாதர்
படாஅ முலைமேல் துகில்.

1087

kadAak kaLiRRinmael katpadAm mAthar
padAa mulaimael thukil

The chemise lace on the buxom breasts of this belle
is like the face-shield put on a rutting tusker

ஒள்நுதற் கோஒ உடைந்ததே ஞாட்பினுள்
நண்ணாரும் உட்கும்என் பீடு.

1088

oLn-uthaR kOo udain-thathae njAtpinuL
n-aNNArum utkumen peedu

Can I trust my might and fame, feared by foes on the
field, shattering at her bright browed face?

பிணையேர் மடநோக்கும் நாணும் உடையாட்கு
அணிஎவனோ ஏதில தந்து.

1089

piNaiaer madan-Okkum n-ANum udaiyAtku
aNievanO aethila than-thu

For the damsel decked in modesty, and dazed
fawnlike looks, of what avail are other jewels?

உண்டார்கண் அல்லது அடுநறாக் காமம்போல்
கண்டார் மகிழ்செய்தல் இன்று.

1090

uNdArkaN allathu adun-aRAk kAmampOl
kaNdAr makizseythal inRu

Seasoned wine deludes only those who drink it;
nothing delights like love at first sight

110. குறிப்பு அறிதல்
kuRippu aRithal
SIGNS OF LOVE

(AN INVITING LOOK CONCEALED BY MODESTY, A HIDDEN SMILE
AND FALTERING STEPS SIGNAL THE SYMPTOMS OF LOVE)

இருநோக்கு இவளுண்கண் உள்ளது ஒருநோக்கு
நோய்நோக்குஒன்று அந்நோய் மருந்து.   1091

*irun-Okku ivaLuNkaN uLLathu orun-Okku
n-Oyn-OkkuonRu an-n-Oy marun-thu*

Her brow-painted eyes have dual intent in looks; one
that inflicts pain of love, the other that balms

கண்களவு கொள்ளும் சிறுநோக்கம் காமத்தில்
செம்பாகம் அன்று பெரிது.   1092

*kaNkaLavu koLLum siRun-Okkam kAmaththil
sempAkam anRu perithu*

Her stealthy glances have a language that speaks
the major part of love and sexual lore

நோக்கினாள் நோக்கி இறைஞ்சினாள் அஃதுஅவள்
யாப்பினுள் அட்டிய நீர்.   1093

*n-OkkinAL n-Okki iRainjsinAL aqthuavaL
yAppinuL attiya n-eer*

Her eager looks besiege in hope and wish; that is
the pail of water she sprays for love to grow

யான்நோக்குங் காலை நிலன்நோக்கும் நோக்காக்கால்
தான்நோக்கி மெல்ல நகும்.   1094

*yAnn-Okkung kAlai n-ilann-Okkum n-OkkAkkAl
thAnn-Okki mella n-akum*

She blushes and bows in modesty at my loving glances;
other times she eyes me secretly and smiles

குறிக்கொண்டு நோக்காமை அல்லால் ஒருகண்
சிறக்கணித்தாள் போல நகும்.   1095

*kuRikkoNdu n-OkkAmai allAl orukaN
siRakkaNiththAL pOla n-akum*

She avoids a direct gaze; but sideways she
glances at me with a darting smile

உறாஅ தவர்போல் சொலினும் செறாஅர்சொல்
ஒல்லை உணரப் படும்.   1096

uRAa thavarpOl solinum seRAarsol
ollai uNarap padum

Her words may pretend alien sounds, concealing love;
but her facial expressions expose her true to form

செறாஅச் சிறுசொல்லும் செற்றார்போல் நோக்கும்
உறாஅர்போன்று உற்றார் குறிப்பு.   1097

seRAach siRusollum setRArpOl n-Okkum
uRAarpOnRu utRRAr kuRippu

Hard little words sans malice, offensive looks without
fire are feigned tricks of love-lorn consent

அசையியற்கு உண்டுஆண்டோர் ஏள்யான் நோக்கப்
பசையினள் பைய நகும்.   1098

asaiyiyaRku uNduaaNduoor aeeryAn n-Okkap
pasaiyinaL paiya n-akum

Beauty is her slim waist that swings in grace;
she returns my gaze with a lovely smile

ஏதிலார் போலப் பொதுநோக்கு நோக்குதல்
காதலார் கண்ணே யுள.   1099

aethilAr pOlap pothun-Okku n-Okkuthal
kAthalar kaNNae uLa

A common look of strangers unconcern, is the hallmark
of lovers, who discern postures in public

கண்ணொடு கண்ணிணை நோக்குஒக்கின் வாய்ச்சொற்கள்
என்ன பயனும் இல.   1100

kaNNodu kaNNiNai n-Okkuokkin vAychchoRkaL
enna payanum ila

When two pairs of eyes meet to converse in
unison, words of mouth are of little use

111. புணர்ச்சி மகிழ்தல்
puNarchchi makizthal
JOY OF UNION (INTIMACY)
(LOVERS DELIGHT IN SHARING SWEET THOUGHTS, TO KNOW EACH OTHER AND UNITE IN MINDS)

கண்டுகேட்டு உண்டுடயிர்த்து உற்றுஅறியும் ஐம்புலனும்
ஒண்தொடி கண்ணே உள. **1101**

kaNdukaettu uNduuyirththu uRRuaRiyum aimpulanum
oNthodi kaNNae uLa

In the bright bangled belle's beauty I sense the
joy of touch, sight, sound, smell and taste

பிணிக்கு மருந்து பிறமன் அணியிழை
தன்நோய்க்குத் தானே மருந்து. **1102**

piNikku marun-thu piRaman aNiizai
thann-Oykkuth thAnae marun-thu

Medicines cure other ailments but, for the bejewelled
beauty's love sickness she herself is the cure

தாம்வீழ்வார் மென்தோள் துயிலின் இனிதுகொல்
தாமரைக் கண்ணான் உலகு. **1103**

thAmveezvAr men-thOL thuyilin inithukol
thAmaraik kaNNAn ulaku

Is there in life a brighter joy than the comfort of
arms of the loved one, beaming like a lotus?

நீங்கின் தெறூஉம் குறுகுங்கால் தண்ணென்னும்
தீயாண்டுப் பெற்றாள் இவள். **1104**

n-eengkin theRUum kuRukungkAl thaNennum
theeyANdup petRRAL ivaL

Separation is scorching summer sun, intimacy is cool
spring; wherefrom she gained this warmth!

வேட்ட பொழுதின் அவையவை போலுமே
தோட்டார் கதுப்பினாள் தோள். **1105**

vaetta pozuthin avaiavai pOlumae
thOttAr kathuppinAL thOL

The damsel of flower-decked locks and cheeky face
has her shoulders of bamboo or whatever to my fancy

உறுதோறு உயிர்தளிர்ப்பத் தீண்டலால் பேதைக்கு
அமிழ்தின் இயன்றன தோள்.   1106

*uRuthORu uyirthaLirppath theeNdalAl paethaikku
amizthin iyanRana thOL*

The simple artless belle has shoulders of nectar's
charm in embrace, that thrills my life each time

தம்மில் இருந்து தமதுபாத்து உண்டற்றால்
அம்மா அறிவை முயக்கு.   1107

*thammil irun-thu thamathupAththu uNdatRRAl
ammA arivai muyakku*

Embracing the better-half is life in sweet home, where
you share with kin the fruits of hard labour with joy

வீழும் இருவர்க்கு இனிதே வளியிடை
போழப் படாஅ முயக்கு.   1108

*veezum iruvarkku inithae vaLiidai
pOzap padAa muyakku*

The thick embrace of longing love does not admit
even a whiff of breeze to dart in-between

ஊடல் உணர்தல் புணர்தல் இவைகாமம்
கூடியார் பெற்ற பயன்.   1109

*uudal uNarthal puNarthal ivaikAmam
kUdiyAr petRRa payan*

Sulking in envy, feeling fine and clasping fast in love
are the sweet accomplishments of sexual lore

அறிதோறு அறியாமை கண்டற்றால் காமம்
செறிதோறும் சேயிழை மாட்டு.   1110

*aRithORu aRiyAmai kaNdaRRAl kAmam
seRithORum saeyizai mAttu*

As love's lust gets closer and closer, the belle's finesse
reveals in fresher knowledge, past ignorance

112. நலம் புனைந்து உரைத்தல்
n-alam punain-thu uraiththal
EXTOLLING THE LOVE'S BEAUTY
(RUMINATING THOUGHTS ABOUT EACH OTHER LOVERS RIDE
HIGH IN IMAGINATION TO PORTRAY THEIR QUALITIES)

நன்னீரை வாழி அனிச்சமே நின்னினும்
மென்னீரள் யாம்வீழ் பவள்.   1111

n-anneerai vAzi anichchamae n-inninum
menneeraL yAmveez pavaL

**Hail thee, soft petalled 'Anicha' flower, the
damsel I dote is far softer than you**

மலர்காணின் மையாத்தி நெஞ்சே இவள்கண்
பலர்காணும் பூஒக்கும் என்று.   1112

malarkANin maiyAththi n-enjsae ivaLkaN
palarkANum pUokkum endRu

**O my mind, you are baffled by the sight of flowers of
different hues, likening them to her beaming eyes**

முறிமேனி முத்தம் முறுவல் வெறிநாற்றம்
வேலுண்கண் வேய்த்தோள் அவட்கு.   1113

muRimaeni muthththam muruval veRin-AtRRam
vaeluNkaN vaeyththOL avatku

**How shall I extol her splendour? bamboo shoulders, silken
skin, pearly smiles, lancing eyes and fragrant locks!**

காணின் குவளை கவிழ்ந்து நிலன்நோக்கும்
மாணிழை கண்ஒவ்வேம் என்று.   1114

kANin kuvaLai kavizn-thu n-ilann-Okkum
mANizai kaNovvaem enRu

**The lily droops down in shame: 'I cannot stand
the bright eyes of this bejewelled beauty'**

அனிச்சப்பூக் கால்களையாள் பெய்தாள் நுசுப்பிற்கு
நல்ல படாஅ பறை.   1115

anichchappUk kAlkaLaiyAL peythAL n-usuppiRku
n-alla padAa paRai

The drums blare a solemn sound, alas! her waist is crushed
by the weight of 'anicha' flowers with stems she wears

மதியும் மடந்தை முகனும் அறியா
பதியிற் கலங்கிய மீன்.   1116

mathiyum madan-thai mukanum aRiyA
pathiyiR kalangkiya meen

Stars in the sky stare confused, failing to clearly
distinguish the moon and the maid's face

அறுவாய் நிறைந்த அவிர்மதிக்குப் போல
மறுஉண்டோ மாதர் முகத்து.   1117

aRuvAy n-iRaintha avirmathikkup pOla
maRu-uNdO mAthar mukaththu

The moon that wanes and waxes has dark craters;
my darling's face is spotless in virgin beauty

மாதர் முகம்போல் ஒளிவிட வல்லையேல்
காதலை வாழி மதி.   1118

mAthar mukampOl oLivida vallaiyael
kAthalai vAzi mathi

If you can shine in radiance like the face of my lady,
O dear moon, I shall hail thee in blessed love

மலரன்ன கண்ணாள் முகம்ஒத்தி யாயின்
பலர்காணத் தோன்றல் மதி.   1119

malaranna kaNNAL mukamoththi yAyin
palarkANath thOnRal mathi

If you can compete in beauty with the fairy of flowery
eyes, O moon! why this shameless shine in open sky?

அனிச்சமும் அன்னத்தின் தூவியும் மாதர்
அடிக்கு நெருஞ்சிப் பழம்.   1120

anichchamum annaththin thUviyum mAthar
adikku n-erunjsip pazam

The stems of soft 'anicha' flowers and swan's
feathers are nettles to the fairy's soft feet

113. காதற் சிறப்புரைத்தல்
kAthal siRappu uraiththal
IN PRAISE OF LOVE'S ECSTASY

(LOVERS BITTEN BY THE BUG EXPRESS THEIR INTENSE FEELINGS
OF ATTACHMENT TO EACH OTHER)

பாலொடு தேன்கலந்து அற்றே பணிமொழி
வாலெயிறு ஊறிய நீர்.   1121

pAlodu thaenkalan-thu atRRae paNimozi
vAleyiRu uuriya n-eer

The soft parroting pretty's dew of pearls
on her lips is so sweet like honey in milk

உடம்பொடு உயிரிடை என்னமற்று அன்ன
மடந்தையொடு எம்மிடை நட்பு.   1122

udampodu uyiridai ennamatRRu anna
madan-thaiyodu emmidai n-atpu

The love of the lovely doe sustains my existence
like the life instinct motivating the body

கருமணியின் பாவாய்நீ போதாய்யாம் வீழும்
திருநுதற்கு இல்லை இடம்.   1123

karumaNiyin pAvAyn-ee pOthAyyAm veezum
thirun-uthaRku illai idam

Depart dear pupil of my eye to make room for
the fair browed belle I love and long for

வாழ்தல் உயிர்க்குஅன்னள் ஆயிழை சாதல்
அதற்குஅன்னள் நீங்கும் இடத்து.   1124

vAzthal uyirkkuannaL aayizai sAthal
athaRkuannaL n-eengkum idaththu

Life has meaning in living with my precious jewelled
beauty; death it is that tortures when she departs

உள்ளுவன் மன்யான் மறப்பின் மறப்புஅறியேன்
ஒள்ளமர்க் கண்ணாள் குணம்.   1125

uLLuvan manyAn maRappin maRappuaRiyaen
oLLamark kaNNAL kuNam

I never forget, nor need to recall, as I always cherish
the charm of the bright eyed, darting me in battle

கண்ணுள்ளின் போகார் இமைப்பின் பருவரார்
நுண்ணியர்எங் காத லவர்.   1126

kaNNuLLin pOkAr imaippin paruvarAr
n-uNNiyareng kAtha lavar

Subtle and beautiful is my lover; he never leaves
my eyes, and is not harmed by winking brows

கண்ணுள்ளார் காத லவராகக் கண்ணும்
எழுதேம் கரப்பாக்கு அறிந்து.   1127

kaNuLLAr kAtha lavarAkak kaNNUm
ezuthaem karappAkku aRin-thu

He resides in my eyes; I avoid painting my brows,
lest they conceal him from my constant view

நெஞ்சத்தார் காத லவராக வெய்துண்டல்
அஞ்சுதும் வேபாக்கு அறிந்து.   1128

n-enjsaththAr kAtha lavarAka veythuNdal
anjsuthum vaepAkku aRin-thu

My lover dwells in my soul; I am afraid of taking
food hot, lest it harms his tender form

இமைப்பின் கரப்பாக்கு அறிவல் அனைத்திற்கே
ஏதிலர் என்னும்இவ் வூர்.   1129

imaippin karappAkku aRivaL anaiththiRkae
aethilar ennumiv vUr

I know, when my brows wink they conceal him; even
for that folks around blame him as unfriendly

உவந்துஉறைவர் உள்ளத்துள் என்றும் இகந்துஉறைவர்
ஏதிலர் என்னும்இவ் வூர்.   1130

uvan-thuuRaivar uLLaththuL endRum ikan-thu-uRaivar
aethilar ennumiv vUr

Happy he resides in my soul forever; when he
departs on duties, people mistake he is apart

114. நாணுத் துறவு உரைத்தல்
n-ANuth thuRavu uraiththal
LOVE'S PAIN DEFYING MODESTY

(MADAL is a horse made of Palmyra leaves and hands, ridden by the lovelorn male, exposing the torture of burning passion in separation and
seeking sympathy of folks around for gaining the hand of the beloved)

காமம் உழந்து வருந்தினார்க்கு ஏமம்
மடல்அல்லது இல்லை வலி.   1131

*kAmam uzan-thu varun-thinArkku aemam
madalallathu illai vali*

Pangs of lovelorn passion find no recourse to safety,
save riding a palmyra horse to exhibit it

நோனா உடம்பும் உயிரும் மடலேறும்
நாணினை நீக்கி நிறுத்து.   1132

*n-OnA udampum uyirum madalaeRum
n-ANinai n-eekki n-iRuththu*

Paining body and soul of life defy shame and
take recourse to riding of the palmyra horse

நாணெடு நல்லாண்மை பண்டுடையேன் இன்றுடையேன்
காமுற்றார் ஏறும் மடல்.   1133

*n-ANodu n-allANmai paNdu-udaiyaen inRu-udaiyaen
kAmutRRAr aeRum madal*

Times were when I prided manly exploits and geniality;
now I am pushed to the madal of the lovelorn

காமக் கடும்புனல் உய்க்குமே நாணெடு
நல்லாண்மை என்னும் புணை.   1134

*kAmak kadumpunal uykkumae n-ANodu
n-allANmai ennum puNai*

The wild flood of love's passion sweeps away the raft
of firmness and the paddle of modesty, without a trace

தொடலைக் குறுந்தொடி தந்தாள் மடலொடு
மாலை உழக்கும் துயர்.   1135

thodalaik kurun-thodi than-thAL madalodu
mAlai uzakkum thuyar

Her linked hip-brace and bright little bangles have cast
on me pain and passion of a dull eve, besides madal

மடல்ஊர்தல் யாமத்தும் உள்ளுவேன் மன்ற
படல்ஒல்லா பேதைக்குஎன் கண்.   1136

madalUrthal yAmaththum uLLuvaen manRa
padalollA paethaikkuen kaN

My sombre eyes do not permit me to catch any sleep
at night, always brooding over the madal option

கடலன்ன காமம் உழந்தும் மடலேறாப்
பெண்ணின் பெருந்தக்கது இல்.   1137

kadalanna kAmam uzan-thum madalaeRAp
peNNin perun-thakkathu il

Sea deep in the pangs of love's lust, it is the serene
glory of women folk, who think not of the madal

நிறையறியர் மன்அளியர் என்னாது காமம்
மறையிறந்து மன்று படும்.   1138

n-iRaiariyar maNaLiyar ennAthu kAmam
maRaiiRan-thu manRu padum

Lust betrays and brandishes without sympathy, even
chaste women, ignoring their frailty to conceal mind

அறிகிலார் எல்லாரும் என்றேஎன் காமம்
மறுகில் மறுகும் மருண்டு.   1139

aRikilAr ellOrum enRaeen kAmam
maRukil maRukum maruNdu

Perplexed is my passion raving in public, in delusion,
that secret modesty in love does not hold any sway

யாம்கண்ணின் காண நகுப அறிவில்லார்
யாம்பட்ட தாம்படா வாறு.   1140

yAmkaNNin kANa n-akupa aRivillaar
yAmpatta thAmpadA vARu

Those who have not experienced the pangs of love sway before
my eyes when I am undergoing trials and tribulations of love

115. அலர் அறிவுறுத்தல்
alar aRivuRuththal
CLAMOUR AND GOSSIP

(OF FOLKS AROUND, THE BUD OF LOVE BLOSSOMS, WHICH HELP
THE LOVERS TO FRUITION OF THEIR RELATIONSHIP IN WEDLOCK)

அலர்எழ ஆருயிர் நிற்கும் அதனைப்
பலர்அறியார் பாக்கியத் தால்.   1141

alareza aaruyir n-iRkum athanaip
palaraRiyAr pAkkiyath thAl

The clamour of gossip sustains my love life;
by chance, many know not its secrets

மலர்அன்ன கண்ணாள் அருமை அறியாது
அலர்எமக்கு ஈந்ததுஇவ் வூர்.   1142

malaranna kaNNAL arumai aRiyAthu
alaremakku een-thathuiv vUr

Rumours and gossip have gifted me this flowery-eyed
belle; the public know not her preciousness

உறாஅதோ ஊர்அறிந்த கௌவை அதனைப்
பெறாஅது பெற்றுஅன்ன நீர்த்து.   1143

uRAathO uuraRin-tha kovvai athanaip
peRAathu petRRuanna n-eerththu

Will not the gossip groups develop into a public clamour;
that will help me to have the rarest to have in joy

கௌவையால் கௌவிது காமம் அதுஇன்றேல்
தவ்வென்னும் தன்மை இழந்து.   1144

kavvaiyAl kavviyathu kAmam athuinRael
thavennum thanmai izan-thu

Seeds of love sown have sprouted in health, watered
by gossip and rumour; or else would have withered

களித்தொறும் கள்ளுண்டல் வேட்டற்றால் காமம்
வெளிப்படும் தோறும் இனிது.   1145

kaLiththoRum kaLLuNNal vaeNdatRRAl kAmam
veLippadum thORum inithu

Craving for liquor grows as it flows in and delights;
gossip fans and flares our love to sweet delight

கண்டது மன்னும் ஒருநாள் அலர்மன்னும்
திங்களைப் பாம்புகொண் டற்று.   1146

kaNdathu mannum orun-AL alarmannum
thingkaLaip pAmpukoN datRu

Like the earth's shadow eclipsing the moon, rarely we
met alone; but rumours on it spread fast and wide

ஊரவர் கௌவை எருவாக அன்னைசொல்
நீராக நீளும்இந் நோய்.   1147

uuravar kovvai eruvAka annaisol
n-eerAka n-eeLumin n-Oy

With public gossip as manure and mother's reproach
as water, the pain of passion grows up in no time

நெய்யால் எரிநுதுப்பேம் என்றுஅற்றால் கௌவையால்
காமம் நுதுப்பேம் எனல்.   1148

n-eyyAl erin-uthuppaem enRuatRRAl kovvaiyAl
kAmam n-uthuppaem enal

Quenching the lust of love by the fountain of rumour, is
like seeking to put out a fire, by pouring in ghee

அலர்நாண ஒல்வதோ அஞ்சல்ஓம்பு என்றார்
பலர்நாண நீத்தக் கடை.   1149

alarn-ANa olvathO anjsal Ompu endRAr
palarn-ANa n-eeththak kadai

'We are one in one, fear not separation'; that assurance
stands me in blushing modesty, from clamouring gossip

தாம்வேண்டின் நல்குவர் காதலர் யாம்வேண்டும்
கௌவை எடுக்கும்இவ் ஊர்.   1150

thAmvaeNdin n-alkuvar kAthalar yAmvaeNdum
kovvai edukkumiv vUr

A rising pitch of clamouring gossip of the public is to my
liking; that makes my lover's job easy to get consent

116. பிரிவு ஆற்றாமை
pirivu aatRAmai
PANGS OF SEPARATION

(AFTER LOVE BLOSSOMS, WHEN THE MALE HAS TO GO ON
DUTIES OF DEFENCE, OF THE GOVERNMENT, FOR EDUCATION,
TRADE ETC. THE THOUGHTS OF SEPARATION DESPAIRS)

செல்லாமை உண்டேல் எனக்குரை மற்றுநின்
வல்வரவு வாழ்வார்க்கு உரை.   1151

sellAmai uNdael enakku-urai matRRun-in
valvaravu vAzvArkku urai

If it is happy news, tell me you are not leaving; I cannot
bear separation, convey it to one who survives to see

இன்கண் உடைத்துஅவர் பார்வல் பிரிவுஅஞ்சும்
புன்கண் உடைத்தால் புணர்வு.   1152

inkaN udaiththuavar pArval pirivuanjsum
punkaN udaiththAl puNarvu

The absorbing looks of love have enduring pleasure;
the despair in embrace throbs pain of separation

அரிதரோ தேற்றம் அறிவுடையார் கண்ணும்
பிரிவோர் இடத்துஉண்மை யான்.   1153

aritharO thaetRam aRivu-udaiyAr kaNNum
pirivuoor idaththu-uNmai yAn

Even as he knows that separation lurks, hard to take
at face value, the assurance: 'I will not leave you',

அளித்துஅஞ்சல் என்றவர் நீப்பின் தெளித்தசொல்
தேறியார்க்கு உண்டோ தவறு.   1154

aLiththuanjsal enRavar n-eeppin theLiththasol
thaeriyArkku uNdO thavaRu

When he bestows love and comfort in words 'fear not
separation', am I at fault in believing him earnest?

ஓம்பின் அமைந்தார் பிரிவுஓம்பல் மற்றுஅவர்
நீங்கின் அரிதால் புணர்வு.   1155

Ompin amain-thAr pirivuOmpal matRuavar
n-eeppin arithAl puNarvu

As I surmise, he may leave on intrigue, reunion may be
hard; best to defeat his plans in binding love and comfort

பிரிவுஉரைக்கும் வன்கண்ணர் ஆயின் அரிதுஅவர்
நல்குவர் என்னும் நசை.   1156

pirivu-uraikkum vankaNNar aayin arithuavar
n-alkuvar ennum n-asai

When he is stubborn to announce separation, it will
be futile to nourish any fond hope of reunion

துறைவன் துறந்தமை தூற்றாகொல் முன்கை
இறைஇறவா நின்ற வளை.   1157

thuRaivan thuRan-thamai thURRAkol munkai
iRaiiRavA n-inRa vaLai

Bangles sliding down my thin arms are prone to
betray my lord's separation and cause ridicule

இன்னாது இனன்இல்ஊர் வாழ்தல் அதனினும்
இன்னாது இனியார்ப் பிரிவு.   1158

innAthu inaniluur vAzthal athaninum
innAthu iniyArp pirivu

Life in an alien land, away from kith and kin, is bitter;
still worse is separation from sweet embrace in love

தொடிஇன்சுடல் அல்லது காமநோய் போல
விடிஇன்சுடல் ஆற்றுமோ தீ.   1159

thodinsudal allathu kAman-Oy pOla
vidinsudal aatRRumO thee

Fire can burn you on touch; the embers in the souls
of love-sick couples burn hot in separation

அரிதுஆற்றி அல்லல்நோய் நீக்கிப் பிரிவுஆற்றிப்
பின்இருந்து வாழ்வார் பலர்.   1160

arithuaatRRi allaln-Oy n-eekkip pirivuaatRRip
pinirun-thu vAzvAr palar

Many take with rare courage and survive pangs of separation,
desertion, of widow-hood to live on, but not I.

117. படர்மெலிந்து இரங்கல்
padarmelin-thu irangkal
PINING IN SEPARATION
(LANGUISHING IN SORROW)
(LUST CLOUDED BY SHYNESS, LANGUISHING IN PAIN, SORROW SURROUNDS IN FLOODS)

மறைப்பேன்மன் யானிஃதோ நோயை இறைப்பவர்க்கு
ஊற்றுநீர் போல மிகும்.　　　　1161

*maRaippaenman yAniqthO n-Oyai iRaippavarkku
uutRun-eer pOla mikum*

The harder I try to hide my love-sickness, the greater
it grows, like the swelling up of a drained spring

கரத்தலும் ஆற்றேன்இந் நோயைநோய் செய்தார்க்கு
உரைத்தலும் நாணுத் தரும்.　　　　1162

*karaththalum aatRaenin n-Oyai-n-Oy saeythArkku
uraiththalum n-ANuth tharum*

I can neither conceal this pain of love nor complain
to my lover to know it, for fear of shame

காமமும் நாணும் உயிர்காவாத் தூங்கும்என்
நோனா உடம்பின் அகத்து.　　　　1163

*kAmamum n-ANum uyirkAvAth thUngkumen
n-OnA udampin akaththu*

My lifeline as shoulder pole, both lust and shyness
at either end weigh down my weared body

காமக் கடல்மன்னும் உண்டே அதுநீந்தும்
ஏமப் புணைமன்னும் இல்.　　　　1164

*kAmak kadalmannum uNdae athun-een-thum
aemap puNaimannum il*

The lure of lust is roaring like a sea; I do not
see a raft to sail on it in safety

துப்பின் எவனாவர் மன்கொல் துயர்வரவு
நட்பினுள் ஆற்று பவர்.　　　　1165

thuppin evanAvar mankol thuyarvaravu
n-atpinuL aatRRu pavar

My soul grieveth, he who can leave me in sorrow in
friendship, what woes will befall if he leaves in enmity

இன்பம் கடல்மற்றுக் காமம் அஃதுஅடுங்கால்
துன்பம் அதனின் பெரிது.   1166

inbam kadalmatRRuk kAmam aqthuadungkAl
thunbam athanin perithu

The pleasure of love is brimming like an ocean, when it
hurts, the pangs of lust swell up higher than the waves

காமக் கடும்புனல் நீந்திக் கரைகாணேன்
யாமத்தும் யானே உளேன்.   1167

kAmak kadumpunal n-een-thik karaikANaen
yAmaththum yAnae uLaen

Unable to swim and shore up the flood of wild lust, in the
dead of night, I languish alone longing for my lover

மன்னுயிர் எல்லாம் துயிற்றி அளித்திரா
என்னல்லது இல்லை துணை.   1168

mannuyir ellAm thuyiRRi aLiththirA
enallathu illai thuNai

All living creatures are lulled to sleep by the wakeful
night; mercy it, I am its lonely companion to wit

கொடியார் கொடுமையின் தாம்கொடிய இந்நாள்
நெடிய கழியும் இரா.   1169

kodiyAr kodumaiyin thAmkodiya in-n-AL
n-ediya kaziyum irA

The endless nights passing slowly, are more cruel to me
than the soul-less one torturing me in separation

உள்ளம்போன்று உள்வழிச் செல்கிற்பின் வெள்ளநீர்
நீந்தல மன்னோஎன் கண்.   1170

uLLampOnRu uLvazich selkiRpin veLLan-eer
n-een-thala mannOen kaN

Like my soul, if my eyes can fly fast to my lover living
yonder, they will not swim in a flood of tears

118. கண்விதுப்பு அழிதல்
kaNvithuppu azithal
GRIEF OF EAGER EYES

(IN SEPARATION THE EYES DO NOT CONTAIN TEARS AND THE
MIND FINDS FAULT WITH THE EYES FOR THEIR FICKLENESS)

கண்தாம் கலுழ்வது எவன்கொலோ தண்டாநோய்
தாம்காட்ட யாம்கண் டது.　　　　　1171

kaNthAn kaluzhvathu evankolO thaNdAṇ-Oy
thAmkAtta yAmkaN dathu

These wistful eyes have in their looks brought on me the
lasting malady of love and lust, what for do they weep?

தெரிந்துஉணரா நோக்கிய உண்கண் பரிந்துஉணராப்
பைதல் உழப்பது எவன்.　　　　　1172

therin-thu-uNarA n-Okkiya uNkaN parin-thu-uNarAp
paithal uzappathu evan

Should these eyes of painted brows, that went eagerly
after him grieve, sans regrets for their thoughtless acts

கதும்எனத் தாம்நோக்கித் தாமே கலுழும்
இதுநகத் தக்கது உடைத்து.　　　　　1173

kathumenath thAmn-Okkith thAmae kaluzhum
ithun-akath thakkathu udaiththu

These mystical eyes, having cast their hurried glances,
pine in grief to see him; they evoke but a pathetic laugh

பெயல்ஆற்றா நீருலந்த உண்கண் உயல்ஆற்றா
உய்வில்நோய் என்கண் நிறுத்து.　　　　　1174

peyalaatRRA n-eerularn-tha uNkaN uyalaatRRA
uyviln-Oy enkaN n-iRuththu

Tears having dried up, the eyes can weep no more, but
have caused endless grief, in interminable pain of lust

படல்ஆற்றா பைதல் உழக்கும் கடல்ஆற்றாக்
காமநோய் செய்தஎன் கண்.　　　　　1175

padalaatRRA paithaluzakkum kadalaaRRAk
kAman-Oy seythaen kaN

My eyes have caused me the pain of lust, greater than the sea, and have now to suffer sleepless nights

ஓஓ இனிதே எமக்குஇந்நோய் செய்தகண்
தாஅம் இதற்பட் டது.

1176

*Ooo inithae emakkuinnOy seythakaN
thAam ithaRpat tathu*

It is soothing sweetness to mind, eyes that have caused me pain of passion, have themselves to suffer regrets

உழந்துஉழந்து உள்நீர் அறுக விழைந்துஇழைந்து
வேண்டி யவர்க்கண்ட கண்.

1177

*uzan-thu-uzan-thu uLn-eer aRuka vizain-thu-izainthu
vaeNdi yavarkkaNda kaN*

Let these eyes that gazed intently on the beloved languish in pining pain, tears having dried up

பேணாது பெட்டார் உளர்மன்னோ மற்றுஅவர்க்
காணாது அமைவில கண்.

1178

*paeNAthu pettAr uLarmannO matRuavark
kANAthu amaivila kaN*

He is the one who lured me with sweet words of love, sans spirit, still my eyes are listless, pining to see him

வாராக்கால் துஞ்சா வரின்துஞ்சா ஆயிடை
ஆரஞர் உற்றன கண்.

1179

*vArAkkAl thunjsA varinthunjsA aayidai
aaranjayar utRRana kaN*

My eyes lose sleep eagerly awaiting his return; when he is here, anxious they lose sleep and suffer endless grief

மறைபெறல் ஊரார்க்கு அரிதுஅன்றால் எம்போல்
அறைபறை கண்ணார் அகத்து.

1180

*maRaipeRal uurArkku arithuanRAl empOl
aRaipaRai kaNNAr akaththu*

My eye-brows drum up and declare my grief, can I then conceal anything from probing minds of folks around?

119. பசப்புறு பருவரல்
pasappuRu paruvaral
PAIN OF PALLOR AND SALLOWNESS
(AFFLICTED BY SEPARATION, PALING OF THE BODY TO SICKLY GREEN OR BROWN)

நயந்தவர்க்கு நல்காமை நேர்ந்தேன் பசந்தளன்
பண்புயார்க்கு உரைக்கோ பிற.   1181

n-ayan-thavarkku n-alkAmai n-aern-thaen pasan-thaen
paNpuyArkku uraikkO piRa

In folly I consented my lover to depart, to whom shall I
relate the woes of sallowness paining my body?

அவர்தந்தார் என்னும் தகையால் இவர்தந்துளன்
மேனிமேல் ஊரும் பசப்பு.   1182

avarthan-thAr ennum thakaiyAl ivarthan-thuen
maenimael uurum pasappu

With unjust pride pallor fills the void of my lover
and rides happily creeping on my body

சாயலும் நாணும் அவர்கொண்டார் கைம்மாறா
நோயும் பசலையும் தந்து.   1183

sAyalum n-ANum avarkoNdAr kaimmARA
n-Oyum pasalaiyum than-thu

He has robbed me of my tender beauty and modesty;
but in return, unfairly left me in pain and pallor

உள்ளுவன் மன்யான் உரைப்பது அவர்திறமால்
கள்ளம் பிறவோ பசப்பு.   1184

uLLuvan manyAn uraippathu avarthiRamAl
kaLLam piravO pasappu

He is in all my thoughts, I praise his excellence, yet
pallor steals my body, paining in sexual passion

உவக்காண்ளம் காதலர் செல்வார் இவக்காண் என்
மேனி பசப்புஊர் வது.   1185

uvakkANem kAthalar selvAr ivakkANen
maeni pasappu-uur vathu

My lover is just departing, still in my view, but lo!
sallowness has already started usurping my body

விளக்குஅற்றம் பார்க்கும் இருளேபோல் கொண்கண்
முயக்குஅற்றம் பார்க்கும் பசப்பு.   1186

viLakkuatRam pArkkum iruLaepOl koNkan
muyakkuatRam pArkkum pasappu

As darkness seen in the absence of light, I became conscious
of pangs of pallor in the absence of my lover

புல்லிக் கிடந்தேன் புடைபெயர்ந்தேன் அவ்வளவில்
அள்ளிக்கொள் வற்றே பசப்பு.   1187

pullik kidan-thaen pudaipeyarn-thaen avvaLavil
aLLikkoL vatRae pasappu

From his close embrace I just turned a nonce; as if
waiting for the chance, pallor seized me in a trance

பசந்தாள் இவள்என்பது அல்லால் இவளைத்
துறந்தார் அவர்என்பார் இல்.   1188

pasan-thAL ivaLenpathu allAl ivaLaith
thuRan-thAr avarenpAr il

Folks comment on my sallowness in separation, but do
not sympathize with me that he has left me in despair

பசக்கமன் பட்டாங்குஎன் மேனி நயப்பித்தார்
நல்நிலையர் ஆவர் எனின்.   1189

pasakkaman pattAngkuen maeni n-ayappiththAr
n-aln-ilaiyar aavAr enin

For return of the one who took leave in consent, let his
mission fare well, I am willing to bear pangs of pallor

பசப்புஎனப் பேர்பெறுதல் நன்றே நயப்பித்தார்
நல்காமை தூற்றார் எனின்.   1190

pasappuenap paerperuthal n-anRae n-ayappiththAr
n-alkAmai thUtRRAar enin

The branding of pallid I can take in its stride, if my
beloved's unkindness, people do not deride

120. தனிப்படர் மிகுதி
thanippadar mikuthi
ANGUISH OF LONELINESS
(SORROW OF SOLITUDE)
(SORROW OF SOLITUDE EXPRESSES IN PATHOS OVER LONG
SEPARATION AND LURKING DOUBTS)

தாம்வீழ்வார் தம்வீழப் பெற்றவர் பெற்றாரே

காமத்துக் காழில் கனி.   1191

thAmvIzvAr thamvIzap petravar peRRArae
kAmaththuk kAzil kani

The blessed luck of being loved by the beloved
is the seedless fruit of sexual delight

வாழ்வார்க்கு வானம் பயந்தற்றால் வீழ்வார்க்கு

வீழ்வார் அளிக்கும் அளி.   1192

vAzvArkku vAnam payan-thatRAl veezvArkku
veezvAr aLikkum aLi

The bestowal of love by the beloved, is like the gift
of rains from the sky, for life to survive on earth

வீழுநர் வீழப் படுவார்க்கு அமையுமே

வாழுநம் என்னும் செருக்கு.   1193

veezun-ar veezap paduvArkku amaiyumae
vAzun-am ennum serukku

The happiness and pride of a fuller life is only to those
endowed with the intimacy of love in body and soul

வீழப் படுவார் கெழீஇயிலர் தாம்வீழ்வார்

வீழப் படாஅர் எனின்.   1194

veezappaduvAr kaezeeiyilar thAmveezvAr
veezap padAar enin

Who miss the pleasure of life in loving hands, may be
highly placed, but do not achieve fame or greatness

நாம்காதல் கொண்டார் நமக்கெவன் செய்பவோ

தாம்காதல் கொள்ளாக் கடை.   1195

n-AmkAthal koNdAr n-amakkuevan seypavO
thAmkAthal koLLAk kadai

Whom I long for in love, will he return me the same
kindness, in case he is not in love with me?

ஒருதலையான் இன்னாது காமம்காப் போல
இருதலை யானும் இனிது.   **1196**

oruthalaiyAn innAthu kAmamkAp pOla
iruthalai yAnum inithu

Love's lust is sweet, when poised even, on both sides of
a shoulder pole; one sided infatuation pains in despair

பருவரலும் பைதலும் காணான்கொல் காமன்
ஒருவர்கண் நின்றுஒழுகு வான்.   **1197**

paruvaralum paithalum kANAnkol kAman
oruvarkaN n-inRuozuku vAn

Cupid is partial to his pals; he aims his arrows
of love, unmindful of my pain and pallor

வீழ்வாரின் இன்சொல் பெறாஅது உலகத்து
வாழ்வாரின் வன்கணார் இல்.   **1198**

veezvArin insol peRAathu ulakaththu
vAzvArin vankaNAr il

Are the fairer sex so hard-headed to live on, without
words to console, from him whom they dote in love?

நசைஇயார் நல்கார் எனினும் அவர்மாட்டு
இசையும் இனிய செவிக்கு.   **1199**

n-asaiyiyAr n-alkAr eninum avarmAttu
isaiyum iniya sevikku

Though my beloved accords not my desires yet, the
tidings of praise and fame are sweet music to my ears

உறாஅர்க்கு உறுநோய் உரைப்பாய் கடலைச்
செறாஅஅய் வாழிய நெஞ்சு.   **1200**

uRAarkku uRun-Oy uraippAy kadalaich
seRAaay vAziya n-enjsu

O my poor soul ! Blessed be thee, listless to relate
sorrows to strangers, rather dry up the sea of tears

121. நினைந்து அவர் புலம்பல்
n-inaiththu avar pulampal
BEMOANING PAIN OF SEPARATION
(OVERCOME BY SELF PITY, REMINISCING
THE SWEET TIMES ENJOYED EARLIER)

உள்ளினும் தீராப் பெருமகிழ் செய்தலால்
கள்ளினும் காமம் இனிது.   1201

uLLinum theerAp perumakiz seythalAl
kaLLinum kAmam inithu

Liquor stimulates the drunk; it lacks the rapturous delight
of sweet sexual passion all the time, in thoughts

எனைத்துஒன்று இனிதேகாண் காமந்தாம் வீழ்வார்
நினைப்ப வருவதுஒன்று இல்.   1202

enaiththuonRu inithaekAN kAmamthAm veezvAr
n-inaippa varuvathuonRu il

Pleasure is there in the arms of the beloved, and in fond
thoughts on him; sweet sexual passion is all pervasive

நினைப்பவர் போன்று நினையார்கொல் தும்மல்
சினைப்பது போன்று கெடும்.   1203

n-inaippavar pOnRu n-inaiyArkol thummal
sinaippathu pOnRu kedum

A sneeze prods my nose, but does not beget; perhaps
the beloved tried to think of me, but forgot

யாமும் உளேங்கொல் அவர்நெஞ்சத்து எம்நெஞ்சத்து
ஓஓ உளரே அவர்.   1204

yAmum uLaengkol avarn-enjsaththu emn-enjsaththu
Ooo uLarae avar

My beloved darling has a permanent place in my
soul; do I have any room left for me within him

தம்நெஞ்சத்து எம்மைக் கடிகொண்டார் நாணார்கொல்
எம்நெஞ்சத்து ஓவா வரல்.   1205

thamn-enjsaththu emmaik kadikoNdAr n-ANArkol
emn-enjsaththu oovA varal

Inexplicably he resists entry to me in his mind; he should
be ashamed of bothering my thoughts ceaselessly

மற்றுயான் என்னுளேன் மன்னோ அவரொடுயான்
உற்றநாள் உள்ள உளேன்.   1206

matRuyAn enuLaen mannO avaroduyAn
uRRAn-AL uLLa uLaen

Enduring memories of the beautiful days enjoyed
with him sustain life in me, even in separation

மறப்பின் எவனாவன் மன்கொல் மறப்புஅறியேன்
உள்ளினும் உள்ளம் சுடும்.   1207

maRappin evanAvan mankol maRappuaRiyAn
uLLinum uLLam sudum

His memory burns in me ceaselessly, in his absence;
I deter to think what will happen in case I forget

எனைத்து நினைப்பினும் காயார் அனைத்துஅன்றோ
காதலர் செய்யும் சிறப்பு.   1208

enaiththu n-inaippinum kAyAr anaiththuanRO
kAthalar seyyum siRappu

He chids not my possessing his memory in depth; in any
dire context, it is a great favour my beloved extends

விளியும்என் இன்னுயிர் வேறுஅல்லம் என்பார்
அளியின்மை ஆற்ற நினைந்து.   1209

viLiyumen innuyir vaeRuallam enpAr
aLiinmai aatRRa n-inainthu

He assured: 'we are one, not apart', but has departed
without mercy, leaving my precious life to ebb and sink

விடாஅது சென்றாரைக் கண்ணினால் காணப்
படாஅதி வாழி மதி.   1210

vidAathu senRAraik kaNNinAl kANap
padAathi vAzi mathi

Hail thee, moon! guide me without hiding, to trace
my beloved, who departed, not quitting my mind

122. கனவுநிலை உரைத்தல்
kanavu n-ilai uraiththal
SWEET SOLACE OF DREAMS

(THE PAIN OF SEPARATION SUSTAINS WHILE AWAKE. DREAMY SLEEP
HAS BETTER COMFORT AND HENCE PREFERRED AS SWEET)

காதலர் தூதொடு வந்த கனவினுக்கு
யாதுசெய் வேன்கொல் விருந்து.   **1211**

kAthalar thUthodu van-tha kanavinukku
yAthusey vaenkol virun-thu

What shall I feast in return, to the sweet dreams
on a pleasant mission from my beloved

கயலுண்கண் யானிரப்பத் துஞ்சின் கலந்தார்க்கு
உயலுண்மை சாற்றுவேன் மன்.   **1212**

kayaluNkaN yAnirappath thunjsin kalan-thArkku
uyaluNmai sAtRRuvaen mun

I besiege my fish-like eyes to sleep, so that I reach my
lover in dreams and confide the motivation of my life

நனவினால் நல்கா தவரைக் கனவினால்
காண்டலின் உண்டுஎன் உயிர்.   **1213**

n-anavinAl n-alkA thavaraik kanavinAl
kANdalin uNduen uyir

In wakeful hours I miss him badly, but life
lingers on, with his vision in my dreams

கனவினால் உண்டாகும் காமம் நனவினால்
நல்காரை நாடித் தரற்கு.   **1214**

kanavinAl uNdAkum kAmam n-anavinAl
n-alkArai n-Adith tharaRku

Dreams goad my lovelorn passion to seek after
in reality, the one who has left me forlorn

நனவினால் கண்டதூஉம் ஆங்கே கனவுந்தான்
கண்ட பொழுதே இனிது.   **1215**

n-anavinAl kaNdathUum aangkae kanavun-thAn
kaNda pozuthae inithu

Sweet was the pleasure at sight; the delight
persists whenever I meet him in my dreams

நனவுஎன ஒன்றுஇல்லை யாயின் கனவினால்
காதலர் நீங்கலர் மன்.   1216

*n-anavuena onRuillai yAyin kanavinAl
kAthalar n-eengkalar mun*

If wakefulness does not interrupt my sweet dreams
I will not like my lover to depart in fantasy,

நனவினால் நல்காக் கொடியார் கனவினால்
என்எம்மைப் பீழிப் பது.   1217

*n-anavinAl n-alkAk kodiyAr kanavinAl
enemmaip peezip pathu*

The cruel minded one who does not return to
reassure, is unfair to torture me in dreams

துஞ்சுங்கால் தோள்மேலர் ஆகி விழிக்குங்கால்
நெஞ்சத்தர் ஆவர் விரைந்து.   1218

*thunjsungkAl thOLmaelar aaki vizikkungkAl
n-enjsaththar aavar virain-thu*

He is adept at the magic of embracing my shoulders
in sleepy dreams and hiding in my soul, when awake

நனவினால் நல்காரை நோவர் கனவினால்
காதலர்க் காணா தவர்.   1219

*n-anavinAl n-alkArai n-OvAr kanavinAl
kAthalark kANA thavar*

Those starved of pleasant imagination in dreams,
rue missing their beloved in wakefulness

நனவினால் நம்நீத்தார் என்பர் கனவினால்
காணார்கொல் இவ்வூ ரவர்.   1220

*n-anavinAl n-amn-eeththAr enpAr kanavinAl
kANArkol ivvU ravar*

Folks failing to see him close, are prone to gossip, when they
fail to see the lovers enjoy themselves in dreams.

123. பொழுதுகண்டு இரங்கல்
pozuthu kaNdu irangkal
DISTRESS OF THE EVENING

(THE DIM EVE AND THE PALLID MIST BEWILDER THE THOUGHTS
AND ACCENTUATE THE MISERIES OF LONELY MAIDS)

மாலையோ அல்லை மணந்தார் உயிர்உண்ணும்
வேலைநீ வாழி பொழுது.   1221

mAlaiyO allai maNan-thAr uyiruNNum
vaelain-I vAzi pozuthu

Hail thee, even tide! you are not the garland on
Sunset, but a lance darting at wedded brides

புன்கண்ணை வாழி மருள்மாலை எம்கேள்போல்
வன்கண்ண தோநின் துணை.   1222

punkaNNai vAzi maruLmAlai emkaeLpOl
vankaNNa thOn-in thuNai

O dim and sad evening, is your mate like mine, merciless
on your miseries, blessed be thy life!

பனிஅரும்பிப் பைதல்கொள் மாலை துனிஅரும்பித்
துன்பம் வளர வரும்.   1223

paniarumpip paithalkoL mAlai thuniarumpith
thunpam vaLara varum

The eve of pallid mist slowly spreads chillness
to tremble wedded women in growing pain

காதலர் இல்வழி மாலை கொலைக்களத்து
ஏதிலர் போல வரும்.   1224

kAthalar ilvazi mAlai kolaikkaLaththu
aethilar pOla varum

With my beloved far away, the cruel evening comes
on me, like a slayer's sword at the slaughter house

காலைக்குச் செய்தநன்று என்கொல் எவன்கொல்யான்
மாலைக்குச் செய்த பகை.   1225

kAlaikkuch seythan-anRu enkol evankolyAn
mAlaikuch seytha pakai

The invigorating dawn is kind to me in hopes, what
harm have I done to the spiteful eve that tortures

மாலைநோய் செய்தல் மணந்தார் அகலாத
காலை அறிந்தது இலேன்.   1226

mAlain-Oy seythal maNan-thAr akalAtha
kAlai aRin-thathu ilaen

When my beloved was bound in affection, I had no
occasion to know, the eve could pain in separation

காலை அரும்பிப் பகலெல்லாம் போதாகி
மாலை மலரும்இந் நோய்.   1227

kAlai arumpip pakalelAm pOthuaaki
mAlai malarumin- n-Oy

The pain of passion is a bud at morn, blossoms all
through day and blooms on the eve to beguile

அழல்போலும் மாலைக்குத் தூதுஆகி ஆயன்
குழல்போலும் கொல்லும் படை.   1228

azalpOlum mAlaikkuth thUthuaaki aayan
kuzalpOlum kollum padai

The sweet music of shepherd's flute enters my ears
in the fiery eve of forlorn, as a conch call of battle

பதிமருண்டு பைதல் உழக்கும் மதிமருண்டு
மாலை படர்தரும் போழ்து.   1229

pathimaruNdu paithal uzakkum mathimaruNdu
mAlai padartharum pOzthu

When the eve spreads paleness to bewilder the mind,
the whole commune plunges into the pangs of love

பொருள்மாலை யாளரை உள்ளி மருள்மாலை
மாயும்என் மாயா உயிர்.   1230

poruLmAlai yALarai uLLi maruLmAlai
mAyumen mAyA uyir

Love sustains fond memory of one who left in quest of
wealth and fame; the deluding dark eve sucks my life

124. உறுப்புநலன் அழிதல்
uRuppu n-alan azithal
WITHERING OF BEAUTY
(BEMOANING THE WOES OF SEPARATION DULLED EYES,
WITHERED SHOULDERS, SLIDING BANGLES AND PALED FACE
SPOIL HER BEAUTY)

சிறுமை நமக்குழியச் சேண்சென்றார் உள்ளி
நறுமலர் நாணின கண்.　　　　　1231

siRumai n-amakkuoziyach saeNsenRAr uLLi
n-aRumalar n-ANina kaN

He has left me afar to earn and lift us from want, my eyes
dulled in tears, shy at the beauty of fragrant flowers

நயந்தவர் நல்காமை சொல்லுவ போலும்
பசந்து பனிவாரும் கண்.　　　　　1232

n-ayan-thavar n-alkAmai solluva pOlum
pasan-thu panivArum kaN

My pallid eyes floating in tears, seem to betray
the unkindness of my beloved husband

தணந்தமை சால அறிவிப்ப போலும்
மணந்தநாள் வீங்கிய தோள்.　　　　　1233

thaNan-thamai sAla aRivippa pOlum
maNan-than-AL veengkiya thOL

My shoulders swelled plump in nuptial bliss; now they
are shrinking to proclaim the pain of his separation

பணைநீங்கிப் பைந்தொடி சோரும் துணைநீங்கித்
தொல்கவின் வாடிய தோள்.　　　　　1234

paNain-eengkip pain-thodi sOrum thuNain-eengkith
tholkavin vAdiya thOL

Beauty has withered from my shoulders, shying for him;
bangles of pure gold are slipping off my shrunk arms

கொடியார் கொடுமை உரைக்கும் தொடியொடு
தொல்கவின் வாடிய தோள்.　　　　　1235

kodiyAr kodumai uraikkum thodiyodu
tholkavin vAdiya thOL

Bangles hang loose, shoulders have faded from bridal
beauty, exposing his soulless cruelty in deserting me

தொடியொடு தோள்நெகிழ நோவல் அவரைக்
கொடியர் எனக்கூறல் நொந்து.   1236

thodiyodu thOLn-ekiza n-Oval avaraik
kodiyar enakkURal n-on-thu

Unable to bear sting of tongues branding my beloved
as cruel, shoulders thin out and bangles loosen in pain

பாடு பெறுதியோ நெஞ்சே கொடியார்க்குஎன்
வாடுதோள் பூசல் உரைத்து.   1237

pAdu peRuthiyO n-enjsae kodiyArkkuen
vAduthOL pUsal uraiththu

Would you seek glory, O my mind! by relating the
woes of my fading shoulders, to the soulless self

முயங்கிய கைகளை ஊக்கப் பசந்தது
பைந்தொடிப் பேதை நுதல்.   1238

muyangkiya kaikaLai uukkap pasan-thathu
pain-thodip paethai n-uthal

Startled by the slackening of my clasping hands this bangled
beauty's hapless body paled in her forehead

முயக்கிடைத் தண்வளி போழப் பசப்புஉற்ற
பேதை பெருமழைக் கண்.   1239

muyakkuidaith thaNvaLi pOzap pasappu-utRRa
paethai perumazaik kaN

As a cool breeze stole into our tight embrace, unable to
bear it, pallor covered her eyes in a flood of tears

கண்ணின் பசப்போ பருவரல் எய்தின்றே
ஒண்ணுதல் செய்தது கண்டு.   1240

kaNNin pasappO paruvaral eythinRe
oNn-uthal seythathu kaNdu

Sensing the brightness of her forehead paling
her eyes took on the pain of sallowness

125. நெஞ்சொடு கிளத்தல்
n-enjsodu kiLaththal
CONVERSING WITH THY SOUL
(SOLILOQUY)
(SEEKING SOLACE IN SOLILOQUY WITH THE MIND IN AGONY AND DISBELIEF)

நினைத்தொன்று சொல்லாயோ நெஞ்சே எனைத்தொன்றும்
எவ்வநோய் தீர்க்கும் மருந்து.　　　　　　　　1241

*n-inaiththonRu sollAyO n-enjsae enaiththuonRum
evvan-Oy theerkkum marun-thu*

O my mind! could you not invent some rare medicine
that can cure this chronic malady of passion

காதல் அவரில ராகநீ நோவது
பேதைமை வாழிஎன் நெஞ்சு.　　　　　　　　1242

*kAthal avarila rAkan-ee n-Ovathu
paethaimai vAzien n-enjsu*

His non-return I surmise as lack of love, still you are
willing to suffer folly, my mind, may success be yours!

இருந்துஉள்ளி என்பரிதல் நெஞ்சே பரிந்துஉள்ளல்
பைதல்நோய் செய்தார்கண் இல்.　　　　　　　　1243

*irun-thu-uLLi enparithal n-enjsae parin-thu-uLLal
paithaln-Oy seythArkaN il*

Your brooding and longing are of no avail, the one
who caused the pain of pallor has no compassion

கண்ணும் கொளச்சேறி நெஞ்சே இவையென்னைத்
தின்னும் அவர்காண ஊற்று.　　　　　　　　1244

*kaNNum koLachchaeRi n-enjsae ivaiennaith
thinnum avarkkANa lutRRu*

My kind soul, take these eyes as you seek to meet him,
lest they pester and finish me off in their passion

செற்றார் எனக்கை விடல்உண்டோ நெஞ்சேயாம்
உற்றால் உறாஅ தவர்.　　　　　　　　1245

setRRAr enakkai vidaluNdO n-enjsaeyAm
utRRAr uRAa thavar

He spurns my love, O my soul! may be on a mission
important; it will be unfair to misconstrue and hate

கலந்துஉணர்த்தும் காதலர்க் கண்டால் புலந்துஉணராய்
பொய்க்காய்வு காய்திளன் நெஞ்சு.   **1246**

kalan-thu-uNarththum kAthalark kaNdAl pulanthu-uNarAy
poykkAyvu kAythien n-enjsu

When you see the beloved who enthrals in embrace,
sulking falls in a huff, and falsifies your wrath, my mind

காமம் விடுஒன்றோ நாண்விடு நன்னெஞ்சே
யானோ பொறேன்இவ் விரண்டு.   **1247**

kAmam viduondRO n-ANvidu n-ann-enjsae
yAnou poRaeniv viraNdu

O my dear mind! I have lost myself in the lust of love,
modesty has to give way, as I can forebear neither

பரிந்தவர் நல்கார்என்று ஏங்கிப் பிரிந்தவர்
பின்செல்வாய் பேதைதன் நெஞ்சு.   **1248**

parin-thavar n-alkArenRu aengkip pirin-thavar
pinselvAy paethaien n-enjsu

O my poor soul ! you persist in pursuit of the one
departed, sighing in fond hope for his favours

உள்ளத்தார் காத லவராக உள்ளிநீ
யாருழைச் சேறிஎன் நெஞ்சு.   **1249**

uLLaththAr katha lavarAka uLLin-ee
yAruzaich saeRien n-enjsu

The beloved has returned to reside in my soul, then my
mind, whom do you think, you are after in search?

துன்னாத் துறந்தாரை நெஞ்சத்து உடையேமா
இன்னும் இழத்தும் கவின்.   **1250**

thunnAth thuRan-thArai n-enjsaththu udaiyaemA
innum izaththum kavin

I have retained in my soul, the one who departed our
home; still despair destroys my beauty day by day

126. நிறையழிதல்
n-iRai azithal
LOVE FAILS FEMININE MODESTY
(THE PASSION OF LUST IS IN FULL FORCE IN SEPARATION
MERCILESSLY TORTURING THE LOVERS)

காமக் கணிச்சி உடைக்கும் நிறையென்னும்
நாணுத்தாழ் வீழ்ந்த கதவு.   1251

kAmak kaNichchi udaikkum n-iRaiennum
n-ANuththAL veezn-tha kathavu

Passion of love is in full force, to break the door
of chastity, secured by the bolt of modesty

காமம் எனவொன்றோ கண்ணின்றுஎன் நெஞ்சத்தை
யாமத்தும் ஆளும் தொழில்.   1252

kAmam enaonRO kaNNinRuen n-enjsaththai
yAmaththum aaLum thozil

Merciless is lovelorn passion, that sways my
mind through the blind night of despair

மறைப்பேன்மன் காமத்தை யானோ குறிப்பின்றித்
தும்மல்போல் தோன்றி விடும்.   1253

maRaippaenman kAmaththai yAnO kuRippuinRith
thummalpOl thOnRi vidum

Can I hide in any way this lust of love that
breaks out unawares like a loud sneeze

நிறைஉடையேன் என்பேன்மன் யானோஎன் காமம்
மறையிறந்து மன்று படும்.   1254

n-iRaiudaiyaen enpaenman yAnOen kAmam
maRaiiRan-thu manRu padum

Can I be proud of my chastity, when feminine
modesty betrays to proclaim my love in lust?

செற்றார்பின் செல்லாப் பெருந்தகைமை காமநோய்
உற்றார் அறிவதுஒன்று அன்று.   1255

setRRArpin sellAp perun-thakaimai kAman-Oy
uRRAr aRivathuonRu anRu

The dignity to desist seeking after a deserter
is not known to those bitten by the love bug

செற்றவர் பின்சேறல் வேண்டி அளித்தரோ
எற்றென்னை உற்ற துயர்.

1256

setRavar pinsaeRal vaeNdi aLiththarO
eRRennai utRRa thuyar

He left me in caprice, O grief, passion of love
is cruel that forces me to seek him still

நாண்என ஒன்றோ அறியலம் காமத்தால்
பேணியார் பெட்ப செயின்.

1257

n-ANena onRO aRiyalam kAmaththAl
paeNiyAr petpa seyin

I am not aware of anything like shame or modesty
when the beloved fulfils the desires of my love

பன்மாயக் கள்வன் பணிமொழி அன்றோநம்
பெண்மை உடைக்கும் படை.

1258

panmAyak kaLvan paNimozi anROn-am
peNmai udaikkum padai

The enticing words of this worthy of wily-arts
is all-pervasive to break feminine resolve

புலப்பல் எனச்சென்றேன் புல்லினேன் நெஞ்சம்
கலத்தல் உறுவது கண்டு.

1259

pulappal enachchenRaen pullinaen n-enjsam
kalaththal uRuvathu kaNdu

Determined I went to sulk in feigned dislike; my mind and
soul merged in his embrace, the moment I saw him

நினைந்தீயில் இட்டன்ன நெஞ்சினார்க்கு உண்டோ
புணர்ந்துஊடி நிற்பேம் எனல்.

1260

n-iNan-theeyil ittanna n-enjsinArkku uNdO
puNarn-thu-uudi n-iRpOm enal

For mates, whose souls melt as fat on fire, it is hard
to sustain feigned sulking in fondly embrace

127. அவர்வயின் விதும்பல்
avarvayin vithumpal
THROB OF LONGING FOR LOVER
(LENGTHENING DAYS OF SEPARATION SPOILS LUSTRE OF EYES
AND BEAUTY OF BODY, DESPERATION INTENSIFIES
DISAPPOINTMENT AND SHAKES CONFIDENCE)

வாளற்றுப் புற்குன்ற கண்ணும் அவர்சென்ற
நாள்ஒற்றித் தேய்ந்த விரல்.   1261

vALatRRup puRkkuenRa kaNNum avarsenRa
n-ALoRRith thaeyn-tha viral

Raving eyes lose their lustre and dim in disappointment;
weary fingers wear out, marking days away from me

இலங்கிழாய்! இன்று மறப்பின்என் தோள்மேல்
கலம்கழியும் காரிகை நீத்து.   1262

ilangkizAy! indRu maRappinen thOLmael
kalamkaziyum kArikai n-eeththu

O my bright maid! I survive by thoughts on him; the day
I forget, beauty fades and bracelets slide off my shoulders

உரன்நசைஇ உள்ளம் துணையாகச் சென்றார்
வரல்நசைஇ இன்னும் உளேன்.   1263

uran-n-asaie uLLam thuNaiyAkach senRAr
varal-n-asaie innum uLaen

Motivated by will, valour as aide, he went to win fame;
I still survive in the fond hope of his early return

கூடிய காமம் பிரிந்தார் வரவுஉள்ளிக்
கோடுகொடு ஏறும்என் நெஞ்சு.   1264

kUdiya kAmam pirin-thAr varavuuLLik
kOduǩOdu aeRumen n-enjsu

He enthralled me in ecstatic embraces, my soul throbs in
raptures and mind climbs high, longing for his return

காண்கமன் கொண்கனைக் கண்ணாரக் கண்டபின்
நீங்கும்என் மென்தோள் பசப்பு.   1265

kANkaman koNkanaik kaNNArak kaNdapin
n-eengkumen men-thOL pasappu

I gaze in delight to feast my eyes with his appearance;
sallowness flies off my soft shoulders without a trace

வருகமன் கொண்கன் ஒருநாள் பருகுவன்
பைதல்நோய் எல்லாம் கெட.   1266

varukaman koNkan orun-AL parukuvan
paithaln-Oy ellAm keda

My beloved will be back soon, mind brims with pleasure
of his embrace, and drives out agonising pain

புலப்பேன்கொல் புல்லுவேன் கொல்லோ கலப்பேன்கொல்
கண்அன்ன கேளிர் வரின்.   1267

pulappaenkol pulluvaen kollO kalappaenkol
kaNanna kaeLir varin

The lord of my life is returning in grace; as I see him, I am
at a loss to know, to sulk or clasp or merge in him

வினைகலந்து வென்றீக வேந்தன் மனைகலந்து
மாலை அயர்கம் விருந்து.   1268

vinaikalan-thu venReeka vaen-than manaikalan-thu
mAlai ayarkam virun-thu

My hero shall shine in his exploits and win; I shall
feast him on the eve, in a way to amaze him

ஒருநாள் எழுநாள்போல் செல்லும்சேண் சென்றார்
வருநாள்வைத்து ஏங்கு பவர்க்கு.   1269

orun-AL ezun-AlpOl seilumsaeN senRAr
varun-ALvaiththu eengku pavarkku

For yearning spouses, on the tidings of reunion,
a day moves on at a snail's pace, over a week

பெறின்என்னாம் பெற்றக்கால் என்னாம் உறின்என்னாம்
உள்ளம் உடைந்துஉக்கக் கால்.   1270

peRin-ennAm petRRakkAl ennAm uRin-ennAm
uLLam udain-thu-ukkak kAl

When my fragile soul lies shatters, of what avail
are his retun, embrace and possession?

128. குறிப்பு அறிவுறுத்தல்
kuRippu aRivuRuththal
SIGNALLING SYMPTOMS OF LOVE
(ON RETURN FROM SEPARATION THE LOVER EXPRESSES ADMIRATION
OF HER BEAUTY AND LOVE; SHE IN TURN FALLS FOR HIM, BUT
INDICATES HER FEAR THAT HE MAY LEAVE HER AGAIN IN PAIN)

கரப்பினும் கையிகந்து ஒல்லாநின் உண்கண்
உரைக்கல் உறுவதுஒன்று உண்டு.　　　　　1271

karappinum kaiikan-thu ollAn-in uNkan
uraikkal uRuvathuonRu uNdu

O my love! your eyes ignore to hide modesty and
come to me to convey the message of love

கண்நிறைந்த காரிகைக் காம்புஎர்தோள் பேதைக்குப்
பெண்நிறைந்த நீர்மை பெரிது.　　　　　1272

kaNn-iRain-tha kArikai kAmpu-earthOL paethaikkup
peNn-iRain-tha n-eermai perithu

Her serene beauty fills my eyes in grace, ample charm
of her smooth shoulders, enhance modesty in simplicity

மணியில் திகழ்தரு நூல்போல் மடந்தை
அணியில் திகழ்வதுஒன்று உண்டு.　　　　　1273

maNiyil thikaztharu n-UlpOl madan-thai
aNiyil thikazvathuonRu uNdu

Like the thread shining with pearls it holds, there is a
message of love shining through her bejewelled smile

முகைமொக்குள் உள்ளது நாற்றம்போல் பேதை
நகைமொக்குள் உள்ளதுஒன்று உண்டு.　　　　　1274

mukaimokkuL uLLathu n-AtRRampOl paethai
n-akaimokkuL uLLathuonRu uNdu

Like the fragrance of scent enclosed in a bud, there are
secret symptoms in the blossom of her broad lips

செறிதொடி செய்துஇறந்த கள்ளம் உறுதுயர்
தீர்க்கும் மருந்துஒன்று உடைத்து.　　　　　1275

seRithodi seythuiRan-tha kaLLam uRuthuyar
theerkkum marun-thuonRu udaiththu

In the mischief of her piled bangles sliding off, there is a
signal of the remedy, that relieves my mind and body

பெரிதுஆற்றிப் பெட்பக் கலத்தல் அரிதுஆற்றி
அன்புஇன்மை சூழ்வது உடைத்து.   1276

*perithu-aatRRip petpak kalaththal arithu-aatRRi
anpuinmai sUzvathu udaiththu*

His overflowing love and embrace has the gleanings
of painful parting, drowning me in a sea of sorrow

தண்ணம் துறைவன் தணந்தமை நம்மினும்
முன்னம் உணர்ந்த வளை.   1277

*thaNNam thuRaivan thuNan-thamai n-amminum
munnam uNarn-tha vaLai*

My bangles are quicker than my mind to read, the
grief of parting in my lord of the cool seashore

நெருநற்றுச் சென்றார்எம் காதலர் யாமும்
எழுநாளேம் மேனி பசந்து.   1278

*n-erun-atRRuch chenRArem kAthalar yAmum
ezun-ALaem maeni pasan-thu*

It is but yesterday he departed; sallow is dominating my
body, as a seven day wonder, refusing to depart

தொடிநோக்கி மென்தோளும் நோக்கி அடிநோக்கி
அஃதுஆண்டு அவள்செய் தது.   1279

*thodin-Okki menthouLum n-Okki adin-Okki
aqthu-aaNdu avaLsey thathu*

Her keen looks on loose bangles, tender shoulders and
swollen feet, speak of her norms, and intent to seek him

பெண்ணினால் பெண்மை உடைத்துஎன்ப கண்ணினால்
காமநோய் சொல்லி இரவு.   1280

*peNNinAl peNmai udaiththu-enpa kaNNinAl
kaaman-Oy solli iravu*

Modesty that silences her lips; the keen message of her
eyes, ~~not~~ to depart, are hallmarks of feminine excellence

129. புணர்ச்சி விதும்பல்

(காதலருடன் கூடத் துடித்தல்)

puNarchchi vithumpal (kAthalarudan kUdath thudiththal)

THROBBING FOR REUNION

(THOUGHTS OF REUNION KINDLE IMAGINATION OF THE
SITUATION WHEN HER EAGER LOVER RETURNS)

உள்ளக் களித்தலும் காண மகிழ்தலும்
கள்ளுக்குஇல் காமத்திற்கு உண்டு.
     1281

uLLak kaLiththalum kANa makizthalum
kaLLUkkuil kAmaththiRku uNdu

Throbbing at thought and cheering by sight are
special qualities of love-lore, not of liquor

தினைத்துணையும் ஊடாமை வேண்டும் பனைத்துணையும்
காமம் நிறைய வரின்.
     1282

thinaiththuNaiyum uudAmai vaeNdum panaiththuNaiyum
kAmam n-iRaya varin

As passion for love grows like a palmyra, it is not
appropriate to feign sulking, even of a millet size

பேணாது பெட்பவே செய்யினும் கொண்கனைக்
காணாது அமையல கண்.
     1283

paeNAthu petpavae seyyinum koNkanaik
kANAthu amaiyala kaN

Even when the beloved wilfully slights me, these
listless eyes refuse to rest without seeing him

ஊடற்கண் சென்றேன்மன் தோழி அதுமறந்து
கூடற்கண் சென்றதுஎன் நெஞ்சு.
     1284

UdaRkaN sendRaenmun thOzi athumaRan-thu
kUdaRkaN senRathen n-enjsu

At last when he returned, I wanted to confront him in
sulking, but alas! I forgot everything and fell for him

எழுதுங்கால் கோல்காணாக் கண்ணேபோல் கொண்கன்
பழிகாணேன் கண்ட விடத்து.
     1285

ezuthungkAl kOlkANAk kaNNaepOl koNkan
pazikANaen kaNda idaththu

My eyes cannot see the brush painting my brows; I do
not see any blemish, when my lord is here to comfort

காணுங்கால் காணேன் தவறுஆய காணாக்கால்
காணேன் தவறுஅல் லவை.　　　　　1286

kANungkAl kANaen thavaRu-aaya kANAkkAl
kANaen thavaRual lavai

When I see him closeby, everything seems to be in place;
when he is away, nothing seems going right for me

உய்த்தல் அறிந்து புனல்பாய் பவரேபோல்
பொய்த்தல் அறிந்துஉள் புலந்து.　　　　　1287

uyththal aRin-thu punalpAy pavaraepOl
poyththal aRin-thuen pulanthu

For a beloved wife to feign sulking, knowing its futility,
is like leaping into swirling floods that can fool

இளித்தக்க இன்னா செயினும் களித்தார்க்குக்
கள்ளற்றே கள்வநின் மார்பு.　　　　　1288

iLiththakka innA seyinum kaLiththArkkuk
kaLLatRRae kaLvan-in nnArpu

Like liquor that disgraces addicts, O my crafty! is an
embrace of your bosom, for my madness in love

மலரினும் மெல்லிது காமம் சிலர்அதன்
செவ்வி தலைப்படு வார்.　　　　　1289

malarinum mellithu kAmam silarathan
sevvi thalaippadu vAr

Love is softer and more delicate than a flower; not
many handle it tenderly, knowing its finesse

கண்ணின் துனித்தே கலங்கினாள் புல்லுதல்
என்னினும் தான்விதுப் புற்று.　　　　　1290

kaNNin thuniththae kalangkinAL pulluthal
enninum thAnvithuppu utRRu

Her eyes feigned dislike for once, but cried unable to
bear it, and flew into an embrace eager than me.

130. நெஞ்சொடு புலத்தல் (மனத்துடன் ஊடுதல்)
n-enjsodu pulaththal (manaththudan uuduthal)
CHIDING THY SOUL

(ON SEEING THE LOVER, HER SOUL HOPS FOR HIM HER MIND
AND BODY ABANDONING FEIGNED SULKING AND
PRETENSIONS)

அவர்நெஞ்சு அவர்க்குஆதல் கண்டும் எவன்நெஞ்சே
நீலமக்கு ஆகா தது.　　　　　　　　　　　1291

avarn-enjsu avarkkuaathal kaNdum evann-enjsae
n-eemakku aakA thathu

O my soul! his mind abides by him, ignoring me;
why then you discard me and seek after him?

உறாஅ தவர்க்கண்ட கண்ணும் அவரைச்
செறாஅரெனச் சேறிஎன் நெஞ்சு.　　　　　1292

uRAa thavark-kanda kaNNum avaraich
seRAarenach saeRien n-enjsu

O my mind! what is your intention; deserting a fallen
friend, or to besiege pity of the beloved on me?

கெட்டார்க்கு நட்டார்இல் என்பதோ நெஞ்சேநீ
பெட்டாங்கு அவர்பின் செலல்.　　　　　1293

kettArkku n-attAril enpathO n-enjsaen-ee
pettAngku avarpin selal

O my mind! you have seen his lovelorn slights; still
my soul seeks him in fond hope of friendly clasp

இனிஅன்ன நின்னொடு சூழ்வார்யார் நெஞ்சே
துனிசெய்து துவ்வாய்காண் மற்று.　　　1294

inianna n-innodu sUzvAryAr n-enjsae
thunisaeythu thuvvAykAN matRu

O my mind! you are not anxious to sulk or seek his
embrace; it is futile to counsel you on this phase

பெறாஅமை அஞ்சும் பெறின்பிரிவு அஞ்சும்
அறாஅ இடும்பைத்துஉள் என் நெஞ்சு.　　1295

peRAmai anjsum peRinpirivu anjsum
aRAa idumpaiththuen n-enjsu

My soul is in incessant pain of fear; fretting to fetch him
back, and having gained, not to lose him again

தனியே இருந்து நினைத்தக்கால் என்னைத்
தினிய இருந்ததுஎன் நெஞ்சு.　　　　　1296

thaniyae irun-thu n-inaiththakkAl ennaith
thiniya irun-thathuen n-enjsu

As I muse over my beloved in desperate solitude,
my itching soul eats into me in great anger

நானும் மறந்தேன் அவர்மறக் கல்லாஎன்
மாணா மடநெஞ்சில் பட்டு.　　　　　1297

n-ANum maRan-thaen avarmaRak kallAen
mANA madan-enjsil pattu

My foolish mind of ill-repute, has relentlessly fixed me
to his thought, forcing me to forget modesty

எள்ளின் இளிவாம்என்று எண்ணி அவர்திறம்
உள்ளும் உயிர்க்காதல் நெஞ்சு.　　　　1298

eLLin iLivAmendRu eNNi avarthiRam
uLLum uyirkkAthal n-enjsu

My soul clings to the love of my life, ignoring the
blame of separation on him, and hails his glory

துன்பத்திற்கு யாரே துணையாவார் தாமுடைய
நெஞ்சம் துணையல் வழி.　　　　　1299

thunpaththiRku yArae thuNaiaavAr thAmudaiya
n-enjsam thuNaiyal vazi

When one's own mind is reluctant to support in
distress, who else will stand by me to relieve?

தஞ்சம் தமரல்லர் ஏதிலார் தாமுடைய
நெஞ்சம் தமரல் வழி.　　　　　1300

thanjsam thamarallar aethilAr thAmudaiya
n-enjsam thamaral vazi

It is hard to expect aliens to perform as trusted
folks, when one's own soul stands estranged

131. புலவி

pulavi

BOUDERIE (FEIGNED DISLIKE, ANGER, FROWNING)

(FEIGNED, PRETENTIOUS SULKING, DISLIKE, FROWNING ON
REUNION TO EXPRESS ANGUISH OF SEPARATION; THE
SWEETNESS OF IT AND THE ADROITNESS IN OVERCOMING IT)

புல்லா திராஅப் புலத்தை அவர்உறும்
அல்லல்நோய் காண்கம் சிறிது.   1301

pullA thirAap pulaththai avaruRum
allaln-Oy kANkam siRithu

I will elude and dodge his embrace, feigning sulking; be
witness to his distress and suffering, and the fun of it

உப்புஅமைந் தற்றால் புலவி அதுசிறிது
மிக்குஅற்றால் நீள விடல்.   1302

uppu-amain-thu atRRAl pulavi athusiRithu
mikku-atRRAl n-eeLa vidal

Sulking and feigned dislike in love are like salt in food;
too much of these spoil the taste and pleasure of it

அலந்தாரை அல்லல்நோய் செய்தற்றால் தம்மைப்
புலந்தாரைப் புல்லா விடல்.   1303

alan-thArai allaln-Oy seythatRRAl thammaip
pulan-thAraip pullA vidal

Failing to comfort the eager spouse by embrace, is
to torture him unkindly by adding pain to grief

ஊடி யவரை உணராமை வாடிய
வள்ளி முதல்அரிந் தற்று.   1304

uudiya varai uNarAmai vAdiya
vaLLi muthalarin- thatRRu

Not to reconcile the feigned sulking of a spouse, in
time, is like cutting off a fading plant at its roots

நலத்தகை நல்லவர்க்கு ஏஎர் புலத்தகை
பூஅன்ன கண்ணார் அகத்து.   1305

n-alaththakai n-allavarkku aeer pulaththakai
pUvanna kaNnAr akaththu

Virtuous husbands of lovely grace overcome sulking
and excel in pleasing their flowery eyed damsels

துனியும் புலவியும் இல்லாயின் காமம்
கனியும் கருக்காயும் அற்று.   1306

thuniyum pulaviyum illAyin kAmam
kaniyum karukkAyum atRu

Family life will be raw or over-ripe, sans the sweet
pleasures of frowns and feigned sulking in love

ஊடலின் உண்டுஆங்கோர் துன்பம் புணர்வது
நீடுவது அன்றுகொல் என்று.   1307

uudalin uNdu-aangkuor thunpam puNarvathu
n-eeduvathu anRukol enRu

Sulking in feigned displeasure exhilarates, but it risks
exasperating extension of wait for precious union

நோதல் எவன்மற்று நொந்தார்என்று அஃதுஅறியும்
காதலர் இல்லா வழி.   1308

n-Othal evanmatRRu n-on-thAr-enRu aqthuaRiyum
kAthalar illA vazi

Of what avail lamenting in grief is, when the beloved
who alone can heal the pain of passion, is not there

நீரும் நிழலது இனிதே புலவியும்
வீழுநர் கண்ணே இனிது.   1309

n-eerum n-izalathu inithae pulaviyum
veezun-ar kaNNae inithu

Water is delicious in the coolness of a shade; and
feigned sulking is sweet with those deep in love

ஊடல் உணங்க விடுவாரொடு என்நெஞ்சம்
கூடுவேம் என்பது அவா.   1310

uudal uNangka viduvArOdu enn-enjsam
kUduvaem enpathu avA

The beloved has left me alone to wither in sulking pain;
it is hard desire that my mind persists to unite in love

132. புலவி நுணுக்கம்
pulavi n-uNukkam
FINESSE OF BOUDERIE

(TO SUSTAIN FEIGNED SULKING TEASING HIM IN PRETENTIOUS
POSTURES FOR THE PAIN CAUSED BY SEPARATION)

பெண்ணியலாள் எல்லாரும் கண்ணின் பொதுஉண்பர்
நண்ணேன் பரத்தநின் மார்பு.　　　　　1311

peNNiyalAr ellArum kaNNin pothu-uNpar
n-aNNaen paraththan-in mArpu

'You have not known chastity as a code, and your bosom
is exposed for all women to gaze; I will have none of it'

ஊடி யிருந்தேமாத் தும்மினார் யாம்தம்மை
நீடுவாழ் கென்பாக்கு அறிந்து.　　　　1312

uudi irun-thaemAth thumminAr yAmthammai
n-eeduvAz kenpAkku aRin-thu

When sulking prevailed, he sneezed expecting me
to come out with the customary 'long live'

கோட்டுப்பூச் சூடினும் காயும் ஒருத்தியைக்
காட்டிய சூடினீர் என்று.　　　　1313

kOttuppUch chUdinum kAyum oruththiyaik
kAttiya sUdineer enRu

Seeing my garland of new flowers, she complains in
sulk, 'you do this to please another lady'

யாரினும் காதலம் என்றேனா ஊடினாள்
யாரினும் யாரினும் என்று.　　　　1314

yArinum kAthalam enRaenA uudinAL
yArinum yArinum enRu

When I assured 'my love is incomparable', she sulked
to tease me, 'to whom, with whom you compare me?'

இம்மைப் பிறப்பில் பிரியலம் என்றேனாக்
கண்ணிறை நீர்கொண் டனாள்.　　　　1315

immaip piRappil piriyalam enRaenAk
kaNNiRai n-eerkoN danAL

I assured her 'I will not depart from the sanctity of wedlock';
she was in tears longing 'could it be for ever'

உள்ளினேன் என்றேன்மற்று என்மறந்தீர் என்றுஎன்னைப்
புல்லாள் புலத்தக் கனல். 1316

*uLLinaen enRaen-matRRu enmaRan-theer enRuennaip
pullAL pulaththak kanaL*

I said I was thinking of her; she sulked and left saying
'how come you forget me often, to think afresh'

வழுத்தினாள் தும்மினே னாக அழித்துஅழுதாள்
யாருள்ளித் தும்மினீர் என்று. 1317

*vazuththinAL thumminae nAka aziththu-azuthAL
yAruLLith thummineer enRu*

When I sneezed, customarily she blessed by instinct; but
retracted to sulk and weep 'at whose calling you did it'

தும்முச் செறுப்ப அழுதாள் நுமர்உள்ளல்
எம்மை மறைத்திரோ என்று. 1318

*thummuch seRuppa azuthAL n-umaruLLal
emmai maRaiththirO enRu*

I suppress a sneeze; she weeps bitterly sulking, 'whose
thoughts you are trying to conceal from me'

தன்னை உணர்த்தினும் காயும் பிறர்க்குநீர்
இந்நீரர் ஆகுதிர் என்று. 1319

*thannai uNarththinum kAyum piRarkkun-eer
in-n-eerar aakuthir enRu*

I offer to come clean on my love; still she blames me:
'you are so adept at coaxing others as well'

நினைத்திருந்து நோக்கினும் காயும் அனைத்துநீர்
யாருள்ளி நோக்கினீர் என்று. 1320

*n-inaiththirun-thu n-Okkinum kAyum anaiththun-eer
yAruLLi n-Okkineer enRu*

I gaze at her sulking beauty in contemplation; displeased
she questions 'you scan me to compare with whom?'

133. ஊடலுவகை
uudal uvakai
THE DELIGHT OF BOUDERIE
(SULKING ENHANCES PASSION OF LOVE AND UNITES COUPLES IN WEDLOCK)

இல்லை தவறுஅவர்க்கு ஆயினும் ஊடுதல்
வல்லது அவர்அளிக்கு மாறு.   1321

illai thavaRu-avarkku aayinum uuduthal
vallathu avaraLikkum aaRu

I know he is free from flaws; still I feign to pout,
for him to show up his excellence in embrace

ஊடலில் தோன்றும் சிறுதுனி நல்லளி
வாடினும் பாடு பெறும்.   1322

uudalil thOnRum siRuthuni n-allaLi
vAdinum pAdu peRum

I sulk at his pleadings, to annoy and distress, testing depth
of our love; but the pleasure that blooms outlives pain

புலத்தலின் புத்தேள்நாடு உண்டோ நிலத்தொடு
நீரியைந் தன்னா ரகத்து.   1323

pulaththalin puththaeLn-Adu uNdO n-ilaththodu
n-eeriyain- thannA rakaththu

We have united in wedlock like water and earth; is there
a pleasure greater than sulking love, in the life ahead!

புல்லி விடாஅப் புலவியுள் தோன்றுமென்
உள்ளம் உடைக்கும் படை.   1324

pulli vidAap pulaviyuL thOnRumen
uLLam udaikkum padai

Prolonged pout and sulking, with the beloved in sweet
embrace, is a weapon rising to shatter my soul

தவறுஇலர் ஆயினும் தாம்வீழ்வார் மென்தோள்
அகறலின் ஆங்கொன்று உடைத்து.   1325

thavaRuilar aayinum thAmveezvAr menthOL
akaRalin aangkonRu udaiththu

He is free from faults, yet my beloved's separation is
mystic; his feigned sulk has undefined pleasure

உணலினும் உண்டது அறல்இனிது காமம்
புணர்தலின் ஊடல் இனிது.   1326

uNalinum uNdathu aRalinithu kAmam
puNarthalin uudal inithu

The feeling of assimilation is sweeter than the meal;
sulking passion of love is more pleasant in the union

ஊடலில் தோற்றவர் வென்றார் அதுமன்னும்
கூடலில் காணப் படும்.   1327

uudalil thOtRavar venRaar athumannum
kUdalil kANap padum

The yielder in sulking contest is the winner in love,
the resultant union that delights brings this out

ஊடிப் பெறுகுவங் கொல்லோ நுதல்வெயர்ப்பக்
கூடலில் தோன்றிய உப்பு.   1328

uudip peRukuvang kollO n-uthalveyarppak
kUdalil thOnRiya uppu

Intense union in love making swells the salt of sweated
brows; will not my sweety sulk again, to sweat again!

ஊடுக மன்னோ ஒளியிழை யாமிரப்ப
நீடுக மன்னோ இரா.   1329

uuduka mannO oLiizai yAmirappa
n-eeduka mannO irA

The bright jewelled belle thrills me in tender sulk;
O peaceful night, I plead thee to prolong

ஊடுதல் காமத்திற்கு இன்பம் அதற்குஇன்பம்
கூடி முயங்கப் பெறின்.   1330

uuduthal kAmaththiRku inpam athaRku-inpam
kUdi muyangkap peRin

Sulking stimulates passion of love; the pleasure of
union in wedlock affords protection to family life.

❀ ❀ ❀

arunjsol-poruL akaravarisai
English version of
Thamizh words in KuRaL

akadu	elastic (stomach)
akaththathu	in the mind
akazvAr	diggers
akanRAr	developed
aqki	subtle
aqkAmai	staying close
angkaNam	courtyard
asAvA	un-shaken
asai	shaking ·
anjyar	grief
anjsaloumpu	fear not
adal, adum	control, overcome
adiyaLanthAn	measure by feet
aduthth-Urrvathu	coming next
adun-aRA	fermented toddy
adumuraN	club, pludgeon
attiya,	poured, sprayed
aNangku	damsel
aNiyum	decorate, beautify
aNikalan	ornament
aNiyizhai	jewellery
aNdam	space (universe)
aNNAththal	looking up, open
atharvinAy	searching the way
athin-utpam	intricate knowledge
anthaNar	people of grace
amarakaththu	in war field
amaiyAmai	discordance
amiztham	Elixir, nectar
amai	bamboo, fitting
amaivil	·not suiting

ayarkam	surprise
araN	fort, safety
aritharO	is ind't rare
arithARRi	do rare things
arivai	young lady
arungkEdu	non-ruinous
arunjsevvi	rare face
arumaRai	rare scripture
arumpu arA	keeping fresh
alakudai	cobs of grain
alakai	spirit of evil
alan-thArai	the confounded
alar	gossip in intrigue
alaimERkoNdu	tossed by tide
allavai	non-virtuous
allidam	hostile place
avam	waste, blameful
avalam	grief, sorrow
avi,aviththal	cooked, seasoned
avir	shining
avviththu	perverted envy
avvadhu	feasible way
avvulaku	renouncers world
azal	burning pain
azipasi	destructive hunger
azivinavai	destroying forces
azivinkaN	in desperation
azukkARu	envy
aLavaLA	confabulation
aLaRu	ire (watery grave)
aLavinAl	within the mind
aLAval	stirring up
aLi	Grace, munificence
aLikkum	granting, donating
aLiththhanjsal	shun fear

aLiththirA	(aLiththu+irA) pitiable night
aLaiyee	embrace
aRangkURum	protect mental virtue
aRam n-ANa	virtues shy in shame
aRal,aRuthal	cut off, disconnect
aRivuru	knowledge & shape
aRivallathu	ignorance
aRikonRu	blunting knowledge
arin-thARRi	knowing & doing
aRuthozilOr	mental labourers
aRuvAy	curved form (moon)
aRai	wile trick
aRaipaRai	beating drums
aRkaa	unstable
atRam, atRal	diminishing, disgust
anaiyarAl	similar
antRaRivAm	see later
aRRu	things not good
avalAka	dip (low surface)
aa aathum	rise, grow up
aakUz	positive environment
aakARu	income
aasAram (aasu aRal)	faultless code
aaNmai	managing skill,
aathi	primordial, basic
aayam	profit, assembly
aaytum	analyse, research
aaythodi	fine bangle
aara	full
aaRa	subdued heat, hunger
aarayar	un-subsiding grief
aarkkum	tying
aarvalar	enterprising, seeking
aavAr	amenable, compatible
aazi	deep (sea)

aazvinai	pervading effort
aaRu	pathway (of river)
aatRa	to fulfil
aatRal	strength, to cool
aatRAthu	non-performing
aatRuvAr	performers (of duties)
aanmA	subconscious mind, soul
aanRa	perfect
ikal	discordance
ikavAmai	concordance, amity
isai	music, consonance,
idam	space, vacuum
idan	facility
idipurin-thu	poked, thumbed at
idumpai	pain
idukkaN	crisis
idai	(space) in between
idaikkodka	expose in the middle
iNaruuzn-thu	tied together
iNar eri	hot flame
immai	here, in life
imaiyArin	highest in fame
iyalpinmai	unnatural, unusual
iyalpudaiyamUvar	natural three (parents, spouse, children)
iyaRkai	natural way, tradition
iyaRpAla	which attracts, usual
iyatRal	to produce, make
iyaipu	in tune, in line
iravanmin	do not beg
iravu	night, begging
irunjAlam	universe of light and darkness
irun-ilam	land of water, earth
irupunal	rain and subsoil water
irumai,	good and bad;

iruvina	what has happened, that may occur
iruL	darkness
ilakkam	target, number
iLangkizaay	jewelled maid
ilangku	that shines, light of knowledge
il, illam	home, house-wife, family
illANmai	management of home
ivaN	here, now
ivarthan-thu	inflicting pain
ivaRal,	miserliness,
ivaRanmi	stingy, selfish
izavU	adverse situations
izivu	descent, degrade
izukku	stain, blame,shame
izaiththathu	committed
iLi	disgrace
iRan-thu amain-tha	unlimited, extended
iRan-thAr	insecure, destitute
iRappu	death, crossing, exceeding
iRappinai	losing patience
iRappae purin-tha	transgressing limits
iRal	pain, disaster, death
iRuthi	end
iRai	protector, tax, fodder/food
iRai iRavA	loose, not lost
iRainjchi	besiege
iRpiRan-thAr	of good tradition
inaththARRi	moving with clan
inaiyar	related like
inmai arithE	ignorance revealed
eeakai	munificence
eeathal	contributing
eeaNdu	in family/society
eearngkai	wet hand
eearngkaN	compassionate (wet eye)

eearum	cutting (into two)
ukA	not disclosed
ukka	spilled
unjaRRi	promote with effort
udaRRupavar	spoiler
utkam, utkum	respect
udukkai	loin cloth
uNangka, uNakkin	withering
uNkaN	painted brow
uNmai aRivu	true wisdom
uNarththinum	make to understand
uNarvu	feeling
uthavi	help
uppakkam	inside
uyir achcham	fear of life
uytha	duly enjoy
uythal, uyal	survival
uyiththal	drowning
uruL aayam	rolling dice
ulaku-	ordainer of
iyaRRiyAn	worldly life
ulku	customs duty
ulai, ulaivu	furnace, destruction
uvakai	happiness
uvakkAN	just now
uvan-thavar	pally
uvar	salty
uzanRum	suffer in toil
uzai	circumstance, environment
uLathAkum	staying, sustain
uLazikkalAkA	safe from destruction
uLLaRivAn	know intricacies
uLoRRi	weighing in mind
uLn-Ir	tears
uLLam	mind, soul

uLLam uLLath	conscience
uLLi	thinking
uLvazi	way to where is
uLvIzn-tha	reduced, scaled down
uRAthavar	alien to friends
uRin	if distressed
uRukaN	grief & pain
uRuppinuL	component of
uRuppun-alan	health of limbs
uRuporuL	revenue
uRuvathu	benefiting
uRai	residence, cloud
uRain-thathu	settled
utRavai	gains, results
uukka	lifting up
uungku	higher
uuN	food, consumable
uuthiyam	remuneration
uur uNi	commune well
uurn-thu	ride, slide
uuzi	outer space
uuz	force of nature
uuRu	obstruction, harm
uuRu anjsA	fearless to pain
uuRu orAl	not inflicting pain
uuR eaythi	striking the mind
uun	flesh
uunkuRiththa	life lives in flesh
uunRum	taking roots
echcham,	remnant
enjnjal	left behind
enjsAthu	completely, fully
edukkum	praise, speak out
eNsErn-tha	thinking, calculating
eNpatham	simple in appearance

eNporuLavAka	considered opinion
eyiRu	tooth
eytha	target, achive,
eyyAmai	in natural course, un-aimed, or sought
eri	fire
eRithal	throwing, attack
ellaikkaN	frontier of friendship
evvam	pain
evvathu	in what way
ezili	cloud
ezil	beauty
ezumai	seven-fold, uprise
ezupiRappu	rospering life
ezuvAr	who leave off
eLLuvar	who ridicule
etRA	beyond, endless
etRu	oh how, oh what
enparithal	self pity
enpAkku	what kind
enpilathu	boneless, invertebrate
enpu	bone
ennAm	like that, similar
ennai	my leader
eangkaRRu	seek studiously
eatham	troublesome burden
eathilAr	aliens
ean-thiya	adopt, undertake
eaemam	security
eamaRA	unsecure, unprotected
eamuRRa	insane
ear	beauty, glory
eaval	command, errand
eavavum	directed
eeRu	lion, bull, chieftain
oh ohthal	to sideline, keep off

okkal	relations
ottAr	do not stick, differ
otpam	higher position
ottu	attachment, sticking
oNmai	brightness
oNthodi	bright bangles
oNporuL	glittering gold
oppathAm oppu	uniting parity
oppu	comparable, likeness
oppuravu	social sense
orAl	guarding against
orIi	keep away
orumai	single, unitary
orungku	integrated
oruthalaiyA	straight & firm
oruvan-tham	totally, completely
oruvuka, oruvum	cut off, leave out
olkAr	do not let down
ollAthu	doesn't occur
ollum	possible,agreeable
ollai	fast, quickly
ozukku	discipline, flow
oLi izai	bright jewellery
oLiyodu	light, knowledge,
oLLiyAr	bright, learned
oLn-uthal	bright forehead
oRuththal	punishing, convicting
ooRkaththu	in primeness
otRi	attached, hidden
ondRupOl-kAtti	time indicator
ondRal	uniting
onnAr	foes
oochi	show up, govern
oothi,ooththu	read, memorise
oompal	undertake, patronise

oorayn-thu	five senses
oorthal,oorum	attach, continue
oovA,	without let up
oovAthae	or slackness
kasadu aRa	with clarity, pure
kadappAdu	natural duty
kadan	impelled duty
kadA	bold and brisk
kattaLaikkal	touch-stone
kattu	bound, integral
kadi	reprimand, remove
kadithu	hard, fast
kadiyan	tyrant, despot
kadin-tha	detestable
kaduki	diminish
kadumpunal	jungle stream
kaduththathu	frozen, frown
kadin-thorAl	not giving up
kadaikkodka	fully to the end
kaN anjsA	fearless face
kaNara	without sympathy
kaNpadu	closing eye lids, sleep
kaNdam	land mass
kaNNin	of the eye, sight
kaNn-inRu	on the face
kaNNOttam	mercy, humaneness
kaNichi	axe, spear
katham	heat, anger
kathuppu	long hasir
kathumena	fast look
kan-thA	immature
kayamai	cowardice
kayal	fish
karathal	conceal
kari	witness

karumam	imminent duty
karain-thu	call by crowing
kalam	fittings of beauty
kalaththal	mingling, mixing
kalaththImai	defective container
kalan-tthu Narththum	interacting
kallA mA	untrained horse
kavaRu	gambling on dice
kazakam	assembly
kazal	ornaments on legs
kazA	impure, unwashed
kaziperum	overwhelming glee
kazulvathu	swivelling
kaLar	marshy swamp
kaLiththorum	as you enjoy
kaL oRRi	attached to toddy
kaLLal, kaLLam	stealing
kaRuththu	darkened
kanRiya	ripened
kAtchi	true perception
kAdi	gruel
kANAthAn	blind, ignorant
kAthal	love, desire
kAthanmai	out of affection
kAmam	passion, lust
kAmakkalan	raft of passion
kAmpu	bamboo pole
kAmpErthOL	bamboo like shoulder
kAraNam	aim, reason
kAraNam-kAttal	enlightening, reasoning out
kAraRivu	dim, dark view
kArikai	beautiful (woman)
kAl	prout from seed
kAva, kA	shoulder pole
kAz	seed

kAzththa	aged
kAzppu	hatred
kidan-thamai	contained
kizamai,	right to
kizavan	rightful owner
kiLainjsar	close relative
kiLaththal	express clearly
keezn-Ir -	drowned in
kuLiththAn	deep water
keezn-thidA	un-deteriorating
kudangkar	(snake) hold, cave
kudampai	nest, egg shell
kudi	community
kuzavi	child
kuzAm	gathering
kuRiyethirppa	recompense
kuRiththathu	aimed, signalled
kuRukungkAl	nearing, closing
kuRun-thodi	small bangles
kuRaipeRin	in dire need
kunRa	small
kunRuva	mean
kUmpal	shrinking, closing
kUrn-thu	sharp. surround
kUz	gruel
kURAmai	without saying
kURRu,kURRAm	force of death
kURRuvan	messenger of death
kezher	pally
kezuthakaimai	fitness for camaraderie
kaeNi	water source
kaeNmai	fellowship
kaeLAthu	not listening
kaeLizukkam	fault of fellows
kaeLir	fellows

kaeLvi	listening
kaiseythu	handicraft
kaithUvEn	without let down
kOdu kOdu	out and out
kOtti	competition
kOL	code, policy
kORal	Goring
salam	unsteady, deceit
sAkkAdu	death, degenerate
sAppullal	get rid off
sAyal	beauty,personality
sArbu,	connection,
sArthal	attach, depend
sAlpu	worthiness, sublimity
sAlum	enough, fully
sARRuvan	submit, dedicate
simizthal	netting
sinaippathu	appearing, sprout
siRak-kaNiththal	shrinking brows
siRun-Okkam	side view
siRukAppu	easily defendable
siRusol	hard word
siRumai	smallness, poverty
siRai	security, control
sil ozukku	sharp discipline
seer	beauty, fame, fine
seerthUkkum	refine, assess,
seerAr	great, famous
uthai	whiteness, lime
surukkaththu	in shrinking, reducing
sutRam	related, surround
sUzal	surround, counsel
sUzum	take up
sUzchi	examine, planning
sUzthal	seizeing, think out

sekun-thu	separate, divide
sen-thaNmai	refined manners
seppam	equity, impartial
semmal	head, superiority
semmAkkum	riding
semporuL	clear truth
seyak-kidaththal	complete, achieve
seyiRu	sickness, pain
seyyAL	wealth (figurative form)
seyka	produce, create
seykai	action, conduct
seyAmai	not to do (unfit)
seyumneera	fit to do, worthy
serukku	pride, haughty
selachcholli	dinning in acceptably
sellA	cannot pass or enter
sellidam	habitat, hard place to enter
sevichchol	into the ear
sevili	nurse, nanni
sevvi	appearance, manner
seru	war, enmity
seRuppa	control, suppress
seRithodi	lined up bangles
seRivu	density, integrity
setRu	immobilise
sollAda	hard word, curse
saeN	distance, lasting
saeyizai	refined ornament
saeri	reach, community
saerntha-nakai	drumming up
sO(kAppar)	sorrow (end up in)
sOravidal	let down, give up
gnaadpu	war field
gnaalam	universe (suspended)
thangka-	equals,

NaththAr	of same skills
thakavilAr	unequal, unworthy
thakuthi,	fitness,
thaka	suitability
thanjsam	refuge
thaNanthamai	separation, leaving
thaNdA	unceasing, afflicting
thaN-	weakness,
pathaththAn	inability
thaN vaLi	cool, gentle breeze
thappA	without fail
thamar	related
thalaisellA	non-recurring,
thalaippaduvar	take up, engage
thalaippattAr	taken to lead
thalaippiriyA	backing up, without let up
thavam	penance
thavA vinai	unfailing job, action
thav enum	slakening, feeble
thavvai	sister (darkness)
thazhAl	embracing
thaLLum	push aside, end
tharukku	respect
thatRcheythu	strengthen
thaRukaN	strength, firmness
thanmai	quality, kindness
thanippadar	pain of separation
thAmaraik-kaNNan	bright eyed
thAmaraiyin	An bright like lotus
thAya	embraced, held
thAvil	lasting
thAzhchi	degradation, delay
thAn kANAn	ignorant, blind
thAL	enterprise, effort
thidpam,	firmness,

thiNmai	resolve
thiru	wealth, beauty
thirin-thu	change,deteriorate
thiniya	eat in, herass
thiRai	levy, tax
theeththurI	flame torch
theerAmai	held together
theeyuzi	harmful situation
theernthAr	the lost ones
thuchchil	obscure corner
thunjsin	sleep, slumber
thuNai n-alam	good aid
thuppu	truth, consumable
thuppuravu	wherewithal
thuppuaakki	shape, bring into
thunbin	in distress
thuyththal	relish, enjoy
thulangkal	bright, shining
thulai	quality, balance
thuvara	fully
thuvvAr	destitutes
thuLakku	polish
thuLangkAthu	dim, stained
thuRai	harbour, way
thuRaivan	sea farer
thuni	pain, worry
thunnAthu	non-comforting
thunniyAr	folks
thUkkumkOl	balancing rod
thUvA	not spilled or spoiled
theyvam	bright guide, path leader
thevvar	foes, hostile
theruLAthAn	un-intelligent
theLLiyAr	knowledgeable
theRal	conquering

theRUvum	burn, hurt
thetRu, theruL	clarity
thenpulaththAr	ancestors
thaerthal,thaeruthal	examining, knowing
thEyam	country
thaevar	the bright, the great
thaetRRam	strength, clarity
thokai	total
thokku	added
thodarAr	persist not
thodi	bangles, (volume measure-palam)
thOythal	attach, embrace
tholaividaththu	ancestral
tholkavin	sustaining beauty
tholvaravu	tradition
thollaikkaN	in the face of crisis
thozil	profession, occupation
thozil-vaetRRumai	vocational pattern
thoziRRAl	by actions
thOl	kinship
thOlvi koLal	accepting defeat
thOLmael kalam	shoulder anklets
thOdka	pierce
thOttAr	flowered (locks)
thOtti	elephant goad
n-akal	laughing
n-akai	ornament
n-akaiyaenum	even in jest
n-akai mokku	budding smile
n-akai-vakaiyar	laughing face
n-achchap-padAthavar	not sought after
n-asai,n-achchal	desire
nanjsu	poison
n-aduoreei	partiality
n-attAr	friends, seekers

n-aNi, n-aNiyam	near, proximity
n-aNNaen	will not seek
n-aNpuaatRAr	unfriendly
n-aththam	stable fame
n-ayanthavar	who seek, adore
n-ayap-piththavar	made to agree
n-ayan	soft manner
n-alam-purin-tha	do good
n-alaththinkan	on health of, demeanour
n-alkAmai	not favouring
n-alkuravu	indigence
n-alkuvar	will grant
n-avilthal	saying, expressing
n-aLLA	as inappropriate
n-ani	abundance
n-anaikavuL	musking, rutting
n-ankalam	precious ornament
n-anneerai	in good health
nantRaRivAr	healthy, discerning
n-antRAkum	positive, useful
n-antRi	thankful, duty
n-antRikkaN	conscious of duty
n-antRiyil	thankless, wasteful
n-antRikku	for goodness
n-AdAthu	without probing
n-ANam	dignity of honour
n-ANun-thuRavu	foregoing honour
n-Amaneer-	sea surrounded
vaippu	land
n-Arinmai	callous
n-AvAy	ship, boat
n-AL izukkam	a faulted day
ந-AL oRRi	counting days
n-ARRam	smell
n-ichcha(m)	sure, continuing

n-iNam	fat
n-irappiya	accumulated
n-iran-thu	cogently
n-irappu	poverty
n-ilai	stability, status
n-illAthavai	unstable
n-iRam	colour, quality
n-iRai	fullness
n-iRai azithal	spoiling of poise
n-iRain-enjsam	satisfaction
n-inaikkap-padum	will be thought of
n-inaippa varuvathu	pain of memory
n-inRa	stay stable
neettal;	
neeLum	elongation
neeththAr,	renouncers
n-iRai, neermai	purity, fullness
neeLvinai	continuing effort
n-eRunatRu	like yesterday
n-usumpu	waist
n-uN, n-uNNiyam	subtleness
n-uNangkiya	minute, sharp
n-uthuppOm	put out (fire)
n-uzaipulan	penetrative, keen mind, intellect
n-Ul	book, thought, plan
n-eduneer	prolong, delay
n-erun-al,	yesterday
naerA	un-matching
naern-thaen	agreed
n-Okku	thought, perception
n-Oy seythal	inflicting pain
n-OnA	unbearable (pain)
n-Onmai, n-Onbu	fasting, penance
n-ORkippavar	forbearer (in fasting)
pakadu	bullock

pakavu	part (half)
pakal	day time, enmity
pakAn	without antagonising
pakuthiyAl	by reasoning
pakaiyakaththu	against the foe
pasappu	pallid, pale complexion
pasaiyinaL	attachment, affection
padar	spreading
padal	closing, falling
padA	not bend or lean
padAthu	without hiding
padAm	face shield (of elephant, horse)
padiRu	fraud, mischief
padiyudaiyAr	bards, benevolent
padivam	copy, replica,
paduthal	getting hit, experiencing
paduppar	cause to perish
padai	arms
pattadai	anvil
pattAngku	true state, moral text
paNimozi	parrot like talk
pathadi	chaff, husk
pathi	staying, resting place
pathiyuL payakkum	status
payan-tha	useful
payamilarae	useless
paran-thu	in distress, loitering
pariyinum	seeking, going for
paraththa(n)	polygamist
parukuvar	sip, drink
paruvaththOdu	in tune with seasons
paruvaral	getting pimples
palkuzu	in many groups
palakudai	many umbrella
palasolla	to say variously

pala pala n-alla	good many
pallavai	so many
pallArmuniya	wrath of many
pallARtRin	in many ways
pazakiyaselvam	cultivated wealth
pazakiyan-atpu	traditional friendship
pazamai enap	ancient
pazaiyam	old friendship
pazi anjsi	fear of blame
pazimalain-thu	full of blame
pazuthu eNNum	scheming envy
paLLi	pure, sacred place
paRRividA	attachment
patRAtRi	safeguarding
panivArum	soaked with tears
panuval	rare scriptures
pAkkiyam	chance
pAdu	glory, fame, manners
pAthaip-paduththu	canalise
pAththu	divide
pAriththu	cultivate, gather
pArppAn	guide, reciter
pAlalla	not deserted
pAl	belong to
pAvam	pretence, sin
pARpattu	straight forward
piNai	female deer
piNi	sickness, ailment
piNikkum	getting together
pizaiththa	missed, lost
piRangki	bright, highlight
piRa n-alam	other benefits
piRappu	birth (its objective of life)
piRappennum-	wrong notion
pEthaimai	of pain in life

piRavAmai	curbing desires
piRappu aRukkl	sinking of life
pin neera	waning moon
pinnOkkAn	ignoring consequence
peedu	fame, dignity
peeli	peacock's plume
peezai	continuing grief
pukkil	refuge
pudai	turning to a side
puL	bird
puran-thAr	patron
puraiyilA	w/o rise, or scope
pulaththal, pulavi	sulking in love
pulaththakai	worthy of sulking
pulan	senses
pulAl	meat
pullaRivu	shallowness
pullAr	the mean, the low
pulli	embraced, cuddled
pullividAp-	sulking delaying
pulavi	embrace
puRangkURal	back-baiting
puRam	wedded life
puRaththARu	life in renunciation
puRanazi	concealing the mind
puRkai, puRku	gruel, dimmed embers
punai	hand-cuffs
punaithal	outer form, imaginary creation (poetry, art)
punmai	smallness, lowness
pUsal	loud expression, exhibition
pUsanai	propitiation ceremony
pUthangkaL	elements
pUppar	flower, rise up
pUriyar	lowly

petpam	liking
peyal	rain, pour, put on
peridARRi	in large measure
perung kAmam	overwhelming desire
perumitham	pride
perum iRai	great harm
perumporuL	worthy wealth
peRAthu	rare to gain
peRukuvam	gain, attain
petRam	cow
petRi	skill, might
pEthaimai	ignorance
pENi	patronise, safeguard
pEramarkkaN	battling arrows (eyes)
pErA	stable, steady
pErAthu	neglecting duty
pErum	move back
paing kUz	young plants
paithal	sorrow
pain-thodi	delicate bangles
paiya	softly
pochchAppu	forget, weary
pothu vuNpar	freely gaze, grasp
poyyA viLakku	veracity, sunlight
porutha	fit in to cut
poruthakar	fighting goat
poruththal	joining, matching
poruLAka	useful wealth
poruL	matter, material
poruL mAlai	fame of wealth
pozuthu	time of day
poRuththAn	one who forbears
poRai	patience
ponRAmai	longevity, sustenance
pOkARu	out go

pOkUz	losing situation
pOthu	bud of flowering
pOza	enter, sneak in
pORRal	protect, praise
mangkalam	bright ornament
madal	puppet horse
madavarAl	young lady
madavAr	fools, idiots
madpakai	potter's knife
madi	laziness
madithaRRu	in earnestness
madimadi	lapping laziness
madiyum	dies, ends
maduththa	dips on the way
maNiaNi	ornament of red stones
maNin-Ir	moat canal
mayakkam	stupor
marungku	relatives
marungkOdi	leaving relatives
marutti	activating
maruvum	accept, get
malarmisai	on the flower
malain-thu	multiplied
mallal	might
maziththal	tonsures
maRavi	forgetfulness
maRan	valour
maRu	black spot
maRukil	foyer
maRuku	narrow way
maRukum	roll, swivel
maRuththu	refusing desires
maRuvuka	accept, take
maRumai	future, renunciation
maRuththu	opposing, in return

maRai	concealed
maRaippAn	protector, saver
maRaimozi	Books on virtue
maRRinpam	other pleasures
matRReeNdu-vArA	yet to discover
manaikezee	praise in private
manaivizaivAr	subserve wife
man aLiyar	pitiable
manRupadum	expose in public
mannuthal	stay firm, survive
mA	horse, big, black
mAsaRu-kAtchi	faultless view
mAgnAlam	wide universe
mAdu	wealth of toil
mAtchi	greatness, glory
mANAp-piRappu	listless life
mANizai	bright ornament
mANdAr	respectable great
mAththirai	capsule, measure of time (2.5 sec)
mAmukadi	big lid, darkness
mAyiru	universe of light and darkness
mAri	rain
mAlai	garland, glory
mArththal	protecting
mARalla	congenial, harmonious
mAREththal	oppose
mAtRRal	change, finish
mAtRRAr	foes, alien
mAnam karutha	affecting honour
mAnam varin	damage to honour
mikkAr	the better, the high
misai	upon
misaiyAka	high, above
michchil	the remnant
mIkkURum	praise high

muttA	unobstructed
mudiveythum	conclude, succeed
muthukkuRaithal	experienced
muththu am	like pearl
mun-thuRum	in the forefront
muyangkiya	embraced
muRai	right way, justice
muRaiseyyA	just rule
muRaikOdi	unjust, bent
mutRRiyum	surround, ripened
muRi	young, tender
muniya	provoking anger
munai	war front, edge
meypporuL	real meaning
meyyuNarvu	self realization
meyvaruththa	straining the body
maekapakai	level up enmity
maelallar	not higher
maelulakam	better life
maevaRka	do not confide
maevana	desired, superficial
maevAr	not satisfied
maevuvAr	will fulfil
main-thURum	acting senseless
maiyyal	infatuation, madness
maiyAththi	mystified
moyppu	strength, support
yAkkai	body
yAngkaNum	everywhere
yAthenin	anything
yAppu	growing, evolving
yAruzai	with whom
yArinum	better than whom
vakuththal	organising, arranging
vakai	method of action

vakaimai	categorise
vakaiyaRa	analysing methods
vakaiyaRin-thu	knowing the ways
vasai	blame
vattu	dice
vadu	scar
vaduppu-ariyum	erasing blame
vadu-mAtRRam	faltering words
varan	highly placed
varisaiyA	according to merit
varin	reach the stage,
varupunal	rain, river
varaivin(l)	out of virtues
vali	might, strength
val, vallai	fast, quickly
vazakku	custom
vazi	emissary, missive
vazich selavu	tradition
vazipAdu	adopt the path
vazimuRai	succession, right path
vaziyadaikkum	paving, forming path
vaLaththakkAr	according to means
vaLavarai	growth
vaLi	air
vaLimuthalA	pulse of breath
vaLLi	creeper
vaLLiyam	benevolence
vaRan	valuable
vaRangku	drought
vaRumai	poverty, indigence
vaRRAki	dry up, wither
vanmai	violent, harsh
vanpAdu	cruelty
vanpAr(l)	hard, dry desert
vAy	mouth, opportunity

vAysAnRa	in fullness
vAymai	veracity, purity
vAy uNarvu	sense of tongue
vAri	income
vALn-uthal	bright forehead
vAnOr	high in fame
visumpu	sky, space
vidal	give up, expose
vidu mAtRRam	envoy's missive
viththakar	wise, skilled, mysterious
vithumpal	throbbing desire
vithuppu	avoid
viyanpulam	wide knowledge
vizu,vizuppam	greatness
vizumiyAr	the excellent
vizuppuN	scars on the bosom of warriors
vizumam	grief, pain
vizai-thakaiyar	fit to seek
vizaithal	desire, eagerness
vizaiyAr	who despise
viLiththal	beckon
viLin-thAr	dead
viLiyum	end up, pass away
viLaiyuL	arable land
viLaivu	produce, consequence
viRal	success, gain
vinaikalan-thu	heroic action
vinaikedal	complete job
vinaikku ariya	rare to perform
vinaikku urimai	suitable to perform
vinaikkuRai	incomplete job
vinaimukaththu	in performing
vinaivizaivAr	seeking to perform
veedu	secure home

veengkiya	swelled up
veeyAthu,	unrelenting
veeyA	certain, sure
veevar	will fall
veezthal	falling for
veez n-AL	day in vain
veeRu eythi	in heroism
vekuLi	anger, guileless
veqki	in covet
veNmai	white, blank
ven-thuppu	great might
veythu	hot, foment
veLi	space
veLiRu	open, manifest
veRu, veRi	hate, detest
veRi n-ARRAm	deluding smell
veRukkai	resolve, willpower
veRuththakka	strong, suitable
vRUm	fears
veRRivinai	winning performing
venReeka	come successful
vaettal	seeking desire
vaeNdAp-	family life-
piRappu	left off by sages
vaeNdin -vaeNdum	desire to attain
vaen-thu avAm	sought by ruler

VOCABULARY GUIDE

A

abhor	treat in disgust, hate
abide	adhere, remain
abjure	renounce, abstain/refrain from, keep away
accentuate	stress on , intensify
accolade	act of praise, recognition
accomplish	succeed in doing; achieve
accord	harmony; agreement; give
acumen	keen perception; penetration
adept	capable; thoroughly proficient
addict	habitually devoted, sticking
adore	admire, revere, deeply respect
adorn	add beauty to, deck with
adultery	spurious, extramarital sex
adversary	opponent, unfavourable
aesthetics	appreciation of beauty
afflict	trouble, affect, distress
agony	intense, severe pain
ailment	illness, troublesomeness
akin	related, likeness, similar
alacrity	alertness, briskness
alibi	excuse, elsewhere
alien	foreign, differing character
alleviate	mitigate, lessen, relieve
altar	flat topped block at a height
amaze	overwhelm with wonder
amity	friendship, unity
anguish	severe mental pain
anklet	support, ornament for ankle
antagonize	oppose actively, adversity
anvil	iron block of a smith
appetite	desire, craving for food
apprehend	perceive, understand

archer	shooter with bow & arrow
ardour	zeal, enthusiasm
ascetic	severe in self discipline
aspire	earnest desire
assail	attack
assimilate	absorb into system
astute	subtle, sagacious
attribute	ascribed, characteristic
aught	if there be (to know)
augment	increase, enlarge, enhance
austerity	morally strict, severely simple
avocation	minor occupation, calling

B

babble	innocent talk (like a child)
babble	confused sounds
balm	ointment, healing, soothing
banal	trivial, degrading
banal	ruinous, harming
banish	eradicate, dismiss from mind
banter	make fun of, humorous ridicule
bay	keep in bounds, sea gap
beguile	cheat, deceive, delude
behoves	fit to do, incumbent on
belle	handsome woman, reining beauty
bemoan	lament, express grief
benevolent	charitable, do good character
benign	favourable, kind, gracious
benumb	paralyse, desensitize
bereft	deprived, robed, dispossessed
beset	obstruct, assail, hem in
besiege	lay seize to, assail requests
bestow	confer, grant
betray	lead astray, reveal treacherously
bile	bitter liver fluid, derangement

blabber	indiscreet loose talk
blemish	flaw, stain, mar, spoil
bliss	gladness, perfect joy,
bosom	heart, breast, enclosure
bounding	committed, encircled
bounty	generous, profuse gift (of nature)
bracelet	arm chain, ornamental band
brandish	wave, exhibit, flourish
brood	ponder, hatch, sit on egg
buxom	plump, comely, stunning

C

cajole	persuade by flatter, cunningly
calamities	grave disaster
cauldron	boiling vessel
callus	insensible, unsympathetic
caprice	fancy, freak mind, flimsy conduct
cardinal	central, fundamental, basic moral
cease	stop, desist, end
chastity	pure, disciplined life, integrity
chemise	women's breast cover garment
cherish	keep in mind, lovingly
chest	large treasury box, front of body
chide	rebuke, scold to correct
chronic	persistent, recurring
clamour	shout, loud protest, demand
clenched	tightly closed, confirmed
cling	maintain grasp, hang holding on
coax	persuade to good temper
code	rules of ethics, set of norms
cogent	orderly, convincing, in-line
cognizance	being aware, taking note of
compassion	pity to spare or help
compatible	capable of coexistence
comprehend	understand, grasp mentally

comrade	fellow, mate, familiar pair
conch	sea shell trumpet
conceit	vanity, notion of pride
concise	brief, compact, a few in words
confabulation	talk together, consult
congenial	kind temper, pleasurable
considerate	thoughtfully kind, deliberate
consonance	in tune, same wave length
consummate	highest perfection, skill
contemplation	study with eye/ mind
contrive	devise, find a way, think out
conversant	familiar, well acquainted
convulsion	upheaval, eruption, shaking
corpse	dead body
council	assembly of deliberative body
counsel	advice, views
court (v)	to seek favour of, love of
covet	envy others, long to possess
crave	vehement desire, ask for
cross	not in agreement, transverse
crore	ten million
cultivate	develop, befriend, domesticate
cupid	symbol of sexual love
curb	contain, restrain, suppress

D

damsel	mystic lady, girl
darting	throwing pointed missile
daunt	frighten, dissuade
dazed	bewildered, overpowering sight
dearth	scarcity, deficiency
decay	rot, decline in quality
deceit	cheat, deceive, mislead
dedication	solemn devotion to service
defy	refuse, to obey, challenge

deliberation	careful consideration
delude	deceive, false belief
deluge	flood, overflow, devastation
demean	lower dignity, beneath one
demeanour	form of manner, ones bearings
dementi	mental disorder, baser motives
deplete	reduce, exhaust
deprivation	feeling of loss
deride, derision	scoff, ridicule, scorn
descent	way down, succession, despair bemoan, loss, regard doom
despicable	vile, morally contemptible
despise	look with contempt
despot	tyrant, oppressor, autocrat
destitute	devoid of means of support
deter	prevent, make to abstain
detest	hate, loathe
devious	leaving straight path, erratic
devour	gulp greedily, beasts of prey
dice	cube used in gambling
diktat	edict, code of law, order of ruler
diction	choice of words
diligence	application to knowledge/work
dinning	ram into ears, roar of noise
dire	dreadful, terrible
disaster	sudden or great mishap
discard	reject, cast away
discern	make out, distinguish
disdain	treat as unworthy, keep off
dismay	despair, horrified amazement
disparage	lower dignity, disrepute
disposition	inclination, arrangement
disseminate	spread, reach around
divulge	reveal, bring out

doe	female deer, hare, rabbit
dote	bestow passionate affection
dousing	sedating, quietening, immersing
dread	fear of, terror of, awe
droop	hang down, languish, hang head
drought	dry weather, thirst, failed rain
dud	scare crow figure, inactive
duress	restraint, forcible threats
dwindle	diminish, waste away, lose

E

earnest	serious, ardent, genuine
ebb	reflex of tide, decline, decay
ecstasy	rapture, exalted poetic frenzy
edict	order of authority
elation	high spirit
elicit	draw out, obtain, bring out
elixir	alchemists' preparation to prolong life; sovereign remedy
eloquence	fluent powerful speech
elude	escape stealthily, avoid skilfully
embers	simmering coal, ash covered
embitter	make bitter, aggravate
emissary	envoy sent on a mission
encomiums	formal or high praise
encore	inner voice, deep insight, covered out
encrypt	condensed text
endow	assign, invest, empower
enmity	hostility, hatred
entrepreneurs	bold venturers to achieve, risking enterprise
enticing	alluring, attractive persuasion
environment	surroundings, circumstances
envoy	messenger, ambassador
equanimous	composed, balanced, equitable fair, just, valid

equity	just position, risk capital for profit/loss
errand	short assignment, message pass
eschew	avoid, shun, keep away, not relish
estranged	alienated, treated strange
eulogise	extol, praise
eve	feminine, evening before event
even	evening of day, eventide
exalt	rise in position, lofty, noble
exhilarate	enliven, gladden, hilarious
extol	praise enthusiastically
exploit	utilise for own selfish ends
extort	get, fleece by threat or force
exude	ooze out, give off
exult	rejoice, elate in triumph

F

facet	one side, part, appearance
facility	easy fluency, opportunity
faculty	aptitude, inherent power
fantasy	mental image, fanciful design
fatal	deadly, destructive
fatigue	weariness from exertion, tiredness
fawn	fallow deer, cringe, affection
feasible	practicable, doable, economically
feign	pretend, simulate
ferocious	fierce, cruel, fast vigour
fervour	intensity, ardent, hot
feud	lasting hostility, assaulting enmity
file	reduce, make uniform
fleeting	glide away, pass, fly rapidly
flex	bend without breaking, versatility
fling	rush, throw to hurt
flock	large gathering of people, animals
foil	baffle, parry, repulse, spoil
folklore	traditional songs of country folks

folly	foolishness, committing without knowing
forbear	abstain from, be patient
forbid	prevent, not allow to act
forlorn	forsaken, desperate, pitiful
foster	tend to, promote, encourage
fowler	who catches birds by net
fragile	weak, delicate, brittle
fragrance	pleasant smell (of scent) fret irritation, vexation, annoy
frustrate	baffle, destroy, counteract, futile useless, frivolous

G

garb	cover, characteristic dress
genial	conducive to growth, jovial
girded	encircled (with waist belt)
glasnost	open view, approach
gleaming	subdued, transient light
gleanings	select collections from pile
goad	urge, incite, push
gore	pierce with horn or tusk
gorgeous	splendid, dazzling, extravagant
gruel	liquid food in water
guile	treachery, deceit, cheat

H

hail	greet, salute, praise
hallmark	marking standard of gold
hanker	crave, hang after
hapless	unlucky, without help
harbinger	forerunner, preface
harlot	prostitute
harness	low means, hard existence
heaves	lifts, display, utter

heed	careful attention, take notice, listen to
herald	usher in, proclaim, approach
heritage	tradition, inheritance
hiccup	involuntary spasm of respiration
hindrance	obstruction, impediment
hoard	stock store avidly, amass greedily
hostile	opposed, unfavourable
hue	colour, tint, outcry
huff	bully, anger, annoy
humility	humbleness, meekness
hypocrite	pretender, guilty dissembler

I

impediment	hindrance, hurdle
impel	drive, proper, force
imposter	false person, swindler
impregnable	impossible of entry
incense	spice smell, perfume, anger
incessant	continuous, without break
indolence	sloth, laziness
inept	silly, absurd out of place
infatuation	extravagant passion/ folly
ingredient	component part, input
inhabit	dwell, occupy, live in
innate	natural, inborn
inquisitive	curious, anxious to know
insatiable	greedy, not satisfiable
insouciant	forgetful, indifferent
instinct	impulse, intuition,
interminable	endless, tediously long
intricate	entangled, inner complexity
intrigue	underhand plot, secret influence
intrude	enter uninvited, stealthily, thrust in
invigorate	strengthen to act
ire	anger

itch	irritation, impatient desire
jest	joke, fun, banter, derision

L

lackadaisical	affecting delicacy, eschew enthusiasm
lament	express or feel grief
lance	horseman's spear
languish	lose vitally, feebly suffer
largesse	extravagance in rejoicing
lasting	enduring, sustaining
laudable	praiseworthy, commendable
laurel	garland or emblem of victory
legacy	gift by will, by predecessor
lethargy	laziness by lack of interest
lewd	indecent, base, worthless
lynch pin	axle end-pin to protect wheels
lineage	lineal descent, ancestry
linger	be slow, stay about, dally
listless	without inclination, agitated
locks	plaits, tresses of hair
logger(head)	in dispute, on bad terms
loiter	linger, roam, hang around, degenerate
longevity	long life, sustenance
lore	body of tradition, erudiction
lorn	desolate, isolate
loveless	lacking learning, w/o affinity
lure	entice, attract by deceit
lurk	hide, elude out of sight
lust	sensuous appetite, passion
lustre	gloss, shine, brilliance

M

malady	ailment, persisting disease
malice	ill will, evil intent, hatred
malign	destructive virus, slander

manoeuvre	tactical movement, adroit manipulation
manifest	appear clear, come to light
mars	impairs, spoils
meek	tame spirited, submissive
menace	trouble, apparent danger
minister(v)	serve, contribute, console
mire	mud pool, swampy ground
mirth	happiness, being merry
mishap	bad, evil event
mission	task of envoys, self conceived objective
mitigate	reduce, alleviate serenity
mode	method, form, manner, medium
modesty	unassuming, pure minded
morbid	unhealthy, sick sentiment
motley	unworthy as dust
multifarious	of many kinds, variety
mundane	earthly, worldly
munificence	generosity in giving
muse	ponder, think over, reflect
muster	collect and hold
mystic	bewildering, esoteric

N

nectar	sweet fluid of plants, delicious drink
nemesis	cause and effect, retribution
nettles	thorns, pins, stinging hair
niggard	stingy person, grudger
nocturnal	nightly, active by night
nonce	a little for the act

O

obtrusive	thrusting forward
omnipotent	all powerful, infinitely capable
oscillation	swing, vary end to end

P

pal	comrade, of a tribe
palanquin	covered, human carriage
pallor/ pallid	wane, pale, sickly looking, mental suffering, sudden sharp pain, grief
paramount	supreme, superior, main
passion	strong emotion, sexual love
pathetic	suffering emotion
peerless	unequalled
pelf	contemptible wealth
penance	self inflicted discipline
penitent	repentant, contrite, sorrowing, atoning
penetrate	find access, seep into
penury	poverty, lack of means
perfidy	breach of faith, treachery
periphery	bounding line, esp.of circle
perish	suffer destruction, die
perplex	puzzle, complicated
perceive	see, aware of sense, understand
persist	insist on, continue to do
perseverance	be steadfast, maintain endeavour
personify	give image to abstracts, symbolise
perspective	view, dimensional drawing
pervasive	spread thro', be rife among
pester	noxious, spreading infection
phlegm	viscous substance secreted by mucus membrane, coughed
pining	wasting in grief, longing
plight	predicament of distress
plume	feather segment
poise	balance, equilibrium
ponder	think over, muse, heave dull
port(v)	convey, deport, transport
potential	latent power, strength

pout	thrust out lips, displeasure
predict	forecast, foretell, prophesy
prevail	gain mastery, attain object
privy	hidden, secret, entrusted
probing	exploring, investigating
prod	poke with
produce(n)	agricultural product
prone	tending to , inclined to
propitiate	appease, seek favour
prop up	hold up in support
prowess	strength, bravery, valour
proximity	nearness, closeness
pursuit	seeking after, with intent
purveyor	procurer and supplier with right of pre-emption

Q

quack	pretender, charlatan
quagmire	treacherous mud pool, marsh
qualms	sick feeling, scruples
quantum	as much as suffices
quell	put down, crush, suppress
quench	extinguish, stifle, slake

R

raft	floating structure of timber
rage	violent anger, vehement desire
raise	make higher, cause to ascend
rakes	immoral people, fakes
rapture	ecstatic delight, emotional height
rattle	rapid shaking noise, alarm
recapitulate	recall in summary
recompense	return, repay
reckoning	ascertain, take into account
recoup	restore, recover

redeem	reclaim, rescue, repay
redress	remedy, make up for
refute	rebut, deny, prove false
rein	pull up, means of control
reins	steeples of horses
relent	relax security or stubbornness
reluctance	unwillingness, hesitation
remorse	repentance, compassion
renounce	give up, abandon, leave off
replete	filled, stuffed, well stocked
repose	place faith, trust, lay to rest
reprimand	command to put down, suppress
reprieve	suspend or remit sentence
reproach	scold, censure, upbraid
reprove	rebuke, chide
repulse	drive back, foil, rebuff, reject
requisite	rightly needed thing, requirement
respite	interval of rest or relief
restraint	keep in check, confinement
retort	reply sharply, repay, pay back
retract	withdraw, go back, pull off
retribution	retrieval, recompense
revel	make merry, delight
revered	regarded, respected
revile	abuse, rail at, contempt
revolve	come around, going in orbit
rhythm	musical motion
rip	cut, split, tear
rot	decay, deteriorate
rotate	swirl on own axis
rove	wander without direction
rue	repent, feel dismal, regret
rut	musk, sexual excitement (madness) of male elephant, deer etc.

S

sagacity	insight, shrewdness, wisdom
sallow	sickly yellow, pale brown
sanctity	piety, holiness, saintliness
saner	sensible, of sound mind
sans	without, less
sapless	dried up, w/o vital juice
savant	distinguished learned, erudite scholar
scheming	secret underhand planning
scorch	dry heat burning surface
scorn	contempt, despise, deride
seep	ooze, trickle, leak
seers	visionaries, prophets
serene	clear and calm, placid
servitude	slavery, bondage
sham	false, useless, pretension
shatters	broken to pieces, wreak
shimmer	faint diffused light
shrewd	astute, sharp, penetrating
simmer	suppressed anger, bubble below boiling
shun	keep clear, avoid, eschew
sigh	aspire, yearn, long for
sinister	evil, ill, wicked, vile
sine qua non	inevitable, cannot do without
slight	fail respect, discourtesy, dishonour
sloth	laziness, weariness, indolence
slush	thawing snow, thin mud
slur	blame, stain on reputation
snob	meritless person/ wealth
snub	reprove, rebuff, nose-cut
solitude	loneliness, isolation
sombre	gloomy, dismal, dark, dull
soothing	calming, cooling, composing
spasm	sudden convulsive motion, hiccup

spinster	unmarried woman
spiteful	dictated by ill-will, malice, revengeful
spouts	rises as a jet of liquid
spurn	repel, refuse, reject, in contempt
staff	support pole, stick
stagnate	inert, unchanging, motionless
startle	give shock or surprise
stature	high appearance, status
steadfast	immovable, unwavering
stew	soak hot, sweat, swelter
stimulate	rouse, evoke, spur to act
stoop	bend forward, condescend
strain(n)	breed or stock
straits	narrow passage, difficulty
strangle	deadly grip, squeeze
stride	without changing step, on line
strife	dispute, quarrel
subjugation	subduedness, submit to
sublime	surpassing, inspire awe, purified, exalted virtue
subsist	support life, exist on support
suffocate	choke respiration, impede
suitor	wooer, petitioner
sulk	resent, sullen, morose
surmise	infer, assess by guess
swagger	superior air, boast
sways	rules over, swings unsteady, overpowers
swirl	rotary sucking motion
swollen	expanded, bulged
symptom	sign, signal, manifestation
syntax	rules of construction of verses in poetry

T

talent	high mental ability
tangling	intertwining, ensnaring

tenet	code of doctrine
terminator	one who brings to an end
thrift	saving ways, sparing expenses
tidings	news (received in waves)
timid	shy, easily frightened
tonsure	shaving off hair on head
torment	severe body or mental pain
trait	trace, trend of character
trample	tread heavily to spoil
trance	suspended consciousness, intense mental concentration
tranquillity	serene calmness
travails	suffering, pangs, labour pains
tread	set foot on, put down
treachery	violation of faith, stealthy acts
torpidity	agitation, flurry, perturbation
trifle	small, flippant, insignificant
tusker	male elephant
tyrant	oppressive, cruel ruler

U

ultimate	final, last, at the end
unmitigated	not reduced or relieved from severity
unravel	disentangle, separate, find out
unruffled	calm, unmoved
usurp	seize wrongfully
unversed	unskilled, inexperienced, unknowing

V

vacillate	waver, show indecision, swing
valour	battle courage
vamp	crafty, wicked, boastful vanity
vantage	advantage, preferable
venality	corrupt, influence of bribe
veracity	truth (as seen or believed)

verily	truth (as assumed)
vexed	annoyed, disturbed
vile	despicable, depraved
vilification	slander, speaking ill of

W

wanes	decreases, declines, falls, wings
wary	cautious of dangers
waxes	grows larger
wean	induce to give up, cure of weakening feeble person
whiff	puff of wind, breathe of air
whore	indecent prostitute, fornicator
wink	move eyebrows
wistful	betraying vague desires
wither	dry up, fade, loose form
woe	bitter grief, mishap
wontage	inherent advantage
wrath	anger
wrest	snatch, wrench away
wriggle	evade, avoid, twist about
wry	grim, distorted

Y

yearn	long for, craving wish
yonder	over there, distant
yore	the past

Z

| zeal | fervour, enthusiasm |

ɼ   ɼ   ɼ